The Anabaptist Writings of
David Joris

Portrait of David Joris, Frisian School, c. 1550/55
Courtesy of the Öffentliche Kunstsammlung, Basel, Kunstmuseum

The Anabaptist Writings of

David Joris

1535-1543

Translated and edited by

Gary K. Waite

HERALD PRESS
Waterloo, Ontario
Scottdale, Pennsylvania

Canadian Cataloguing in Publication Data
Joris, David, 1501 or 2-1556.
    The Anabaptist writings of David Joris
(Classics of the radical Reformation ; 7)
Includes bibliographical references and index.
ISBN 0-8361-3113-4
1. Anabaptists - Doctrines - Early works to 1800.
2. Theology, Doctrinal - Early works to 1800.
3. Anaptists - Netherlands - History - 16th century. 4. Netherlands -
Church history - 16th century. 5. Joris, David, 1501 or 2-1556.
I. Waite, Gary K., 1955- . II. Title. III. Series.
BX4930.J67 1993 284'.3 C93-094900-5

BX
4930
.J59
1994

The paper used in this publication is recycled and meets the minimum re-
quirements of American National Standard for Information Sciences—Per-
manence of Paper for Printed Library Materials, ANSI Z39.48-1984.

THE ANABAPTIST WRITINGS OF DAVID JORIS
Copyright © 1994 by Herald Press, Waterloo, Ontario N2L 6H7
      Published simultaneously in the United States by Herald Press,
      Scottdale, Pa. 15683. All rights reserved
Library of Congress Catalog Number: 93-61141
International Standard Book Number: 0-8361-3113-4
Printed in the United States of America
Book design by Gwen M. Stamm/Hand lettering by Jan Gleysteen

02 01 00 99 98 97 96 95 94 93 10 9 8 7 6 5 4 3 2 1

CLASSICS OF THE RADICAL REFORMATION

H. Wayne Pipkin, *Editor*
Institute of Mennonite Studies

Honorary Editor: C. J. Dyck, Elkhart, Indiana

Advisory Editors: E. J. Furcha, Montreal, Quebec; Walter Klaassen, Vernon, British Columbia; John S. Oyer, Goshen, Indiana; C. Arnold Snyder, Waterloo, Ontario

Classics of the Radical Reformation is an English-language series of Anabaptist and free church documents translated and annotated under the direction of the Institute of Mennonite Studies (the research agency of Associated Mennonite Biblical Seminaries, 3003 Benham Avenue, Elkhart, Indiana 46517) and published by Mennonite Publishing House (Herald Press, Scottdale, Pennsylvania 15683).

1. *The Legacy of Michael Sattler.*
Translated and edited by John H. Yoder, 1973.

2. *The Writings of Pilgram Marpeck.*
Translated and edited by William Klassen and Walter Klaassen, 1978.

3. *Anabaptism in Outline: Selected Primary Sources.*
Edited by Walter Klaassen, 1981.

4. *The Sources of Swiss Anabaptism: The Grebel Letters and Related Documents.*
Edited by Leland Harder, 1985.

5. *Balthasar Hubmaier: Theologian of the Anabaptists.*
Translated and edited by H. Wayne Pipkin and John H. Yoder, 1989.

6. *The Writings of Dirk Philips, 1504-1568.*
Translated and edited by Cornelius J. Dyck, William E. Keeney, and Alvin J. Beachy, 1992.

7. *The Anabaptist Writings of David Joris.*
Translated and edited by Gary K. Waite, 1993.

To Kate, Jess, and Brian
for love, life, support

Contents

List of Illustrations

General Editor's Preface

The last three decades have witnessed a change in the understanding of the origins, nature, and development of the Radical Reformation in general and the Anabaptists in particular. A growing awareness of the diversity and variety of the Radical Reformers has emerged. Essential to a grasp of the divergences and convergences of the early Anabaptists is the availability of the primary source materials of these reformers. It has been the vision of the Institute of Mennonite Studies to make such sources available in English in the series Classics of the Radical Reformation (CRR).

The editions of CRR, though scholarly and critical, are intended also for the wider audience of those interested in the Anabaptist and free-church writers of the late fifteenth, sixteenth, and early seventeenth centuries. The translations are intended to be true and polished yet not excessively literal or wooden. With this seventh volume in the series, professor Gary Waite makes available the Anabaptist writings of David Joris—the major Anabaptist theologian in northern Europe between the fall of Münster and the emergence of Menno Simons. The list of current volumes in CRR may be found on page five. Further volumes are in process on a variety of radical reformers.

Appreciation is hereby expressed to the Institute of Mennonite Studies and its sponsoring institution, the Associated Mennonite Biblical Seminaries, for the continuing support of this series. Gratitude is due to Herald Press for its willingness to make available works of this kind to the broader church and academic publics. A final word of thankfulness is expressed to C. J. Dyck, the founding editor of CRR, who, while carrying the burden of multiple responsibilities over two decades, saw the first six volumes of CRR through to publication.

—*H. Wayne Pipkin, Editor, CRR*
Institute of Mennonite Studies

Editor's Acknowledgments

As with any worthwhile scholarly endeavor, a great debt of gratitude has been accumulated in the completion of this volume. While words of thanks cannot come close to repaying that debt, I would like to express my appreciation for the encouragement and assistance I have received from friends and colleagues on both sides of the ocean. Their support has helped considerably to improve the quality of the book. The fault for any remaining errors can be laid at my feet alone.

In Europe, Piet Visser, curator of the Mennonite Library, University of Amsterdam, provided not only the efficient and helpful service one has come to expect from his institution, but also considerable advice and hospitality. I am also thankful to José Bouman of the Bibliotheca Philosophica Hermetica, Amsterdam, for her kind help while I perused the Joris materials in that remarkable private library.

My all-too-brief stay in Basel in the summer of 1986 was made unusually profitable by the proficient service of the staff of the Rare Book and Manuscript Department of the University Library of Basel. On this side of the ocean, Sam Steiner and his staff at the Conrad Grebel College Library, University of Waterloo, were also extremely important in the collection of materials. A note of appreciation is also due to the staff of the Interlibrary Loan department of the Harriet Irving Library, University of New Brunswick.

I must record a major debt of gratitude owed to Werner O. Packull of Conrad Grebel College, Waterloo. For many Friday afternoons, Professor Packull patiently waded through Joris's writings with me while I was a graduate student and a novice in the art of translation. Samme Zijlstra also assisted me in the translation of several difficult passages.

I am very thankful to the former editor of the CRR Series, Cornelius J. Dyck, for his constant and unwavering encouragement and advice, without which this project would not have been completed. The advice and support of the current editor, H. Wayne Pipkin, have also been extremely valuable.

I have learned much about editing and translating as a result of the tireless efforts of John S. Oyer and the staff of the *Mennonite Quarterly Review*, which published two of my Joris translations and which have graciously permitted their inclusion here. I have also profited immensely from informal discussions about Joris with many other scholars and friends, as well as from the support of the University of New Brunswick History Department. I would like to thank all for their patience and interest.

—*Gary K. Waite*
Fredericton, New Brunswick

Explanation of Biblical References

Where possible, Joris's biblical references are listed in the translations. Verse numbers, when they could be identified, have been added to the original marginal scriptural notations (in square brackets where there is some uncertainty). In the cases of tracts published in the seventeenth century, many of these verse numbers had already been included.

It should be noted that following the conventions of the sixteenth century, Joris quoted freely from the Apocrypha. For the purposes of clarity, Joris's Ecclei. is listed here as Ecclesiasticus; Sapi. as Wisdom of Solomon; 1 Esdras as Ezra; 2 Esdras as Nehemiah; 3 and 4 Esdras as 1 and 2 Esdras.

All quoted scriptural passages in the texts of Joris's works are translated from his renderings. Page numbers of the original texts are noted in square brackets. Where possible, gender neutral language has been used, hence Joris's "nieuw mensch" is translated here as "new being."

The Anabaptist Writings of
David Joris

1
The Life and Works of David Joris

David Joris (1500/1-1556) has always been an enigma whose importance to the Dutch Anabaptist movement has only recently been acknowledged.[1] Mennonites have naturally been suspicious of Joris's reputation as a spiritualist who denied the necessity of a separated church and who purposely avoided martyrdom with a conscious program of Nicodemism—concealing unorthodox beliefs under a cover of conformity. But these were, by and large, characteristics of his later career, especially after he had moved to Basel in 1544.

Between the fall of Anabaptist Münster in 1535 and the ascendancy of Menno Simons by the mid-1540s, Joris was clearly the most important Anabaptist leader in the Low Countries. He provided the major pacifist alternative to the revolutionary Anabaptists, such as the violent guerrilla group around the nobleman Jan van Batenburg.[2] And while Joris certainly diverged from mainstream Anabaptism later in his career, there is no denying that he was an extremely influential figure for the Anabaptist movement for some time after the debacle of Münster. At the very least, his writings illustrate the variety within sixteenth-century Anabaptism. They are, therefore, invaluable sources for our understanding of what it meant to be an Anabaptist in the Low Countries immediately after the fall of Münster.

By trade Joris was a glass painter. Recent studies have shown that his skill at this craft was considerable.[3] But aside from the fact that he left behind only a handful of known artistic creations, there are good reasons Joris is not famous as a Dutch artist. His career as a radical religious reformer overshadowed his artistic achievements, intentionally so. Around 1537 Joris gave up his craft to devote himself full-time to his spiritual mission. This mission had begun around 1524 when he became excited by the message of the German Reformer, Martin Luther. In his home city of Delft, Holland, Joris preached informally and distributed anticlerical pamphlets throughout the streets and churches.

In 1528, however, Joris was too bold. His public denunciation of the veneration of the Virgin Mary during a procession in her honor led to his arrest and eventual punishment. As part of this punishment he was banned for three years, and, like many of his fellow religious dissenters in Holland, he traveled to more tolerant East Frisia. Here he eventually met with supporters of Melchior Hoffman, if not with the South-German lay-preacher himself.[4] Joris was early entranced by Hoffman's apocalyptic message. In spite of this ideological affinity, Joris seems to have returned to Delft after the expiration of his ban as a mere sympathetic observer of Anabaptism. His earlier punishment, which (according to the court records) had included the boring of his tongue, must surely have made him reluctant to engage in further illegal activities.

It was therefore not until the winter of 1534-1535, during the siege of Anabaptist Münster, that Joris publicly joined the Melchiorites (the followers of Hoffman) and allowed himself to be baptized into the movement. His talents were immediately recognized by his new brethren. Two prominent Anabaptist leaders, Obbe Philips and Damas van Hoorn, selected him for a leadership role in the movement. He appears, however, to have been initially reticent to fulfill his spiritual office, although he is known to have participated in a conference in the Waterland district in the winter of 1534-1535 on the issue of the use of the sword on the part of Anabaptists. He also composed a tract on the dilemma of the fall of Münster.[5]

The failure of the Münster Anabaptist kingdom was a pivotal event for Anabaptists in the Netherlands. Many Anabaptists, disillusioned with the failed prophecies of Hoffman and the Münsterites, seem to have left the movement entirely. Others, such as Obbe Philips, moved in the direction of Spiritualism.[6] Some fled the Netherlands in search of refuge. Hoffman himself was in prison in Strasbourg. Menno Simons, with the assistance of Dirk Philips (the brother of Obbe Philips), sought to rebuild what survived of Hoffman's charismatic movement into an organized, separatist, and theologically uniform church.

In the Low Countries of the late 1530s and 1540s, however, open sectarianism was an extremely dangerous approach, especially for those Anabaptists still residing in the urban centers. Until the mid-1540s, therefore, most of Simon's success came from his own province of Friesland, in part because he communicated in the eastern Dutch dialect that was related more to the Low German of the Saxon territories rather than in the Holland Dutch spoken by Joris. The approach of the surviving revolutionary Anabaptists, such as the remnant of Münsterites around Heinrich Krechting in Oldenburg or the Batenburgers, was perceived by many as suicidal.

In 1536 Joris stepped into this apparent vacuum of moderate leadership, hoping to revive the religious devotion of many Dutch Anabaptists. Considering the obstacles which he faced, Joris's success was noteworthy. He gained a large and devoted following, especially in Holland's cities, which also spread throughout the Low Countries, East Frisia and Westphalia. His success at winning supporters from other Anabaptist camps also earned for him the ire of other leaders such as the pacifist Menno and the violent Batenburg.

The most important event in Joris's career as an Anabaptist leader occurred in August 1536. In that month he managed to mediate an agreement, short-lived as it turned out, between revolutionary and pacifist Anabaptists at a meeting in Bocholt, Westphalia. Then, in December 1536, he experienced some visions that finally imbued him with the missing sense of divine calling. He developed an exalted view of his mission and authority, based on his concept of the apocalyptic third David.

While perhaps strange to modern readers, Joris's conception was a moderate one compared either to those of the former king of Münster, Jan Boeckelsz van Leiden, or to Batenburg and was not at all surprising to his contemporary Anabaptists. Boeckelsz, as king of Münster, had sought to replicate the physical and earthly kingdom of the first David. Joris's claims were much more modest and he never explicitly identified himself as the third David, although one can easily infer such an identification from his writings and from the comments of his followers. In Joris's scheme, the third David—acting on behalf of the second David, Jesus Christ—would usher in the new spiritual age.

Unlike the conception of Boeckelsz, Joris saw his role as a purely spiritual one, as the authoritative messenger of the Lord. What later leaders such as Menno Simons viewed as arrogance and presumption, Joris saw merely as fulfilling the call of the Lord. In any respect, from the time of his visions on, Joris's previous doubts about his religious vocation seem to have vanished.

On the strength of these visions, Joris set out on an ambitious program to unite under his leadership the scattered and divided Dutch Melchiorites. At this time he gave up his menial task of glass painting to take up full-time his spiritual vocation. He directed his energies to the unification of Melchiorite and Münsterite groups both by means of a vigorous writing campaign and by his participation in several crucial meetings of Anabaptist leaders, particularly conferences in Oldenburg and Strasbourg in 1538. He opposed, at the risk of his own life, the violent activities of the Batenburgers, those Anabaptists who sought not only to maintain the revolutionary spirit of Münster, but also its polygamy. Joris was only partially successful, for while several Batenburgers and Münsterites joined his camp, there were still bands of Batenburgers continuing their lawbreaking activities well after Joris's death.

Joris's industry in his mission was indeed remarkable. As an Anabaptist and later spiritualist, Joris composed some 241 published literary works of various sizes, from four folio page pamphlets to the two editions of the massive *Wonder Book*.[7] He achieved a degree of infamy in his own day that rivaled that of better-remembered Anabaptists such as Menno Simons. His contemporaries certainly viewed him as the leading figure in Dutch Anabaptism after Münster.[8] His opinion on a variety of controversial issues was highly sought after and his presence at conferences enthusiastically received.

Joris's achievements, however, also attracted the attention of the authorities, and he and his followers were mercilessly hounded; in 1539 alone, over one hundred Davidites were put to death for their Anabaptist faith and devotion to the teachings of Joris.[9] As a result the prophet was forced more than once to leave Holland in search of refuge. In 1539 he settled in Antwerp and five years later he moved to the Swiss city of Basel where he was to end his days.[10]

Joris's Early Ideas

Joris's reform thought appears to have shifted with the changes in his geographical locale and state of personal security. His writings can be roughly divided into the three periods which correspond to his location. The first period includes the years between 1524 and 1539 when he was an active and enthusiastic Reformer and then Anabaptist. Although frequently on the run, during this time Joris was usually based in his home city of Delft, Holland. After his baptism, Joris sought to blend the ideas of Hoffman and the Münster propagandist Bernhard Rothmann.

In most respects Joris's concepts were in line with those of his fellow Dutch Anabaptists. Joris's compromise solution at the Bocholt colloquium, for example, saw agreement reached on several major doctrinal areas. The importance of the rites of believers baptism and of the Lord's Supper were maintained. Accepted was the Melchiorite conception of the incarnation, which stipulated that Jesus Christ had brought his humanity with him from heaven and therefore had derived nothing from his mother Mary.[11] The doctrines of human free will in salvation and the perfectibility of believers were also affirmed.[12]

The slippery issue of the use of the sword in bringing in the kingdom of God was worded by Joris in such an obtuse fashion that both sides saw it as a victory. Although a permanent settlement was out of reach, Joris's success at this conference was the beginning of the dominant role he would play in leadership over Dutch Anabaptism for the next several years.

Joris was like Hoffman in several other respects. For example, he believed that Anabaptism could remain true to its original mission only by maintaining the charismatic form of leadership which had been Hoffman's inspiration. Joris was therefore quite dismayed that those closest to Hoffman, the Strasbourg Melchiorites, had left this path of spiritual safety. In one sense his concern was appropriate, for after Joris's meeting with the Strasbourg leadership, these stalwarts of Dutch Anabaptism orchestrated the dismantling of the Melchiorite fellowships in the area and the return of hundreds of Anabaptists to the Reformed Church of Strasbourg.[13] Joris was like Hoffman also in emphasizing spiritual or inner truth over externals such as ecclesiastical ceremonies or the literal Scriptures.

Joris in the 1530s, also promoted a Hoffmanite form of Anabaptist congregational organization, with elders, pastors and teachers providing the local leadership under the guidance of the Holy Spirit. The Spirit's instruction was mediated by the prophet, in this case Joris. Ordinary believers were to obey and support the approved leaders, as well as love and assist their brothers and sisters. In his unpublished correspondence it seems that baptism, when combined with the proper spiritual disposition, was employed in Joris's fellowships. In his published works, however, Joris more commonly described baptism in terms of the baptism of suffering. Moreover, in contrast to their reputation, neither Joris nor his followers were strangers to suffering and martyrdom. As noted elsewhere, it was only because of the devotion and sacrifice of his supporters as well as fortuitous circumstances that Joris barely escaped death at the stake.[14]

In response, Joris, like most Anabaptists throughout Europe, emphasized the spiritual rewards of suffering and praised those who died a martyr's death. He expended much energy encouraging his followers in the face of their terror and castigating the authorities for their brutality.[15] Throughout his life Joris remained a vigorous opponent of religious persecution. His activity in this regard reached a climax in 1553 with his famous letter to the magistrates of Calvinist Geneva pleading for the release of the brilliant Spanish physician and anti-trinitarian, Michael Servetus.[16]

This is not to suggest, however, that Joris was in every respect a typical Anabaptist. On top of the commonplaces mentioned above, he developed several idiosyncratic concepts or practices which largely account for the poor state of his reputation. The most obvious was his frustratingly unbending stance regarding his divine calling. Joris's eventual depreciation of the outward rite of baptism and his elevation of his personal authority, moreover, became the special targets of Menno Simons. The Frisian Menno, one of only a few Dutch Anabaptists with a priestly training,[17] had joined Anabaptism in 1536, although it seems that he, like Joris, had flirted with Melchiorite ideas well before his baptism.[18]

However, Menno, unlike Joris appears not to have adopted the full Melchiorite vision in its apocalyptic fervor. It was natural, therefore, that the two leaders would not see eye to eye. Their written debate and oral discussions, at the latter of which Joris was represented by his lieutenants, Jorien Ketel and Nicolaas Meyndertsz van Blesdijk, proved often to be virulent and uncharitable, to say the least.[19]

The main issue was whether leadership of the remaining Dutch Anabaptists was to be based on Hoffman's and Joris's charismatic claims of divine inspiration, or on a more formal leadership trained in biblical exegesis. Menno's position eventually won the day. During the 1540s, however, many of his supporters were lost to Joris. Although this debate necessarily polemicized the two positions, one must be careful not to distinguish too greatly between the Anabaptism of Joris and Menno,[20] nor to assume that Joris ignored the authority of the Bible. His knowledge of the Scriptures, including the apocryphal books, was outstanding, especially when one recalls that aside from his participation in the reform conventicles of the 1520s, he had no formal theological training. Scriptural references and paraphrases fill the texts of all of his writings.

What was distinctive about Joris in this regard is that he claimed to have received the true meaning of those passages directly from the Holy Spirit and not through human education or wisdom. Here again Joris was in many respects following in the footsteps of Hoffman, as well as the late medieval mystical tradition of the Lower Rhineland.

Perhaps the most cryptic of all of Joris's teachings was his sexual ethic. He sought to maintain the rigorous sexual code of the Melchiorites and Münsterites—sexual intercourse only for procreation—within a monogamous framework.[21] For a time Joris's asceticism went to the extreme of requiring candidates for marriage to prove that they had completely eradicated sexual desire from their relationship by a ceremony that bred misunderstanding and rumor-mongering among his opponents.[22] Similar to this was the practice which Joris termed "public confession of sins" during which believers would confess all of the trespasses which they had committed "from their childhood on" and bare their souls before the other believers.

Joris's practice, based on James 5:16, "confess your sins to one another," was a democratization of the contemporary Catholic practice which involved the private confession of a believer to a priest. Both public confession and sexual purity would prove to be major bones of contention between Joris and other Anabaptist leaders.[23] While these teachings of Joris led to a major division between him and Menno in the 1540s, during the last years of the 1530s Joris clearly represented what remained of the mainstream Dutch Anabaptist tradition.

Joris's Later Ideas

The second period of Joris's thought falls between the late summer of 1539 and the summer of 1544, during which time he lived in Antwerp. This was a transitional phase in the prophet's life. Here Joris gained the patronage of a wealthy noble family, led by the matriarch Anna van Etten, the Lady of Schilde, and her son-in-law, Cornelius van Lier, the Lord of Berchem.[24] In the rich cultural atmosphere of the Schilde manor and the city of Antwerp, Joris returned to his artistic endeavors and broadened his intellectual interests, although always for a spiritual purpose.

Joris also quickened the pace of his spiritualization of Anabaptist tenets. This tendency had begun in earnest after the frustrating conferences of 1538. As part of this spiritualization, Joris developed his concept of a "spiritual language" which could be understood only by a spiritually enlightened elite.[25] His writings, always difficult to understand, became even more turgid, inspiring one well-educated contemporary to remark: "It was difficult for me to understand the meaning of the thoughts because of the terribly obscure and confused style of the writing."[26]

His ideas in this middle period are best reflected in the first edition of *The Wonder Book* which probably came off the press in 1543.[27] In this quite sophisticated work, Joris sought to bring all knowledge into the service of the Holy Spirit. Here the divinely inspired third David was the center for all true wisdom. However, he toned down the more blatant aspects of Hoffmanite apocalypticism which had so predominated in his earlier writings. While the length and date of composition of this magnum opus precludes its inclusion in this volume, the *Apology to Countess Anna* provides an example of Joris's writings in this middle period.

The final stage in Joris's career embraces the years after he had moved to Basel. The situation within Antwerp for Joris and his followers had been insecure at best. Antwerp magistrates had taken frequent and severe actions against religious dissent, and during the early 1540s several more suspected heretics were publicly executed.[28] While the patronage of an important nobleman offered some protection, Joris and his fellows could not take the chance of exposure.

After an exploratory trip to the Swiss city of Basel, the fugitives decided it would provide the ideal location for the New Jerusalem, where they could establish the kingdom of God in their own hearts. Joris's noble supporters not only underwrote the relocation, but also escaped with him, bringing along considerable wealth before the imperial authorities could confiscate it. The move, complete with families, took place in August 1544 and symbolized a new stage in Joris's career, as did his adoption of a pseudonym, Johan von Brugge. Joris took on the life of a leisured gentlemen. Neither Joris nor any of his companions experienced any qualms in giving the oath of allegiance, in providing their assent to the city's statement of faith, or in having their infants baptized.[29]

Joris's Nicodemism was now fully formed. Removed geographically from the center of Dutch Anabaptism, Joris allowed his spiritualism to develop more fully and his Anabaptism receded to the background. Joris's move to a complete form of spiritualism is seen in the significantly revised second edition of *The Wonder Book*, completed in 1551. Most visible in this later edition are the changes in Joris's attitudes concerning the third David. The first edition had brought to a climax his self-conception as the apocalyptic agent of God. It is clear that Joris had made some quite subtle revisions by 1551. For example,

Joris in the 1551 *Wonder Book* edition added a section explaining his current view of the promised David and the kingdom. He closely identified the third David with the Spirit, and spiritualized the kingdom of the promised David to mean little more than the community of those who had experienced the rebirth of Christ.[30]

While Joris in his later career maintained a doctrine of the third David, he had lessened the implication that he and the third David were the same and instead identified the apocalyptic figure with the Holy Spirit. In any event, as a result of Joris's physical and ideological movement away from Dutch Anabaptism, leadership of the movement left his hands, and others, such as Menno Simons, were able more completely to take control.

The end of Joris's life was quite an unexpected one for such a notorious heretic. Joris, sick and distraught over recent divisions among the colonists, died of natural causes on August 25, 1556. With his death, the Basel Davidites split into two factions, one led by a devoted noble supporter, Joachim van Berchem, while the other, consisting of the disillusioned, surrounded Joris's son-in-law, Blesdijk.[31] Within three years of his death, Joris's true identity had become public knowledge.[32] Sentence was passed against Joris at the end of April 1559. In the following month his body was disinterred and burned at the stake along with his books and portraits.

Joris's Abiding Influence

Although Joris himself was dead, many in the Low Countries, Germany, and even France continued to publish and purchase his writings. If the worries of a Reformed Synod are any indication, as late as the 1620s there were still many followers of Joris's teaching in the Netherlands.[33] Through the second half of the sixteenth century, disciples of Joris took it upon themselves to respond to what they regarded as the slander of those who accused him of heresy.[34]

In the 1580s, several dozen works, including the second edition of *The Wonder Book*, were reissued in the printing establishments of Dirk Mullem of Rotterdam and Jan Canin of Dordrecht.[35] Another of those accused with sponsoring the reproduction of Joris's works was the Reformed pastor Herman Herberts of Dordrecht and Gouda, who appears to have been a devotee of Joris's teachings.[36]

Joris's writings therefore continued not only to provoke controversy through the next centuries, but perhaps also to influence attitudes of succeeding generations of reformers in the Low Countries.

Joris's Anabaptist Writings

We are most concerned with the Anabaptist writings of this controversial figure. Joris's compositions during his early Reform and Anabaptist career are relatively few in number but extremely important for understanding the nature of post-Münster Dutch Anabaptism. Unlike most of his later spiritualistic writings, many of these early treatises are relatively clear and contain important and historically relevant details.

Joris also composed a number of spiritual songs, twenty-six of which survive in a collection entitled *A Spiritual Song Book*.[37] Several of these provide the only known surviving literary works which can be dated to Joris's pre-Anabaptist phase.[38] While Joris was not above revising his song texts in line with later concerns,[39] by and large the songs in this collection remain accurate reflectors of the early period of the Dutch radical reformation. Many of them are intensely apocalyptical and as such, are among the few windows into the mentality of Anabaptists living in the Netherlands during the high point of the Münsterite kingdom.[40] Two of these will suffice as examples here.

There are at least fourteen tracts which can be confidently dated to the period up to the end of 1539, and more could be discovered simply by a careful perusal of the known Joris corpus.[41] Three of these are included here as representatives of Joris's early published compositions. These works mirror Joris's nearly frantic attempts to keep alive the apocalyptic excitement that had characterized Dutch Anabaptism before the fall of Münster in the summer of 1535. Dulled somewhat by the failure of apocalyptic predictions, the sword of the vengeance of the Lord still threatened the enemies of the Lord's anointed in writings of this period.

First among Joris's early tracts is *Of the Wonderful Working of God*, apparently written in 1535 in an attempt to account for the failure of Münster. The changes brought about by Joris's visions of December 1536 are clearly evident in a long and repetitive tract, *Hear, Hear, Hear, Great Wonder, Great Wonder, Great Wonder*, written immediately after the revelations, purportedly under the direction of the Holy Spirit. Because of its repetitive nature, only excerpts of this important tract are included here.

Shortly after the visions, Joris received what he believed to be a divine mandate to proclaim the message to the remaining Melchiorites, particularly those in England, East Frisia, and Strasbourg. The unpublished "Hydeckel" contains many letters from 1537 to 1543 which indicate that he took this mission very seriously. Translated here are three important letters from this volume.

Joris furthermore penned several tracts relating to this mission (again under the direction of the Spirit). These include the 1537 *An Admonition in Order to Bridle the Tongue*, a work intended both to announce his mission and to warn his readers from speaking presumptuously about the things of the Lord.[42] The contents of this tract lead one to suspect that it was among the works sent by Joris to the Strasbourg Melchiorite leadership, the "elders in Israel," in 1537 and 1538. Its contents, however, are largely duplicated in the letters from this year which are part of our collection. It therefore has not been included here.

Although no dated tracts survive from 1538, this year is notable for the manuscript record of the disputation between Joris and the "elders in Israel" held in June of 1538. This record is not extant in a published form, and we do not know whether this record actually went to press or was even intended for publication. It is nevertheless an extremely important source—not only for its depiction of how Joris publicly defended his teaching and calling, but for its rare insight into the frame of mind of the followers of Hoffman in Strasbourg. The disputation therefore provides a important chapter here.

Several works have survived from 1539. Those which have been dated include *A Very Beautiful Tract or Examination of Humanity's Enemies*;[43] *A Very Beautiful Tract on the Beauty of the Beloved*;[44] *An Announcement of the Coming of the Bridegroom*;[45] "Behold, and Wake up My Children," in *The Third Handbook*;[46]"Behold, a Vision, Seen Openly in the Daylight, of One Who Loves the Truth and Justice of God";[47] *A Very Good Examination of Wisdom*;[48] and *The Eight Blessings*.[49] This last work is Joris's written attempt to encourage his followers in the face of the horrendous persecution which they were experiencing in 1539. Because of the length of this tract, however, we have instead included here a letter written by Joris in 1539 on the same subject.

While this summary includes all the known extant works composed by the Dutch prophet before the decade of the 1540s, there are several undated tracts that can be safely assigned to this early period. The criteria for such selection include evidence of intense apocalypticism (still to be fulfilled on earth) and references to specific events and severe persecution.

It is therefore possible to suggest that at least the following works belong to Joris's "Anabaptist phase": *Of the Principle or Trust of the*

Heavenly Marriage;[50] *The End Comes, the End Comes over All the Four Corners of the Earth;*[51] *A Blessed Instruction for the Hungering, Anxious Souls* (included here);[52] and *How the Believer, Who Takes to Himself a Sister or Wife, Should Support Her.*[53]

These last two cited works appear to be related to Joris's experience at the Strasbourg disputation in 1538. *A Blessed Instruction* will be discussed below. *How the Believer* may have been the work on marriage that Joris promised to send to the Strasbourg Melchiorite leadership after the disputation.[54]

Perhaps the most valuable work for our knowledge of Joris's life—and even state of mind during his time as an Anabaptist—is an anonymous biography composed ostensibly by a close associate of the leader, sometime after Joris's move to Basel. The account is so richly detailed it is likely that Joris was personally involved in its production. In any event, it carries the stamp of autobiography. Its extraordinary insight into Joris's mental and emotional condition during periods of severe persecution makes it one of the most remarkable documents in the field of the radical reformation and provides a good introduction to the writings of Joris included here.[55] The biography, together with the other selections from the tracts and letters of the Anabaptist leader David Joris, provides English readers with their first glimpses into the thought of this extremely important if controversial figure.

A note about biblical references in Joris's writings may be in order. While the specific Dutch translation of the Bible used by Joris is unknown, it could very well have been Jacob van Liesvelt's translation, which first appeared in print in 1522. At the Strasbourg disputation, Joris remarked to his opponents that scriptural proof texts were not necessary for the "simple, God-fearing believers," but only for the "unbelievers and scribes."[56] True religious knowledge was mediated directly to the individual from the Holy Spirit, not merely from the text.

In spite of this seeming depreciation of biblical authority, Joris, as these works indicate, was unusually well-versed in a wide range of biblical passages, rivaling most of his Anabaptist colleagues.[57] As can be readily discerned, however, there was a wide gulf between Joris and his more literalist fellows when it came to the interpretation of those passages. For Joris, the true, spiritual meaning of scriptural passages had been given only to "the small and simple ones who worship [God] reverentially and who are his beloved,"[58] in other words, to Joris's own community of faith. For their part, his opponents complained that Joris's Spirit-illuminated exegesis played fast and loose with the literal text.

Glass round portraying the allegorical virtue of Love; c. 1544-56
Ascribed to David Joris
Courtesy of Historisches Museum, Basel

2

The Anonymous Biography of Joris

The anonymous biography is easily the most informative document arising out of the Davidite circle. In it we learn much about the life and teachings of David Joris, including his state of mind during periods of intense persecution and stress. Interesting details also emerge relative to the experience of Anabaptists in the Netherlands and incidentally to Dutch society under the rule of Charles V. Although the issues of its authorship and transmission are problematical, the account's historical reliability has been confirmed at several points.[1]

The only extant version of the biography is in German translation in the eighteenth-century Lutheran Pietist Gottfried Arnold's collection of sources relating to the history of heresy.[2] Arnold translated the work into High German, but did not provide information about its origin, aside from his affirmation that it was an old manuscript. Since the original is no longer extant, a direct comparison with the known works of Joris or his followers is impossible.

An answer to the question of authorship is a matter of speculation which need not long detain us here. The most active writer in Joris's group was Nicolaas Meyndertsz van Blesdijk, who composed both defenses and later exposés of his father-in-law, as well as a history of the early Melchiorite movement entitled "Concerning the Origin and Beginning of the Sect Which Is Called Anabaptists."[3]

Blesdijk's works, however, do not normally evidence the same kind of psychological insight which we see in the anonymous biography. The anonymous author, moreover, seems to have known or been with Joris before 1539, the year Blesdijk joined Joris's group. A similar problem arises with Joris's secretary, Henrich van Schor, who did not join Joris and the van Berchem family until 1541.

Given the amazing depth of insight and biographical detail which mark this account, the question must be asked whether Joris himself penned the work. Most scholars who have read it have come to the conclusion that it is autobiography.[4] This supposition is not without problems of its own. Joris's known writings are usually obscurely written, with only rare references to specific events. The presentation in this anonymous work is fairly straightforward, with specific events, dates, and locations frequently provided.

It is possible to speculate, however, that Joris composed a rough draft of the work or narrated the relevant stories to one of his better educated associates such as van Schor or Blesdijk, who then polished Joris's utterances into this account, adding quotations and references from Joris's other writings. The only firm conclusion that can be made is that Joris clearly played a major role in the formulation of the anonymous account, if he was not specifically its author.

The biography on the whole is the most detailed source for the study of Joris and his movement up to 1540. The only major problem associated with the use of the biography on the part of the modern researcher is the anonymous author's unquestioning loyalty to Joris. Fortunately it is not the only biographical study of this important Anabaptist leader. Blesdijk, who later became a Reformed pastor, wrote a history of the Davidite movement after he had left it.[5] Although highly critical of Joris's teachings and practices, Blesdijk was fairly reliable on questions of historical detail.

The anonymous account translated here reveals several interesting facts about Joris. He was, like a "Renaissance Man," talented and trained in drawing and painting as well as accomplished in song writing and perhaps also in drama. He was from a merchant family and his mother was a member of Delft's upper class. He had received an adequate grammar education, although he apparently retained little of his Latin. His form of writing and thought revealed a penchant for "hidden meanings" and intentional obscurity common among Renaissance Neo-Platonists.

This is not to say that Joris was a humanist, for his lack of ability in Latin closed to him the cultural world of the humanist elite. Although providing considerable detail about Joris's life, the anonymous author clearly intended to present Joris first and foremost as an individual inspired with a religious mission, the importance of which made the composition of this extraordinary biography worth the considerable effort involved.

❂ ❂ ❂ ❂ ❂

David Joris's Extraordinary Biography from a Manuscript[6]

[703] In God I will, to the best of my ability, try to do enough to satisfy you, my beloved, regarding your request about David Joris, of whom you desire to know more. I surely will, for I can only do that which is the daily public practice concerning all those who are regarded as pious, learned and wise. For I know how the stories of the holy fathers, patriarchs and prophets of previous times, yes, of the saints and even more of the Lord Christ Jesus, were told for improvement. I desire only that my written history be well received. I desire nothing more than to do everything possible (believe it or not if you will) to place it freely and unhindered before all eyes, whether it is beneficial or unbeneficial. For I, more than any other, am the one to do this, because his entire life and being on earth is well known to me. God is my and his witness that I do not lie. I believe the same things that this man taught and I perceive myself to be like him. Namely, that he might honor only his God, to whose praise I also desire to write or speak this. Otherwise, if this were not true, then it would be much better for both me and him to refrain from such, even though it has been dearly wished for and requested by many.

One observes that many different people during their lives and even after death obtain a reputation as good or evil. One may easily know what kind of fruit this will bring to the readers, for it will uncover their own honor and praiseworthiness, just as much as his. For it provides a comparison to what they have desired, sought, or lusted after and what they have done and commanded (as I hear). But this purpose must remain far from me, from him and his people. All of this has occurred only to great amazement and to the praise of God. One is able to imagine, as far as one is able to feel, observe, or consider the matter, the kind of powerful, almighty hand and foresight God has displayed above his people in all respects, that he, to his praise, would protect and preserve this man's life from the world. Therefore I was moved to write this, desiring to say something about the aforementioned words, for I am amazed about the hand of God on his beloved. [704] To do otherwise would not be good, but evil. May my Lord God and Christ Jesus guard me in his Spirit. Amen.

I must confess that I know little that is worthwhile to narrate concerning this man's beginning or youth; nor concerning the business and conduct of his outward life and nature; yes, even less of his end in the same. It has been requested, as one should modestly expect, to hear only about the nature of his inner heart in his will and spirit. I will therefore (if God wills) do what I can. How the Lord, in the very beginning, took him by the hand and gradually removed him from the world with all its flesh and raised him in his Spirit and nature according to his heart, and to his praise.

Firstly, he was a firstborn son, born in sin like any other boy. He was born into the daylight in the city where his mother (of blessed memory)[7] was forced to reside because of the disagreement and great injustice of the world, having fled from her parents or friends like a runaway into this strange land (it is so amazing to hear). Because he was the second son on her mother's side, some wanted to name him Peter and others Jacob, but neither was selected. Furthermore, because six godparents had been chosen and they wanted to give the child their own name, one of the six finally spoke up, saying: "He should not have any of these; the child should be called David, because his father is now playing him."[8] His first name came about in this way, in which he had recognized little of God. I believe, however, that God had preordained and known it before the foundation of the world [cf. Eph. 1:4] and he desired to prove the truth of the name. One must admit that no other conclusion is possible about this matter.

A little time after this (when he was twelve or thirteen years old) he was confirmed by a suffragan bishop and given the name of his grandfather John. His first name David, however, was most commonly used, because he was best known to everyone by this name. After he had grown up and came first to the Lutherans and afterwards to the Covenanters,[9] it was desired that he return to his first baptismal name. He did this and it is also not incorrect to call him David after this time, until he journeyed with wife and child to Germany, where he again took on the name Johan von Brugge.[10] Nevertheless, one must bear one's name, which, without the true deed, is vain and unseemly. Nothing else is due to anyone, nor to any outward thing upon the earth created either by God or people, other than to honor the thing that is, although in this case the name is indeed revealing. Therefore the holy, eternal God himself did not designate himself with any name (although Moses or the people had wished for such), because the time was not yet ready for the people. For which reason, he, blessed, would say nothing else to Moses, according to my knowledge, except "I am who I am" [Exod. 3:13-14]. Because he had not yet revealed himself in the power, not to mention in the Spirit and eternal truth. He therefore proclaimed his name through the prophet or the understanding one. For he is a God of the past, present, and future [cf. Heb. 13:8] and he proclaimed these clear words: "I am who I am." Because this described his essence, he could not have proclaimed any other designation. Truly all of us are therefore responsible to observe that we neither accept nor draw to ourselves either honor or harm concerning our names until they are manifestly joined to the Spirit of power and truth, or until one is what one should be, eternally provided by God.

Now to come again to our purpose. The names which he received have been briefly narrated, and he grew up as a very fine, chaste man in an honorable fashion. Through many different pestilences and sickness he was raised up in all manner of simplicity and modesty of the world. Furthermore, he was not by nature false, bad, ill tempered, cunning, proud, lying, nor deceptive (as one naturally makes one's way by necessity). Instead, even when he was tempted or had only put his finger into the ashes or did anything bad or talked too quickly (which can easily come to pass due to the old corrupt childish nature) it was just as quickly driven out of him by his parents and also by strangers; sometimes by his teacher, other times by God himself in his heart. He never or very rarely had a completely pleasant, quiet day. He was like any other in the manner of inborn childish naughtiness, although he was always sorrowful, maintaining a humbled nature. He had to leave behind his own nature, for he was also tempted by the evil of the flesh or the world and would not have followed after any decency had God not oppressed him.[11]

Like any other pupil he was sent first to a small, then later to a large school.[12] But what did this mean? Although he had, like his fellows, the ability to learn (as is commonly found), he experienced no lust or desire for it. Nevertheless, he finally ascended so far that he soon came into the fourth grade. He has, however, after all this time remembered nothing of it, except a most inferior merchant's Latin. He has not retained even that very well, but in a completely absurd form, as he often heard said about himself. On account of this he said "that we should perceive God's hand on him and in his nature and spirit, because he would not put up with any learned wisdom and intelligence." Whenever he was supposed to study, he would instead paint figures. Although he had no heart for study, he was extraordinarily religious and he displayed it like any other, enjoying especially godliness and holy things. [705] He was one in a thousand in this respect, not driven back or led astray. But it pleased him to serve God with outward religion, for at that time he was deeply concerned about the superstitious and idolatrous things of his youth. Now because he had no desire to learn, but possessed a great love for art and was always making pictures from nature, they said to each other, "Yes, it is a pity that he is not an artist." And then each one had their own desire regarding the artistic crafts. His father and mother gave him the choice that whichever he loved the most, they would allow him to learn it. His grandmother desired that he become an organist and his mother that he be a goldsmith, because in these occupations there existed no anxiety or danger to the soul. But he desired to learn glass writing or painting, but not to become a gold-beater.

This desire to learn glasspainting came to him from a merely human understanding of a particular story, when he saw another youth do the same. Furthermore, the grandiose rich people, who had a great name, taught such to their children. Whoever learned this art would be held in great esteem, yes, even by emperors, kings, bishops, popes and cardinals. For their part they could travel and reside with the highest nobility and be able to wear gold, silk and jewels on their clothes. This was what aroused him particularly (as one can imagine) to learn the art. When this was now confirmed and he was taken away from it again because of a bad constitution and other related conditions, he was for two or three years placed in his father's small shop and in everything served his father's needs. Then his father, together with two brothers, four sisters, and several others in the household were killed by the plague. After this he came to a rich, powerful merchant, who was very wealthy. And if this had not been the case, he would have been brought into the chancellery of the court by one of his mother's friends.[13] But God brought it to pass that he would come to this splendid and experienced man, who offered to give him (when he became eighteen or nineteen years old) his own daughter if he served well. Joris heard this promised in his presence, for the rich man truly liked him. I believe, that he, without a doubt, was worth more than a hundred thousand guilders, because this youth recorded all his money, rents and everything else that was income.[14]

On top of this he also had a large chest full of money, which the young man saw. And one time around 4 a.m., with David sitting nearby, the man opened it before his eyes, and he left him sitting nearby and went into his writing chamber to write a letter. This chamber was right above the chest, so that he could look over everything. But the youth was so innocent that he thought nothing of it and was not tempted by the money. Nevertheless, it was unbelievable. But what could it mean to him when he was that young? There was a corner in the chest divided by a middle shelf, which was completely full of large pieces of gold, so tightly packed that I believe they could not have been hammered more tightly together with a hammer, so that one could look at but not examine a single piece. All of this was pure gold. The silver was much more abundant, probably worth 100,000 florins if it was as tightly packed to the bottom as can be easily imagined. The merchant had neither wife nor child, except the one, and was subsequently elected as burgomaster of the city. He had a very great reputation, and kept a house alone with his daughter, two maids, and a servant girl.[15] The youth, however, could not stay here because of the offense of the chest, because he found himself disposed to something better and believed that one should overcome such a money God. For that could not satisfy him, however many great things and commitments this rich man promised. And if he would have stayed with him, then he would in the meantime not have learned the art which was his true love and desire.

He could not endure it and stay. He instead left, on the pretext of his mother's business. He asked for a leave of absence from him, and it was agreed. David stayed instead in the shop in the place of his father until he found another master under whom he completed his apprenticeship in only one year. After he had finished the year he was sent out and was able to earn twelve pounds for a work, yes, as time went on even more, for he was well taught. Moreover, all of his good masters were pleased with his profit, for he served without charge. But it would not always be this way and he desired his freedom. He therefore left on a trip to France and went with some of his guild from Antwerp to Valencia, where he did not remain long because of incentive elsewhere.[16] Instead, they journeyed through Lille and Calais, where they contracted themselves out to the treasurer of the King of England,[17] who hired them for a price which would give them as much as they could earn in one year. From there they, together with his entire family, moved to London and he brought them from there into the land near Lasing and Basingstoke, fifty-five miles from London.[18] I have forgotten the house, but not one out of ten wanted to stay there and cut glass. But God let him get into a quarrel, on account of which he and his journeymen departed secretly from there. They still had a little to use up of what they had earned with some garments and believed to find their lord and master, millord Sandys, at London in England, because the emperor had come at that time into England. Sandys, however, had not come, staying instead at Calais. They therefore stayed in England because of the unfriendly waters,[19] and earned much money and thought they were doing wonderfully with their

great earnings. But God soon assailed David, so that he bled so strongly from his nose that he was regarded as dead. [706] He therefore
found it impossible to live there. This sickness consumed him so much
that he either had to leave or die, because he could not endure the nature of the land or air. On this account he departed, and returned in a
short time to Antwerp in 1524.[20] From there he went to Delft and was
married.[21] Now at the time when this occurred, David immediately
began to seriously consider Luther's teaching (according to his own
assertion) about which he had heard something here and there. He
took it to his heart to pay devout attention to understanding it. Also,
for quite a while, there was not one sermon preached from which his
love of knowledge did not increase greatly in his heart. This preoccupation, furthermore, consumed all of his mind, like the working of
physical love. Yes, he nearly drowned in this knowledge, for there was
in him such a desire and sight for it, which increased and grew daily.
He learned more than one can believe, much of it on his own. He continued in this even though he was as a result forced to retain many
household servants. But this knowledge began around the time the
gospel broke into the land, bringing everywhere a new manner of
thinking. People were unaccustomed to this, so that all who took the
knowledge to heart could not surrender their hearts to it and thereby
become masters over others.

Reason for His First Zeal

The principal reason for the zeal by which he was attracted to the
great unmeasurable sweetness was in a sermon in which this Psalm
was expounded: "How blessed and well is he who does not walk on
the path of the godless, but who has his desire and joy in the law of the
Lord, and therein day and night he will be as a tree, etc." [Ps. 1:1-3].
Also, the passage where Mary had chosen the best portion [Luke
10:42]. These were only two especially notable speeches which
struck David Joris's heart and attracted him to become involved in the
movement with hunger and longing. Furthermore, he went about
boldly in this same mind and was always zealous and continually asking questions of the teachers of the Lord so that all of it was instilled
in his heart.[22] And he never tired of listening to them. Nevertheless,
temptation still countered him, even in the years when he stood in
such good zeal. For he still sighed and grieved over his godless, fleshy,
vain life. He developed for a while such a fiery spirit that he could not
look at a door or window (so to speak) without courting danger. For

everywhere he wanted to bear witness to the evil and good (according to his understanding) and he made himself black and abominable to the papists. In this zeal he sought out and encouraged the prisoners, some of whom were put to death with the sword, some on the other hand were led to fire, some to the wheel.[23] In summary, in every street and alley, he reproved the honoring or worshiping of the images of Mary or other wooden idols. One time, after long prayers (since he was clothed with power and ability) he did so too boldly and too loudly. For he desired to be innocent of all their errors, about which he testified in writing here and there. It therefore happened that if the Burgomaster had not removed him, some would have wounded or even slain him. They struck him indeed on his cheeks [cf. Matt. 26:67], but his heart still burned within him to carry out his work. He had borne with affliction all of this in his mind for so long, having to watch the idolatry of those who boasted of being Christians. And because he would not permit it and keep quiet, he was imprisoned on this account for eleven weeks. He had also written two, three or four letters which were fastened by night to the church doors and scattered here and there on the streets, whenever there was a procession.[24] He also placed them in the confessionals for the clergy. In summary, he did what he had to do and was able to do it from the great desire and zeal for his God, the Lord knows it.

He was still young, and had been married for only a few years, but he did not consider this, nor his wife or child, even though he loved them as much as it is possible to love, regardless of where he was. But this zeal increased even more after he was miraculously released from prison without being forced to recant. For some of his relatives had made a letter of obligation or guarantee, speaking on his behalf without his knowledge and they remained entirely free on his account as was told to him after this. Everyone in the city had a good testimony of his zeal and honesty for the gospel and they feared an insurrection of the common people and poor on behalf of Joris. He had become their friend because of some small outdoor worship services. If they had truly known David Joris, he would never have been released, although he was. Too much happened (as it frequently occurred) to recount everything here. The torture or punishment did not even take place publicly, because he was expelled out of the city at sunrise and was not to return in three years upon life and goods, except with the pleasure of the judge if he desired or demanded it.[25] After this it happened that around seven or nine of these people were thrown into the prison in The Hague.[26] When they were to be beheaded on account of rebaptism, they spoke to the same David Joris and called to him: "Brother, are you here? See, we are going here to testify to our faith for the name of the Lord Jesus Christ." One of them, who was called their bishop, knew David Joris and formerly had disputed with him two years before concerning the deity of Christ, denying the same and claiming that Christ was only a mere human servant of God. David Joris, along with his assistants, however, were most important in convincing him and [707] God brought it about, without harm and bloodshed. This one now spoke to David Joris and said: "Are you here? Were you not he, with whom I formerly disputed of Christ?" "Yes, I," spoke David. "Indeed," spoke the bishop, "now I am completely free and delivered from it, and believe in Christ my Savior." And many more similar things befell the same man. But David Joris took it to heart, and thanked God greatly, that he had heard this before his death.

From this time on he became more famous and subsequently when the baptists or covenanters arose and many followed after them, David Joris remained in his own way. This amazed many who also disputed with him, desiring to persuade him and to convert him to their beliefs or mind, but that was not possible. For they could not do so with the Scriptures, for he was very gifted therein and many others were forbidden to dispute or to speak with him at all, as he was regarded as an opponent of God. This, however, passed soon in one year. In the next year, however, there was a procession of the covenanters in the land.[27] I believe that the year, day and month it occurred as well as the complete names of the leaders and from which lands and cities they came has been written elsewhere. With some of these David Joris was somewhat acquainted. Among this crowd he also identified some of his relatives, who, before this had occurred, had wanted to have him in their midst. It is not necessary to relate here everything that these same ones alleged. Suffice it to say that he became very confused in his soul, because these people were among the best, most innocent, faithful and honest persons who inquired after God and sought his kingdom. And then, the sickness of his heart returned, so that if God had not especially forbade and hindered him from it, he would have joined the movement, if only because they were the good simple society, placing themselves in all sorts of danger. On this account David Joris turned to God in his soul with prayers and petitions, seeking and crying to God ceaselessly, beating himself so that he would not be abandoned by the Lord. He therefore had no rest at this time, but admonished his companions daily that they should not look up to him. "For I," he said, "might not be willing to join this thing because my sins or iniquities are keeping me out of it. Therefore, call to God with pure hearts, without regard to any person!" And he distanced himself from them, for he had a great reputation both from within and without. But they desired to discuss it with him, because he was richly endowed with scriptural understanding, able to overcome all heresies. But God did not remove him from such a sensation, but placed him instead on friendly terms with his royal household and land. He had called him (I maintain this because of his wisdom in writing and through his prudence in the truth, which he sought) to convert the simple hearts from their error, of which error people repeatedly accused him, giving him the guilt.

As the matter now stood, he was daily opposed by these ones or those ones. He heard about this, that even his associates in the upper classes in the city were ready to gave him up, like a sacrificial lamb to the slaughter. But he became aware of it in his heart so that he was forced to depart for other places. At this time the apostasy came as foretold by the Scriptures [cf. 2 Thess. 2:3] and it became evident which people or fellowship was pleasing to God. It came about during one winter evening in a house where he found gathered approximately eight or ten people sitting together. Here he spoke to the teacher with arguments to the effect that he was not gifted enough to counter him orally, it was enough that he do so in writing. Then, however, a knowledgeable woman from Rotterdam named N. Kniepers, who is still known today, answered him. Due to her simplicity and innocence and mostly on account of her zeal, he liked her very much.[28] Therefore David Joris asked to go with the teacher to the back part of the room in order to speak more freely with him, so that the other simple, poor sheep would not worry themselves about it and despair. When he now was with this same teacher, he asked him how he had come to this movement or through what sort of spirit, word or doctrine he came into this. But this one answered in a very simple literal fashion, that it was written in the last chapter of St. Mark [Mark 16:15-16] and the Lord had commanded such. He dared to follow Christ, and would confirm such with his blood. See, when he said "with the blood," these words aroused David Joris's heart, and he was struck down in his most inward being about it and said that he desired to speak even further with him. Not long after this it happened on another evening that he came to this same house with three or four other persons, and surrendered himself to the Lord, requesting to be received into their church. He made the condition that he be allowed to speak about the incarnation of Christ (for at that time they promoted it as necessary, in a very fleshy manner). "The same Lord and Master Christ," he said, "who has come down unto the lowermost regions of the earth, I believe that he is the same one who has ascended above all heavens."[29] He furthermore cited from the speech of Paul and with this he was at peace, because he wished to say nothing else against it. Now when some heard that this man had given himself to them and had allowed himself to join them, they were very merry, and boasted much of it.

But some of these (who regarded themselves more learned than this teacher, and yet could not hold a candle to David Joris in debate) refused to believe, but said, "If this were so, it must not have been done correctly." But some, who were still outside and who heard the boasting of others about this man, bore remorse and sorrow of heart. As a result they became increasingly inclined to join them, and the persecution became so harsh against them from this time on, that in every city not a single [708] one of them could go about freely. It was then that he was forced to roam freely upon the earth, and it is known to everyone the kind of edicts and mandates which were issued against these people. Furthermore, this same man was very anxious, and had to run sometimes here, other times there. He was hidden by some for money, by some because of old acquaintances, and by others because of friendship. He had to leave behind wife and child. Then, when it was Easter [March 28, 1535], he was forced to leave by necessity and hardship and went away secretly at great expense.[30] But this was dangerous because he had his wife and infant son (named Joris) with him, which caused him anxiety and danger everywhere. But he found some companions on the way who traveled with him to Strasbourg, where he hoped to support himself and to practice his craft. But even on the same day when he arrived, in the month after Pentecost in the year 1535 [June 1535], he was approached by one named Leonard (a butcher) who was terribly startled to see him, saying: "Brother, what are you doing here in the godless city?"[31] And after speaking with him about those things which were most preoccupying him, he went into a lodging, for the others were not allowed to put him up, neither out of doors nor inside, without the consent of the magistrates of the city. And when he had examined everything and found no service or work for himself, it came to him (on account of the desolate, wild state of the city) when he saw the mercenaries and other scoundrels, as well as the community,[32] he refused to be in such an unsettled lodging, not to mention to remain there alone. For it was just as if they were in a field of soldiers. He therefore wanted to permit his company to leave, for these also wanted to continue on.

But David Joris had not been there for even two days when he left again with much burdensome pain, anxiety, and worry in his heart, just as when he had arrived. For wherever he had been seen before, he must not allow himself to be seen by anyone again. Furthermore, there was not one in ten places where he would not have been interrogated if he were seen. On this account he stayed for one to four days in the bush behind the lodging and wrote a song: "O Christian Spirits," etc., whereof the contents were: "Be always prepared to die."[33] And another (if I am correct): "The Lord is King in Israel," etc., to the tune of "A Mighty Fortress Is Our God."[34] And when this came to pass, one of them desired to go to Vlissingen in Zealand and Joris desired to go to London in England. He, along with those who journeyed with him, were advised to depart, for it was very dangerous there because of his fame. So, in God's name he left by boat, but it was such a wretched ship that it could not have survived much, and they would all have drowned if a strong wind had arisen. When he now arrived in Vlissingen, he was not led immediately into an inn like the others, but into a sleeping house (where each one had to take care of his own board). They would be able to sail when there was a good wind. He could then depart by a ship which had sailed to London and returned. Here in this town, moreover, he was not concealed, but was in much anxiety and fear. Therefore, when a ship was ready to sail with the wind, they led him into it and commended him to God. In the evening the skipper stood on the thwart and said that the next time they stood up, "then we will be in England." Just as soon as he had spoken the words, the wind blew so frightfully, that they had to tie themselves together with a sail or rope around their chests and heads. The wind blew against them, flinging the ship backwards, so that the rudder no longer held. And it was so dark that one could see nothing in one's sight except the tall, mighty waves. By all appearances it seemed to all of them that the ship would be capsized.

But he commended himself to God in these manifold miserable events and thought among other things, "O Lord, if I will and must perish here secretly, I would prefer it for I have longed to die on account of your name. But if it is possible, let us escape from this and become more mature in your Word than we are now." The storm continued throughout the long, dark night, so that the ship's crew knew not where they were and awaited the day in fear. They soon turned back and in this way they returned distressed and with just as many difficulties as when they had left earlier, to await for another day or wind.

When he now arrived at the house, he went straight into the room. Three men then came from England into the house and spoke secretly with those who were residing therein, describing to a stranger the kind of persecution there. They said that one could not enter what was called the roost[35] without being interrogated. There was always someone who was checking out the people, interrogating and examining them to see what kind of people had entered.[36] Then the two who heard this spoke to each other, saying it was not worth it to go there. But one, who is called Martin, a knifesmith, said: "I will go and see where I can dwell."[37]

Then the man remained alone with his wife and child, but his heart was beating in him above all measure. Nevertheless, he would not let himself be observed by the people. For this reason he placed himself in a Dutch ship and dared to sail in it. But the skipper almost observed it. This man was a conceited, careless, carnal person. And he brought him to Dordrecht. Although he would have liked to have departed, the good man was in no way able to hazard it. He sat down and then laid down on the ship, but with fear and anxiety, so that the skipper would not be too suspicious. And he saw his old acquaintances passing close to him, but they did not see him clearly, because of the prevention and protection of the grace of God. [709] In this way they took him to Gorkum on the Waert, where he remained for several days. There he was not afraid to receive some work with a master for whom he worked early and late, all for a modest pay which he received for his considerable effort. Yes, the people must have spoken with amazement that such a skillful journeyman would work merely as hired help. During this time he experienced no little anxiety, for it happened once or twice that he was nearly betrayed by some at the court who had come into the shop, as one says, to spy. Because of this he went into a thatched field-hut, wherein had lain one with the plague. When these officials left, he returned along the road, and lived in Gorkum for some months. After this time he was forced to leave this place because his wife was pregnant and they had to move to Delft where his mother lived in freedom so that his wife could make her childbed.

But he arrived there at night with much anxiety and at great expense, and went to work for a master and he was always with him. But she (because the time had come) went to his mother to give birth, and she bore in time a son, whom they named David, and it was Candlemas in 1536 [February 2, 1536]. He was here for nearly the whole winter and sat upstairs under a low ceiling where he worked and slept. He suffered much cold and much shivering here, and it was amazing that he did not die at this time. He had a heavily burdened and anguished heart for his wife and child, more than anyone has ever heard or seen. It seemed that he too was in labor pains. And if he loved his life and those with whom he was concealed, he had to be quiet and hide himself. He lay in great pain, flat as a worm upon the earth. Then without his cooperation he was pulled up and down at his hips, from one end to another, just like a worm or maggot wriggles up and down. Then it seemed that he was dead. Therefore, he was placed near the fire, where he came to himself and was healthy again. Here he was visited by some of his acquaintances, who, by means of many disputations, desired to bring him around to their beliefs or intentions. This continued through the entire night, but they always left overcome by him. One cannot imagine the words which were said there. They were those of Hazerswoude, among whom was Batenburg.[38] David Joris would not follow the life or ways of these. He had, before they came to him, received a message from God, in this fashion, that they would not overpower him. On account of this they regarded David Joris as nothing and believed that when the vengeance came, he would have to watch out that it did not fall on him as on the others. And they threatened the good man in this fashion with more similar words, but that did not help at all. David Joris always acted only after praying and desiring that God would protect and guard him from all evil, and that he would become a new creature. (I have heard him say that at this time he had known this merely from the letter.) Yet in his heart he hoped for nothing except the purity of God and to love the truth. He furthermore worked constantly and vigorously in all quietness. From time to time he wrote something, which cannot be narrated here. To summarize, he had quarrels with everyone who did not desire the middle way of his understanding. He was therefore defamed by the Batenburgers, as if he had a jealous, evil heart and an angry spirit. Batenburg spoke very badly about the good man, only because Joris would not take up the sword (which he used severely in punishment) and put on Peter's crown. About this David said nothing except that there were already too many Peters who desired to use the sword too quickly [cf. Matt. 16:18-19; John 18:10]. Others said he was an impertinent scribe and continued to oppose him on the other side. But he did not retreat because of this, instead in prayer he always kept his eyes fixed on the very best, namely, on what pleased God, on what was the most loved and necessary for his will and word. Yes, he neither went up or down, nor ahead or behind, without his heart being always inclined to pray and desire.

But there came a great dissension among these people, for one wanted it one way, another the other way; some put forward strange, unusual things, others, hypocrisy; and there was on every side nothing but strong emotions. Everyone was in anxiety, worry and calamity, not knowing who they should follow, whether these teachers or those ones. But David Joris kept himself quiet and came to no one. But whoever came to him, of whom there were few indeed, he spoke to them of the Lord and his Word. He, however, did not claim to be a teacher. For he neither wished nor desired to be one and he never baptized anyone. Even if he had wanted to, he could not do it, for God had certainly not laid it upon him. He however had been chosen to do so by one named Damas[39] and another named Obbe,[40] together with some others, not to mention the church which laid hands on him. He, David Joris, complained, saying continually, "I neither desire it nor am I able, for I feel no calling or power." But, even though he cried bitterly and shed many tears, they did not consider this at all, but commended him to fulfill his ministry. But in his heart he could neither accept nor regard it, as long as he did not have a good feeling about it nor sense a proper authentic calling for it. At this time the books and letters came out of Münster concerning marriage, the kingdom of Christ and the restitution or restoration of all things.[41] He was therefore summoned to the place where a great crowd was to be gathered together in the Waterland to discuss these distributed books. He came along with them, but not without anxiety, for he did not know how or why.[42] When he arrived at this place, where he had never been in all his life, he had to meet with the twelve or fourteen men there. He knew some among them and they finally brought forward their message to him [710] concerning the things about which they wanted to speak to him. They sought to come to an agreement amongst themselves about what was to be done in every city. To them he answered "that he could not present himself as such a teacher or act like one, he had to wait for it from God." On this account they exchanged many words with each other (which are too long to narrate here) and mostly about him, his youth and inexperience, being worried and anxious because of him.

After the meal they then commenced to read the book; with it was a messenger from Münster. And they briefly questioned him [Joris] about everything, if he had anything to add to it. But he said that he was not old and experienced enough to know about it, let someone else answer. He could not agree that one should therefore smite with the sword. But they had on the agenda that if someone saw his brother imprisoned, he should give his life for him, and more similar sayings. But David Joris answered that such was not free to him, the Lord Jesus did not present such an example to him. Neither was it taught by the apostles, but instead to bear the cross and to suffer every injustice. He declared this with many points from the Scriptures, and said, "This is God's Word which must have its fulfillment in you. You had better look after yourselves. This I know, that it is God's Word," he said, "and it abides into eternity." One of them named Damas[43] replied to this: "How? Beloved brother David Joris, it is also God's Word, which is spoken as well from the prophets and the apostles, and likewise abides certainly into eternity. What do you say to this?" David answered, "I say nothing against it, except that I have to study it first, and will let it take its course," and more similar arguments which are too long to narrate here. Therefore, they responded first in this way, then in that way, so that the argument continued for a long time, because each one desired to be better than the others in his reply. Some, as Joris himself admitted, believed themselves to be more highly esteemed than he was in the best understanding and divine insight. David, however, could not agree with them in this matter. He finally kept himself completely quiet, with the condition that he and they would ask God to give his grace and understanding and that they would inquire after the best without looking to anyone.

After this he journeyed away from them with great trouble and haste over the ice, so that he came close to death. What happened to him on the way cannot be described, but he was a man of very delicate and infirm nature, and on account of his own physical condition, he was full of anxiety and fear, so that he could not be left alone. On account of this it was advisable not to leave him alone along the route, neither on the roads nor at the inns where his fellow travelers stayed, because it was feared that he might be all too easily identified. After this the matter was again brought up and discussed by some.[44] And although he abstained from it as something evil, yet he did not want to judge them on account of his ignorance and inexperience outside of the Spirit of truth. He was, however, still reckoned as among them, although his heart and hand were far from it. However, when he soon saw and heard where it was all heading, he felt very badly that such hearts would so soon perish and very many of them would die, because he knew that it would result in this way because of their zeal. On account of this he prayed and pleaded without ceasing that God would grant them mercy and understanding and true knowledge about his Word. Furthermore, he prayed that for the sake of many souls it would produce fruit in every willing heart and also that many might be saved.

After all of this had happened, one of the people of Poeldijk arose, a simple man (as I have heard said) and with him three or four others, who went throughout the land saying, "He has received the Spirit of power from the Father, so that he will soon take vengeance and punishment against all the godless and malicious evildoers and especially against the Court at The Hague, for the innocent blood of their brothers."[45] How things proceeded and ended with him, as well as everything which was done for him and by him, one can learn from the trustworthy witnesses in the region of this same land, who have heard and seen it. To this one the good man, David Joris sent a letter, saying that they should refrain from such things. He furthermore remonstrated them with words and letters, that they should not persist in setting one up so high or claiming him as a king, as was said. He also desired to meet with them, just as he had done and written to those of Hazerswoude. But the letter had hardly come when they were immediately captured; they, however, refused to read the letter, throwing it instead in the fire and speaking against it. They despised him and finally sent him word: "Go there and say to David Joris that I am chosen as a king and a lord and a ruler over the whole world in Christ's place, with more similar words."[46]

But some of these men, who were taken in by him, went and uttered strong words which they had heard from him against David Joris, so that no goodwilled, innocent heart could stand it. But before the morning came, these same had been converted and convinced by David's speeches, realizing that they had erred therein. The result of all this was that Joris was noticed everywhere and his word at that time had as much power and blessing as any other. On account of this he prayed even more fiercely and implored for more Spirit and power. And when this thing with these men at Poeldijk was nearly forgotten, he, David Joris, was now again summoned to Bocholt, where the [711] leaders from Strasbourg and England were to meet along with many others. These included Jan Matthijs, Johann Maastricht, and Johann van Schoonhofen.[47] They were to discuss the restitution or restoration, for those of Münster were to come and present their beliefs concerning it.[48] They hoped to settle it in unity, and to compare everything with each other. For an Englander, by the name of Henry, who formerly had been of one mind with him [Joris], had requested and prayed that the great disunity be ended and that their leaders or elders, as they were called, would be gathered there at his cost, if they were able, so that there might once again be unity.[49] For this reason many who stood on the side of Batenburg were also invited to come along. To this meeting David Joris was also called to appear with the rest of them. His departure and arrival were accomplished with great danger, anxiety, fear, and need. What happened to him on the way and with whom he disputed is too long to narrate here. Briefly, when he heard of the man's [i.e., Batenburg's] all too great freedom and speed, he did not want to appear there. He therefore sat in the room in his mother's house and worked quietly in the stillness, fearing perhaps that they might bring forward something secretly among them. What it may have been I do not know exactly, although I know well that at first he remained away from it. Also Jan Matthijs was forced to come a long way from Strasbourg because of a dream which he had, namely, that all who were gathered together, about twenty or twenty-five, would perish or be imprisoned. And that was the reason why he stayed away from it.

When David Joris finally appeared everyone assailed him, for those from England believed that if David Joris had not been there, they would have been able to talk with, persuade, and convince the others. Nevertheless (although they repeated such things about him behind his back), they did not separate from each other. For David Joris desired that they would depart peacefully from one another, without scolding, quarreling, or reviling. Instead, he desired that they proceed in a brotherly fashion and that everyone sincerely pray that whoever was incorrect at some point or had a misunderstanding, that it should be brought out into the open and examined. But not to scold and examine one another with hateful, unbrotherly words, but instead for their own information. To this they finally assented. But no one was willing to write the manuscript which was to be produced as a statement of testimony and to show how they actually agreed. David (although he was the youngest of them all) had to do this as well. See, it was therefore written and they all received it unanimously, and then departed from one another.[50] But alas, they did not keep to it as it was announced.

After this David became increasingly earnest (as God knows it) and his spirit was enlightened more each day in his zeal and faith. However at this time there was near Faute[51] a great persecution and severe inquisition. Because of this, fear became so widespread that one was not able to find a corner to stay anywhere, regardless of how many places one tried. Therefore, he could sometimes remain in one place for scarcely two or three days, hardly more, and he experienced in this search much misery. All of this cannot be described here. Every day he must take his life into his hands, because he was known by many. But God kept him alive and rescued him out of the city in broad daylight, for the gates were certainly guarded too closely. He was placed like a dog in a basket and covered with skins and rags, and a beloved servant let him down in a sack from a high place[52] into a small boat and they quickly sailed away. Many things happened to him on the way, for all of them were nearly drowned and one time he fell out, but some strangers caught the boat and the sack. Because they were still near Faute, it is unnecessary to narrate. In this way he came out of the city just a few days before it burned.[53] He finally also had to leave this place because of the fear of execution and anxiety of the people and he moved to another region. When he had not been long in this place, he was very heartily invited into a town, being told that he could come there if he was willing.[54] It must happen in this way, otherwise they might not have been willing to shelter him, because there were also no sleeping places there. He walked through the whole night with great vexation to this place. After this he took his leave from his wife and children, which happened lamentably so often, that God in heaven, yes, even a heart of stone, would have pitied them.

When he now came to a shore where a ship was ready, he took his leave from his friends who had accompanied him and went secretly into the ship, although he had to sail inside the strange cargohold to where he wanted to go. Because he arrived there during daylight, they had to hide him for the whole day with all the other cargo which lay in a small chamber in the front of the ship. He lay so still that no one knew of it. At nighttime, perhaps eight or nine o'clock, after it became dark, a grandfather came who, wanting to let him out, tried to quietly remove the lock in the darkness with a bent woodborer. He spent so much time at this that he eventually gave up all hope and wanted to leave it. Finally God allowed him to succeed, and he was released from it and was received joyfully by the God-fearing hearts. Here the table was decked and the food prepared and it was around ten o'clock or later before the meal was finished. While there he was tempted in many different ways, and often was forced to completely quiet himself (whenever the temptations fell on him) among the people, as if he was standing behind a curtain and had to hide. He had to swallow all sorts of pills, [712] which happened to him many times. About this (and many more things), however, he rejoiced in his God and thought: "Well, Lord, you know that it has happened on account of your will." And after this there came to him a peace, whenever he thought about this. In this place he received much understanding from the Scriptures and divine dreams, more than his companions, which were very wonderful to tell. In his dreams the Scriptures were interpreted and the proverbs explained so well that he regarded everything else as worthless compared to them.

There were together in the house two young men and two young women, one of whom was married but not the others, and sometimes a grandfather came in and out. Sometimes the devil and Satan laid hands on them to great temptation, but they prayed always day and night to the Lord, that Satan might not have his will. The Lord was with them, and it happened that David Joris, because of this situation, began to love one in particular and she began to love him, on account of the Holy Spirit, wisdom, perception, and understanding which she saw in him.[55] But nothing came out of their mouths nor was there anything in their hearts except godly fear, their confession of faith, and holy things. If there came to one or the other an evil thought or sight, then they prayed heartily and overcame their tormentor through the grace of God, so that they departed undefiled from one another, in true brotherly love. See, the beloved woman did not know how to praise God about this man's gifts. She had been away from her husband for about two years. This man, who was rude and dissolute in life, came unexpectedly home.[56] But she was now of such a mind (which was then unknown to me) that she refused to sleep with him so that she would not partake of his unfaithfulness. She therefore left the house without his knowledge and approval and would no longer suffer his unclean life. She moreover would not speak with him, except what she had already said. When this happened, they wanted to leave rather than remain there, because they heard that he was very hotheaded. They feared he would think wickedly and that if he did not find her and the men at home, he might inflict harm and suffering on them. In summary, they had to leave it with their God. He came and spoke with them, being dissolute and wild in appearance, as one can easily imagine. In the end he did nothing to the people except to complain about his wife because she, thick-skulled, would not be subject to him according to his will. But they apologized, for they had wanted to keep her in the house, but she had refused. After six or eight days he sailed again without quarrel to England, but he had, alas, spoken very maliciously of David Joris, as if he was keeping his wife from him and had slept with her. But God is witness that he had remained as pure from her, and she from him, as the smallest infant upon the earth. Nevertheless, he secretly spread the rumor among the brothers, although neither David nor she knew of it.

After this two or three brothers came to him from England, who spoke to him concerning this matter in the same house to which he had returned. He gave them a good report, and they committed each other to the Lord, and took leave of it in this manner. After some days, when it was time that these men (presumably from a summons) had to leave, they ate together in the same evening and departed from each other in a friendly fashion. In the night they crossed the water in this way with David Joris. Finally, they by chance arrived at the shore around two o'clock. They then hired a wagon which they drove to the city, desiring to bring it to the gate before four o'clock.[57] It was past five, however, and now everyone was there, standing with many wagons in front of the gates and doors and many knew him. But he cried to his God, asking him that he would help them through it. After this he courageously got up from the wagon and walked right in front of everyone. And the city watchman struck him on the neck with his glove. They risked both their lives in this way because it had to be done. But no one observed it particularly, except a single man, who kept it secret. Therefore, because of the Lord, nothing evil resulted. In this way they walked for a long time along the wall in front of many people, finally arriving at the house where they wanted to be. After they had been in this place for a long time, they went into another. All the while he was faithfully trusting in his soul and truly courageous in faith, because he constantly turned his sight and trust to the Lord. Finally the soul of the man became so ardent, that he weakened himself night and day because of it, troubling himself about the condition of his being. He did not fully know how or what he prayed, whether about this or about that. However, many of the prayers were done at the moment, in order to become or to be this and that.

But he prayed solely for a heart, I say, that might be more firmly attached to his God with even stronger love and to become free from all worry. Namely, free of all anxiety, danger, pain, and lack of desire or feebleness. For he knew that when the heart was surrounded with stronger love, it would permit no incitement, rod, or chastisement which God did not permit [cf. 1 John 3:19-21]. Instead, he was inclined to this and not reticent. He wrote at this time a song, entitled "Our Hands We Wash with Innocence," on the basis that no one should sing it freely, except he who was of a true, sincere, and willing heart.[58] For it vexed him that everyone sang the spiritual songs with a fleshy, impenitent heart, which did not seem proper to him. He thought and spoke about what this meant, saying, "I will make it so that one should not desire to sing them with too sweet a harmony." After this they came into his mother's house to his wife and children. The other one was called Anthon, a very beloved obedient servant who also went into a house to his wife.[59] [713] After this it happened near Faute that he was forced to leave the house where he had wanted to perform his work, being compelled by his need. He worked because his heart was such that he did not complain, nor did he want to burden anyone, yes, not even his own mother. But that such a godly troubled heart was surrounded with such work fell heavily upon him. He groaned, prayed, and implored in many ways. One time he spoke to a person who doubted him, suggesting that he should not continue: "Look, the time hastens for you to observe and progress (namely in the second birth). I must leave your presence, because if I speak further to you or call to you, you will not hear or understand me." But some realized that his heart spoke boldly out of zeal, therefore, they accepted it well.

When all of this had finished, he then came to examine how God was named in the Word and how all people used the holy name of God so immorally and lightly in their speech; swearing, singing, speaking, and blaspheming as much as they wanted. Furthermore, he thought about what to say to them, in particular, what kind of terrible punishment had been proclaimed because of this. This burdened him so heavily that he wrote to all his acquaintances, that they should consider the great holy names of God, and not take the great holy names into their mouths so imprudently and thoughtlessly, for they will not go unpunished. For one will be judged according to one's words, as it was written [Matt. 12:37]. He furthermore believed that the word "Lord," because it was used so much by people, was not as fitting as the word "God," seeing that so much was written about it and the punishment which is threatened to the transgressor. Therefore, he admonished them to no longer use the names so lightly, neither in speech nor in writing. For one could certainly use God's name, he said, but only in holy devotion. One should be afraid to name such a great God with such lightheartedness. Therefore, some quarreled with him, believing that the word "Lord" signified as much as "God." These spurned the Spirit which they did not know. It has not gone well for him because of it, as I know for certain. To David Joris, however, much more advice, understanding, freedom, and knowledge was revealed and given concerning the lighthearted and slanderous use of these names among his contemporaries.[60] And he encountered this in his actual experience, just like a growing child and a maturing adult. Few have examined this. While it was clear to him at this time, it had never come to him before how one can perceive truth in the progression from childhood, to youth and to adulthood; that the child must be nourished with softer, but the adult with stronger food. "When I was a child," spoke Paul, "I spoke and acted as a child, and had a childish understanding, but when I became an adult, I removed whatever was childish" [1 Cor. 13:11].

And even then his ardor did not cease, but he continued to pray and supplicate about himself. He also heartily prayed about Christ's nature, spirit and power. One time he was going to sit down where he always sat to work in front of two or three lights. He became silent, standing enraptured as if he had left his body, so that he did not know if he was living or dead, just like someone examining a face from the outside. He had no idea how long he had been standing, for he then had to take notice of the hour. After it had happened in this way, he saw a great tumult and uproar upon the earth and a gathering together and falling down in dreadful fear of the lords and princes and all the great and powerful authorities, spiritual and secular. All of this was a result of their fear of the small and innocent children.[61] This happened suddenly in his vision and so certainly and amazingly, that its effect cannot be described here. After this vision had passed, he immediately looked around him and saw that the walls were all full of naked women and men, but in the vision it seemed to him that the women were in all manner of shapes and postures and he cried out: "Lord, Lord, I may indeed see everything." Therefore, because the vision had to do with his own understanding, he perhaps knew and understood why it had happened. Namely, that his eyes must be so pure and clear that he must not be vexed or made impure by any created work of God. Thereupon, when he awoke or came to himself, he was as exhausted as if he had run for two miles, so heavily was he breathing from exhaustion. He immediately seized feather and ink with both hands, and wrote while still standing.[62]

....

See, all of this the man wrote down and indeed three, four, or five times more words were said before he could write it with the quill.

After this was written, there came to him a vision in the form of verses, which he quickly wrote down with a swift hand, with the melody: "A Mighty Fortress Is Our God," running in this fashion:

My ears have heard from above,
My eyes have seen from afar.
The innocent sheep of Christ understand the word.
Although they hop, they go a straight way,
totally upright.
Pure in the midst of wickedness.
Spotless like children.
Without shame and without hypocrisy.
As Adam and Eve were in the beginning,
they are at the end.[63]

Through this he received an innocent, restful spirit, so that he thought that he was set free from all his fantasies or fears that his wife would not be able to find another husband after his death. This seemed to him, when he saw what he had received with his still unchanged eyes, to be a gift far greater than 100,000 guilders. He then received a bold, confident spirit, as it were, free from all worry, anxiety, fear, and esteem of the world. He was released, single, and free, and the same radiance always remained with him as a new joyous appearance.

In this spirit he went to a brother, who was amazed about him and thought, "What could have happened to him, that he has such a joyful and happy spirit, heart, mind during such a sad time?" For he was usually a very reticent man, and before this had no pride, but now he was very bold. This brother insisted that David Joris eat, and when they had sat at the table he said, "Eat and do not be afraid," for he believed it was on account of his wife, with whom he was not acquainted. But David Joris answered him and said, "My brother, I have been afraid of everyone now for a long time, but now I am not afraid, not even of an emperor or king. Instead, let them be ashamed of me, I have no need to be ashamed before them." And he continued to converse in this fashion, saying that nothing could be free to them before God, until they had made agreement, friendship, and peace with him. With this he had received a certain assurance or certainty in his soul. When it came time to sleep, he was brought into an unheated attic, under a badly covered roof. Here he lay in a barely (compared to his need) covered bed, in such a way that if God had not provided him during the night with an inner warmth, he would not have been able to endure the pain in his body on account of the great cold. But he was completely at peace and untroubled because of the unbelievable experiences. One must be amazed also concerning the wholeness of his spirit and purity of his thought.

It so happened that the radiance remained constantly in his sight for three months and his mind was just like a little child's. For he thought nothing evil or mischievous during the night, and even when he saw, at that time, images of many mischievous and carnal things, they did not trouble him nor arouse any lust in him. In this state and spirit, he gained a son named Gideon. About a year or year and a half later [715], he received a vision about this one in which he saw him in a long silk gown, as if he was to be raised up as a great man before the Lord and especially according to the wisdom of Samuel [cf. 1 Sam. 1]. But he left it with the other things, although it remained amazing to his mind. In and with this new spirit, he drafted a written outline with only half-completed sentences and meanings and also in great haste and speed, just as he received it from the Spirit. All things in their perfection were given to him to write about and to explain further. It was written on Lombard skin in large format,[64] and many other things were contained in this outline than were published. It was composed in brief form and not all things were published because much of it was never heard. A booklet was, however, published and some other things were printed, as much as was desired by the publisher, who did not understand them.[65]

In this spirit he wrote three letters, one to England, the second to Strasbourg in Germany, and the third to [East] Frisia in Westphalia [sic]. All of these had to be delivered by hand in his name, even if he had to deliver them himself by foot. But it happened that he sent them by another messenger.[66] Now when the letter to England was completed and was ready to be sent, something in it appeared very strange to David, for even though it had flowed out from his quill it was written before he had examined it completely. It read in this fashion: "One will still bring presents and gifts to you." Because it was written in this manner, he feared he would be ashamed of what the brethren might think of it. For some said, "Seeing that the Münsterites desired to fall upon the property of other people, perhaps David Joris was also awakened to this or was planning to do the same." [67] This was said although his heart was far from such and has remained constantly so into eternity. He therefore scratched it out again. He then thought, however, "Do not be proud, but allow it to remain in this fashion." So he had to write it out again. He was inwardly constrained to do it, for it seemed as strange to him as to Sarah when she was supposed to have a son [cf. Gen. 18:12]. One may believe it or not.

At this time he experienced many wonderful inner dreams, sights, and other visions. Indeed, throughout the whole day one heard or saw nothing else from him except what the Lord's Word and Spirit said about what had yet to occur before things could be right according to God's heart, mind, and soul. Finally there came to him the unmistakable witness of the Spirit, extremely strong in its effect. He therefore had to completely separate from all carnal intentions of his heart, for at the time God desired to renew all things by him and in him. The mischievous eyes, carnal thoughts, and all manner of sinful lusts had to depart. The same Spirit impelled him in his heart so forcefully that at times he lay fallen down in the attic from exhaustion, bent over completely in fear and terror of the strict judge, before he could let go of any of this. Everything was in a clear, immediate, and sensitive nature in his heart. One time this affected him so strongly in his heart that he fell down, dead to all appearances, just as if it had happened physically. And though it happened only in his thoughts and heart, he was forced to completely assent to the mind and will of God. There was so much of this in him that he had to be eternally believed with a full soul and heart. And see his prayers never ceased. Furthermore, this and that beautiful thing would come to him from the Lord. He therefore pledged that from henceforth he would see to it that he would never again turn away from this separated mind nor let himself be drawn into any carnal love or sight. Instead, he must allow himself to be spiritualized or divinized. He examined himself to see if his mind truly abode in the spirit of innocence and purity of heart.

In summary, he became entirely drawn out of all mischievousness or carnal vision, just as a little child is turned away from his will and mind and is taught in tangible ways to return to the first wonderful vision. For it produced in him the knowledge that in the kingdom of God nothing impure could endure nor remain. Furthermore, the hearts of people must be entirely pure, innocent, and without faults. On account of this he examined himself frequently and had to test himself to see if he stood firmly established in his mind and will or if he lacked the same. From this point on, when any such danger appeared, his heart had to fight bravely and be assaulted before it could be completely pure and clean. Therefore, his faith and love were strongly tempted. For the Lord had first received him in a fatherly manner, but now he set him down less tenderly or less gently and not without a little danger. He thereby pushed him into mighty deeds, leading him through unbelievable things, which happened beyond any human understanding, things which cannot be told. In truth, if all this had not happened from the Lord, I know very well (as I confess that I have written this after having heard everything from his own mouth) that it would have been impossible for any man. Here I can say with Paul that flesh and blood is weak and human thoughts are too feeble to bear it [1 Cor. 15:50]. He had a constant, heartfelt desire to turn to God in prayer, beseeching God without letup and with all the strength and ability of his soul. He lived so frugally that he lost all his strength, becoming weak in his body. Not only because of the [lack of] food, but also because of his fervor, so that he was nearly completely consumed by it.

Once, in a thought or inner vision, he saw his own heart like a tired-out fish which had another fish inside it. God admonished him in his soul that he should rest somewhat in his [716] mortal being and eat and drink whatever tasted good to him or whatever he desired for nourishment and sustenance, since everything was free to him [cf. Acts 10:9-16]. And see, he had to do it, necessity compelled him to it. Someone prepared a meal of vegetables for him in order to strengthen his heart until he became a bit stronger. Occasionally this person also gave him a drink of wine. Joris, however, desired to avoid all human things, for God gave him light and understanding to know what it was he was seeing. But he now allowed himself to be satisfied with green vegetables and for a long time he would only eat lettuce. But alas, his nature could not endure it. He was forced to give in and to eat moderately just like any other human until he was restored to complete strength. In his soul, however, he remained totally resigned[68] to whatever God willed, whether to eat or to fast, to sleep or to be awake. He was concerned only with the inward life and refrained often from food, so that after some time, having eaten so little, his stomach and bowels shrunk completely and hunger completely left him. Thereafter, one had to force him to eat against his will, more times than he desired. And he was forced to do these acts of mortification secretly before God, without anyone observing or knowing of it. To him this was also a good test and feeling of his inner self. The kind of self-denial he performed every day and night cannot be described here in detail, except that it was an example of the circumcision of his old life and nature. He continually prayed, supplicated, and sighed about his former life, thoroughly examining the time of his youth. He had to confess everything that had happened from the beginning, as much as he could remember. This involved despising himself and everything that had once been so important to him. He did not turn himself to anything that was related in any way to the world. He took refuge only in completely removing everything from his mind and will.

He did not enquire at all after what he ought to eat or drink, whether he should go, sit, stay, lie down, sleep, or get up. All the time the Lord's Word was his way and he kept his proclamations before his eyes. For a whole night he lay without sleep and as usual he was pre-occupied with divine thoughts and concerns until one a.m. Further-more, from time to time he tasted joy and sweetness, although it was always mixed with bitterness. At first it took much effort to bring the Lord into his thoughts, for not one moment went by (I must say this) when there did not come before his eyes human, worldly, or carnal, yes, unnecessary, vile, and ugly thoughts, all of which he had to fling from himself and expel from his mind, turning and departing from them instead of desiring them. For he knew that he must let go of vain practices and fight the whole day long against these attacks. He had to prevail over himself or overcome himself, for without exertion and difficulty of the senses he could not proceed. It was no small difficulty at this time for him to become sensitive and aware of himself before he could progress. Yes, I will say this to you, if God had not held him up by his hand and led him forth, he would not have endured the at-tacks (when they first began). But the Lord first made known to him through his Spirit the entire way through which he had to go and suf-fer, for he always looked after him. Now because of his devotion to godly things and the Spirit's inner work (which he observed many times in many ways in different hearts), he no longer took pleasure in his outward work, but wished to free himself completely from the same. Nevertheless, he worked even harder at this time. But finally the Holy Spirit advised him and inspired him little by little that henceforth he should no longer be the servant of mortals but of God and his Christ. But he was not able to undertake to remove himself from it, for it was still too hard to live only on faith. Moreover, he had gained many valuable jobs through his wife, from those who took par-ticular pleasure in his craft. Yes, much work was brought for his hands from many who loved him because of the gospel and art.

Here he stayed hidden between two walls. He had to concen-trate much harder on the technique of his art than ever before, more than on its beauty. It was as if he had already turned his eyes away from it and instead spent his time praying to God. However, whenev-er he sat down to work, there began to arise in his heart something like a fire in his body, so that he (whether he willed it or not) had to stop and keep himself still. He wondered about this and then he thought to himself, "See, if I do not work, O God, how will I provide for myself and my house?" But the thought came to him, "Let God worry." Even after this he still could not dare to do so immediately, because he was afraid there might be a temptation behind it and the people would not accept it well, believing that he had not kept his word. This continued for several days. The fiery ardor always began from the inside. Finally he became aware that it was his own disbelief and the honor and worries of livelihood which pressed and hindered the true holy service of the Spirit (whereto God had called him). Instead he had to cast it off. When he let himself judge this sincerely (as he previously thought he had), he was admonished to rely solely on God and pay attention to nothing regarding his craft or to anything which might worry him. At the same time, no one had given or promised him anything, nor did he know anyone who would. Those who normally would have done so were absent, either slain or banished. In spite of this (I must credit him with this), in the same year he could have received much money from those who were executed, who had [717] the day before they were imprisoned promised such to him.[69]

But he desired not a penny of it, as it had not been necessary. For this reason he did not take it. O, his heart was sincere and upright, even though it was rumored and lied about him that he had brought in more than 600 florins from it, to which he sent 300 florins to his wife at home and had taken 300 florins along with him. This rumor, however, did not hinder him at all. Not one penny did he take from anyone. Instead he quietly sold some belongings, namely his own and his wife's clothes, or whatever jewelry they may have had. With these funds they went to Strasbourg, consuming what they had, all but 18 florins which he had earned with his own hands, and so they fed themselves in this fashion. Before God it happened in this and no other way. One time, when he was in The Hague after his imprisonment,[70] he did not have much work, except for two large, costly windows which he had nearly completed by his own hands for a city magistrate. Then he came down with a severe fever and thus for well over six or eight weeks he was without work and in great poverty and terrible need, and his wife was also in childbed. Eight or ten florins were given to him from those who were his brothers in the gospel. He did not desire this except as a loan which, as soon as he could, he would repay. Afterwards, when he became healthy enough to work for those who had collected the donation from other people to give to him, he promised he would pay it back or die. He told them to take it off his wages, which no one may refute. This included the old person or old woman with whom he stayed, although (she said) she did not desire it back. And there were people, with whom he had no relations, and desired none, who knew of it and were thought to be his fellows.[71] This had occurred in such a manner that he later discovered that they had boastingly repeated the rumor to his insult. But God brought it about that they had to confess that they had done wrong therein. For such a nature is abominable before God, just as if they had lived in harlotry and roguery until this day. That is, whenever they repeat anything to the detriment and harm of the pious, God-fearing, and sincere hearts (whom God has loved), they would have much preferred (this I say in the truth of God) to have a stone tied around their necks and be cast into the deepest part of the sea to be drowned [cf. Matt. 18:6].

Also, it is indisputable before God, that when he had returned to the city of Delft, he was assessed as to how much tax he should pay from his earnings.[72] And when this came before the brothers, there was one who was the most prominent and noblest of appearance. He went at this time to the brothers and requested from each one a collection or gift for one of their brothers who stood in great need of it, and see, he obtained much at the time. For just about everyone noticed that it was for David. On this account they gave very richly, because they loved him or were favorable to him because of his courageous soul in the Lord. He also had many young children.[73] Some asked, "Is it for our brother David Joris?" But the collector replied that "it is not fitting for you to know. Give only what God tells you in your heart, it is all the same, whoever receives it." David was so moved by all of this and by his poverty that he set out to work under the management of the covenanters, and he must have overheard everything. This happened just as has been testified and the truth of it will appear before God and the Lord Christ on his day, against all the lies which are repeated about him. It came to me to put this to paper, in order to put a stop to these lies. Those who lie had better watch out, for they have been allowed to do so against the man for far too long, not heeding the Lord. Namely, he was forced (whether or not he wanted to) to enter into debt with each person, although he has remained in debt to no one. For he had an upright, modest, and sincere heart, that only sought to fear his God and to teach the gospel and love everyone (especially everyone on the earth) from the bottom of his heart and fullness of his soul. God remains his witness, that there were some who remained in great debt to him; he, however, to his best knowledge, did not reprove anyone.

It is indisputable that this happened just so and no one (even those who are by nature most perverse) can doubt it. God loved him above all and entrusted him with his Word in its most pure and certain form, because he did not have a false, perverse heart. Neither was he able to do anything which was false, for he was a man chosen (I must say it to the praise of God) according to the heart of God, as was David the king, after whom he was named [1 Sam. 13:14]. He sought only sincerity, truth, and trust. He loved peace and mercy, and desired only what was good or best. He chose, loved, and followed after the most sacred faith. He strengthened himself in hope and trusted patiently. Moreover, he was not long able to hold his position against his opponents and persecutors, because he was hated by all people or flesh. His name was cast out and greatly despised, but this was only upon the earth. It has gone so far that it is not even possible to think well of him or even to use his name. For he has been rejected so completely by the world, because he was contrary to it in everything. Furthermore, he was no esteemer of appearances, for he looked only to the truth. But no one on the earth was more useful nor none so necessary to restore the truth as he, because all hidden or secret things about God were revealed to him, such as the new birth of God and the Father and Son. Moreover, in him or in his words (however strange or distant they may seem, [718] in appearance impossible) is everything renewed or transformed. It must be said that everyone must follow him as if they were blind, along the path which he has walked first. This is to be expected at its time. Whoever does not believe this can examine it.

This was shown to his mother (just before the Spirit of truth illumined him)[74] through a vision in the night. In this vision she saw him sitting on a horse with his eyes bound shut, a hat upon his head, a cloak placed on his body, and shoes and spurs. He has forgotten what he held in his hand (he believes that it was a gun or a bow) and at his side was a sword. Some ran alongside his charger, although he rode very quickly. All people were troubled or in an uproar about him. These runners desired to lead the horse by hand along another path. But if they struck down David Joris, then everyone would go his own way, as is very well known. And everyone cried, "This is the way to journey." But David spurred on the horse and desired to go straight ahead. But there was no visible road ahead, nor could anyone find a way to travel, for it was full of thorns and thistles, growing very deserted and wild, and no path was seen nor perceived. But he rode alone straight ahead. The runners (I believe indeed) left him and shouted after him from every side very derisively, harmfully, and abusively, saying that he had run astray and become lost. But he did not listen to their cries, but instead followed after his soul (though as a blind man). He, however, did not know at all the kind of road which was ahead of him, except by experience. And see, after they had cried out after him, screaming and opposing him with these and other comments, and after throwing things at him, they finally stood still. They watched him for a long time, until it was finally revealed to them that all of them must go the same way if they did not want to be lost.

His mother, however, kept this in her heart and said nothing of it to anyone, until she deemed the time was right in the development of doctrine. She then revealed it to David just as she had seen it, with these and further details. At the time he was experiencing much vexation from many who yet were far from him. For the rumor began to resound, being found particularly on the most inexperienced, incompetent, or imprudent tongues. As a result of this, the evil nature and the anti-Christian spirit or world waylaid and pursued him like a hunted animal. And one in particular actually attempted such. This was the noble leader Batenburg, from whom David hoped to have a peaceful welcome.[75] And he wanted to speak with Batenburg and such would have taken place if God had not protected him from it. For he would have fallen into the hands of his greatest enemy. Batenburg was so envious and evil-minded toward him that he would have certainly torn him apart with his teeth. He also said exceedingly godless and abominable things about him, namely that David was a son of a whore and that he fought against the most high God and his kingdom. He regarded David as an Absalom who wanted to seize the kingdom from him [cf. 2 Sam. 13].[76] It seems that about a month before this, Batenburg had come to an understanding or enlightenment through which he felt himself to be aroused or sent from God to establish God's work. Much more of this had taken place previously here and there, but it had no long-term effect. And he furthermore had a special dream wherein it was said to him that he would be Gideon, who would deliver the people of God [cf. Judg. 6:14]. That is why he considered no people to be a people except those who were willing to be obedient to him.[77] About this enough has been revealed regarding how they were to be obedient. This one made so many crude threats that when it came to the attention of David Joris, he was forced to hide himself. For Batenburg noticed that David with his teaching was opposed to him. Furthermore, David was by no means a soldier, nor was he capable of helping Batenburg with his vengeance and execution of the nobility.[78] Instead, he advised the people to proceed only with purity and good deeds, to suffer and endure, but not to be vengeful. And he completely opposed Batenburg's enterprise and quite vigorously taught the opposite. He did not do this because of hatred and envy, but merely from a Christian spirit. On account of this, Batenburg earlier had threatened that he had hired someone with whom he had spoken to stab David to death as soon as he came to him. One said that he was to arrive shortly and would accept him as his brother. Some said that it would certainly come to pass and others that he had already been in David's house. This the good man David Joris could not remember, nor could he hardly believe it. In conclusion, David did so many things to hinder and restrain these evil undertakings, and he remained free from them.

David Joris was also warned to continue to be cautious to whom he gave his hand and the kiss of brotherly love. Yes, along with the many false accusations which they cast upon his neck, many of the Mennonist disciples threatened to slay him if they could only catch him.[79] Similar accusations came from those of Münster and from some of those in Strasbourg and England, not to mention from the whole world and the other Babylonian false-learned. Some of these later turned to David Joris (from the Batenburgers and Mennonites), and became friendly and loving to him.[80] And despite some of their well-known deeds and desire to punish, it was all forgiven them. Their defection resulted in even more hatred about the good man, to such an extent that, above all, he had to protect and guard himself. Again, there were others who came running ten, twenty, or twenty-one miles by foot to bring ten or twelve pieces of gold (more or less) which he received with thanksgiving and amazement. But until this point in time, there was given to him scarcely half a rotten old cheese, [719] although he does not remember if any day there was some bread along with it. And then there were given to him a half or a whole head of a cow and all manner of pieces (it looked like it was something from a cow or oxen and stunk badly), not worth three shillings or pennies.[81] One merely became ill when one smelled it. It could not be eaten, but had to be thrown out. And yet he had to thank someone for it. And God dealt with him in this way. Thereafter there were one or two who would give him a white penny;[82] a few more, others less. How the nature of his blood and his color deteriorated, that is known to God and cannot be described here.

That he was forced to come into such a poverty-stricken, shameful, abominable, and distressful nature hit his wife harder than him, although it was certainly hard enough and annoying to him. But he comforted himself in the Lord Christ. But when he remembered how he, although now in dishonor, would soon be exalted, it was easier to endure. After this six gold coins[83] were given to him which were the most that he received, and at the time it seemed to him to be a truly great wealth. In summary, the Lord did not allow this to go too far, for when his money was all spent, just then more would come, all without a single thought or written plea. No, one cannot find such. He received it even before he could make a request. One time his messengers heard these words from his mouth, that he would like to do without money or bread. This was what he had promised to God in his first decision, surrendering himself to the sacrifice of his body and life. He had thoroughly resolved that nothing could cause him to forsake the Lord his God, not even concern over life or death; hunger or lack of abundance, gold or possessions; nor fear of fire, water, or sword;[84] nor because of high or low birth; nor because of animosity, honor, or harm. This he said willingly and with full awareness, upon his knees in a narrow, small study. He thanked God and received his food with praise and thanksgiving, which was sent secretly to him by his landlady. At first he kept himself alone, concealed in a strange, unfamiliar house, owned by one who afterwards loved him and who gave him the freedom to walk about the house when the door was closed in the evenings. He always sat there in a narrow corner or nook, high in the attic under the roof. One cannot know what things happened to him there. Many, many bitter tears were shed. For the things which he attempted there were completely against his constitution or frail nature. For no one could find joy and pleasure, or love and peace in such stillness. Everyone who was with him at the time or who had traveled with him must confess that he found no pleasure, amusement, or enjoyment in songs, plays, or other diversions without a measure of godlessness and roguishness.[85]

For he was always quiet and lowly of disposition, truly noble and honest. He was the one who brought the Word. He was not deceptive of heart, neither envious, bitter, vengeful, harsh, nor proud, but he testified to the good. He had a nature which could not bear everything. He cultivated a very loving and peaceful spirit, full of sweetness and friendliness, and to the best of his knowledge he loved and feared God from his heart. But it is true that he had an affectionate disposition or nature, though were I to tell the truth according to the people of the day, he liked to love. Now, however, he could not exhibit more love or goodness than the recipients were able to bear (as one does to the beloved). His heart could display a friendly appearance, which many found easy to love. About this he shed many bitter tears. This did not lead to unchastity, as is obvious to all those who accompanied him. For he saw to it that he never presented anything dishonorable or unchaste to any of his traveling companions, for he had a heart that shamed him in this. I am not trying to justify him, but to copy the truth before God just as it will be found before God. More than anyone else he had to bear a hateful, despised, dishonored name, as will be found in eternity according to the truth. Nevertheless, he too happened to fall just like any other sinner in this, more than he would have liked. For he was easily overcome when anyone showed affection to him, as must be confessed as true of all inborn flesh. But no one can truthfully say that he sought this out like a lewd hound or a grunting swine. For I know that no other opinion of him is possible.

The angels, if in human form, would not have acted more purely than he, as is shown of him here through the new amazing Spirit of power. God, however, made him aware of his sickness and inability. It seems to me that no one has endured more or shown greater patience in sickness. Surely it was God who afflicted him with sickness in this way, to chastise him and to make him lovely and pleasant in the fear of the Lord, as it stands written. For in his nature it is true that he was terribly weak, although even in the opinion of heathens he was called a pure dove (by those who were associated with him for a long time). But he was also a human and knew it well enough, that he was born of the complexion of love, which he could not improve. Just like he was given or bore the reputation (by others in fact who were returning blows) of a woman chaser. But it was not so, for it was only pure love (as one uses this proverb in the world); and yet, it was, I confess, nothing but the flesh and blood of a poor, sickly nature. The gist of this was that the Spirit, which he had, improved and perfected all these failings, as one is reminded [720] of what God has done through him and still plans to do.

To briefly conclude all of this, it must be described in many ways the kind of complexion which he had, that all his life he did not provoke the seed or become excited, whether by sight or sound; whether through word or flesh; whether accidentally or in a legitimate way. All of this is a certain sign of a chaste heart, spirit, and nature, to speak in a human fashion. Is this not amazing for one who was of such a loving heart? Yes, truly there is no comparable heart. Indeed I will say to you, that no one can know the intimacy and the unity which God used with the man. For he was also very talkative, although he could never utter things as perfectly as when there was a conversation. At this time (namely when he stood in such a great union of chastity) it happened that he was asked by some to journey with four or five brothers into the land of Cleves or to Oldenburg.[86] They desired him to go with them, because they believed it to be necessary. They wanted to make a report to the man about the Münsterite position (let those who are strong in the truth be warned) so that they might be united with him. I cannot, however, describe the great danger which accompanied them. Along the way he contracted scarlet fever,[87] so that he frequently had to climb down from the wagon and sit down. He finally had to proceed gingerly, step by step, and he could not walk ten steps without turning pale again, but neither he nor they knew how to advise him. When they came to Schwoll,[88] they hired a wagon and drove quickly. For when a highwayman spotted them, he rode up to them, refusing to leave the wagon. He was terrifying in appearance, having with him four or five muskets. Never before has the world seen such an obedient horse. In the evening this one accompanied them to the inn, wherein was nothing to eat. When David sat at the table, all his color left him, and he nearly sank down. They lifted him up and brought him into an unpleasant chamber or little house, and helped him into bed. In the bed he was so quiet, that no one knew if he had lain like a dead person through the whole night, without any knowledge, thought, sight, hearing, or understanding. All of those who had come with him saw that the game with this highwayman would quickly run its course. They therefore went out that same evening and hired a wagon and continued on their journey. The highwayman became angry about this and said that "they were accompanied by numerous devils, because they would not remain until the morning, and he could not follow them with a weary horse." [89] These ones who left had all been with the man and had said good-bye before taking their leave, but David knew nothing of it at all, even though his eyes remained open. In the morning the people (a husband and wife) with whom they had left him gave him a report about it. Then he too desired to depart, and not to have any rest there, however sick he may be. He therefore stood up and desired to leave before the highwayman knew about it. And just as they started to leave, the highwayman was instantly at the wagon, riding beside, behind, in front of, and all around us. He then rode a long distance ahead, then nearly as far behind us, until nearly out of sight. But he was soon there again, riding next to the wagon. He then turned his head and looked at the sick good man, as if to say, "How will I strike you?" He finally said, "I will soon have you" and came riding so close to the wagon that David did not know if he was going to strike off his head in an instant. And because of this he was sorely tried in his faith, to see whether or not he would doubt the promise of God and other wonderful inspirations.

But he gave himself into God's hands and what he desired had to be. And David asked for nothing more than his shelter, according to God's desire or will, and principally that God would protect him in his going out and coming in. In summary, they arrived in the early afternoon at a village (named Raesfeld) where Hackfort's son-in-law was with many servants.[90] One of them remarked that he was searching for his wife who had escaped or run away from him. David Joris had already heard about this and had spoken and written some words about it, in particular, that those who had taken this woman should be careful how and why they did this. When this N. (the one who had carried off a woman from Raesfeld)[91] had heard of this, he became so very angry and enraged, yes, finally so very embittered against David Joris that he undertook to stab him to death, and that under the appearance of a kiss [cf. Luke 22:47-48]. The reason you will hear further. In the meantime, after David Joris had departed the house to continue his journey, the woman was found by Heinrich Kaal[92] and was brought into David Joris's house, so that she would be under his protection and hand. For it was not his right (the one who brought her) to have her for his wife. She had left only to find the truth and godly basis and understanding, and especially a healthy doctrine of victory. All of this had now happened without David Joris's knowledge. He was amazed that N. had permitted her to go under such conditions, that he should bring her to his lord David in order to learn and overcome all truth, wisdom, and understanding, and then to return to him, for he had risked his life in this. When this happened, that he had got rid of her, there came into his head many anxious thoughts, so that he regretted it, and he cursed himself for being so stupid and blind. His heart began to burn against the one whom he called lord (although David Joris was completely innocent in the matter) and promised himself, that if he came to him soon, he would stab him through and through, for he was an abominable [721] soldier, and the other still loved peace.

When now the man saw that there was such a rumor and realized the pride of the highwayman, the others only knew that he was going to journey with him on the way to Stecklenburg.[93] They had promised to depart in the afternoon (about three or four o'clock). They then went out and secretly hired a wagon, which they wanted to ride within the hour to Oldenburg, just as it happened. When they had driven a part of the way, they were not able to see or know if he was going to pursue them from afar, and could not easily believe that they had escaped from him. For David was ready to use the excuse that he had to fix a wheel. When they now arrived in the evening at Oldenburg, it was half full of soldiers and mercenaries, because there was at that time a war between the Bishop of Münster and the Duke.[94] It therefore took a long time before they were able to find an inn. Then in that same evening, the man was sorely tested. For one of those who was with David Joris was summoned to come before the lord by a servant of the lord. This one knew the lord, but David knew no one. After both of them had left, there developed all around him quarrels and troubles, so that he prepared his soul. When the companion returned, he said, "This has happened because of us," and with these and other words, David was disturbed.[95] A short while later he told him about it. The next day, after all of this, they went with this other one and were received in a brotherly fashion. They washed their feet, and received them in the best way that they could.[96] After this some arrived at the meeting from the city and others from the countryside. These came and enquired how they ought to behave and appear. One had a complaint about this master and lord; another a complaint about husband or wife; now this, now that complaint. David instructed them, as God gave him ability, regarding all manner of remorse and suffering. There were also a few who could not live together without quarreling. It is unbelievable the kind of things which happened among them, especially one woman who cried out and shouted loudly. For those seated there merely added to the quarrels among themselves, always accusing each another, and none of them would give in.

And there were also some who continued steadfast in their Münsterite beliefs and that same day they wanted to prove them to be good and right, and to explain how their doctrine was the true word. They said that their doctrine could not coexist with that of David Joris and that he would not be able to prove his teaching. One of them gave a long introduction (because they were brave, well-trained and learned in Latin, and David was among them).[97] "See," he concluded, "this is our judge," and then he placed the Bible upon the table, implying that they desired to be judged by this. After listening to this with longsuffering patience, David put forward his opinion. With the wisdom of God in his speech he said, "See, this is our judge." And while David was pondering his response, with a joyful soul he saw the book (which they had placed in the middle) fall right off the table, striking fear in the hearts of those standing there. After this and even more similar events, they left the house. The next day these ones (who had left the house) summoned the man to come to them in a cellar, where they spoke further about the matter. They desired to understand his position of truth and act on it according to their ability.

But alas, they did not remain long in this frame of mind. For as a result of some misunderstanding and false thinking, they defected once more, preferring to stand by themselves, and they opposed David Joris's doctrines in some places.[98] An older man insisted that he would not be hastily or quickly persuaded, calling David a false prophet. He shied away from David because David had admonished and chastised him, placing his errors in front of him and instructing him in writing about many things. The old man was supposed to read this letter in front of the brothers. Now because David was among them he was not able to avoid doing this. He therefore did as he was admonished, promising to do everything just as David had written to him. He did so, however, only until David had departed from them. Thereafter, the evil false spirit came. Yes, it had a long-lasting and deep effect, so that with a deceitful spirit he falsified everything, turning all the good that he had heard and seen into evil, confusing everyone in the entire land once again, teaching things completely contrary to David.

When David returned home, he could not narrate the trouble and fear which gripped him on account of the false brothers or spies.[99] He found this woman there,[100] who fell upon her knees and begged him to take her into his house as a maidservant, so that she might observe and learn the truth. For he was anointed by his God to this (as far as she knew) and she agreed to everything. When she said this, he gave her his hand and said that she should not remain prostrate, but she should stand up, for he was only a man; she should be careful before whom she prostrated herself. Furthermore, as much as possible he would be happy to do everything she asked as long as the one who had brought her there was at peace about it.[101] Speaking long and quickly, she replied that her rescue had been accomplished through God and she then proceeded to explain how it happened. At the same time another woman came (her relative) who also was taken from another brother. Because she too sought her salvation and the needs of the soul and the doctrine of the kingdom of God, they desired to remain with David. This continued so that many more came to his house. For God caused them to come there with eternally sincere hearts. [722] Many unheard of things happened through the leading of their spirits.

Eight or ten days after this happened, David was called to come to Strasbourg, where some had gathered together to speak with him and to report to each other about who was the best qualified to be the leader who could bring about unity and peace. And see, David was easily persuaded to appear there in order to explain his teaching verbally, frankly and simply (namely, about what they had come to understand as his teaching). He spared no expense and avoided neither trouble, anxiety, nor fear, leaving behind wife and children (one can imagine their reactions) in order to start on the long journey there. They got up early, around four a.m., and traveled to the Hertogenbosch, where they went into a tavern and ate.[102] From here they traveled to another region, where one of David's companions became so sick that he could not eat. This made David suffer as much as the one who was ill, because he was a gifted, intelligent man who desired to stand with David against the learned ones. David had rejoiced greatly about this man, for he relied heavily on him. In any case, they left him sitting at the table to recover. The hostess brought him everything that she thought would help him, but nothing cured him. The next day they took him as quickly as they could to Cologne. At Cologne, he fell flat into bed and they believed that he would die in their hands. He advised them, however, to leave him alone so that they could continue their journey and then return for him. For at the gate he was shown a letter addressed to him, which told him to turn around and not to travel further with them.[103] He showed this to the brothers. They, however, had little regard for it, except that it struck a blow to David Joris's heart. He therefore realized that he could not finish the journey with them. David, however, desired to continue the journey with his cart, and they now attended to this, for the Lord had so provided that it could not be otherwise. They furthermore admonished him so that he not worry about his lack of ability in the literal Scriptures. For David would be richly provided with them. Even if one of those who were learned judged that David did not adequately understand the literal meaning of the Bible, he was so full of the Spirit's understanding and knew the Bible's hidden places and meaning so well that he could make several more bibles out of the one Bible.

For one must realize that the others were concerned with and loved only the letter, not troubling themselves with the deep and true meaning of the Spirit. From this David understood that God was with him and would not establish his Word by this help; he would therefore entrust and resign himself solely to the Lord and not upon the help of people. So they finally departed from each other with tears, everyone going their own way, commending each other to the Lord. When they arrived at Strasbourg, they appeared to be received well enough, and were lodged in the brothers' homes. The other arrived in Strasbourg in 1538 at the time of the Feast of St. John [June 24, 1538].[104] Eight or twelve days later they gathered together with six or eight of the others, of whom four were gifted and learned in Latin.[105] How their conversation proceeded is written down elsewhere.[106] One can find and read this, for there is too much to relate it all here. When the meeting ended, one of them accompanied David Joris and those who were with him, conversing further with him about how Melchior Hoffman, Johann Campanus,[107] and Melchior Rinck[108] (although I am not certain if he was included), were all regarded as Elijah. David replied, "and what do you say about Johann Matthijsz?" (for he had been one of their disciples).[109] But he would not respond to this, except that he himself did not accept this man. The others believed that it was on this issue where one could see which of these were correct. For there can only be one (he said) and now there are already three or four who have been called Elijah. Moreover, he did not mention Batenburg, seeing that he also had been one once.[110] He believed that he would discover who was the most faithful by seeing whose word endured, who had the best law, and which one had life in God so as to increase beyond the others.

At this David answered him, saying that it was nothing. He too would leave it in the hands of the Lord and guard himself. He knew, however, that this would not help him at all. He therefore said, "Do not tell others that I pretend to be an Elijah, for I am what I am. On this I rest myself. This I know," he said, "that the Lord my God has awakened me, and has entrusted me with his word and light and knowledge for holy understanding. Yes, I must proclaim this with my voice so that everyone can be received into Christ, or they all will be punished by God." And he furthermore said that God had not anointed him to baptize with water, nor to make anyone physically holy. But he was anointed to those things which are necessary in this day, in particular, how we can be united with God and received unto him, or how we can be filled with his Spirit. This was the office which he fulfilled in the sight of his Lord. This is what should be proclaimed to those who would hear it.

In such a way David Joris spoke with him, finally saying, "You yourselves are witness that I will be innocent of your blood in the last day, and that I have done my best about this. I have not shied away nor spared myself from the dangerous trip. Be mindful that I said this to you. [723] They separated in this fashion, walking away from them in the same manner as they had come. David also desired to meet with the imprisoned Melchior, but they would not help him in this matter, though they themselves had visited him often enough.[111] To these ones David, while inspired, had sent a letter written to the Jews, asking them to translate it into High German and to give it to the Jews.[112] But they refused to do it, excusing themselves that they did not understand it correctly. He begged them very heartily, until they told him to give them the letter and they would see if they could send it to Melchior to do it. This he did, but it did not turn out well. Nevertheless, David wrote still another letter, to see if they could understand it. He heard (although he did not know this as a certainty) that the Jews had complained that they could not understand the translation and would have much preferred it in the Low rather than in the High German. See, in this way David returned. One can well imagine how the Lord (to whom he gave himself, though not as perfectly as God has provided for and loved him) protected him on the way and helped him return home undiscovered. It is not possible to describe the kinds of danger which they had to endure, particularly from all the cutthroats along the way, and especially the entire village of Moordtjou.[113]

He therefore returned to the place from whence he had departed. He remained unwavering, continuing to grow in the Lord like a sprout or root which shoots out of previously barren soil. Many things were said about him: one saw him here, another saw him there. Some said one thing, others the opposite. One time he was on a horse, then he was dressed like a king, another time he was a master over many servants. Some said that he had gone into this or another city, or that he would betray this city, now that one. He was greatly slandered by all of this (by evil, envious, slanderous, and bloodthirsty people). This, even though the good man was precisely the one who restrained and stopped such in every region and who made the people courageous in heart, mind, and will. All of these rumors were on account of the envy of those who refused to hear or accept him.[114] The opposition to him became so great that people from all sides threatened to murder him. Yes, if God had not done so much through him, there would have taken place even more murders and arson and entire cities would have been ruined and destroyed by treachery. For they had been made completely despairing, frantic, raging, and insane. I must say this to you because each of them had seen either a wife, child, husband, father, mother, sister, brother, friend, or maid murdered and all their possessions taken. Batenburg therefore rose up, being aroused because of this and taking upon himself the spirit of vengeance. Yes, they admonished, taught, and strengthened him daily in this. They became so accomplished in this that they stole from houses and killed a great number of oxen, sheep, and pigs. They also chopped down

trees and cut down the grain with swords or scythes at night. In all of
this he went ahead of them and taught them how to empty an entire
ship by daylight. To summarize, whatever type of injury and ruin
which they possibly could do, they adopted as the best gospel and
Word of God. They became so hardened in this, that if David had not
been awakened by God, and, with many courageous associates, disputed vigorously against them, drawing away many hearts from
Batenburg, then all of Holland, Friesland, Groningen, and Westphalia
would have been utterly destroyed by them.[115] Yes, everyone there,
whether young or old, would have been murdered by night or beaten
to death. Truly, they would not have experienced any rest if God had
not sent this man in his name in order to restore this rotten, mad, evil
world, according to the Scriptures.

This happened to such an extent that they have hated him and
his associates, reproaching them abominably. Yes, some would have
blamed him for the murders which they were zealously planning to
do.[116] Who has ever heard of such malicious beings? Everyone, at the
moment of their death, tends to fear God and to give a confession, repenting and suffering for their lives. Such is not the case with these
people once they are captured. I find this hard to believe. They must
have had the worst plague of blindness placed on their heads on account of this good man, because they have resisted his righteous spirit
with hatred and envy, and continue wilfully to oppose God. But it is
the world's and the antichrist's bloody way of doing things, for they
have placed the innocent blood upon their necks and have well deserved it. Moreover, I cannot describe the great arrogance and evil
deeds, violence, and abominations which they perform. One can hear
these things from every side. I had not intended to relate these in my
account, but only to allude incidentally to them, in order to show the
origin of the hatred and blame which has fallen upon the good man's
neck. I reiterate once more that no one else has opposed and taught
against these ones, as can be seen in his writings. "The reproach of
those who reproach you has fallen upon me" [Ps. 69:9; Rom. 15:3]. If
he had not mightily vindicated the Lord's majesty, name, honor, and
word of truth, then the world would not have become so displeased
with him, not to mention become his enemy. For at one time he was
one of its best friends, but what did that accomplish? God has taken
him from it and has elected him to the derision of all his enemies. He
has also made him more learned, wise, and prudent, yes, more gifted
and more understanding than all his forefathers, or the wise lords and
masters. No one knew this, except he who accepted him in this. He

did not look to the derision, harm, and shame, nor did he go back on account of his own will, knowing that the servant cannot be better than his Lord, of which it also stands written [Matt. 10:24]. Read Isaiah 52 and 53. [724]

One has seen clearly in both city and countryside, that his disciples loved and valued him so much that they suffered all the pains of martyrdom on his account. They refused to reveal where he was, saying that they knew, but they still refused to tell. They proved faithful as God would have it 1 Samuel 20:32. The envious, evil, and ignorant people said all kinds of harmful, abominable, and evil things about him and his own, including how he captured cities and lands, beat the inhabitants to death and stole their goods. God has heard everything and all pious, devout hearts will examine it well, for it is clearly described. For there is no one under the sun, neither before God nor before humanity (no matter how pious) who can prove a shred of truth in any of these shameful, false, abominable, and evil accusations made against him. For what has happened to him here and there, or in front and behind him, is no concern of his, because he had nothing to do with it. Even less has he been with it, this is obvious. What more can anyone expect of him, except that he has been totally and in every way opposed to and has advised against all such things.[117] His whole doctrine or teaching announces this clearly, one can easily find it. Whoever speaks in a contrary fashion about him can nevermore be his nor God's friend. Now in the first editions of his writings (when he was still alone upon the earth in his most serene spirit of light, life, and truth), one might find two or three words which might be misconstrued to suggest that God and his saints will execute the vengeance and hold the judgment.[118] But against this he taught also that they should watch out, that they do not proceed before the time, because there must be angels. And see, it was the case that he wrote in this fashion so that they would listen to him, seeing that they were geared to vengeance, but certainly not without reason, to speak in a human fashion. And this proved wise, for they therefore learned more of the Old and New Testaments, and then better understood the Scriptures in their divine basis. For now they no longer despised him, but heard him well, such as had the poor, beloved society at Poeldijk. However, because his position was far from theirs at the time, they could not or would not read his writings or letters.

However, one must not be surprised about the words which David wrote or spoke at that time, for these have since perished. Nor about the other things which were said about the situation, seeing that they had formerly been said in this same fashion by the Lord himself, as well as by the prophets and apostles. But he refused to accept or acknowledge the raving, enraged, mad, false, bloodthirsty nature. He did not know what kind of mind, heart, will, soul, basis, nature, and spirit or with which words he should act in courage, frankness, and hope against the rebellious ones, especially when he chastised one who was guilty in this who refused to recant. The great diligence and earnestness with which David and the others petitioned the Lord both day and night at this time, cannot be described. The prayers, supplications and cries never ceased. They practiced self-control, fasting, and ceasing from their old evil customs. They sank into deep humility, and bore sorrow over their previous sins. They slept only a little, nor did they lie down comfortably or softly. They wore hair shirts and did not speak loudly. They chastised themselves severely. They ate no pleasant food so that others finally had to admonish them to do so. It appeared that some of them received a completely different human nature in their heart, mind, and soul, as one could see at that time. They were no longer horrified by death, nor did they flee imprisonment, but went gladly to it, just as if they were going to a feast. Yes (if one can believe it), they heard angel voices in the air for eight or ten days singing *Gloria* and *Laetara*, like the sweet harmony of organs. They were amazed, for they did not know where it came from. Yet they did not depend on that. Above all, they experienced a dream about the most beautiful and wonderful divine things.

It is nearly impossible to believe how David Joris was at this time inspired once or twice (since his childhood days) to make free and fearless confessions in order to tread under his feet or to cast away his shame which he had held unjustly against the Lord for so long. This also happened with his wife. For they drove out and bound Belial, the devil and Satan (which had brought them such evil), according to the Scriptures [Rev. 20:2]. One should try to understand or examine the truth of this more carefully. Let the mockers regard this as horrible if they will; they (namely the hearts of these pious people) will be found spiritually pure and clean. On the other hand, those who are outside will be found impure, stinking, and abominable. For they give honor, fear, and respect to mortals and yet withhold these things from God, merely on the judgment of the world and human appearance. It happened that one time David Joris had written to the Batenburgers telling them to stop and requesting, with the permission of his brothers, to meet together over a meal. But Batenburg reprimanded him, saying that Joris was neither called nor sent but instead inspired by the devil in order to hinder God's work in him. This meeting, however, was not to be, because of the many slanderous, unnecessary words of reproach which God soon revealed before too long. David, however, was willing to attend, but Batenburg wanted nothing of it, believing that God would soon lead Joris into his hands, and he would soon find the son of a whore. He thought that it [725] would still turn out this way, so that everyone would have to sing and speak about it.

This came to the attention of the good man David, and he was forced to write quickly, weeping very bitterly. He wrote a letter to Batenburg with such tears, that it would have melted a heart of stone, and this is not the half of it. There was a place in which David went to pray during the day, and there were chamomile flowers strewn about in the attic and a great pile of them elsewhere.[119] Kneeling on these he said his prayers, asking that the Lord would preserve and protect him from the evil ones. He knew, however, that he had been awakened by him to his praise, in order to establish his work. He also knew that he had not done this for his own praise, but so that the Spirit's foundation, together with the certain witness of his pure Word, blessed understanding, and truth might be heard by all people. Now when this happened David was completely alone, for no other creature was there. Early the next morning (he had spent the entire evening there) he wanted to kneel down again, but now where he had slept the roof was completely open with only daylight above him. And then he realized that the same flowers were now set up like small sheaves into three piles, with one in the middle and two on either side which faced the flowers in the middle sheaf. Behold, he understood the meaning of what he saw (how everything was divided and arranged), how they would bow to him, on account of his doctrine, spirit, and truth [cf. Gen. 37:6-8]. He marveled greatly when much of it happened afterward, to the great envy of others. For Batenburg broke away and attempted to make a revolt in city and country and to obtain freedom by force, to impose his will (as it was said). Behold, to put it briefly, he was captured. He confessed shamelessly, implicating David, saying that he was planning all kinds of misfortune, that he would murder these ones and those ones, that he had his mind set on seizing a city, and similar things. "Let me go or give me enough freedom," he said, "I will deliver him and all who follow him to you." And he said he would murder all the remaining covenanters, so that not one of them would be left.[120] This he said. He certainly had the heart for it if God had allowed him. But God gathered the innocent into his own bosom and guarded them from Batenburg's hands, for he was himself imprisoned, as you will soon hear.

The same day, or around the same time that Batenburg was executed [February, 1538] (as David learned later of this), David sat and wrote something about the bride of Christ, according to the ability given to him. For he never wrote anything special unless he was inspired or enlightened to do so. There came a voice to him in the midday, around one p.m., speaking in a perfectly normal manner. It commanded him, "Stand up and pray, Batenburg is in dire need, and he has come into this because he has misused you, therefore God will punish him. For this reason pray for him, that he may receive grace and not be forever lost." At this he wept as bitterly as any human on earth has. He prayed without any limit or doubt, that if it were possible, God would receive him in grace. For before his eyes appeared a vision of how God had eternally cast Batenburg into hell, just after the judge executed him. He saw everything inwardly. He therefore prayed tearfully and for a long time with his face to the earth, and he refused to eat until a voice spoke to his soul that God would be gracious to him. No one can adequately describe the tears. Even though such was just recompense for the unrighteous, why should he be indebted to the same, namely to the unrighteous? What did everyone afterward see of this? Batenburg's gang continued after him (even though his death should have revealed to them that they were not in the true way), fulfilling the measure of their father and teacher. Batenburg himself had said and written with his own hand, that one would be able to see whether David or himself was the one sent by God by whomever was the first to perish. Either he or David would perish in one of these three plagues: by hail, pestilence or the sword.

David saw this letter a half year later when it was brought to him by one who had been Batenburg's principal friend.[121] Although he did not hate David in the same way, he would not allow David to take the letter into his own hands, letting him instead read it with careful attention. He furthermore said that he had not done it so much on Batenburg's account but on David's, he therefore should not be too concerned about it. Then one of David's disciples renounced him. This one was on the way to becoming one of the best and had been with him on the journey to Strasbourg and back. He had previously wished many strange things to poor David. This one had a dream which he thought referred to David. Briefly, he saw in this dream a beautiful, lovely woman, but when he looked at her she became a whore, though he still desired to remain with her and had done so. Afterwards, however, she became an ugly, lewd dog. He was therefore repulsed and refused to go any further or to have anything to do with it, for God had warned him not to allow it to happen. On account of this, he narrated this dream to David Joris and asked him what he thought of it, whether it related to David. "To me," said David, "this is strange. I do not see how it relates to me at all," said David, "for he is the man who does this work himself, [726] therefore it cannot signify me. Let him relate what he saw to himself." A while later he sent a second letter to let him know that he should watch out, he now knew about whom the dream signified, namely that David was the woman and he was the man who at first saw David as an honorable woman with the true teaching. But many were now apostatizing from him without banning or condemnation because he was willing to be impure with the impure. Yes, he had become like a whore and a dog. This hit David hard. He, however, swallowed the bitter cup which was pushed to his mouth, as if he had to drink tears like one drinks beer or wine. But he sent the following by messenger: "If he found hearing and grace before the Most High, he might keep him in his thoughts and pray for him so that it might proceed better with him. For he was not delighted by such words, although he was neither horrified nor humbled by it." To the same one was this message sent, while he gave himself up to fasting and prayer.

Not long afterward he sent a third message to David that he now interpreted the dream to mean that he himself was the man and Batenburg was the woman, and words to that effect which are too lengthy to record here. In front of everyone else, he now called David the foremost lord David, and confessed that he now realized that Batenburg was the woman and he himself the man. It then happened that he came to David when he was preparing to eat. He asked him, uncovering his head (which greatly bothered David who became dissatisfied with this, more than can be reported here) if he too could eat with him. At this David answered, "Brother, why do you need to ask and call me lord, for I am only a human like you. Do you not know how our Lord has severely forbidden anyone to allow himself to be called this? Furthermore, even the angels at times have said that we should set our eyes only upon the Lord, and must never turn our devotion to any other creature," and he gave him a very long speech. After this the other fellow spoke in this fashion: "I know indeed, my lord, everything that you have said to me. I will not take it from God and give it to a person or a child of a mortal, but allow me to speak in this way. For if I sin thereby, the guilt falls on me, for you do not allow yourself to be so named." But David was not satisfied even at this, so little did he regard himself, being far removed from this. In the evening, when it was nearly time to again sit at the table, the aforementioned man fell on his knees, asking if he might eat with him. This pierced right through David's heart and he did not know whether to allow these words about himself, and he sank into even greater humility. Then one came to him, saying, "No harm will come to you, let him have his own way, do not take it upon yourself, you will yet see, be at peace."[122] Now all this seems to have happened at the same time when the esteemed soldier Heinrich Kaal came into his house in the evening after the lights had been lit. This one had been involved in murderous activities and disputations (as reported above), but David did not know this, for he had never seen him before in all his life. When he came in, David took him by the hand, desiring, according to the usual custom, to give him a brotherly kiss. But the man stepped back, bowed down, then fell prostrate, saying: "Oh my lord David, forgive me the evil which I have done against you," and he told him of his evil, disparate activities.

When the good man heard this, he was amazed, and asked him why. Then he said that it was on account of the woman whom he had carried away. David said "You have sinned greatly because I was innocent in the matter, and knew nothing of it. She is furthermore not here, but back in the region from where she came. You may indeed take her again if she wants you, I will not stop you." Then Kaal said, "No, I will not do this, I will allow her to first grow up, I will not know her in the flesh, but regard her according to the spirit as my sister." "Well," said David, "may the Lord grant us that we see the time when everything will be restored to its correct state," as well as more similar words which they exchanged with each other that evening. The next day he was even more smitten in his heart to such an extent that David could not come into Heinrich Kaal's presence, even if he did so twenty times in a day, when Kaal would not stand up before him if he was sitting or fall down onto his knees before him. David wanted to stop him, but he begged that he might not deprive him of this, he must continue to act in this fashion. These things I relate not to honor David, but on account of the wonder of God. After this it happened that when Heinrich Kaal, a stranger, first came to live in the city, that many evil rumors were spread by evil informants regarding the man and his people, saying that he had come to secretly capture the city. It was believed that there was a large number of his people there and that someone supposedly had seen some of them hiding quietly in a large empty house. This rumor was spread so quickly and fearfully that the sheriff,[123] with some servants of the magistrates and the city militia, in summary, a large group of armed men, quietly broke into the place. But when they got inside all they found were beer barrels. Some of them had a good laugh about this and they returned to the city hall by the street where David just happened to be standing near the bridge. This was a terrible ordeal for him, because he had heard that they had come to capture him. One of them, who had formerly been his playmate, saw him on the bridge and ran to the sheriff saying, "Are you, lord mayor, not going to go hither to this David? You will find him there." Then the sheriff, annoyed by his words, said to him (God, who is the avenger, allowed him to say this), "No, master Gerreit, we have had enough for now, let's leave it for another more appropriate time." [727] Then he (obviously) returned and was reprimanded by some who heard about it (as it went further), and was regarded secretly as a traitor and rascal, and he died not long afterwards.

The sheriff came very reluctantly to the man and one reported that he had said "he would rather have suffered the loss of 2,000 florins than to imprison the man." In spite of this he later took all of his and his mother's belongings, yes, even her life and the lives of all those who were later slain. I believe it is evident that he would never have done it had he not been incited to do so by his magistrates and especially by the clergy.[124] On the whole, however, many more people received pardons here than seen or heard of anywhere else. For all the strangers of this sect were released from the city hall and while they were to be locked outside the gates, they were allowed to depart freely and without punishment in broad daylight.[125] Therefore, whenever someone discovered any suspects, they would not arrest them. However, it was now said by an evil rumor that they were planning to capture the city, though that was far from their hearts. It is true, that they (as I myself have heard it said) imprisoned Heinrich Kaal, the foremost of these. They confiscated all his belongings, in which they found a booklet containing written versions of his dreams.[126] In these (as they claim) it was written that Christians would still be given privileges, cities, yes, every territory, or that he had seen this person or that person whom he named, elevated as a lord in his dreams. From this they conjectured even more that all of them had these intentions in their hearts. These men were all killed by the sword, and the women drowned, God have pity on them.[127] The city can still remember it. The whole countryside around it made itself guilty of this blood. May God forgive them of it, whoever was responsible for this.

Finally they imprisoned David's mother, took her houses and inheritance, also her and his belongings, things which he still needed.

His own children helped carry these possessions and place them on the wagon. They did not exempt even the smallest one from this, nor himself, except the one who was not very intelligent even though he was the eldest. The children had to allow it to happen. These same possessions were sold on the public market for the inheritance of the sheriffs. This is what one of his daughters told another who sat nearby, that it was just like what happens in the houses where someone has died, where everyone argues over the possessions. These possessions were worth more than other goods, because they were this person's belongings. Finally, before she was executed, even the houses were sold as well. At first she was very feeble and trembled in the face of her execution, but after this she was given some time to reflect on the kind of death she wanted. She was given three choices: drowning, bloodletting, or execution by the sword.[128] Her prison was in a cloister, in a room where she was allowed to be cared for by a friend or niece, a Magdalene sister.[129] Here she sat and reflected upon her life, how she had not yet walked piously enough. Finally she chose to be put to death by the sword, and regarded herself to be blessed in this by God's grace, because it would occur for his sake. When midday arrived, the same day that she made her decision, one or two from the court were sent with the executioner into the room and asked her, "What kind of death?" She had decided on the sword, but the executioner had nothing with him except a sharp dagger, because they thought she would want to bleed to death, which was the easiest death. Behold, while she was sitting on a chair, he cut off her head together with some of her fingers, because her hands were held high and folded together. After this they attended to her and lamented her life and buried her body behind the altar in the church. This was very respectable, because she was one of the upper class of the city. And it happened in this way with the man's mother, because she had confessed and professed before the council that he, David, was as good and true in his teaching as the prophets and apostles, and with other words she had professed this with a steadfast heart.

But it was not certain that she, who had friends, really had to die for this reason, if she had not opposed the sheriff so vigorously. For her human nature overcame her when she heard that all her belongings, house, and farm would be taken away from her and sold while she still lived. She therefore spoke somewhat foolishly. One was not sure of her state of mind when she said, "If you take my possessions, then take also my blood." At this he spoke, "This will indeed happen." He remained obstinate, because she had disgraced him before the magistrates, asking him what right he had to her possessions. For they were not to go to him, but only to her son's and daughter's children, but not to him or to his; he should be careful what he did. When the wife of David Joris had been forced to flee, she had left behind her small children who had stayed in the house of David's mother. She had been able to take along with her only a nursing infant (named Gideon). But then the mother of her husband, David, was also imprisoned (as described above), and all her belongings, what was left of them, including the house and farm, were taken away. This had been predicted before and written by the Prophet Micah, not to mention described in the gospel [cf. Mic. 2:1-2]. The children were forced to go running about and begging in the streets. Then they were taken to the sheriff, and boarded here and there, wherever it pleased him. He forbade anyone to touch them, neither friend nor relative, for he placed all of them in different locations from each other, one here, another there. Of these, only three or four could speak well, three not very well, and one or two could not speak at all.[130] They had to listen to much derision, vexation, slander, and disgrace, so that if one were to describe it, a devout heart could not read it without [728] weeping. One can imagine how the hearts of father and mother, sisters and brothers were affected. People from all sides beat them, regarding them as rubbish and threatening them with much harm. For they were thoroughly jealous of the gospel and on this account bore hatred and a grudge against their father.

Father and mother could only hear about and observe all of this. There were good hearts who desired to rescue and release them, but their father, David, said that they should keep still and let it be, they must suffer with the father. God has allowed it and has moreover shown him not to permit such. Only if God willed it would he change his mind. But he felt the pain in his heart and was truly consumed by it. Some people did acts of kindness to his children, for such acts it will never go badly for them. But before this had proceeded much further, it occurred through God's counsel and will, that the time came for the good man David to leave the city, for he had remained there long enough and everything was gone. So it happened that he left at great expense, for no one was supposed to conceal him or do him good because it was forbidden to do so on pain of death.[131] They wanted to help, but did so only because they were well-disposed to the gospel. However there was with him a man (I believe) who was not convinced by him and for this reason they drove him to the ship at night. The separation from wife and children cannot be described. There was much bitter suffering and lamentation from his wife and children. This had happened many times before, but the last time was always the hardest. Now they commended everything and each other into the hands of God, the faithful Shepherd and Lord, and he departed from them in this fashion after a few brief words. After remaining there for a little while longer, they too had to depart at night due to some spies or evil reports. They had to entrust everything to unknown people who did not know each other so that no harm would result from it, as could have happened if everyone knew each other. They might have guessed or realized who they were, but they did not want to know the truth.

After they had boarded the ship, they went secretly with their shipmates down into the back section of the ship and three of them lay down to sleep. They could not sleep, however, because it was still early, but the hold had been closed to keep it dark. David lay nearby and his heart was occupied with divine matters. His soul, understanding and thoughts, sight, mind, fate and strength, and everything that one has inwardly, were taken away from him. In an instant a vision was revealed to him. It seemed as if all the wainscotting had been opened up on one side and when he looked outside he saw the ship flying along the coastline like an arrow thrown by a hand. What this meant was written down just after it happened.[132] By this means David came to Haarlem into the home of a young man who had just been married.[133] He was an elect, honorable flower of Israel, and his wife was with him there. He remained for approximately two or three days, and from there he departed, leaving provisions with his wife and their children, to await the outcome. He sat hidden for a long time, never free from thoughts of God or divine matters. While he was lying before the Lord in his illuminated mind and spirit, it happened that (it is not possible to describe how) there came to him the power of an almighty, divine, heavenly being, just like a heavy spiritual burden. It entered the top of his head in a perception of or sensitivity to the resurrection. It pressed inward through his head and all his members, moving down into his legs so that he had to sit down and could no longer remain on his knees because of the weight of the heavy burden. And behold, he felt the power touching him forcefully before it fell upon his head. While it moved about or circulated, he perceived in this same power five new senses from God.[134] These, however, acted and moved about according to the same nature as if he had seen, heard, tasted, smelled, and touched or felt God. For he perceived it as completely different and absolutely marvelous. It was, however, a spiritual understanding in the form of a divine-human being, desirable and sweet, just as if God had revealed and manifested together both human and divine natures in an overlapping taste and desire. It happened in such a manner that he could not contain himself. Before he had finished his prayers, he rose up as if he bore a burdensome sack full of grain around his neck and stumbled about with faltering steps down to the other two who were with him, and he began to speak.

For there came to him around the same time a vision in which he had no body and could no longer recognize himself. He now had different senses and it seemed to him that, as a result, he had a different voice and was a completely changed and renewed person. He sometimes fell down, having to hold himself steady on the bedposts, just like a drunkard or someone who is overburdened with a heavy load. It seemed that he was almost completely out of his mind. What he saw in this condition (that is, in the light) cannot be described here, because it cannot be expressed in words. 1 Sam. 21:13; Psalm 24:1 [?] etc. After this he experienced a daily renewal of his spirit and he was able to see. For before they had come here,[135] a month before his mother had been imprisoned, a light shone upon him which one could neither approach nor leave. For it was a light of the thoughts of God, an uncreated, [729] unnameable being of truth, which cannot be examined by eyes, nor touched by hands, nor understood by the physical senses. The joy which the man experienced is impossible to explain, for he now understood the words eternal, light, and light of truth. Before this he had never seen them, nor had he ever heard them spoken or preached about. No one knew more about it than he, for these were nothing more than words to others. He knew of no other new being such as he, for there was no one at that time (I believe) with the same Spirit of Christ in the truth.

But now the Scriptures, yes, all the words of God were unfolded even further, increasing more and more each day, the like of which has never been heard. He began to speak in new tongues, to comprehend the words in their divine, eternal, spiritual sense, and to examine their true origins. However, no one can taste nor perceive any of this without the same Spirit. It is therefore useless to write about it with mere letters. He was enveloped with such living, heavenly senses and thought, that he had to pray that God might allow him a little rest. Otherwise his body would perish, not being able to bear it unchanged in such an immediate nature. One need remember how the children of Israel could bear such a nature only in its outward form when they heard it from Mount Horab [Exod. 19:21]. If he were to set down all of this in words, he would need much more time. What happened to him throughout these days and the kind of temptations he had to face as he prayed to and petitioned God is well known. Indeed, what he resisted is not possible for anyone upon the earth, but because of something else and to God's praise, it was reduced. One is able to understand the mortal inborn weakness. All people are aware of their own weakness, although not as well as when in temptation. It is said of this: "Whoever ventures nothing, gains nothing; and whoever tries nothing has and knows nothing." One afternoon he lay down to sleep for a little while and although it seemed to him that he was still wide awake and not asleep, in an instant, in the blinking of an eye, he was filled with a divine meditation. When he opened his eyes, they were so renewed by a transformation of the light in his eyes that what he saw was altogether new in his sight. Although the things in themselves had not changed, they had done so in the sight of David. It spoke to him of the many beautiful things of the new future time. Of this event and words he had written much, but because of the coming of the persecution, everything had to be left unfinished. He also received the inspiration of God by the Spirit, which he welcomed every day and night in the form of a very excellent sound and a beautiful promise. For it spoke to him like an inward voice, which (it seemed to him) he heard outwardly. Although its sound was only internally in his mind, he still heard these things very well, but kept it secretly to himself. He did not want to confirm his teachings with it, but instead he kept silent about it. He finally told it to one person, praying and petitioning him that it should come into no one else's hands, which this one promised. All of it was confiscated, however, along with other books and letters, so that he remembered nothing of it.

He also had a heavenly vision, which he saw outwardly. He believed that not even John the Baptist nor any creature upon the earth, indeed not even Stephen [Acts 7:55-56], had seen Jesus Christ more lovely and realistically as he. There was a vision in which his eyes were transformed and converted from the sensual into the supernatural, that is, into the understanding of beauty according to the Spirit. Many, many more visions were revealed to him, such as regarding the fear of the Lord and his wisdom and righteousness. These were wonderfully revealed to him (no one is able to examine or understand these literally) in the most sacred and beautifully sensitive nature, for the human heart can obtain more of this than the mind. Also, during this time, around early Easter morning [April 6, 1539], when he still lay on his bed, a voice spoke to him, saying, "Get up and write!" He however remained prone, listening attentively, thinking, "What is this?" But the voice cried out a second and third time so loud and strong that he was forced to write. Otherwise it would not go well with him, for the voice said "Leap up and write, I say to you!" This is described elsewhere. I leave it out, because my time is short. One can read it in part in the first section of *The Wonder Book*, in the 130 and 131 chapters.[136] Now while they sat continuously in the stillness, David did not write anything down except what was given to him from above. It happened once more that at the same place there was a religious festival or procession and three or four of them wanted to go into the small attic under the roof in order to remain hidden there during the day. While they sat there, David spoke continuously about what was in his heart. One of them (named Leonard van Dam) was listening and saw a spirit and living word come out of David's mouth and enter him, inspiring in him a living mind and an elevated vision. First, a voice spoke to him, saying he should go downstairs where he would observe what would be shown to him. When he did this, he went there and prayed to the Lord, for he felt that something was happening to him which was very troubling and terrifying. At this he stood up and walked the length of this room, then waited to see why he was inspired and where he would be told to go and what would occur. Then, just when he was turned with his back to the light, the voice spoke: "Keep still, remain standing, and behold." Then he saw a man's image standing before him with his back [730] to him, that is, from behind. What followed is here:

> A vision of one (named Leonard von Dam)
> who loves the truth and justice of God,
> which he has seen in the daytime
> during the course of the month of May
> or beginning of June 1539.[137]

Sitting up in the attic in a house it happened that the Spirit of God came suddenly upon a man named David and he began to speak of the power and word of his God, just as the Lord placed into his mouth. When I heard these words, they were inserted into my innermost being, so that the heart and mind of my soul were opened up like a rose. I then could not contain the life and joy of my innermost spirit. I cannot describe this in words, for it remains unspeakable to me. And behold, I was compelled to stop my work. But I was troubled about this and continued to work in order to overcome my laziness and weakness, although I was pressured to stop. Finally there was an inspiration given to me by the voice of the Spirit, without my advance knowledge or advice, running in this fashion: "Truly you have heard today (through the living conversations which have proceeded from David's mouth) and you have listened to, seen, tasted, and felt Jesus in his living, spiritual, true nature, standing at the right hand of God in heaven, even more truly than had Stephen, Acts 7:18. Or like Isaiah, who said in Isaiah 6:1-3, when he saw the glory of God sitting on his seat and throne: 'I am a man of unclean lips.' You too must read and speak freely, without timidity in this way, for you too are a man of unclean lips, and after this you will see in a living fashion in the innermost parts of your heart the majesty of God. After this it was shown to me from the Spirit that I should read Isaiah 6 and Acts 7. I did not know what I would find written there, but I thought, what can it be? At the same time I was full of a living fire and burning in my innermost being, so that I did not know how or what was happening in me. For I was young and did not know the Spirit and in my weakness I could not express what was happening to me. I saw myself as too small and unworthy to speak like a man of God about the exalted word of the Spirit. The Spirit, however, allowed me no rest, but spoke as loudly to me as if it had occurred through a person's mouth, saying that I should go downstairs. I could neither sleep nor rest, neither in the evening nor night, until one summer afternoon, around three or four o'clock, when I answered and said: "Lord, you know what the situation is here and the reason why I cannot go downstairs."[138]

This had happened five or six times when the woman of the house (knowing of it) came up to us in the morning, and said, "Is anyone up here who wants to come down? You can do so, for the people have departed." About this I was full of amazement and decided to go into the hall or room. When I now had gone in and out of the room five or six more times, I finally stopped and stood there in the middle, and a voice said distinctly to me: "Stand and behold." Then I stood with my face toward the wall and away from the light and I saw a naked man, standing before me, also facing away from the light toward the wall, for I saw him only from behind. He stood with his feet upon the surface of the earth, which was amazing to me. Then the Spirit spoke again to me: "Behold." Trembling, I looked and watched as the man quietly sank down, with his feet gradually descending until his head had also gone under and disappeared. I then saw the earth neither opened nor closed. The voice of the Spirit spoke again: "Behold." I then saw the same naked man under the earth just as clearly as I had seen him above the earth. I therefore became dismayed and frightened, and asked in my heart, what does this man rest on; does he stand on his feet or on his head? I observed that he was suspended between heaven and earth, as I have told you, and he moved as a bird does in the sky. But so that you will understand me, he was in the earth, as I have said to you. Then the Spirit or the voice answered me: "His feet stand upon nothing, and rest upon no outer thing, but he is suspended, for where he is, there is an eternal abyss." Thereupon he called me to look again. Then I saw the same naked man growing or rising out of the earth just like a flower or plant. But then I saw all of this from behind him. The head came up first, then afterward the neck, then the shoulders, arms, hips, legs, and gradually the feet, all slowly or little by little.

Take note. The head came up first, then afterwards the neck, so that he once again stood upright upon the earth. I then wanted to touch him, to see if he was living or dead. But such was not permitted to me, for the Spirit answered me: "He is still dead and not yet living." Then I looked at his feet and I became aware that they touched the earth and became impure from it. But from the feet up the body was so pure, beautiful, and shining that one has never heard of nor seen such a clean and majestic image of a human. Furthermore, my eyes fell once more upon the feet and I saw that they were now also pure and beautiful from the earth, for the earth or impurity had disappeared completely from them. And behold, I saw the life enter him; first his hips were pulled to and fro from behind, [731] just like a human or beast that has first been killed and yet lays and wriggles, so that his veins and sinews were pulled to and fro, as is easy to comprehend. A little later he lifted up his arms and let them down again; then he shifted or moved his whole body, until he was completely alive. Finally he lifted up a leg from the earth, or stretched it forward; then the other, and set them down again. See, after this he turned completely around with his face toward mine and against the light, and his face shone like the sun. So brightly, in fact, that one cannot describe it. He also had a beautiful red beard and he came walking toward me, as if he would go right through me.[139] Whether he went through or around my body, I do not know. But when he came up to walk to me, I was so amazed and frightened by the appearance of his movement that it was like I had been outside of my body, although still standing on my feet. I cannot write nor describe this with the quill. He was also so large and amazing, so mighty and frightening, that he feared no one. He, furthermore, saw perfectly that all great rulers, lords, princes, dukes, even the kings and emperors of this world, were in his eyes as worms upon the earth are commonly regarded by people; as worms, which have only a little movement, not even as the beasts, fish, or birds. I say that no one fears to tread upon or near them, killing them or letting them live. Yet even more insignificant than these were all people, both small and great, strong or sick, noble or common, all swept away by a wind.

When I now wanted to look at him, he was gone and I saw him no more. Then the Spirit spoke to me: "That is God, the Messiah, the new creature, the first true man of God from heaven." The name of the person, which was pleasant to me at that time, I will still keep secret, it was very well known to me. He will, according to the word, be heard, known, and loved even more at the right time. I did not relate any of this for seven or eight days afterwards, until it finally broke out of my heart. I am also certain that this vision came right from God. Moreover, I desired to reveal or bring it to them, for even as I had seen it outwardly, so I saw it also according to the Spirit.[140] After this happened, the man was so amazed he did not know what to do, for he thought, what is the meaning of this? During this time he kept it concealed and did not reveal it to David. Then it happened that David was also inspired to go into the entrance hall where the first vision had appeared. When he came before the light, he turned around to come toward the other brothers. At that moment a voice said that he should kneel down, but David did not do it right away because of his concern for the others. Then a voice spoke strongly and loudly to him that he should be obedient. And see, he did it, regardless of whether or not the others might think it to be as strange as he did. Regardless, it had to be done. As soon as he was down, his heart, sense, and mind turned to the Lord and his eyes opened up inwardly. Immediately David found himself staring at a quickly rotating clockwork wheel. It turned quickly, and then after it had rotated for a little time it stopped. The thing which one normally used to wind it turned over and over two or three more times and then stopped.

Then the voice said: "Behold, in this way will I from henceforth awaken the hearts of princes, lords, kings, and mighty ones against each other. There will be no end nor rest until they have all perished, and in this way the blow will fall upon their necks." There were many more words spoken by the voice which have since been forgotten. David believed that it signified that they would not obtain peace and therefore must humble themselves. He was so convinced of this that he placed it in a book.[141] Finally the clearest meaning of the contents came to him, namely, that God wanted to entangle their hearts against each other, or make unrest or trouble for them which would not cease until he had finished and declared his will and word. Be this as it may, it certainly happened in this fashion. For in the same evening that the wonderful vision of the naked man was described to him, David had a divine, glorious incident. God (it seemed to him) pulled him totally away and took David (it appeared) away from his own sight and perception, as if he were no longer the same man. He, in fact, no longer recognized himself. In this same vision he saw himself in Aaron's priestly garments [Exod. 28:2], like a pure bride and a spiritual head of the church. He was asked if "he received joy and peace from it and if he was satisfied with it." For it appeared as if he was not married to a woman but only to God, and that he had never had relations with a woman. Instead he desired to be entirely free of the same. But after this he saw that all his other brothers had wives. He, however, was supposed to be completely divinized, so that he would have no need of such. He chose this as the best portion which would humble his soul, for God had chosen and loved him, he therefore wanted nothing else. When he told a little of this to Leonard van Dam, this one said, "Something special has also happened to me, which I will now tell you. I have been burdened with it for so long, it seems to me it should now be told," and he began (as shown above) to narrate how it happened. All of this is described above. Amazing things like these have never been heard before. [732]

Now after this had passed and his spirit grew stronger, it happened that in the city where David's wife was, that a beloved young man was captured and led away by betrayal and defamation.[142] The way that he perished caused some to become more wary or cautious (due to the advice of some), among whom was David's wife. So she, with her daughter and young son, journeyed to a place where she requested to live with them for one or two months.[143] But as soon as they had left, they tortured the brethren, just as had been done everywhere else. They, however, found nothing evil or false in them (although such was reported of them) except that they highly praised David and were in agreement with his teaching. These ones were badly treated. Others were imprisoned at Leiden but were, through the assistance of a courageous man, rescued by night.[144] All of these were David's fellows and followed after his teaching. And so they wanted to know what David's teaching meant. Well, it was this, that one must perceive the old being through the new and in this way each one could remove it and put on the new being with true understanding and the knowledge of divine righteousness. This must be done through the most holy faith of the eternal, blessed word, which he, David, said he had received above all others in a living fashion in order to reveal and to announce the way of death.

And all of this he clearly proved with much evidence in his own Dutch language. For the time had arrived that all of us who desire to be saved must hasten to die to all things in which we have lived a godless life. We must become blind to those things which we have seen incorrectly. In every way to leave ourselves and enter Christ, receiving the new birth of God in the power of faith according to the Spirit and truth. To serve God willingly and not the flesh; to become completely perceptive in our senses. Once one has received this new birth, one must in time proceed and fulfill what one has been given, more richly each day. One can perceive this clearly in his writings, in which he has truly revealed more than all the wise ones in the world, indeed more clearly than all other writings. The end of this will be further shown.

I wanted to put this here so that one could know a little about his teachings.

For this has not set out one-thousandth of the same. It is impossible to relate it all to anyone who has not been nourished by the same Spirit, or who has not been inspired to speak by the Spirit. For to hear it said does no good. For he teaches nothing except the death and mortification of the carnal being and what is involved in burying the same through mortification and suffering, as well as the overcoming of oneself. In particular, that everyone must forsake, hate, and remove themselves from all the carnal senses, will, lust, and desire; from their own understanding, learning, and opinion. No longer believe themselves, but instead believe the Lord in his eternal gracious word and truth. Be conformed in every way to Christ Jesus [cf. Rom. 8:29; 12:1-2] and be regarded by the world just as he was when he came into it. One must not be worried or offended by it.

However, as soon as the people received such with believing hearts, then they are received by God as his beloved ones, whom he has blessed in his Son and whom he will consecrate or save. They must be found in him, and not outside of him. They must be especially obedient to the eternal truth in their heart, senses, will, and soul.

So now, in the meantime, if there are occasionally any faults and deficiencies (namely human weakness) which appear before this is fulfilled, then they must prove themselves as truly reborn in their hearts, senses, and minds. And they must through sorrow and suffering put on a penitent, sincere heart. For they must evidence a truly childlike, correct perception which does not exist on the outside. For one must first know and perceive oneself, who, how, and what one is, and of what one is able or not able.

He also presented in many different ways the well-founded basis and teaching of this, therefore all tongues are made dumb [Ps. 31:18]. And so in this fashion they made their heartfelt confessions, both publicly and among themselves, in the most faithful and believing fashion, concerning what they knew to be the best. For it had happened in the same way in the first times. He did not baptize, nor did he command anyone to do so, for he said that it was not to be established with water. For while it was sufficient in the period of childhood, if it was to have any meaning at all then it must occur in a truer way in the Holy Spirit. Therein lay the power to live and die, along with many more absolutely beautiful teachings and proofs.

Therefore, he said that they should mortify in their hearts all flesh and beggarly and sinful lusts or turn the senses of the heart away from them. Furthermore, to pluck out the eye and its sight [Matt. 18:9] so that one can instead look at and contemplate everything that God has made and created as good and beautiful, without spot or wrinkle, so that one does not destroy oneself through oneself. To heed the good, not evil, the free, not the bound, and the pure, not the impure. But each one should judge oneself and know that all those things which are forbidden to people as impure are so only because of an impure heart, senses, and soul. For about this the devil has reviled and spoken very harmfully in promoting this error, especially when he remarked that some have been made stinking to him, and have thereby entered into their own suffering and death (I speak of the true and upright ones). It is as if humanity or the world [733] were free, pure, and righteous in this, or that in this one does not commit sin or refrain from touching the good. One must draw near to, hear, and see it. It is as if they had never been born into the world and other gatherings were as holy, or without sickness or misery.

These few points are in brief the correct meaning and basis of the rope woven by the strength, nature, spirit, and life (by God's grace), in order to bind Satan and to become completely free from the old enemy of humanity and to live solely in the new being (God's Son) in eternity. Also, to neither look to nor regard the kind of revilement, harm, insult, and evil rumors which have been spread and heard throughout the whole world about him. He knows that his countenance could have no better and more beautiful experience than, along with the whole naked body of his church, to have looked to the cross of his Lord Jesus Christ as his outward example and victory. This is noted of the servant of the Lord by the prophet Isaiah in chapter 53 [50:7]; "He hardened his heart against his enemies like a flint stone." For before God he knew that he could not be harmed, for his heart truly sought God. He woke up with God. Indeed, he was daily sustained, raised, fed, and taught with the Word of eternal life. He knew, furthermore, that he could not partake of or fulfill such without being condemned by the ignorant and without great vexation. For the Scriptures were freely and clearly revealed and inspired to him in all of their parts (which no one knew, for it was an entirely wild and overgrown desert).

See, when this had happened, the report came to David that even more of his brothers were captured in the city and elsewhere. They, and especially one from Utrecht who was living there, therefore advised and begged him that he should no longer remain in the city. He said that he might come there [i.e., to Utrecht], for he believed that his wife was either there now or would soon arrive. He therefore gathered some things together. I do not know what things exactly, there might have been a cloak or a robe, for David was in no great hurry to escape. For he wondered when all of this was going to end. Now there was a young fellow who had been with them for less than a year who had to travel to Delft.[145] He wanted to rescue and bring back with him some of David's children. But their father, David, would not hear of it, even though the mother would have agreed to it if it would not be too perilous. They therefore desired that he not attempt it, and David, with many fine reasons, forbade it earnestly, saying he would wait until God provided. When this one completed his trip, however, one of the little daughters (who was in the worst condition there) recognized him and ran up behind him, screaming and crying bitterly, saying, "O, Johan, where is my mother? O, where will I find her? I can't stay here, for I am beaten and dragged about by the hair. O! O!" and other similar words. It seemed to the youth that his heart would break. Not wanting to leave her, he said, "Child, do you want to come with me? I will help you find your mother." She cried: "O, I do," and earnestly begged him, clinging to him. For that reason he took her with him and they rode to the Gouwe[146] and then from the Gouwe to Amsterdam. But alas, an archrogue followed them out of the city. This man knew the identity of the child, either by himself or by another. He pretended to be favorably disposed to her father and spoke in an evangelical fashion.[147] The other good man did not guard himself from this man and listened to him with his heart. When the rogue wished, he gave him up to the authorities in Amsterdam in such a way that he was arrested with the child. The child was taken to the mayor who gave her to his wife to spin for her, for she was very competent in this job.[148] They interrogated the child in a special manner, saying this and that, especially that she should tell them where her father was, although she did not know. They threatened to hold her hostage and to take her everywhere with them. She cried out to them, "I will not work any more," and she wept bitterly, for she had a truly innocent spirit. She was finally released to a cloister.

The news of these events was reported to the mother who sent one of the child's relatives there (she was also one of the sisters of Magdalene) who took the child out of their hands and in this way she was returned to her mother. About this there was great rejoicing, not to mention what they concealed in their hearts. But alas! The noble, courageous, fine youth was severely tortured and martyred, for the most part in order to force him to confess where the child's father was. But he refused to tell them, for he did not think it right to bring his brother to his execution. For such was neither his intention nor desire, and he cried to God in his heart that they would not be able to force it out of him. They threatened him severely when he continued to refuse to tell them, hoping thereby to make him so exhausted that he would soon reveal it. They increased the severe torture even more, hoping that he would tell them. Instead he said "I know indeed where he is, but I will not tell you. Do what you want, you will not force it out of me." For it went against his conscience and faith. Furthermore, love did not allow him to say it. Those who desired the information would under different circumstances have commended him greatly, but now he was merely an obstinate or stiff-necked boy. Many who heard of this incident commended and praised him indeed. But now they shamefully destroyed his limbs and the like, which was only the half of it.

Finally they condemned him to death and executed him with the sharp sword, and so shamefully that there certainly would have been a revolt if he had been an evildoer.[149] [734]

But now this did not happen, because they died willingly for Christ and the gospel, and therefore no one lifted a hand, because they were not of this world, neither did they esteem or love the world.

After this the good man David went aboard ship and stayed on the water for a few days because the earth had become too restricted for him. And when he left there, he heard the news that all the brothers at Utrecht had been imprisoned, including his wife.[150] If anyone was troubled about this, it was him, indeed from the bottom of his heart. He therefore left the ship (the skipper has since died) and went to a city called Deventer, thinking to himself that here he could perhaps find some rest so that he could write some more regarding the heavenly stream which had come over him. One can see and read about this in *The Wonder Book*.[151] Such a deep understanding of it is revealed from an unlearned man that it could only have come from his innocent spirit. At this place he was taken by one named Jorien[152] (the other he left behind in the inn) who traveled by foot with him, hoping to bring him to a certain person. They therefore walked quickly for a full night and day, becoming exhausted and weak (when they arrived they were nearly crippled) and after all this they were not as well received as the one who had brought him so far had hoped. It was very difficult, for while they would perhaps allow the person into their home, they did not really desire to, for the house was not well situated. Finally they did well and David Joris and Jorien made the acquaintance of this nobleman (whom David did not know, neither the region where he lived) during a meal. Finally they returned to the region from whence they came. On the way back the good man was so troubled and oppressed that several times he wanted to jump out of the wagon on which they sat and once had actually jumped off, wanting to go to Utrecht to give himself up to the authorities so that they would release his wife. Those who were with him, however, begged him with many words not to do it.

Along the way David, in his torment, saw many strange visions which he regarded as a forceful temptation, for he thought of the great violence and injustice which was done to him and to his own, especially when he thought of his poor, lost, scattered children. For it was said (at the time that it was happening) that when the mother was captured she had to abandon her daughter, who carried their small infant. The child with the infant departed from her imprisoned mother and being in a strange city she was in bitter sadness, as one can imagine. She had to journey alone with strangers and finally arrived with a pounding, weeping heart at the city of Delft where she would have had little help (if one person had not done so). All this the good man, her father, pondered intensely, so that he nearly risked turning himself in, so that the mother might once again join her children. They interrogated her intensely about her husband, wanting her to tell them where he was.

She told them that she did not know, and this was true. The pious heroes who were with her counseled her as best they could so that she would be soon released to join her children, but such could not occur. For the prosecutor or advocate of The Hague (Mr. Reynier),[153] together with Jan Sondersyl,[154] were so bitter and envious of her, that they shamefully accused her and the brothers who had been executed at Delft and Haarlem of desiring to attack the cities. Jan Sondersyl said that he still had their confessions with him. The woman asked permission from the good magistrates and the mayor of Utrecht if she could speak freely and respond to this and she gave her confession about this. She was so enraged and angry about the crude, proud lies which they had told behind David's back, shaming him publicly. She insisted that he prove it or be called an evil and false witness. David had proven himself to be excellent and had spoken to the brothers only about virtue, honor, faithfulness, and piety, which she had seen of them. They desired to execute her swiftly because she had associated, traveled, eaten, and drank with these people, even living and hoping with them. She furthermore told them that she did not need to know what sort of people her husband led. She would not be guilty of condemning or bringing about the death of her husband (if she desired to be an honorable woman) because she knew far better than anyone else that he feared the Lord and loved the truth of Christ, seeking to do good to everyone. He just could not conceal the blessedness which he had received from God. For she could testify only a little about the matter and of what kind of result had come to him. She would say much good if it was not already common knowledge. She was therefore willing to die.

The suffragan or assistant bishop wanted to torture her thoroughly and had selected the day when she would appear before him in the court. But such was not allowed to him, for in that very week he lay down and died. Similarly the prosecutor or advocate (Mr. Reynier) had also wanted to proceed harshly against her, not wanting her to escape. He spoke very shamefully and dishonorably about the woman. But this did not once enter the court, for he did not return. For he fell and had such a pitiful death that he had wished (as one person said) he had instead been a swine butcher or shepherd instead of a prosecutor.[155] It is well known what kind of end he received, so that the good magistrates measured [735] all things and after having drunk all the blood of the other pious heroes, they were no longer thirsty. They executed only one more person who had been in Münster, whose sentence had been delayed until she had given birth.[156] What happened to the good man in the meantime, no one knows; he even had to sleep below the earth. When he could no longer endure this type of concealment, because he was quickly becoming ill, they rented a small room where they stayed as guests and this was not too bad. But David became so aware of the very great judgment over the world that (had not God taken it from his heart) he would never forgive neither emperor nor princes, neither lords nor judges, nor anyone who had been guilty of the persecution. He had to constantly listen to the curses, crying, and screaming. Indeed, even if he sat on the emperor's throne and if authority over the whole land, according to the flesh, was given into his hands, yet all of it was not worth a drop of water compared to what was given to him.[157] Then the news sheet came to him which said that his wife with all the others were to be executed.[158] He lamented this greatly, although he overcame it by prayers and supplications, being one who had placed himself in total submission into God's hands. Every day he prepared himself for this.

After this came the news sheet that she was still alive. At this time he moved again, with great danger, to another place because it was very expensive and not very comfortable or quiet for him in the inn. They had to shy away from the host and hostess, but the maid encouraged them to come in for the night. He did not wish to do so, but one of their company had secretly rented a small house which had once again occurred because he trusted solely in God, as had happened throughout his life up to then. In this house were shown and revealed to David Joris once more many wonderful things, and his spirit continued to increase. There were many others, however, who here or there were saying that God had chosen them and given the Spirit to them, speaking in secret about high matters, believing that they were the one who was to be expected. For example, one rose up at Wesel, who had a strange and amazing spirit, believing that he was the person, and writing amazing things.[159] After this the Norseman arose who said that he knew everything and that he would never die. For he would renew the earth, level the mountains in Norway and establish all things according to the Scriptures.[160] These and similar ones reviled David's disciples (I must speak in this fashion) on account of their immaturity in the Scriptures and the simplicity of their understanding, because they remained standing under the cross and suffering and did not have all the excellent things in mind. But all of this was insignificant in David's sight, even if they were inclining others against him by their words. This was nothing to him, nor did it agitate his soul; however, many set themselves against him. He felt this to be a temptation indeed, but his spirit did not sorrow about it. He also knew that they, devoted to righteousness, must attempt to be purified and cleansed like Christ in their heart, sense, and soul. He furthermore wrote at that time more than three letters to them, composed in an excellent spirit (according to the flesh) which, if read literally, seemed deceptive, as when one brother opens his heart for examination to make others realize their inconsistency.[161] A good result came of all this, working wonderfully and quietly, so that some were finally convinced through much effort.

When by God's grace Dirkgen was released, she settled herself quietly in the city of Delft and all her children (those not stuck in one region) came to her. It came to pass once again that he hurried in the early morning to come there too, intending to arrive before daylight. Because of delays (too many to relate here) it did not work out at all, so that he arrived in front of the gates once again in the bright daylight, around seven o'clock. But God provided them with a heavy fog, so that no one could see very far. If that had not been provided, then everyone would have recognized him. After he had been there secretly for around four or five days, the devil made it known (by the upper class or by those who love people according to the flesh instead of the spirit) all over the city that he was in the city so that someone was going to capture him in the evening. It was also ordered that he should go south and his wife north and that was only a pretense to separate them from each other. They, particularly he, were not happy about this, but he perceived it in his spirit and thought of the dream which he had had in the night, although it was too long to narrate here. He let them know that he would not leave the city without her, let them catch him if they liked. She could not be with him during the daylight for fear of being seen. One must remember that he wanted to remain there on account of his wife. Observing this, they allowed her to journey with him for eight or fourteen days and in this way she moved around with him until it was dark, though not without concern about those who were not favorably disposed to him. Indeed, how it came about I cannot describe here. Now when she had been with him for some days, she desired to be with her children again, as was only natural for good mothers. They therefore separated once more from each other and she stayed alone with a resident who also loved her husband (in the spirit of her trust and faith) [736]. A long time elapsed when David became so troubled that he wrote sharply to her. She replied that she had been advised not to travel until he had obtained a safe place, then she would come again to him as a good wife should for her husband. But she had to, alas, keep secretly in a rented house for some more time, until God provided for her in another land or city, just as he always had provided all too wonderfully.

After this it happened that a brother named Leonard[162] set out and came to a comfortable house where the lord and master was willing and swore with many promises that if the good man would come, then he would support him. David was now advised that he should show himself there to inspect it to see if he wanted to stay there. If so, then his wife and children would perhaps also come there. He did this immediately, driven of necessity, separating once again from wife and child, as it must occur. They rented a wagon to take them through The Hague and not through Leiden. When they set out, the wagon-driver had hired a youth in his place to drive the wagon. This youth was accustomed to driving through Leiden and insisted on going there. What kind of dismay and trouble they experienced cannot be described, for the youth was so obstinate and insolent, crying and screaming because they wanted the horse to go another direction than he did. In summary, he had to make a detour or they would turn around and return by foot, especially David. The others, however, were willing to risk it and they drove inside. The next day they heard the report that three or four of these people had been arrested and that the gate through which they would have had to ride had been closed until eight or nine, but God had prevented it.[163] They rode on and traveled the streets very dangerously in the beautiful light of day, encountering these or those ones on the way, but there was nothing they could do, they had to risk it. They came in this way to the water and got into a small ship sailing to Breda. In summary, they had many annoyances along the way. When they now came to the house, the man had changed his mind on account of his wife's anxiety and fear, and so they had to turn around again.

They took courage, because it could not be otherwise and left on a ship that was in a hurry to shove off. If God had not protected David, he would certainly have drowned, for he was at the portal when the ship started to leave and the ship struck against the wall and he nearly fell in headfirst, but he reached out and grabbed a sail in his hand, holding onto it until he no longer needed it. He had not done this by himself but God had provided that he remain above. They hired this sailor to take them to Dordrecht and he loaded nothing aside from them and two or three other people so that he should continue their journey to Dordrecht. On the way the boat was so full of water that they had to move from the sides to the middle and in this way he set out for Dordrecht. They pumped and worked very hard so the boat would not sink, because it was leaking so badly and was not at all seaworthy. They were very angry at the skipper, insisting that he would keep his word as he had said. Indeed, they spoke so much that the skipper replied in such a way that the people heard him. "What kind of people are you," he said, "that you do not desire to be in the city? I will take you no further, and cannot do so anyway." He truly said this to them. They had to keep quiet and place the matter in God's hands and they said, "All right! Do your best as much as you will and can." David, however, prayed to the Lord and attempted to be of good courage.

When they now came before Dordrecht, they believed he was going to land, but he swore by himself that he would do as he had said. Another stood up and said he "wanted to go to the land" and argued so much that they became angry with him and the skipper was unhappy about him begging and asking him so. He finally went out and called a small barge for him, in which he sat to sail into the city. They had no pleasure in this man. They got out and went into an inn where they were welcomed. The hostess said she would make them comfortable that evening; they, however, were in doubt whether or not to remain because it was late. They decided they could not risk it. So they hired a wagon and drove on. They came very late to Isselmonde, where my Lord of Isselmonde was present and all the peasants were drunk and full.[164] The hostess sat them by the fire because they were cold, tired, and weary. Now one, then another came to their table, and they thought, "Something is going to happen to us," but they submitted themselves to their God because they were not thieves or murderers, so they would not worry. In summary, it happened that they were taken to where they were to sleep, and David thought that he saw a singer who was familiar with him (because of his craft) who was going to sleep in their room. They went to bed before him and hung their clothes upon the trunks. He then came up here and desired to go to sleep but the maid refused to give him a light (so it seemed) so that he had to walk in the dark. He cursed the plague and whatever else he could think of. When he came to the clothes, he felt some here, some there and he became very angry when he touched their clothes. He finally lay down and slept soundly. In the morning they got up early before daybreak and went out the door to continue their trip, because they had paid their bill in the evening. They came to a barge [737] in which they could make the crossing so that they would be able to arrive by wagon in time at Rotterdam. For they had an introduction to a

Hillegont, a fine elderly widow, and it happened in this way.[165] On the right side of the gate of the city, there rode toward them the magistrates of the Court, but because it was dark and they were disguised by the fog, they rode right by them and God was with them so that nothing happened.

They came to Delft at night and one of them called to the doorman, telling him who he was, for he would have known the others quite well if he could have seen them. Leonard von Dam gave him money and directed the others through, because it was night. In this way they remained in a citizen's house, an old beloved, sincere Israelite, until they continued their journey to where his wife was. When they came there, there was joy and sorrow, for they knew that without God's special protection it would be impossible for him to leave again. After this Leonard traveled to Guelders where he found a knight who had assisted in the assault on Münster.[166] This man had been shot at by one of those inside who had only a gun and who was inside under the bulwarks. The bullet fell harmlessly on the knight's helmet, and with the halberd in his hand, he shoved the one who had shot at him down into a pitfall and ran him through. The knight had become quite sorrowful about this, and he was therefore glad to do some good and provide housing for a person such as David. He was told to come to the house. When he now entered the house, the maid of David Joris, who had a heart for running messages, came out with the news that God had allowed them boldly to rent a house inside Antwerp and they had already given the deposit for it. They therefore left the knight because throughout the day many soldiers came and went. The good knight became quite sad about this and died soon afterwards.

So they sailed to that place, but when they were on the trip, David and his brave ones were sorely tempted. For in front of Dordrecht they sent one of them into the city to buy something. They lay hidden in front of the city, looking this way and that. They began to worry when he did not return. Finally they sent another to go to the market and to hear how the matter stood, if this one had become sick or had been captured. But what happened? Why, neither of them returned. Furthermore, the skipper believed that it was not good to stay there much longer and that they must either sail or the ship had to go to the port, something which he had not told them before. They decided to sail and when they had started moving, a small barge rowed out to them from the shore, and the people inside waved their hands, which frightened and caused much anxiety among them until they saw that

it was their own people. No one knew what the problem was in find-
ing what they had set out to buy, but they had to observe a passport,
with stools and benches, therefore it took so long.[167] In this way they
came into the city of Antwerp in Brabant.

The end
of the written report of David Joris's life.

Glass round portraying the allegorical virtue of Righteousness; c. 1544-56
Ascribed to David Joris
Courtesy of the Historisches Museum, Basel

3
Two Songs of David Joris

The following texts are included as two samples of Joris's Anabaptist songs composed after his affiliation with Anabaptism and before the fall of the Münster kingdom in June 1535. Both reflect major concerns of Joris during his career as an Anabaptist leader. The first, "I Heard the Wind Blowing (1534)," illustrates Joris's preoccupation with Jesus's command in John 13:34, to "love one another." The second, "O Christian Spirits," was composed at the end of June 1535, while Joris was seeking refuge near Strasbourg. As noted by the anonymous biographer, not only was he and his family fleeing persecution, but the siege of Münster was in its final stages. In this poetic work we see Joris's attempt to encourage the hounded believers with an affirmation of the nearness of the return of Christ for judgment.

Both texts are from Joris's *Songbook* which was most likely published in the 1580s, probably off the press of Jan Canin.[1] In spite of the late publication of the volume, it is evident that the contents of the individual poetic texts relate very specifically to the period of composition and can be generally regarded as reliable guides to Joris's early ideas.[2] In order to be as faithful as possible to Joris's original meaning, no attempt is made here to rhyme the verses.

✲ ✲ ✲ ✲ ✲

I Heard the Wind Blowing[3]

I heard the wind blowing,
the Spirit breathed in my senses;
And I stopped sowing
my grain, to my loss;
I did not produce any fruit

or blessings.
I must seek them in love,
for they are always gathered for my good.

I grasp in my hands the understanding
which must come from God.
It is love, as you know,
which comes to the pious people.
Esteem love above all,
and do what you will.
Do no other work than this,
And be at peace in it.

All that you do on earth,
protect the ciborium of God.[4]
Highly esteem God's temple,
do all to the glory of God.
Seek the profit of the many,
of one another, but not of yourself.
Heal your brothers' wounds,
Just as love commands us [Luke 10:30-37].

Protect the simple as well as the sick,
Do not let them perish.
Give offense neither to
the Jews nor the Greeks.
Neither injure God's people,
as the Scriptures testify.
For there is no salvation in such action,
For God values such people.

For the nuts are produced in love,
and they will be unmeasured.
It is all concluded
in the Law and Prophets.
It will all be provided for me
without any harvesting.
Store up love to the last measure,
Otherwise it is not preserved.

FINISHED 1534

O Christian Spirits[5]

O Christian Spirits, pay attention here,
all who are living in oppression;
expect Christ's physical coming,
never let your faith die;
let watching and praying be your occupation.
Yes, mortify your flesh as Paul said,
and always be prepared, unto death.

O Christians, do not let yourselves be robbed
of the evangelical Spirit's meekness;
do not believe every spirit,
but first examine if they are good and from God;
stand firm on the ground trod by the apostles.
Separate your heart from this world,
and always be prepared, unto death.

If you have truly died with Christ,
then seek only what is above;
not the earthly, which is completely foul,
but an eternal good which is promised,
although it is damned here in this world.
Therefore be understanding, do not be misled,
and always be prepared, unto death.

Do not set your heart on a long life,
do not allow evil to kill your heart.
If you give yourselves freely to oppression and suffering,
through this you will be exalted as you enter God's kingdom.
be patient, flee the evil life,
walk in the light without delay,
And always be prepared, unto death.

These are truly dangerous times,
in which the elect of God stand in anxiety;
but God will justly fight for them,
their days will be shortened according to his word [Matt. 24:22].
He will joyfully receive the disciples,
for God has prepared the punishment.
And always be prepared, unto death.

All the blessed of God must drink
the clear red wine from the cup of bitterness;
but God shall pour out yeast for the godless,
which they will spit out, vomit, and fall to eternal death.
Grasp understanding, O beloved of Christ,
hold fast your faith and spread God's honor,
and always be prepared, unto death.

Behold your Prince, praise your King,
who was unspotted and without sin;
Like a criminal was he slain,
punished with the evil ones, stretched on the cross.
O slothful one, wake up now,
follow after Christ in his righteousness,
and always be prepared, unto death.

In June, 1535. FINIS

4
Of the Wonderful Working of God, 1535

This tract, *Of the Wonderful Working of God, Who Has Created All Things in His Image in Three*, was apparently written in 1535 in an attempt to account for the failure of Münster.[1] Although it seems to be the oldest surviving prose work from Joris's quill, it does not seem to have been the first of his works off the press; that distinction belongs to *Hear, Hear, Hear*, composed the following year.

Unfortunately, *Of the Wonderful Working of God* is known only in a later edition, one of seventeen tracts in a bound collection of Joris's works printed in 1614. It is therefore not known if or when it was printed before this date or if the available version has been revised at all.[2] That Joris was preoccupied with the theme of this work before the end of 1536 is seen in another tract confidently dated to late 1536, in which he comments that "all things have their perfection in three."[3] In spite of the unknown early provenance of *The Wonderful Working of God*, Joris's usual practice was to date his works by the year of their composition and there is no reason to doubt the veracity of the statement at the bottom the work, "produced [*wtgegaen*] in 1535."

If the tract was written in 1535, then it might be helpful to determine the specific time frame when Joris would have been able to compose it. In the winter of 1534-35, Joris had attended a meeting of Anabaptists in Waterland where, according to his anonymous biographer, he opposed the program of the Münsterite emissary. He returned to Delft sometime in January or February of 1535, but was on the road again by the second week of April, hoping to find refuge first in Strasbourg and then in England. Because of the failure to find a home in either of these locales, Joris and his family were almost continuously on the road until the early autumn of 1535, when Joris found work at Gorkum on the Waert. In December the family returned to Delft. Two periods, therefore, present themselves as the most likely times when Joris could compose this piece: the months of January to March, or September to December of 1535. Considering Joris's apparent reference to Münster in the past tense,[4] the latter period seems best to fit the circumstances.

Great hopes had been pinned on Münster, and after its fall many disillusioned Melchiorite Anabaptists simply left the movement. Unwilling to renounce his own Anabaptist heritage, Joris sought to explain the apparent failure of apocalyptic expectations and to maintain the devotion of other Dutch Anabaptists. To do so, he reshaped Bernhard Rothmann's and Melchior Hoffman's teachings on the final restitution of the people of God in a fashion suitable to the post-Münster situation.[5] His solution was, to say the least, innovative.

❖ ❖ ❖ ❖ ❖

[Title page, 72ʳ]

Of the Divine
and Godly Ordinance
of the Wonderful Working
of God, who has Created and Made
all Things in Three in his own Image.
To the Praise and Laud of his High
Majesty. He alone is all wise, rich, mighty
and full of eternal unspeakable glory;
blessed in eternity, through
Jesus Christ, who is the true
Light and Life,
Amen.

Jer. 31:33[-34]
I will put my law in their hearts and write it in their minds.
And they will be my people, so I will be their God.
And no one shall teach another,
nor will one brother say to the other
know the Lord, for they will all know me, both small and great,
says the Lord.

Published in the Year 1614.

[73ʳ]

Of the Divine and Godly
Ordinance of the Wonderful
Working of God, Blessed in
Eternity.
Greetings to all believing, true, upright hearts.

Rejoice, you heavens! O you earth, be merry! You mountains, exalt! You hills, make a joyous shout! You trees and plants of the Lord, spring up in gladness! Yes, all you rivers and waters, clap your hands together in delight! [Ps. 96:11-12]. Be thankful and let everyone praise the name of God in the highest through Christ Jesus. Through the Word of life, I say, which has proceeded from the mouth of the Most-High. Yes, it was born out of the mouth of the Father, as one in one. He was created the firstborn before all creatures, of one nature and divine essence with God the Father himself [Col. 1:15; cf. John 1]. Whose name "Son" has existed from eternity. He is the true tabernacle, throne, mercy seat, and tabernacle of God blessed. In whom the fullness of the Godhead lives and abides unto eternity [Col. 2:9]. He is the Mother of all true, spiritual children of light and life; through whom and from whom the Father above has brought forth the genuine man of God. [73ᵛ] He has command and authority in heaven and earth; his glory and majesty stands in Jacob and rejoices in Israel. That is, the King of the heavenly hosts of great majesty. To him is the kingdom; to him is multiplied the honor, power, and authority for eternity. Amen [Jude 25].

So now exalt God's wisdom as the cedars of Lebanon [Ps. 148:9; Isa. 14:8]. Glorify his ordinance as the cyprus trees upon Mt. Hermon [Ecclus. 24:13] and as the palm trees in Cades [cf. Ps. 92:12-13]. Beloved, behold the stone foundation upon which you are built, and know the fountain from which you were dug up. Observe this, yes, and be seeing, seeing and single-minded. Hear what I say to you, and of whom or of what I will make known to you or to where I point. Look there, observe with reverence the nature of your Father. See how great and unspeakably holy, pure, wise, and foresighted he, gracious, is. Yes, how mighty, how righteous, how strong, how courteous and merciful, of how much honor he (who alone has authority) is worthy; this is certain. Observe this, yes, pay close attention. Remember beloved, how obedient and careful we ought to be, that he (blessed) is not angry or wrathful against or because of us, and that he has not changed toward us. In other words, that the light does not turn to darkness for us. Pay attention. Therefore, consider the life for which you have been made, the kind of nature or spirit you feel in yourselves. See that you know yourselves, of what you boast or of what you confess to be. Do not further your own name nor preserve [74ʳ] your own honor, which does not belong to you. Do not be fearful Christians, but look upon your Lord, hear what he says, do his will, follow his counsel, rejoice in his Word, keep his commands, obediently fulfill his law, and walk wisely. Proceed with foresight, properly and maturely with those who are among you. Pay attention and allow yet one more thing: do God's work, have his perfect being so that God our Father may be honored, praised, and thanked in us all. This will be when all of us are well humbled, spiritually poor, and are nothing to ourselves. Then we will exalt only the Lord our God, to the praise of his almighty, glorious, and exalted name. To this we have been created, in order to proclaim his praise. Pay attention.

The eternal, invisible, almighty God of heaven, the Father of all good, visible and invisible things, shall now be glorified in the last days. Being rightly known by us, we thank and praise his great grace with joy, through Jesus Christ our Lord and Savior, who has now been discovered by us. Pay attention. For he has renewed all things in heaven and earth, and all things are perfected in him. For he is the eternal-born, elect Son of the Father, the power of God, the word of God, the life of God, and the Spirit of God, the true likeness and image of the invisible God, brought down out of and from him. [74ᵛ] The church of Christ has been made just like Eve and Adam, flesh of his flesh and bone of his bone [Gen. 2:23]. Pay attention here, and rejoice greatly in the knowledge of God and his Son Jesus Christ, blessed into eternity.

See also, it is now possible to hear with high understanding that Christ is this same image of which he spoke, namely, the living word of the Father, which has proceeded from the Father and became flesh [John 1:1,14]. Yes, a true, visible, and tangible human of flesh and blood, but from heaven; heavenly, spiritual, holy, without sin.[6] Pay attention.

See, this only beloved, elect Son of the Father, who from eternity to eternity is one with the Father and came forth from God without the doing of visible hands, is made a Lord and Christ for us. He has subjected himself to God his Father and Lord of heaven and earth, with all humility and great obedience, to the death of the cross. Therefore, God has also placed him above all heavens, to be Lord (I say) over all. It is said also, that before him everything will bow, and must be laid and brought under his feet, since he is worthy of the honor. He made himself subject to him in everything; although he was Lord of everything, he was nevertheless a servant of everyone, yes, a servant [75ʳ] of servants [Phil. 2:8-11]. The Most High did this and made him into the lowest and humblest, to the praise of God his Father. This is surely a great wisdom, a victorious, earnest love and a mighty humility, which has gone forth from God, who also is exalted and to whom belongs alone the praise, overall gracious in eternity. Amen.

This only Son, Jesus Christ, has returned, renewed and restored us in the Spirit. Yes, he has made us free in everything, through faith in his name. Yes, he has moved us from death to life in the Spirit [1 John 3:14], I say, into heavenly beings. But not everyone has their perfection, strength, and age in this, so that they might know victory over death and over all our enemies. These fight against us and seek to bring us from life to death, through the desires of the flesh and lusts of the wild nature or through the evil will, in which we have been drowned. But we thank God through Jesus Christ, who has given us victory in his name [1 Cor. 15:57]. Namely, to all the obedient who prove themselves to the death of the cross and who proceed to the perfection or victory. There the flags or banners of righteousness have been raised up in victory, under which all of us must be gathered, before they can be displayed visibly, flying over all, in full power and majesty, to the punishment of all the disobedient, disbelieving, and evil.[7] Pay heed to this.

Therefore, let everyone, as beloved children, [75ᵛ] be obedient to your Lord and humble before your God. Keep your eyes upon your pastor, Jesus, who has walked ahead and preceeded us in everything, until you have won and passed through [Heb. 12:2]. Be full of the Holy Spirit, filled in all wisdom and intelligence, according to the good pleasure of God [Eph. 5:18]. And do not let up, nor let go, until all things are restored to perfection, visibly renewed and changed. In particular, from the flesh into the spirit, from death into life, from earthly into heavenly, from the old into the new, from metal into gold,[8] from the letter into the perfect way. Take heed. To this end have all things been foreseen, made, and ordained.

For only God of heaven has power and authority overall, for he alone is the head of all and in all. From whom all things have proceeded, are made living and visible. He has given himself (Jesus Christ) to us. In whom all heavenly things have received their beginning and end, in order to restore the children of God to their glorious divine freedom in rest [Rom. 8:21]. Therefore, we must begin and end in his ways. That is, without speaking against the truth. So that because of us, none of you may be ignorant of what he has taught, ordered, and commanded us. Those who have not done so will be ashamed. Pay attention and be obedient in everything. Be found true and upright; that is the will of God eternally blessed. [76ʳ]

Now just as God is the head and Lord over Christ, to whom the praise and the honor are God's, also is Christ placed as a Lord and head over humankind. And the third, even is the man ordained to be (understand) a lord and head of the wife [Eph. 5:22-24]. Pay attention here. Of this is Christ an example of one who has gone before; poor, humble, meek and lowly, yes, he was obedient to his Father and Lord, even though he stood in the form of God in rank, riches, honor, and glory. Even so must everyone in their order, the man to the Lord, and the woman to the man, prove obedient and humble to the death. For that is the certain example which Christ has left to us as a teaching, so that the servant may be satisfied that he has been like his lord [Matt. 10:24-25]. Yes, everyone who desires to live well with him and to be made divine and exalted must die, suffer, and be brought low with him here. Is it not right? Well then, so must we deny ourselves and subject ourselves under the wise and powerful hand and ordinance of God. Be despised, hated, and rejected in this world, finally be crucified and killed. Why? Because he gave witness that their works were evil [John 7:7], and whoever does not do this will remain in their favor and not be hated. Pay attention. And though everything in the world belonged to him for free use, yet he was damned as an evildoer. Yes, [76ᵛ] he was repudiated and killed as a criminal, without justice. For this reason, therefore, the same is given to us, all with him and through him. See, so must we demonstrate meekness and longsuffering against violence and injustice, and strength in suffering, so that all things will be restored in us as in the beginning.⁹ And put on the garment of holy simplicity and innocence. Pay close attention.

I say once more, although the entire earth with everything that is in the world and all its fullness belongs to the Lord and to his anointed or children [Ps. 24:1], nevertheless, we must forgo that and die to it, letting all of it go. I say that it is, however, our own property, our Father's portion or possession through Christ Jesus, until the time of the renewal and restitution. Everything must be first renewed and restored in us together. The summary of this is named the five senses, which are entirely renewed and replaced. They must be restored to how they were in the beginning. This is expected and produced through faith in the Spirit. It is worked and achieved by praying with tears. By this they will see and obtain their desire and health, by grace through faith in Christ Jesus.

These same ones, once they are clean and pure, will thereafter, at the right time, in a perfect and unhindered way, certainly receive their promise and property in the rest and divine freedom, with power, and they will possess all things [77ʳ] and have the victory [Rom. 8:14-27]. I say, therefore, that it is good not to stand still now. Instead, go forward on the path of righteousness and peace, awake and with endurance, possessing your soul, looking forward to the deliverance, just as the farmer expects his fruits. Pay attention.

So therefore fear your Lord and God, you men,[10] and hear what the Spirit, not flesh and blood, says to you. Also, do not threaten your enemy, for as long as (I say) you have not overcome, so that there is no admixture of flesh. Turn yourselves not to foolishness, but do as your Lord, who, although as perfect as his Father, gave it up to those who make judgments. Pay attention and know what I say to you. Do not deceive yourselves, but understand. Be nothing but prudent. The Spirit who impels you speaks clearly in you, so that it is all well. When you then are so far and know that your flesh is mortified, that it neither seeks nor wills nor works of itself nor has anything therein, then be ablaze with wrath, with Moses, Phinehas,[11] Ehud,[12] Jael,[13] David, Christ, etc., against the evil and the rebellious, proud enemies of God and the opponents of the truth. These demand the perfect jealous, burning love, and such earnest, zealous love will be aroused.

In this way, be obedient in everything, stand in the fear of the Lord, and serve him with willing, humble hearts. In this way will you honor the Father. O you men, take heed that you resolve not to follow your own spirit, [77ᵛ] but submissively let the Lord rule and act in you. Behold, behold, let him frighten you in the flesh, for if you do not show him the honor which truly and only belongs to him, he will not let you go unpunished. Instead, be guilty in nothing. Keep his commands, and endure to the end the despising and shame of the cross, until you triumph and pass through death in everything. And be set into the Most Holy, that is in the life. Walk prudently and wisely. Do not neglect yourselves or be disobedient by hiding your back to those who smite you, or who pull, catch, or grasp at your cheek [Matt. 5:39]. Do not hide your face from the reviling and spitting [Matt. 27:29-31]. Behold, guard yourselves from the ingenious. Instead, let all of you learn how to awaken your ears in the morning, until you are gray-headed and are unpunished. Summary: Be a mirror of your Lord, who

did not cease or let up. He did not do this until he had fulfilled all of
his Father's commands and had obtained the victory over his enemies. He has also walked before us into the Most Holy, namely, into
love, and has opened a glorious, immortal, eternal way into heaven,
where he has also left us an example [1 Pet. 2:21]. Pay good attention.

The third: Likewise must the woman stand humbly, with great
tolerance and obedience, under the husband her lord, in everything
to do his will in the Lord. Not doing nor willing, in works, words, nor
actions, other than to please her beloved lord and Christian husband.
[78ʳ] For that is the will of the one who has perfected, created, and
prepared all things well to his glory. So that everyone will carry out
their work, service, and office, reasonably and truly with trembling,
obedience, and willingness, in order to become united with or like his
only Son Jesus Christ, the living Word and the wisdom of the Father.
He will eternally abide and dominate over, fulfill, and complete all
things. The Father's pleasure is for us to be a mirror, student, judge,
and as the white of a target. Weep, all who do not regulate or conduct
their life after this, when what is to come arrives. O, then they will
weep bitterly! For although it is a word of mercy, of salvation and
grace, it is also a word of righteousness and of severe judgment, each
one adding according to what each has worked or said [Matt. 25:31-
40]. Pay attention.

Make captive your understanding, you women, under the obedience of the Christian husband [Eph. 5:22-24]. Assent to his wise
speech, which has been spoken from the fear of the Spirit. Quarrel
not against him, but bow your understanding under his. Be obedient
from the fear of the Lord. And you shall rise as a great light, shine as a
great salvation [Isa. 58:8 or 62:1]. God will judge and punish the evil
and unrighteous ones. Fulfill the will of the Almighty. Do not look after the husband to see that he fears the Lord; but let him look after
you, for he was made first, [78ᵛ] then the woman [1 Cor. 11:8, 1 Tim.
2:13]. He is also her head, but Christ is before and above all of these.
Therefore, he has the preeminence in all things. He preceeds us in a
legal and human fashion. Behind him follows the man, then the woman must follow the man. But she must attend to the children, so that
they will learn correctly and properly from her and be maintained
and taught to virtue in the fear of the Lord. But Christ attends to the
man and the man to the woman, who is his concern. Pay attention and
know what I say to you.

See, in this way you women and you men stand together under
the obedience of Christ, just like Christ also stood under the obedi-

ence of his Father. For he came not to follow his own will, nor to speak his own word, but to do the things of him who sent him, his Father. He maintained all of his commands, honoring his Father and Lord. Learn from this, you men and women, both young and old. Yes, you women, honor your husband and rejoice in him because of the Spirit which lives and works in him. With this he is able to cleave firmly to the Lord, becoming one body with him. Therefore, always be obedient to him; be afraid to anger him on account of the Lord and his Spirit. Just like the man should be obedient to the Lord on account of God. Therefore, do not sin. Be not divided in mind or spirit. Know what I say to you. Beloved, take heed. It is the Word of the Lord [79ʳ] which has come through and from his Spirit. Therefore, pay attention, and be at one in every way with your lord or husband. This must be so. Yes, it must be, if you are to be one body like the church is one body or corpus with Christ. Not Christ with the church or the husband with the wife, but the wife with the husband, who is the head and lord, whom one follows in everything, and in his entire will. Pay attention.

Allow this also in the name of the Lord, without murmuring. Be innocent in this. First, you men, follow your Lord with joy and with thankful hearts. Do the will of God the Father. Similarly you women, follow such men and always stand under the obedience of the Spirit. And be humble and meek, not regarding yourselves. Instead desire passionately to be the least and not the greatest. Not only outwardly in appearances, but also in the heart. So that you might please the Most High, the Lord above all. He knows and sees everything that you do. Let this happen with each one, work toward this. The Lord will indeed find the contumacious ones. Yes, the God of Israel will condemn those who have opposed his Spirit.

You men, let your beards grow and your strength increase in Christ which you, in the first Adam, have allowed the woman (your own flesh) to shave off [cf. Judg. 16:4-21; Lev. 19:27]. By this you have lost the seven Spirits of God,[14] namely, the entire [79ᵛ] strength and power of God in every manner. You have gone the way of Samson, being bound with bands and straps of darkness, and you will be defeated by death, that is certain [Judg. 16:21, 30]. Therefore, each of you watch what you are doing. Do not let your beard be cut off. Behold your strength and honor, which God has given you to his praise.[15] Do not look upon the beauty of the woman, nor upon her temptation and enchanting, so that you not be softened to her covetousness. Instead, turn from all covetousness of the evil flesh and of the belly; let it be far from you. Do not be imprisoned by the lusts of the prostitutes

and concubines. Beloved, see this and pay attention. This is enough
admonition, I say to you. Neither you nor anyone else shall be innocent of foolishness, but you will be ashamed before all the angels.
Take heed.

See, from the woman has come the beginning of sins in humanity,
and through her we all die [Rom. 5:19]. Also, she must consider her
will as an abomination and completely disregard it, so that she will not
again soften the man, nor rob him of his honor and love. From this the
woman must now fight and struggle in a praiseworthy fashion, as a
warrioress and woman of war against her enemies, and gain the victory over them through obedience and humility of the heart. You
church in the Spirit, as an image, watch that you now do not grieve
your teachers of wisdom. Behold, show yourselves strongly obedient
to those who teach and serve you, so that they may always [80ʳ] increasingly produce in you in the Spirit. And furthermore, be perfect
in all knowledge, wisdom, and understanding. Watch that no one
grieves the Holy Spirit [Eph. 4:30]. Beloved, be on guard; be innocent
of pride and scorning which goes before a fall [Prov. 16:18]. Instead,
make sure that your pastors complete their service peacefully in the
Lord, so that you will be blessed, in order to bear much fruit in the
Spirit through your obedience and humility. Pay attention. Let the
church do this first, thereafter the flesh; in everything according to
the will of the Spirit. Also, let everything in the church be handled under man and woman, so that whoever is not faithful to the Word might
be won through the obedience of the good woman's conversation,
without having to speak the Word [1 Pet. 3:1-2]. See, all manner of
fruit will be produced among us through the conversation of the wom-
en; through their humble, honorable ways and obedient ears and
hearts. Then let the man come to the fore.

See, unless all of this is done, the three restitutions will not follow
each other. For only those who first begin to will and to work will receive all things in their first beginning. The same eternal, incomprehensible, fearful, mighty God will correctly restore all things and give
us the promises. We must allow him to work and we must be obedient
and desire to cast out our reason. Do without ceasing what he has
commanded us [Matt. 28:20], so that the same [80ᵛ] will be fulfilled by
deeds. Furthermore, we must stand submissive in things that are
above our understanding and pray always with trust; then it shall be
well. But weep, all those who speak against their Maker or who, murmuring against him, have looked back [Luke 9:62]. Weep, all those
who think they are knowledgeable or who remain in the first school-

ing, not proceeding any further to the perfection and human maturity. Beloved, take heed, and do all that the Most High, only wise God
wills. Stand still, examine your will, discretion, and resolve. It has begun without your wisdom, will, or resolve; it must therefore be completed without them. Stand fast, merely fulfill the Word. This Word
which he, blessed, has commanded and ordered, is to keep the faith,
hope and love with perseverence [1 Cor. 13:13]; to be poor, humble,
meek, and longsuffering, simple, foolish and innocent as children.
Work for this, abandon the wisdom of the letter or discretion. Only be
obedient and faithful in the least as in the greatest, in the first as in the
last [Luke 16:10]. Understand this and pay attention.

From now on the church or temple of the Lord will be purified
and sanctified, examined, exalted, and made praiseworthy. Then will
there be songs of praise and thanksgiving to God, with joy and jubila-
tion. Exclude the devil and he will flee far from here [James 4:7]. Let
us all be full of faith and full of love; [81ʳ] obedient hearts, poor, humble, and foolish [cf. 1 Cor. 1:18-25]. Put on the clothes of simplicity
and innocence, and be as children, yes, as children. But this will cost
much struggle and suffering; we must crucify and mortify the flesh,
before it is fulfilled. Yes, it will cost many tears, much crying and
weeping, much sighing, moaning, regrets, and great longing, being
hungry and thirsty. Once the devil flees, the flesh in its lusts and covetousness will be dead, but in no other way. This I say to you as a certainty, that those who count their goods and blood, the beauty of the
flesh, all of their things, and disregard them, they will win Christ.
They alone, (I say), shall be received [Matt. 19:29]. They will therefore receive truth and faith, for only the doers shall enter therein. Beloved, pay attention to this.

Therefore, work to become a child, for Satan has no will nor work
therein [Matt. 18:3]. But be obedient and do not neglect yourselves;
neither mock the Lord in his grace, but fulfill the command of Christ
toward your brother [John 13:34]. Pay attention. That is, improve all
things, make peace, seek love, love, love. Have no regard for the flesh,
renounce it, regardless of whether it is rich or poor, noble or common.
Chastise it without regard, and let each one be obedient to the other
in the fear of God, so that the Lord may be praised and honored in
this. We have shown much shame, dishonor, and disobedience to God
and to the Lord Jesus Christ; now spit it out, confess, and consume it
in [81ᵛ] anger. O let us now have different minds! And if we are now
truly regretful, then let us show honor and obedience to him, wherever we may and can. Beloved, let all of you have one desire; yes, to be

thankful and strongly reverent. In everything be afraid to make him angry. Let it happen in this way. And the same will receive much honor and grace; my soul will be his soul and his soul my soul, one hand with him. But he damns those who will and act otherwise.

See, in this way Christ's spirit abides in God's spirit, since he hears and follows him, for he can do nothing else, for he was one with him [John 5:19, 30, 10:30]. Nevertheless, he asked his Father what was his pleasure or will [Matt. 26:42]. How much more should we? Therefore, pay attention. In this same way the believing man's spirit abides with Christ's spirit, and the woman's spirit with the man's spirit; both together, one in one, unto one likeness and image of God. But so that you will always understand, I believe that just as Christ is like his Father, so must the man be like Christ, and the woman be like the man. Furthermore, the children should and must be just like the woman; all stand under the obedience of God [Eph. 5:21-24]. For it must be completed through the obedience and humility of the heart. Be they many or few, God knows his own [John 14:14]. It will no longer be an abandoned, but an agreeable, approved state of heart. Before the Lord it will be divine and will have authority over all things. Then God will be blessed in everything. [82ʳ] He will be thanked and praised, and offered a true, unspotted sacrifice of hands. From whom, out of whom and for whom are all things, just as we are, through Christ, to God's majesty.

See, at this time there will be only one good will, one heart, one spirit, and one body, of which Christ will be the head and God, Lord of humanity, with dominion overall. And then none of us will continue to walk according to their own intentions, nor do anything according to their own will, nor speak their own words, but everything through the Lord. For the flesh will be entirely mortified, subdued, and defeated. Therefore, no flesh will be able to desire or do any work. Nor will it be looked at or known, but only the Lord of hosts, whom people shall magnify, honor, praise, and know rightly. Yes, we will be kissed and embraced, and be pressed to his breast. Pay attention. And the Lord admonishes us to come to this through his Spirit or messengers of the Most High, whom we must receive thankfully and joyfully. For they have been sent as ambassadors and messengers in the name of Jesus, proclaiming peace and rejoicing to those who have no rest, who are burdened and in mourning, or oppressed with anxiety and suffering, on account of sin and erring wills.

Therefore, let everyone prepare themselves to be obedient to their Lord. See that you do not oppose God's ordinance, or you will weep. For disobedience is a bewitching[16] sin, and [82ᵛ] contumacy is trouble and idolatry. And those who intend trouble with God's law will have no fellowship with Christ, the Lord of hosts. Instead they will be cast out and punished. For those who are found to be like the idolaters will not be forgiven. Pay attention.

So everyone together obtain one will in Christ and one good mind in the Spirit. Adorn yourselves gloriously, then your Lord will no longer hide himself, but your prayers and tears will go up and be received by him. Be always obedient to the voice of the Lord in his servant of servants, and please the Lord. Cast away all flesh as abominable. Let the world (understand this) be a cross and a pain to you, and perceive the world as a heavy cross. Guard yourselves, then it will go well. O you men, do not remain women. Do not dishonor God's majesty. Do not be chastened, but be men in the Spirit. Do not allow yourselves to be made dead or moved by any woman. Instead, be her lord, and bring all things under you. For all that you have subdued, such as sin, the world, or the entire earth, is given to you. O you images and children of God, do not be defeated by the evil, especially in yourselves. Instead, defeat the evil by the good [Rom. 12:21], first in yourselves, then you can possess all things that have been given to you as your possessions (but do not honor them). This is how to win. Pay close attention. The Lord has given you much wisdom and power from above, in order to come to the victory. This will not come about through [83ʳ] the knowledge of the letter, but through that of the Spirit. Pay attention to this.

See, this will be obtained now in the last days, when all things are restored in three perfect ways or fullnesses of perfection. There are many who write about the restitution, but they have only come to two parts. Although one has run southward and the other northward, they fight against each other. I wish to join these together in a true middle way, so that we might have one mind and have peace.[17] In this way is Satan excluded. This is surely the will of the Lord, to the end that there be unity, unity which the restitution completely reinstates in Christ.[18] The first restitution is that all images, shadows or figures have been fulfilled in the Spirit; everything has been established spiritually by his apostles. Moreover, one should expect no other restitution or glory aside from the reestablishment of that which has been decayed and torn down through the apostasy of the antichrist. But only in the form and ordinance established by the apostles.[19] Pay attention. The second restitution was that of Münster, which was a great light and joyous brilliance.[20] They all believed it to be the restitution, thinking that they were to exercise it in a completely external fashion, in full power and might over the whole earth, ruling over all powers and forces of the world, which they thought they could bring under themselves in the name of Jesus. And they had faith in God, [83ᵛ] blessed in eternity, hoping for freedom, space, refreshment, and mercy. But the third restitution or renewal (to speak in this fashion) must be situated in the middle position.[21] This has been neglected and has not been attended to as it should, leaping from the first restitution to the last or third. It has had, therefore, no full power nor might, nor could it stand or be preserved. For all things exist in three, of which marriage is a figure or likeness, leading to Christ and his bride or wife.[22]

Therefore, all you willing, humble, lowly hearts, learn well how we must be fit for the time when all things are reinstituted or restored. For the word restitution does not in the first place concern the prefigures, whether the visible or literal things in Israel, or Adam, Noah, Abraham, Isaac, Jacob, David, Solomon, and Zerubbabel; for their nature is that of all images and shadows. Therefore, these do not of themselves make a restitution, for the things which they pointed to were envisioned long before them. They therefore could not remain, having no true meaning on their own. For they are completely imperfect and are placed merely as prefigures and as a trust of a better hope which would happen through Christ, whom they expected to bring all things to the right. Although Joshua brought Israel to rest, it was not the true rest, nor were they the true people. Even the best of them were fleshly and infirm and expected the [84ʳ] Messiah, who was promised through Moses. Yes, he was also prophesied in Abraham, Isaac, and Jacob. Those who were upright believed in him, for they drank from the rock which followed them, said Paul [1 Cor. 10:4]. Thus, these figures could not bring a restitution, because they had no true being or perfection.[23] If anyone sees this as a cause of dispute, I will gladly be in the wrong. I do not wish to quarrel about it. May we instead bear with one another in those things hidden from our salvation.

So I maintain that the true restitution is the first, which has thus occurred in Christ. Put briefly, everything we have lost in the first Adam, by disobedience through the devil, is restored by and through the obedience of Jesus Christ [Rom. 5:12ff.]. Also, that those who now believe in the name of Jesus, that he is Christ, and call upon him as his head and Lord and prove to be obedient, in these people all things will be restored and renewed; changed from flesh into spirit, from death into life, from the earthly into the heavenly beings, until they have become once again the likeness and true image of God through Christ Jesus, by grace. They will be just as God made Adam in the beginning as an image of God: immortal, pure, without spot or sin, simple and innocent, just like God. We must again put on these clean, unspotted, white garments of simplicity and innocence, else we cannot enter into Eden, [84ᵛ] that is, into the life and kingdom of God. Pay attention.

These are the pure wedding garments which few people upon the earth have known.[24] Yes, these are the garments of faith, in which exist the union and incorporation. These were given first to Adam from the rising of the sun, and now have been entrusted to me through grace, from the rising of the sun. Yes, to me, unworthy, in order to admonish and proclaim to all those who desire to be saved how to come to victory. See, all of it must be completed in us. The beloved or the saved of the Father will be seen publicly and all things will be restored in their first condition, as God has promised from the beginning through his holy prophets. To say this briefly, it is the abandonment of evil. To this we ought to pray, that we might receive the glorious divine freedom of the children of God, for which we long and seek [Rom. 8:21]. Pay attention.

See, this then is the restitution, of which we are a surety and for which we are all sealed through the Spirit of faith in Christ Jesus [Eph. 1:13-14; 4:30]. Although we have not yet received it in its power, nor does it shine before our eyes, we nevertheless possess it devoutly in our hearts, patiently hoping and expecting it without doubt. And all things will also obtain their perfect way and living spirit, for it must be in this way and not otherwise. Yes, the reasons are evident, the words acquire meaning, the [85ʳ] Scriptures testify to, and the Spirit confirms all of this. Therefore, all the adversaries or opponents, who oppose the beloved and glorious ones of God or the kingdom of our Lord Jesus Christ in its power, must fix their tongues or shut their mouths. For only the saints or the small ones can proclaim this, as it is written [cf. Matt. 1:14]. Yes, only they will be received, for to no other is it given.

See in this way all things have their fulfillment and full perfection in three, according to which we should work with many tears. We who will, desire, and seek to uphold the Holy One in Israel and to bring honor, glory and strength, thanksgiving and praise to the Lord of hosts. Who (I say), seek the kingdom of God and his righteousness [Matt. 6:33]. Take heed. Therefore, seek humility, seek righteousness, all of you who are kept by the Lord's right hand, so that you may be protected in the day of the wrath of the Lord [cf. Rom. 5:9; 1 Thess. 1:10]. Watch out, pay attention.

Whenever this has come so far, that each one is obedient to his Lord and Master, when each one has been subjected under him to whom everyone must bow [1 Cor. 15:25; Phil. 2:10] and has become a captive under the obedience of Christ [2 Cor. 10:5], through the small and simple ones, through the lowly, humble hearts, then they will appear rejoicing in Zion [Isa. 35:10]. The small, lowly hearts will be lifted up, the fearful will obtain space, the enslaved become free, the workers of the vineyard obtain rest, and the wretched ones [85ʳ] be honored. This secret of the kingdom has been given to no one to proclaim, not to mention to see or know it, except to the small ones, who are as simple and innocent as children, without deceit, poor and right. All to the praise of God the Father, who is pleased with this. Take heed and pay attention. Yes, purify your house, the Spirit of the Lord has said [cf. 2 Chron. 29:5, 15-16], and seek, pray, supplicate, and work in order to please the Lord, not mortals. Beloved, guard yourselves from all flesh. Be obedient, poor, humble and lowly, simple and innocent. For in this way will the devil, the prince of this world, the king and head of the angels of the abyss and of the haughty children of disbelief and disobedience, be defeated completely. Yes, death will be swallowed up in victory [1 Cor. 15:54]. At this time its members will be forced to flee and they will come to fear or to an incomprehensible terror. Indeed, one will be able to frighten and drive before him one thousand, and two will frighten two thousand [Isa. 30:17]. Believe that it will happen in this manner. Be poor, full of humility and obedience; that is, full of the fear of the Lord. Take heed and know what I say to you.

Thus, at the last day there will be a holy mountain and a beloved city of the Lord, which shall be very blessed and be made fruitful by the beautiful bridegroom of righteousness [cf. Rev. 21-22]. For the citizens inside it will bloom as the grass upon the meadow [Ps. 72:16]. Yes, they will increase, grow, and become great. They will then fill the whole earth [86ʳ] and possess it, bringing it under them [Gen. 1:28].[25] This the mountain of the Lord will do, and the city of the Lord will have authority over everything, as it is written.[26] Blessed are they who first receive the benediction and blessing in the Spirit, for they will observe and produce fruit in the Lord. These ones are circumcised in their hearts from all the lusts of the flesh. They serve Christ as clean virgins, without lingering lusts, untainted by sin, pure in their spirit, doing everything in complete obedience only to please the Lord. Understand, this is like the obedient wife, who is an honor to her husband. For they die and are mortified to all things of the world and in peace they leave behind the goods of this life for the faith of Jesus Christ. In particular, they forsake and abandon the evil will, and stand against the lusts of the flesh, the covetousness of the eyes, the haughtiness of life. They are brought low, to absolute nothing: poor, humble, meek, needy, simple, innocent, foolish in the flesh. They suffer violence and injustice on account of the faith of Jesus, on account of the gospel, on account of righteousness, or on account of the kingdom of our Lord, without quarreling or murmuring [Phil. 2:14]. See, they will receive again here a hundredfold, and will come into the glorious freedom of the children of God [Rom. 8:21; Mark 10:29-30]. They will forever possess eternal life and find rest from all the work of the Spirit; that is, those (I say) who rest now from the work and evil labor of the sinful flesh, which is eternally damned with its seed. Pay attention. Yes, pay attention indeed, and always and eternally praise the Lord, [86ʲ] the Lord Sabbaoth, Amen. Alleluias will be sung by the victorious.

Receive as truthful my admonition in the Lord, for the word was brought forth with power from the Spirit above, for warning, teaching and edification, in order to fulfill all things and restore what has been long lost, depraved, forgotten, and unknown. Pay attention, yes, take heed, just as you do to the Word of the Lord our God, and pray for me.

The peace, for which I work,
which exceeds all understanding,

guard your hearts
and minds in Christ Jesus
our Lord and Master [Phil. 4:7]. Amen.

THE END
PRODUCED IN THE YEAR 1535

5

Hear, Hear, Hear, Great Wonder, Great Wonder, Great Wonder, 1536

The visions Joris experienced in December of 1536 dramatically altered his sense of mission and in turn his writing style. The change is evident in this tract, *Hear, Hear, Hear, Great Wonder, Great Wonder, Great Wonder*, a long and, as the title suggests, repetitious work hastily written after the revelations, presumably under the direction of the Holy Spirit.[1] Not only is the work repetitious in thoughts, but also in language. For this tract Joris adopted a rhetorical style which is much more suited to the realm of vigorous oral proclamation than to the written word. For example, the title of the work, "Hear, Hear, Hear," takes its cue from the proclamations of city heralds who used the phrase to call attention to their announcements. The overall effect is a sense of immediacy, almost as if one is listening to, rather than reading, a text of Joris.

Although undated, the tract must have been completed by late December 1536 or January 1537. It was probably his first prose work to be published. In a later work Joris remarked that *Hear, Hear, Hear* was his first tract, and there is no reason to dispute this claim, at least in terms of printing.[2] An early copy of the work has survived, printed, it appears, either by Albert Pafraet or Dirk van Borne, Joris's major printers in Deventer. The typeface is identical to other works known to have come from these presses in the late 1530s. *Hear, Hear, Hear* therefore provides an excellent window into the mentality of David

Joris during the period when he began to develop his dynamic sense of mission.

Joris's anonymous biographer described in detail the visions which proved to be so effective in overcoming the Delft prophet's hesitancy to fully adopt the mantle of leadership over the Dutch Anabaptists. According to this source, Joris had a vision in which he saw secular and spiritual princes falling down in terror before the children of God. The anonymous author continues then to quote verbatim the first few pages from *Hear, Hear, Hear*.[3] Joris saw his visions as the major turning point in his career and therefore placed much authority in this particular work. In spite of its frequently repetitive style, it is important that *Hear, Hear, Hear* be represented in this collection. To spare the reader unnecessary tedium, however, only segments of the tract have been included, particularly where they illuminate the major aspects of Joris's thought as it had developed by 1536-37. The places where omissions occur will be appropriately noted.

In comparison with *The Wonderful Working of God* of the previous year, we see in this piece several new themes or emphases in Joris's continuing reflections on post-Münster Anabaptism. Certainly this is the first work to clearly delineate Joris's prophetic status and his conception of the third David, whom he obliquely identified with himself. Moreover, the theme of the true inward restitution is more fully developed here, as is the maintenance of personal spiritual purity among believers.

❁ ❁ ❁ ❁ ❁

[1ʳ]   # HEAR, HEAR, HEAR.

Great Wonder, Great Wonder, Great Wonder

See upon the mountains come the feet of a good messenger, who brings good news and tidings. O Judah, celebrate your feasts, rest from your labor and pay your vows [Nah. 1:15]. Pay attention, you children in the flesh. People of the Spirit, rejoice, for the rogue shall no more overcome you. He is completely exterminated. Therefore, praise the Lord gloriously and thank him with all your might, with your full strength. Pay attention.

Behold a high thing, yes, a flowing principle of the Spirit, and hear what the Spirit says to the true covenanters and holy fellowship of God. O how blessed are those who dare to depreciate themselves and who are counted among the simple. They have sought after and loved the fear of the Lord and the knowledge of the Spirit as the only things upon the earth. Blessing to them all. Take heed.

Be blinded, you people of sin. But not in the outward eyes, for covetousness and lust must vanish and no longer hinder your vision. Understand this, understand this and pay attention, pay attention. All roguishness, deceit, falsehood, and darkness must disappear. All that God has not created, [1ʳ] but which the devil has created, must be cleansed away, away, away. Behold, behold. Know what I say to you, taste this fruit and be healed, and praise the Lord.

Become seeing, become seeing, become seeing, through the eyes of the true person, of the true person, his eyes, his eyes. He has light, light, light, and not darkness in him, not in him. See that you do it quickly, do it quickly. Do not neglect yourselves, see to it, see to it. Become like a child, a child, a child, without guile, without roguishness; simple, simple in your eyes; straight and upright, straight and upright; spirit, spirit, spirit, without flesh, without sin, without spot or wrinkle; innocent, innocent as lambs [Matt. 18:1-5; 1 Pet. 1:19]. Take heed.

Behold the angel of light [Col. 1:12], and the truth of God spoken in words from the Holy Spirit above. Believe, believe, believe, and fulfill it and praise the Lord, praise him. Amen.

Break forth. Come to the day, you children of light, truth, and Spirit. Appear now with power, you kingdom of God. Now the world will perish and her glory will be extinguished, this is certain and it will appear in this way. My mouth will have spoken lies and not spoken through the Lord if it does not happen in this way. Pay attention. When the time has come that the children of God are fit to enter or receive their glorious divine [2ʳ] freedom [Rom. 8:21], then they are the elect, beloved flower of Jacob. Take heed.

In this spirit is the Song of Songs sung and proclaimed as at the first.[4] Pay attention. The veil or cloth which covers the eyes of all people will be removed and death itself will also be destroyed [2 Cor. 3:14-18]. Herein is the complete purification for those who desire to understand all things which are pure, free, holy, and good. Take this to heart.

Anticipate from now on that eternal light, eternal life, eternal rest, eternal peace, and joy without end, without suffering or stain, and without shouting. For death shall be swallowed up [1 Cor. 15:54]. Understand fully, yes, pay close attention.

Now burn, flame, yes, become a furious blaze. Acquire deer's feet [Ps. 18:33], you fiery children, and triumph in and through love and affection, and nothing else. Take heed. Receive what has been said above as good truth. This is a quickly running, hasty, and joyous messenger; receive him in the name of the one who sent him, and thank the Lord through him or in him. Do it so. For he comes to all of you to admonish you about the seduction of temptation which shall come over all the earth. Observe this well.

O how I must work now. This falls upon me as a vexation. Lord, how long, how long, Lord, will it endure? [2ʸ] I hope not long, Lord, Lord. Allow me, allow me, allow that my desire, my desire be, be, be, only upon your saints and to my house.

All that the Lord makes good and holy and public is not shameful before him, because it is created and made by him. See that it shall also not be shamed before people. Therefore, we must be holy, as he is holy [1 Pet. 1:15].

Take heed.

All iniquity and sin will be eradicated from the earth and come to an end. Take heed. Therefore be pure, be pure. Receive the truth, wake up and praise the Lord.

Those who are found impure or naked watch out, for they shall be like Adam and Eve who attempted to hide from the Lord. They will not enter into the living garden [Gen. 3:24]. Pay attention. You who are advancing by the Spirit to God's praise alone—first children, then youths, then old adults—are those who have sought to be thoroughly pure and have opened their senses. These alone will obtain the perfection in the Spirit. Behold, you virgins, O you young women, keep your hearts pure, and be pure in your hands, feet, and eyes, without guile. For I say to you, observe it if you will. You must without thinking yourselves wise be clean, pure, unspotted, sincere virgins of the kingdom in the Spirit, in order to be the Lord's bride and queen. [3ʳ] The one who is called God by all the world is the Lord and King of all beauty. Therefore, behold, he will not be friendly disposed to whores, impure persons, and adulterers; nor will he be contaminated by the impure, be it with anger, judgment, or unrighteousness. But he will receive to himself the pure virgins who are circumcised in their hearts from all heathendom or flesh, and sit them next to him as his beloved. Pay attention.

Here God has given us an image, namely, the circumcision of the flesh, when Abraham was old in the flesh [Gen. 17:1, 10-11]. Observe it. Through this God brought about his covenant and placed it in his flesh. Therefore, Isaac came upon the earth. Pay attention. In a fashion this is concealed from all of us, namely, that the lusts must yet be circumcised in our flesh, even if we have come into old age in our understanding. Pay attention. Therefore, a separation from pride must happen among those whom the Lord has chosen to be his sole heritage and principal flower. For we must always and completely avoid the heathen way and nevermore remember the old being, not to mention to walk in it. Understand this. Therefore, be pure, be pure, wash yourselves thoroughly from all the ungodly being. In everything be pure of heart, light of eyes, undefiled in feet and hands [cf. Exod. 30:21]. Beloved, struggle and suffer in this work. Do not seek to live any other way. The Lord will hear your prayers. [3ᵛ] He will turn your miseries and fears to joy and your suffering and trembling he will change into an eternal joy. Therefore, suffer the work, stand tall and strong. Do not be defeated by evil but overcome evil with the good [Rom. 12:21]. And be entirely delivered from evil and completely healed from your mortal wounds. Enter the true life. Take this to heart.

You men, arm yourselves well and fight against death, which has for so long hidden in the beggarly lusts of the flesh. Oppose mightily and heartily the invincible serpent and cast death away from you into the hell of the abyss [Rev. 20:1-3]. Strike him in the loins, defeat him with your perseverance of spirit, with prayers and singing from a good will and a humble, broken, and meek heart.[5] Set yourselves freely against him and betroth yourselves seriously in earnest love, which is powerful against death. Therefore, fight piously and overcome by your faith. Do not cease, I say, until the day appears and the morning star brings life to your heart [Rev. 2:28]. Pay attention.

You female warriors, fight knowledgeably against the cursed, crooked, sly serpent which has deceived and beaten you. Strike him upon his neck and crush him. Stand upon his head which has been given to you, and do to him what he has done to you [Gen. 3:14-16]. Neither respect him nor trust him. [4ʳ] No longer be children nor women, but be like men, and men like angels. Here is understanding. Therefore, grasp understanding. Do not run from his face, but be strong, clean of hands, and pure of heart. See to it, and do as I say. Do not concern yourselves with being rich and well dressed, but desire first to be poor. Therefore, pray for wisdom, knowledge, and understanding. Pay attention.

Behold, the corrupter is out to pull you into the hole and draw you into destruction. Out of this you were once pulled by faith. But you do not yet seek this faith to the utmost. Be found completely pure and thoroughly cleansed, because your eyes are not always clear of sight. Instead, much blindness and thick darkness remain clinging to them. You should be able easily to expel Satan. Therefore, everyone see to it, know what I say to you. Believe me, I am saying the truth to you, and I lie not. Beloved, wash yourselves thoroughly, and anoint your eyes with eye salve [Rev. 3:18], otherwise you will be deceived by the seducer. Especially now that in the last day you have come to the final park[6] and end, to your full understanding. Satan has for so long kept you in childhood and from running after it, thinking that you have been completely veiled by sadness, terror, and fear. And his desire has been to cool your love. For he is very strong and hates you who have been made especially [4ʳ] righteous in the faith. Therefore, watch, arm yourselves, pray, and stay awake and do not neglect yourselves. See to it. Observe this well.

.... [7ʳ]

Beloved, look at, carefully observe and understand correctly the kind of wondrous abilities which God gave to the man and his wife when he stood in the form of God. When he bore his true image, untainted or unchanged, when he had strength and might over all his handiwork [cf. Gen. 1-2]. For he was placed over it as a duke or lord, to use the same according to the meaning of the Lord. To this was he made, namely as spiritual and holy or good. God commanded him to grow and increase in this nature. He had created him for this according to his divine will and had given him both strength and power, according to his will and pleasure, to the praise of the glory of his high majesty and wonderful power. Look now at what has become of the authority of the man and of the woman, and how it has been used or handled for so long. Yes, the devil has had his complete desire and play here. Indeed, it has been truly found in this way from the beginning until now. Just as each of us is able to observe on our own the kind [7ᵛ] of spirit with which we have begotten our children, reflecting on the abominable work of the devil, his impurity and unchastity. Look to the Lord, the Creator or Maker or father of all things. He should be honored, praised, and magnified, just as in the beginning of the creatures, that is, in the generation of humanity.[7] Who should appear clean, pure, and holy without spot or devil, according to the meaning of the Spirit, and not as the heathens according to the fleshly lusts or sinful desires. The unchaste, old, vile being runs after and desires these. But not the new creature in Christ Jesus, which is created in the image of God and is born from the Spirit [2 Cor. 5:17] and desires, seeks, and wills only that which is of a similar nature, image, or form. To these things alone does he have great lust and desire, and he uses the Spirit's will or desire in this, according to the pleasure and word of the living God, who is an enemy of all flesh and heathendom. Pay attention.

Therefore, all of you be admonished by the Spirit of the Lord. In brief, no longer to approach your wife in the lusts of the flesh as do the heathens in their sinful desire. For they are totally children of roguishness, children of the devil, impure, deathlike in their nature, children of wrath, abominable to the Lord, seeds of destruction, full of evil desire and sinful lust. I say that the [8ʳ] serpent is their lord and father until the rebirth. Pay close attention. For they were produced in a dishonorable bed without the Lord, according to the flesh, according to the devil's lust and senses, namely in sin, in darkness, where the devil alone is present and visible. Take heed.

.... [11ʳ]

For you must progress so far until you hate—in words, works, and thoughts—every kind of sin which the old being clings to or permits. For the vain thoughts must be completely removed and opposed, for from these grow all manner of evil. This must be so if anyone desires to obtain the victory and complete perfection. We must regard everything in which we still live as an abomination, and not admire them. Just as it stands written: "I have hated those who love vanity and have not measured truth" [Ps. 31:6 or Prov. 8:13]. Take heed. We must likewise hate all of God's enemies from the ground of our hearts. We must feel the Father's heart in us and not love or be favorably inclined to whatever he hates. Each one who wishes to remain unspoiled and free of sin, see to this. O take this to heart indeed.

But so that you might find or see a basis for and an end to this, the Holy Spirit of God, the angel of light, gives you this advice and good admonition. Blessed are they who heed it. You goodwilled, humble hearts, understand me, all those who will understand, otherwise no one can even begin. I am certain. [11ᵛ] Recognize that which has sat upon the seat of honor, for the longest time dominating over and in you. Namely, the first born son of the devil, the fleshly being of sin, which hinders Christ and his Spirit and his life in you. Understand it. Repel and strike him, I say, to the death. Shed all his blood and do not hold back your sword. Do not neglect this, or you will be damned. For the old serpent grows in his blood and its light is hidden in his life. I say this to you as a word of the Lord. You will find it so. Therefore, take it to heart, it must be so. Tread upon him with your feet, shame him publicly. Become his enemy; do not stand any longer on the fence,[8] but display to him your heart's lust and will. And become a holy vessel useful to the honor of the lord of the house, prepared for every good work [2 Tim. 2:21]. Free yourselves from the public sinners. Do not remain like the Pharisees, who instead of denying themselves or walking in humility, insisted on being seen in the foremost places in the temple and being esteemed with the greatest honor [Matt. 23:6-7; Luke 11:43, etc]. Pay attention. For here is the explanation of the parable. Therefore, you must choose one of the two sides, in particular, to be happily regarded and placed among the least and to be willingly reckoned with and truly regarded as the public sinners [Luke 18:9-14]. So confess and perceive your sin, your guilt and iniquity. Let [12ʳ] whatever the old being has wrought, fulfilled, willed, and desired in you through the devil be publicly known. Therefore, if you desire to be delivered from it and to become pure and completely released, then shame it. Take off its clothes, unclothe its abominations. Hate it and its works, such as murder, thievery, buggery, adultery, unchastity, whoredom, misery, wrath, bitterness, and roguishness. Yes, even its avarice, together with all its unrighteousness which it brings forth in people. Beloved, do not champion its honor any longer. It is none other than your enemy, I say, so unclothe its shame. Cast out the devils, the impure spirits with all their counsel, lust, and will. See to it. Remain no longer possessed, led, or compelled by that which lives in you. Instead, seek to enter the kingdom of God and his perfection or victory. Do not let this go in one ear and out the other. Watch out so that you no longer excuse the devil or his seed, the sinful flesh, nor that in any way you gloss over his evil parts. Do nothing from his life. But if you desire to do well, unclothe his shame, from the time you had a child's body, with all the ugly sins which have followed since then. Willingly suffer pain, grief, shame, and great mourning in this before the Lord. For although these sins have been long forgotten by you, they have not been by the Lord. To those who are found pure, without [12ᵛ] guilt or iniquity, they shall not be moved by these sins, nor found in any other fashion. Therefore, thoroughly examine your iniquity and guilt. Remember all of them and confess and reveal them publicly in the presence of the Lord, before whose face you have shamelessly committed them. Do not conceal your great roguishness and iniquity. Fetch them all out of the corners; let them appear for a time. Do not hide your sins. O beloved, no, do not do this. But look at their ugliness, smell how they stink. For this is what they are to the Lord. Phew, I am certain that their ugliness will disgust you. But do not complain about nor hide them, else they cannot be reduced or destroyed to ashes. Dear brothers, cast them far away from you, spit them out. Throw away the stained coat, the vile trash, the stinking lusts. Bear the Lord's punishment patiently. I say to you, hasten to do this, before you come into damnation and be ashamed when you come before the Lord. For they are the things which have truly deceived you. Yes, you will be accused, if they are still found in you.

.... [16ʳ]

See, we exist to reveal publicly this day of the Lord, first in the Spirit, the angel of the covenant. This day cannot be endured by any flesh, except by a very few. For it is like the fire of the goldsmith and like the soap of the washers. This day will burn like a glowing oven. Therefore, purify yourselves, you sons of Levi [Mal. 3:2-3]. O you hard, stony hearts, become weak and soft in your manners. Yes, be melted, filtered, swept, and purified from all dross and impurity. See to it or you will mightily and eternally lament. If you do not allow yourselves to be chastised now, you will find yourselves among the evil and godless ones in eternal death. Therefore, be purified from the earth before it is too late for you and this day comes over you with power. Then you will wish, but you will not be able to do it. Therefore, see, the Lord admonishes you through his messenger to proceed and to listen to his voice. Yes, the angels of God announce to proceed and to cry bitterly, because what is of the earth is so miserably condemned and remains so lamentable. So behold the voice of the angel, receive the true token of the living God on your forehead [Rev. 7:3, 9:4].⁹ Do not be ashamed of this. Cast away from you all shame in the flesh, or you will remain lost. Become children, simple and innocent. Put on the bride's pure, unsoiled, white, clean garment. In this way [16ᵛ] the servant of God will be sealed, and will remain standing in the fearful and terrifying day of the Lord, without punishment. He will be sheltered and protected. For this reason I say, put on the white, clean garments of innocence and simplicity, which were given at the rising of the sun [Rev. 3:4-5; 6:11]. These ones, and no one else, will be incorporated into the true unity with God and his son Jesus Christ. Pay attention.

Here will the wide open fountain of grace and of the glorious life be known and sought, so that Judah and Jerusalem can be completely cleansed and purified. Observe this and praise the saints in Israel.

.... [26ᵛ]

Therefore, we must work and desire greatly this glorious divine freedom and rest of the true children of God. Yes, for the creation itself cries out and wishes for the revelation of the children of God, so that it will be subjected without its vain will on account of the will of the one who has subjected it, and it must remain bowed down in all submissiveness. So it waits for this; hoping for, expecting, and desiring the childhood and revelation of the children of God, so that it will be subjected without its vain will. For this reason it will yet be freed from the service of the perishable nature, to the glorious, divine freedom of the elect children of God [Rom. 8:9-22]. For this reason we must proceed roughly in pain and suffering, like the burdened. But we have great longing for the time of the restitution and the deliverance from evil and service to the perishable nature, and to see the transfiguration; so that we might experience the rest in the garden, [27ʳ] the eternal life. Therefore, fight and pray that you might be delivered. Pay attention, you seed of Jacob and David.

The sincere Israelites will be known from the struggle and victory in which they must persevere and not lose, or they are not Israelites in deed. And the final struggle is against death, which is concealed in the flesh and which wounds the living. Indeed, its defeat must be completed by the Spirit, through the power of the Spirit. You will not die in this, but instead be victorious, for the Spirit is stronger and greater in power than the flesh [cf. Rom. 8:1-15]. Therefore, blessed are those who are united in this, yes, those who have lusted after and desired this. These ones will not be ashamed but are able to remain standing against the death in the flesh. Observe this well. Now death is, I say, the last enemy [1 Cor. 15:26]. Therefore, arm yourselves, it comes upon you. Do not be defeated by it, else it will remain your lord and eternally gnaw at you. Pay attention.

The victors and knights of Christ, who inherit the crown of glory and life, do not come to this laughingly, that is in lightheartedness and vanity. No. Instead, they pass through great tribulation, much anxiety, and [27ᵛ] fear as a result of the struggle, or they have been tested through it. Therefore, do not hate nor cast it away from you. But love it, do not hate it, if you desire to do wisely. Otherwise you will come to harm or into eternal suffering. That is, all who have refused to die or to be deprived here, and who have instead maintained the life of the flesh. These ones will eternally die the second death and be cast out of the presence of the Lord [Rev. 20:14-15]. That is, all who have rejected the counsel of the Lord and who have not accepted his chastisement. Take heed. And remember my warning when it comes upon you, for it will indeed come upon your proud, inflexible hearts, you proud spirits. Therefore, behold, and do this quickly. But the poor, miserable crowd will have much rejoicing and joy. Namely, those who have removed the old being, who have washed themselves clean from all impurities in the blood of the innocent lamb, Christ Jesus [1 Pet. 1:19]. They too suffer and live an unspotted life before God and his angels, which stand night and day before the throne and seat of God in his temple [cf. Rev. 4-5]. Pay attention. These are the ones who have fulfilled the gospel, the law of Christ. They have been burdened with his name, they have walked in the light and in the Spirit according to the will of God. They have received the shining coats and crowns of honor have been placed on their heads [Rev. 4:4]. In this way was David victorious, and he is a true image of all believing, fighting, humble, [28ʳ] kingly hearts of the Spirit. They have descended from him and they must share his nature. Understand this well.

Goliath, the great Philistine, the last abominable enemy, terrified and frightened all of Israel. He was defeated by the humble, small David, a man after the heart of God [1 Sam. 13:14]. First, with his strong faith, he slung the stone of the power of God in the name of the Lord, striking him down in weakness. Finally, like a knight he cut off Goliath's head with his own sword. Thus the songs of praise, victory, and joy were sung in Israel and rejoicing went through the heights to heaven itself [1 Sam. 17:50-52]. Take it to heart. But now it is revealed that against this great Goliath, namely death, the spiritual Israel must appear in great power or terror on the last day. Then Jerusalem will be glorified and rebuilt. Then the Spirit of grace will be poured out upon the inhabitants of Jerusalem unto eternity [Joel 2:28; Ezek. 39:29]. This cannot be seen before they fully realize their weakness, lowliness, poverty, and nothingness. And in this way they will be full of oppression, mourning, suffering, and need. Yes, appearing to be abandoned, they tremble until they have been thoroughly examined and totally humbled, lying crushed in the ashes and dust [Job 42:6]. In such need they will call [28ᵛ] faithfully to the Lord. Everyone must taste and feel this for themselves by deliberating over their past sins. They must completely spit out all their evil and stand ashamed of it. Behold. For this reason you poor in spirit will become first [Matt.

19:30]. Behold, I say this to you so that you will do it. Else you will remain lost and become eternally ashamed.

Therefore, neither conceal your sin nor hide your guilt and iniquity. Instead, be crushed, destroyed to the flesh of evil, just like the public sinners, if you wish to enter your house as more righteous than the Pharisees and if you do not wish to defile your baptism [Luke 18:13-14]. Do not allow the devil to make you wise. But if you spit out, destroy, and confess all the evil things which you have done in the meantime, then they will not defile you nor shame you in the flesh. See to this, I testify openly that whoever does not do this will come to harm and will never win the victory. Beloved, do not be proud. I do not speak this from myself. Therefore, see to this, know what you do. Pray therefore that your eyes be blinded to the deceptions of sin. Guard yourselves, that you do not cease from this. [29ʳ]

The suffering and oppression must come over everyone. This is the dying and death to the things for which you have lived. This must be true of all who desire to gain the victory against their enemy, the last and precarious danger and abominable dark valley [Ps. 23:4]. For here death appears to threaten us from all sides. We must therefore penetrate into the living hope [1 Pet. 1:3]. Yes, you must drink from all manner of bitter cups, be baptized with all manner of trembling, and stand in barren need [Mark 10:38-39]. Then we can be examined and tempered to the uttermost. Then the faith in which we glory can be made public and have its work. Then we can see the kind of calling, lust, and desire which should result to our profit and to the praise of God's righteousness and divine grace. But this first has to be known and desired. Pay attention, I say to you.

Therefore, it is from our great need and as an examination that he allows trembling, suffering, and all manner of pain to come upon us, unto death. But it is not amazing that we are struck dead in the flesh of sin by the life and the light which is set in the midst of our darkness [John 1:5]. For this comes to open our eyes completely, so that we can see what it is we still lack. From this comes the fear of the Lord, which drives out sin and evil [Prov. 16:6]. [29ᵛ] For our strength must fail, and our wisdom must cease. Our laughing must turn to weeping, our rejoicing into mourning [James 4:9]. We must put on the clothes of mourning and suffering and willingly sit in the ashes of the destruction or the humiliation; strew the ashes on your head, cover yourself with shame. . . . Bear your wounds and pain, for like David, you have deserved them [cf. 2 Sam. 12 and Ps. 51]. Display your patience and obedience, [30ʳ] you worthy children, sons and daughters of Ephraim,

Judah, and Jerusalem. Observe this well. And always praise the name of the Lord, with full, pure hearts.

Now death is the last, terrifying enemy, which will be brought to nought or slain in the victory of the man Jesus Christ and saints in Israel [Rev. 20:13-14; 21:4]. The Spirit made this known at the first and now to me. This will appear also through a young servant and child of David, who is blessed by God. He will be revealed in time, in a new life. The Spirit of the Lord will rest upon him in power, to the rejoicing of the houses of Jacob and David [cf. Jer. 23:5; 33:15; Zech. 12:10]. This dwelling the Lord will build and it will be fortunate. Let no one be amazed about this, for all things have their perfection in three. The first David was a clear image of God Almighty, who is threefold. It is therefore possible that three Davids are to be identified or expected, who will be brought to one. God's Spirit and power was in the first David. The second was Christ, in whom the entire Godhead was perfected [Col. 2:9]. The Spirit of Christ will rest on the third. He is the least, although he will appear to do the most. For this David has to do nothing less than boldly cut off the head of Goliath, the great Philistine or uncircumcised, whom Christ has cast to the ground and taken away his might, binding him through the [30ᵛ] power of the Spirit [cf. Rev. 20:2; 1 Sam. 17:13-51]. That is, to cut off his pride and trust, which is done through faith in the name of the Lord. So it remains that the one who came in the middle is the most and greatest. To him was the first set as an image, and he himself sent the third after him, who receives the power from him. Moreover, by himself the third David is merely a reflected light who smites off the head. The last is very little compared to the middle one. For he spoke, "Truly I have overcome the world" [John 16:33], "I have taken away the power of death" [Rom. 6:9], "I have trod upon the head of the devil" [Luke 10:19]. What more is there left to do? He alone maintains the prize, yes, certainly. He remains the Lord, the others are the servants. Pay close attention. He receives whom he will, just as it happens with me. The outcome for all the living is that he remains a king above all kings and a lord over all lords; not only in this world, but also in the future [Rev. 17:14, 19:16]. It is good to observe here that there are to be three risings of kings who will become one prince, who has been the faithful servant. The Lord, when he comes, will set this one over all his house. O behold well. Just as Joseph [cf. Gen. 39:3-4], Christ, and God above over all.

Behold the little children and young Davids, who will be as strong as David, in order to be able to stand against Goliath, the death in the flesh. They will cut off his head with his own sword [31ʳ] and destroy him. Understand this well. That is, they will capture him with his own eyes (let him who can understand this, understand). In this way will the world be brought low by the slinging stone. In other words, it will be struck down impotent to the earth, and be cast into powerlessness through the power of God. This had happened to the previous David, so that he was able to defeat Goliath, who was the head of the Philistines. For as long as David looked to the flesh, he could not become tall enough. In this case he would have had to wait even longer, for his enemy was much too large and too mighty for him, too strong for anyone in Israel. Those who avail themselves of the sword, who trust in the strength of their hands of flesh, or in stone and wood, find an example in this. Beloved, become established in the power, be well armed in this, above all like David. If you use the one, then also use the other weapons for your own profit. For in this way he surprised the Philistines with his slinging stone, for he did not hold it in front of him. Take heed and be understanding. For this reason, if you desire to win the exterior fight, first win it inside you. If you desire to bring the members under you, then first bring the head under you. That is the king of the abyss and the children of [31ᵛ] pride or the un-believers. Therefore, become small and insignificant young children —simple, innocent, level, and straight. Be seen as nothing, completely powerless in the flesh. Instead be people of the strength of the Spirit's nature, as those who are well trained in battle. This Spirit will gain the victory before you and will imprison your enemies, all of whom will be brought into powerlessness, fear, and terror. . . . Woe to those who fight against you, both outwardly and inwardly. For you will be like a glowing oven or a flaming brand in a forest, consuming all people around you, both to your right and to your left hand, as is written: "The righteous will shine like sparks running through reeds. They will judge the nations and they will rule the peoples" [Wis. of Sol. 3:7]. There is much to write about this, but there is too much to cover it here.

.... [32ʳ]

In summary, Belial will be driven out by Christ, Satan's spirit by God's Spirit. See, I say this to you as a certain word of the Lord. Un-derstand it well. For here is the end of all things; here will the king-dom of God, the divine freedom of the children of God, be revealed publicly. For the greatest will no longer be the least who are submis-

sive, shamed, and bowed down. But the least, who have been so unjustly, will become the greatest, in a clear transfiguration and restoration [Matt. 19:28-30]. This will be a great wonder upon the earth.
Then all mouths will be made dumb. Therefore, purify and sanctify
yourselves for victory. Become completely childlike: simple, innocent, level and straight, without roguishness. Take it to heart. [32ᵛ]

The female warrior or the woman of war, namely the bride of
Christ, will then appear shining as the daybreak, as the chosen people, just as awful and brilliant as the sun.

....

Do not first see the lord, but first the servant who has been
placed by the lord over his house. He is entrusted with distributing
the food at the right time. God knows him and will reveal him in Israel
at the last day.¹⁰

Behold the guard, whom the Lord has set over his house. Therefore, pray that you might come to know him.

Behold the man, whom the Lord has chosen as a ruler or pastor
and captain of his people.

[33ʳ] Behold the rentmaster.¹¹ Pay attention to the procurator.¹²
Observe the vine worker who first had the ten pounds, and still received more before the others [Matt. 20:1-16].

Behold in your hearts the strong angel of heaven who stands
upon the sea and earth, or has them under his feet [Rev. 10:5]. He will
be the sword after this time of improvement, but waiting no longer.
He will be behind this last, third prophet. O become thinking.

Behold Michael, the spirit and angel of light, who is called the
most pious and greatest prince. He too stands for the protection of the
people of God [cf. Jude 9; Dan. 10:13, 21, esp. 12:1]. Pay heed to this.

Behold the young, small David. I mean the Spirit of the Lord in
its full power. All flesh will perish through him, for he will punish the
world for its disbelief.

Behold the voice of an archangel, namely, the earthly angel
[1 Thess. 4:16], who will make a command or warning to all who desire to become holy and to remain standing in the face of the Lord. If
they will follow and fulfill his voice, then they will be the humble and
sincere of heart.

Behold now the teacher, the Spirit of truth, which shall always
and continually increase. Yes, behold the ambassador of the Lord,
sent to bring the message of good news and tidings. This angel will

sound the final trumpet [Rev. 11:15]. He must be welcomed, [33ᵛ] honored, and praised at the right time, just like the Lord. For he comes to terrify and to kill. See, the life follows afterwards. Take it to heart. O look to this, pay attention to this without roguishness.

.... [37ʳ]

Therefore the blessed Lord God will at once give might and power to his children. Namely, to the bride who has come to maturity in order to stand against the devil and death. For the devil has been allowed an ordained time, in order to torment and to rule, or so that he may be led to the scene of the last battle [Rev. 20:7-10]. This does not mean that the thorns will do damage to the flowers of life. Let them grow up unhindered and as abominable as they will [Matt. 13:39-43]. Pay attention and understand it well, beloved. There exists a time for conversion and restoration. Hasten therefore [37ᵛ] to the time of renewal. In this time the Leviathan, the wily devil, will be captured between the teeth and his head will be split open [cf. Ps. 74:14]. Furthermore, he will be bound and placed under our knees or feet [Rev. 20:2]. Nevertheless, the bride is chased by him to old age. But when the morning star rises and draws near in her heart, she will be strengthened against the deceiver so that she can stand against the strong devil [1 Pet. 5:8-9]. She can then turn freely to him, asking him what he wants and freely and unconcernedly examining him in his light. For in her the love of her Lord is perfected. She will shame him in his vile, evil lusts or look in his face, to see that he is still proud and that he has not ceased from his path. See, she becomes inflamed with wrath from the earnest love of her God. She therefore grasps him by the head and devours or defeats the power or the force of death. She brings it all under her through the power of God in the name of Jesus her Lord whom she loves alone with a full heart. She hates what he hates. The struggle is a witness of this. In this way will he be captured by his own eyes. He will be repudiated and his might will be robbed. Then the brilliant banner of righteousness will be raised up or it will appear. And she will appropriate the crown of life which belongs to her by the right of inheritance [Rom. 8:17]. Observe this well.

.... [47ᵛ]

This must first happen in the upright of heart, who are found working for this. Yes, they are blessed. They work in order to go forth on the path of perfection with lust, will, and desire. But more blessed are those who have come to the truth. But above all the most blessed are the purest chosen ones or the beloved who will be found in the life of the Most High. Observe this. Furthermore, the Spirit will flow out from the heart of each of these. But for those who [48ʳ] will be outside of Christ Jesus, a fearful, miserable, and great suffering will come upon them. I say to you that this must happen first, because all flesh must perish. For the children of God must become his identical image or bear his nature [Rom. 8:29; 2 Cor. 3:18]. Comprehend this first in the spirit in the earthen vessel, of which the earthenware vessel was also an image [Isa. 30:14; Rom. 9:21]. Desire to trod upon the seed of the serpent and destroy their might [Gen. 3:15; Rom. 16:20]. This is certain. For they must be deprived of their might and creep along the earth like the damned. And they will lick the dust off the feet of the children of God [Mic. 7:17; Isa. 49:23]. Let them persecute for a little while longer, for all of them will soon bow down when their force is taken away from them and given to the holy people of the Most High. This will happen when they are fully pure and the others are fully vile. But the others will not be able to bring the earth under them before their authority and force is taken away from them and given to the saints of God. I say that these ones are the victorious, who will become pure and perfect likenesses or images of Christ. For the light is powerful against the darkness and the life or the earnest, zealous, perfect love is powerful against death; the new world against the old. Take heed.

No one else has strength against the enemy of Christ and the great city of evil, or against the earth, except those who are completely pure of [48ᵛ] heart. These ones have felt the great terror and pain of childbirth, believing it in themselves, but they have defeated all of it with the power. For God himself in the full power of his right hand is with you [Matt. 22:44], so that they will be killed with the slingstone cast in weakness, through the breath of his lips and the staff of his mouth. Then their head will be easily cut off with their own sword, which must pierce through their own heart. Take it to heart.

Therefore, become humble and meek children; at the start simple, innocent, straight, and true, pious Davids, whose house will be like God's house. For one devil cannot expel others. This is always how we must proceed as long as one devil remains. Therefore, let us be victorious and become completely full of light and spiritual, or our work, which has begun before this day, will be for nought, as is written. For the ordained time must come to an end and all things will be fulfilled [cf. Matt. 24; Mark 13; Luke 21]. For this the church of God, the bride herself, prays for her entrance and day [1 Pet. 3:11-14]. He will not wake her up before this, until, I say, it has become her own will, lust, desire, and greatest pleasure [Song of Sol. 2:7, 3:5, 8:4]. Therefore, can those who do not work strongly and forcefully on behalf of the kingdom presume that [49ʳ] it will not come upon them? No. Therefore, make your reckoning. When the number is fulfilled, Zion will declare her number closed. These will be all those who have desired and fulfilled the law of Christ and of the Lord.¹³ Pay close attention.

Therefore, behold the creation of God, who has created all things out of nothing. Thus we must in a similar way become nothing. Then we are made worthy, noble, and pure, an undefiled person, which is formed into the image of God, created without stain or darkness [Col. 3:10]. This occurs through the kind of faith which works powerfully and in a living fashion. Only this person, I say, is made a lord and duke, given authority over the entire earth and all that is in it, in order to bring it under him [Rev. 5:10]. Therefore, do not let any of us transgress in this. Instead, we should become small, purified, cleansed, washed, and humbled in our senses, so that we can win and possess all things. Take it to heart. See, in this way is heaven and earth perfected, with all their adornment. Pay attention. And in this way God rested on the seventh day, which day the Lord has blessed or exalted, to remain for him [Gen. 2:2-3]. All the others have an end. Pay attention. [49ᵛ] Work so as to enter into the rest and so that you might receive the glorious freedom [Heb. 4:3-11]. Pay attention.

See, the books will be opened in the presence of the firmaments, and everyone will see; that is, the veil over their understanding will be completely removed [Rev. 20:12; Dan. 7:10]. This veil has concealed or covered the eyes of all flesh on account of the darkness or roguishness of the world [2 Cor. 3:13-18]. This must come to be known first in us, through the key of David [cf. Isa. 22:22; Rev. 3:7].¹⁴ Blessed is the one who has found this.

Here is the time of the renewal of all things, in which wisdom has her perfection. All things will be restored, namely everything that the devil has robbed from and spoiled in us. God, through his servant, has truly proclaimed and promised from the beginning that he would heal them, that he would give them the previous health or life, kingdom, freedom, and peace, and restore them to the place from which they had been cast out on account of their evil and disobedience. Here the new heaven and new earth will be in which righteousness shall dwell

[2 Pet. 3:13]. For no unrighteousness can remain standing therein and have one heart, will, spirit, and flesh and bone with Christ.

.... [60ʳ]

The glorious, divine freedom in part is this. Therefore, rejoice, all of you faithful, true children of God, who have been enslaved, imprisoned, and bound in suffering and pain on account of the name of the Lord and righteousness. You have put to death your lusts or life, leaving these things behind you and depriving yourselves of all things. For this reason you will receive it all back in manifold. See, it is therefore called a true freedom, so that you will become one body, one heart, and one will, bearing the image and likeness of God, pure and without [60ᵛ] stain. What command will be there? None. Why not? For there will no longer be any transgressions, nor any evil will, nor fleshly, heathenish lusts, nor the desires of the devil; only goodness and nothing else. Therefore, there will be no commandments. For people will neither love nor cherish anything else except God the Lord alone. And they will love all things for his sake and in him. Therefore there will no longer be any commandment or transgression, for there will be no sin, which has been their enemy unto death. And why no longer? Because there all things will be free. There will be neither avarice nor any flesh. Nor will anyone possess anything, for people will no longer steal nor commit adultery. They will no longer desire any unchastity, fornication, or murder, or any form of evil. Nor will they kill. For there will be only those who are one body with Christ in the blessed God. See, in this way will all things be changed and sealed. And all things will become free to us, and we will possess them as our father's goods [Rom. 8:17-23]. I say this now to all who have died to the flesh; to those who have fulfilled all things in themselves, such as the law or commands of Christ. For they will become a better spirit—pure, clean, and innocent, humble and meek. They will have one father and one family, one house and fold. They will be like the children of honor and will possess everything which belongs to their father, including the entire kingdom of the earth [61ʳ] and all its fullness [Ps. 24:1]. You must first become his true form and likeness. For he will distribute the kingdom to all of you together, and give you everything to possess, all of which has been prepared for you from the beginning [Matt. 25:34]. Pay attention and praise the Lord.

This is and will be the divine, unspeakable, glorious freedom of the children of God. Blessed are they who come to this and receive it.

These are the ones who have abandoned the old world. Take it to heart. See that no one places himself in the highest place, for he will be brought down in shame to the lowest.

Therefore, everyone, both small and great, go now to the Lord.
Enquire of his mouth and learn from him.
This was prophesied long ago
by the prophet, that they
all should be taught by God [Isa. 54:13]. And the time has arrived.
Behold that you do it now.
Amen. [61ˇ]

The love of your house has consumed and devoured me [Ps. 69:9] (O Lord Master, if you give no strength). You know it. Praise to you, praise, praise, eternally blessed, Amen.

O you hard hearts, become dust. You must become dust and ashes again. For you must become gold. Are you darkness? You must become light. Examine what you are now, according to your calling. See, see, I warn you all, yes, everyone.

See, I began to set down the texts in the margins as evidence. But the Spirit was adverse to my doing any more of this, therefore, I stopped.[15] Also, there came into my body a great fatigue, which still continues at this time. Everyone be careful that they have the Spirit, through which they will be able to judge best. For although I have after all set down some of the texts here—the first ones that occurred to me—they surely will not be received by everyone to that end. Therefore, receive the Spirit, and pay heed indeed to it. See Jeremiah 30 from the beginning to the end and also chapter 31, where wisdom is entirely concealed in this matter. Read Wisdom of Solomon 1, 2, 3; Malachi 3, 4. Pay attention to these. In summary, I have announced to you that which has been given to me in its power for all of you. And you, beloved brothers, be careful to desire the same when you pray. I will be innocent of all your blood. But if you do not find these things from the ground of the blessed God, then all of it must be revealed to me through your prayer. [62ʳ] In any event I also know and confess openly to the death my goal that I desire to do well, yes I indeed. But I am certain that I will not presume or boast too much, for the Lord alone knows how he has taught and directed me from the beginning. For there entered into me some lofty words; it was if I could hear them as they were placed upon me. Yet you should realize that these words were written through a pure Spirit of God, for I am not so foolish or blind. The Lord be praised. I examined them well, however impossible it may be to believe it. But they were nevertheless written with urgency, in a humble, lowly spirit. I had desired not to write any more of it down, but the Lord took away my volition. Take this to heart. For in this I fear him who is blessed in eternity.

And what I have written here is for all the truly faithful—not just the others but also myself—for the Lord is pleased to see and hear such willing messengers or servants, when they seek to sincerely and purely praise the Lord. Therefore, everyone put out that roguish eye, and let us have one heart among each other, without suspicion and fear. Woe to whomever shall be found guilty therein. Yes, let each one esteem the other as better than himself [Phil. 2:3]. Take it to heart. We have one Father. For we best know the Lord, the Father of lights, [62ᵛ] when we are in the light or when we walk according to his will and heart. Each one see to it. I expect neither praise nor contempt from people, for the Lord shall judge me; to him be praise in eternity. To conclude: however it goes with me, my teaching is sincere.

I pray for you all through the merciful God and our Lord Jesus Christ, that you will not be offended by any lofty words which have been written by me in this book. Though they appear to have been composed and said by me, yet they have flowed out of the pen through the Holy Spirit which has spoken in me. Believe it if you will, the Lord is my witness. But if my heart had been free before the Lord Master, with his will and good pleasure, I would have erased these things. But see, they were received, therefore, those things which were written, must remain written. I am so free of haughtiness, pride, honor, arrogance, or inflation with pride, that these things are an enemy to me and I am completely against them. In this way I seek nothing but unity, faithfulness, truth, peace, and love, as well as the Lord's will and praise. O if all those who seek the truth and Jesus had true love; if they had such a heart that each might be pleased to be the least, truly fearing the Lord. O that they spoke with one mouth, and resounded with one sound. Then the world would fear. Believe this, [63ʳ] for then the devil would go through a fire, for he must be emptied and his foundation broken up, his kingdom must come to disgrace before the eyes of all the heathen [Rev. 20:10]. Therefore, seek unity, peace, and love. Love from pure hearts, so that you will abide eternally. Receive this with a spirit of praise and rejoicing. Do not look to me for whoever seeks, like a thief, to take my crown and the Lord's glory from me must be damned [Rev. 3:11]. Do not do so. See, I do not regard myself higher than the least. Yes, I desire from my heart to be the least in prestige. Now the Lord knows what I desire and seek, yes, whatever people may think. I desire not to spare or preserve my life here. But I will offer it up from day to day as

> the Lord wills, for the name of Jesus
> and the righteousness of God,
> my hope and trust,
> my only refuge
> and security.

" 'Hear, my elect,' says the Lord. 'Behold, the days of tribulation are nearby and from them I will deliver you. Therefore, neither fear nor waver, for the blessed God is your chief' " [2 Esd. 16:74-75]. Receive this in your hearts.

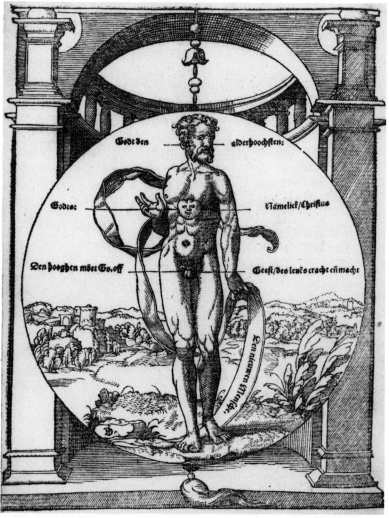

David Joris, "The New Man," *The Wonder Book*, Part II, fol. 211v.
Courtesy of the Mennonite Library, University of Amsterdam

6

The Early Correspondence

By any standard Joris was a prolific letter writer. Four volumes of his correspondence still exist. Three of these were published in the early decades of the seventeenth century.[1] Unfortunately, these volumes contain only a few letters pertaining to Joris's career before 1544. The fourth volume, however, is quite different. Until recently thought to have been lost, the now rediscovered "Hydeckel" contains in manuscript about 130 of Joris's missives composed between the years 1537 and 1543. The fact that approximately 120 folio pages are missing from the extant volume indicates that it probably at one time contained even more. This tome, along with fourteen other volumes of Joris material, is now located in the Manuscript Department at the University of Basel.[2] Fortunately for the modern reader, the letters are in the hand of Joris's secretary, Henrich van Schor, and are therefore legible.[3] Joris's more obscure hand is discovered in the cifered code indicating the date, recipient, and place of composition included at the bottom of most letters.[4] A copy of Joris's woodcut illustration of the Lamb of God/Lion of Judah, presumably drawn for *The Wonder Book*, is also found on the frontispiece.

Unfortunately, what is largely true about Joris's published correspondence is also true of the "Hydeckel." Aside from the encoded addresses, most letters contain little direct information about Joris or his following. Instead they are filled with his typical and repetitive spiritual admonitions. But the letters do reveal that Joris took seriously the mandate which he had received in the winter of 1536-1537 to proclaim the Word of God to the scattered Melchiorites, especially those in England, East Frisia, and Germany (mainly Westphalia and Strasbourg). There are also noteworthy exceptions to the rule of historical irrelevance in Joris's correspondence. For example, there are missives to Henrich Niclaes, the founder of the House of Love; to the Silesian Spiritualist Caspar van Schwenckfeld; to the German Reformer Martin Luther; to Countess Agnes van Limburg, Abbess of the Freckenhorst Cloister near Münster; and to the Evangelical Rentmaster of Groningen, Hieronymus Wilhelmi.[5] While I have translated only three of the "Hydeckel" letters, they are perhaps the most important ones for the Anabaptist career of Joris. One of these is the controversial letter to the Strasbourg Melchiorite leadership in 1537, a letter which, by its previous unavailability, has caused a considerable amount of misunderstanding about Joris. Another is Joris's missive to his supporters in northern Westphalia regarding the organization of the church and their discussions with the Münsterite refugees, who, under the leadership of Heinrich Krechting, had found a secure haven in the Duchy of Oldenburg.

The first letter included here was composed sometime in 1537, apparently in response to several questions directed to Joris by some unidentified followers.[6] While brief, it reveals Joris's attitudes toward specific issues, including the problem of unattached women, the relative importance of water baptism and church discipline, and the spiritual problems surrounding the offices of merchants, military commanders, and goldsmiths.

As elsewhere, his comments about women are less than complimentary. He clearly did not believe that women were able to understand the Word of God for themselves. On other issues Joris is less clear. His comments in this letter do illustrate, however, that at this moment in his career, he encouraged an organized leadership and discipline within his fellowship, and allowed the practice of water baptism. His followers also closely examined potential recruits (the Edomites) and set high standards for their behavior. It is also evident that Joris maintained a relatively neutral position regarding those in positions of authority. In all of these issues, it is readily apparent that Joris was most concerned about the inner spiritual state of the person concerned. Outward forms or practices were secondary.

o o o o o

To the Praise of Our Lord and the Instruction of His People, 1537

Behold.

One should not allow any woman to be alone without an over-seer[7] or head, whether she is old or a young girl, if she does not have a father or master. It is the will of God among us that such should not be allowed to continue. Therefore, each old or young woman who does not have a lord must be placed under a lord or head, who will be her patron and support. He will teach and look after her. He will advise according to her speech, question, or need, to oversee how she is progressing or carrying herself [cf. 1 Cor. 14:34-35]. He is to see if she desires to be obedient and if, like an infant, she will allow herself to be instructed by good advice. He will command and forbid her according to the truth and wisdom which comes from God. The purified will stand and all hearts will be revealed. But this must be true of the God-fearing, for one should make sure that they seek and love the righteousness and the eternal life which is in Christ Jesus. For from these come great wisdom and understanding and fitness. Believe this. Yes, one is able to take four, six, or eight birds under him for instruction and oversight, so that they might be questioned, examined, and taught how to enter the kingdom of God.[8] O, let this happen so. Woe to the disobedient, for upon them will the vengeance come. By doing this no one will be idle in virtue. Instead each will find reason to watch [292[r]] and to be earnest in good works, and to pray, which is right and blessed. This concerns, I say, those who are not our wives, whom we also have to govern. This must happen among those who are qualified and sincere, which must be us all. We must walk wisely and as children of the light. We must be like construction workers. For if this happens in the wisdom and fear of God (each one observe this), then the women will consent to it and submit to such a head in the obedience of the truth. They will honor him as the church of Christ or as the teacher or messenger of Christ. But pay attention to this. Pray, and you will understand the mind of the Spirit and the great wisdom so much deeper and better. Woe to the men who do not conduct themselves well with crying, admonition, understanding and examination, showing her the way to go. For the men will give an account for those placed under their charge [Heb. 13:17], but not for the unbelievers. Dear brothers, we must become fiery children of the Lord's righteousness and grace, who walk in the light and wisdom, full of faith, as sons and daughters of the living God. Pay attention. We must fulfill the deed or he will not remember our names. Whoever is found, unwilling or disobedient will be punished. He will have nothing to do with them. Nevertheless, let each one exercise love and seek to preserve each other, if you desire to be preserved, found and taught. Whoever has an evil will is outside of God. Pay attention. Show to all people love, humility, meekness, and long-suffering, friendliness, and a liberated heart.

[292ʸ]   **Concerning Children**

Concerning those who are children in the nature of their flesh. They must honor their elders in all things and be obedient to the elders of the Lord to the death. But if you mean the children or youths, then I note what I have written about the children who are born in faith. These must stand under their elders, namely under the teachers, who are their pastors. As children they must be taught in all things, and grow up into fitness in order to become elders and pastors. This must be so. "For the Lord will come suddenly to his holy temple" [Mal. 3:1]. Blessed are they who are found adorned and resolute, properly constructed on the foundation of the apostles and the prophets, namely upon Christ Jesus [1 Cor. 3:10-11]. Being like him as obedient children, or as it is fitting for women to their lord, servants to their lord, and a disciple to his master [Matt. 10:24]. Pay attention. Pray and watch, O I admonish you strongly. Become fervent and alert. Do not sleep. Do not slow down, but win many prizes for the Lord. O fulfill this and greet all those who are submissive in this. For I regard these as my brothers and sisters, as Christ's members.

Everyone pray for a clear understanding, that is, for simple eyes, for Spirit wisdom, so that your thoughts might be found holy and pure, without bitterness or impurity of heart. See, these ones will see the King God in his beauty [Ps. 27:4].

All the men or sincere brothers who from their lowliness [293ʳ] believe with their hearts and confess with their mouths his glorification [Rom. 10:9], who, with their full hearts seek their God's honor or praise in every way, these ones the Father will allow to honor him. And the women who are sincere, humble, and loving of heart should honor his servants and hold them in great worth [cf. Eph. 5:22—6:3]. Yes, the Spirit gives this to the one brother as to the other. The children are commanded in a like manner, for they should also be images. This is what pleases God and is fitting for his eyes. This is profitable for the learning of submissiveness and humility. But let it happen willingly and from the love and mind of the Spirit. Everyone guard themselves from glorying in vanity. Let us give honor to God alone and scorn ourselves in shame and disgrace. Understand that as long as we are mortified in all things and have struggled vigorously, then it is proper for us to cherish love rather than honor. Obtain understanding, and cherish humility. Sela.

Concerning Baptism

One should allow it for those who have an earnest heart, who believe they have received it in simplicity or without pride. But only if they secure it through evidence of good works of faith. But if this is not so, then it has happened to the damnation of those who have been baptized. If they desire to submit themselves under the obedience of the truth, then the iniquity and dishonor which they have done against God [293'] and the angels will be borne. They will pray and patiently bear their humility or abandonment and revilement.

Concerning Edomites, Edom[9]

If he has been publicly revealed, then the matter can be easily judged. If not, then they must be visited and examined through and in the Spirit, in order to see the kind of spirit which is leading him. If he is sincere, then one can let him retain both of them,[10] if he desires and seeks to proceed in a manly and correct fashion. First, they must bear their chastisement, even if they have been masters in Edom, and now have gone backwards [Obad. 8]. If they were once with the evil, then they are excluded, and he must ensure that he keep himself pure from them until it is revealed what God has in his mind.

Concerning Mother and Daughter[11]

If it is true that he has completely nullified himself under the humility and obedience of the truth, but still feels himself to be in sin and iniquity, thinking[12] without the counsel and maturity of the Holy Spirit, but by his own thoughts and human advice, which shall cease [1 Cor. 13:8], then he must pray and humble himself before the Lord, grieving over his fleshly freedom which has worked without the Spirit, but instead in a fleshly manner before the time. He must abide with the last;[13] not disconcerting nor concerning himself about it, but he must give them over to the Lord. For the Lord joins them to whomever he will, to this man or to another, and they must place themselves in humility and submissiveness and confess this to the Lord.

Concerning Merchants

The occupation of the merchant is beautified[14] only with difficulty [294ʳ] because of neglect. But if anyone has moved his sin under him, so that he is lord of his senses and mind, if he can do such freely in order to help his brothers, then he can do it. If this is not the case, then I advise against it. The time is short and valuable, accept it as true.

Concerning Commanders

Judges and commanders stand in great peril. If they have love, so they will perish as a result. Understand this. But if they petition to be released from it, then it is free to them, as long as they do all things correctly in the faith and do not hinder Christians nor the gospel, but instead further it. If this is not the case, then it is better to abandon it with Moses and to suffer trouble with the people of God, rather than to have the temporary pleasure of sin, esteeming the reproach of Christ as much better.[15] So forth.

Concerning Goldsmiths

Goldsmiths carry out their work according to their heart and faith, whether pure or impure. The Lord will judge them according to their heart and the purity of their faith. If they are pure therein, and if they support good works toward eternal life and are prepared to do or to tolerate all things according to the counsel of their servants whom the Holy Spirit loves and directs, then it is free to them according to the temporal opportunity.

Concerning Outward Punishment

If there is a brother who has transgressed from righteousness into sin, God has prepared for him a sword. Furthermore, a brother has given him over to the devil and his sins have served to death [1 Cor. 5:5]. In this way he should be admonished once, twice, or three times [Matt. 18:15-18]. Nevertheless, it is said that if he continues in his unrighteousness, he will be guilty in the flesh. Namely, he will bear his guilt and punishment. But if he [294ᵛ] will pray and plead with the Lord and the brothers, then the leaders should not make a ruling except in mercy. See, then he can be saved on account of the blessed time, submitting himself to his humiliation and conversion and for all the virtues of God. But those who remain hardened on account of their sin and unrighteousness and who have gone away to some others among whom they seek to be saved, instructed, and taught, they will remain there and not return. Without murmuring they must bear and suffer their guilt, for they have brought it upon themselves. If there are any people, men or women who do not seek God nor walk according to God's fear, then reject them as whores and hold their derision above them through the Holy Spirit or the Lord.

Blessed is he who does not think anything iniquitous against the Lord, or who does not sin with his tongue [Ps. 34:3]. Moreover, you dear brothers, pray in order to understand and judge what is right. Whatever agrees with your Spirit, do it. For if any witness a greater Spirit about this or that, I do not contradict them. For I want to be innocent. I have here revealed to you what I, unworthy, have received, and what the Lord through his Spirit has given to me as a sign.

From Delft, in the Year 1537

David Joris's Response to Johannes Eisenburg, 1537[16]

This missive was a written response by David Joris to a tract of Johannes Eisenburg concerning marriage and divorce.[17] As far as we know, the letter was never published and for years was assumed to have been lost along with the "Hydeckel." Unlike most of the letters in this collection, Joris noted the recipient of this work, Johannes Eisenburg, in the title instead of in the code.

Johannes Eisenburg was a major leader of the Melchiorite group in Strasbourg. Regarded as intellectually superior to his fellows, Eisenburg had been chosen as one of Hoffman's prophets of the last days.[18] The Strasbourg leaders as a group were revered by many Dutch Anabaptists as the "elders in Israel" and thereby carried a great deal of religious authority. The most influential of these "elders" had been, of course, Hoffman himself, but his esteem had diminished somewhat since he was still in the Strasbourg prison and was to remain there for the rest of his life.[19] Joris sought to fill this authority vacuum when he agreed to meet with the Strasbourg leaders in the summer of 1538. During this disputation, Joris told the "elders" to submit without question to his personal authority, which Eisenburg and his compatriots naturally refused to do. Even in this letter, which was composed the year before the conference, Joris affirmed that his message could be received only by those who had entered into the highest level of spiritual perfection, the holy of holies. It is therefore not surprising that Eisenburg's confrontation with the pretensions of this self-proclaimed "third David" accelerated his dissatisfaction with the movement as a whole. Just one year after the disputation Eisenburg and Peter Tasch, another prominent Strasbourg Melchiorite, sought to disband the remaining groups of Melchiorites in Hesse and Strasbourg. With the cooperation of the Strasbourg Reformer Martin Bucer, many of the Melchiorites joined the Reformed Church.[20] The role that Joris played in heightening the disillusionment of these "elders" may have been considerable.

The subject of Joris's missive to Eisenburg was one of the most controversial which confronted the heirs of Hoffman. Since the debacle of Münster, during which the Old Testament patriarchs' practice of polygamy was reinstated by Jan Boeckelsz van Leiden and rationalized by Bernhard Rothmann, the Dutch Anabaptists had sought to redefine their concept of marriage. Most, including Melchior Hoffman himself, rejected Münsterite polygamy, although Jan van Batenburg and his coterie of violent Anabaptists maintained its use. Compounding the difficulties related to the Münster heritage was the very serious dilemma of whether or not marriages between believers and unbelievers remained valid. Joris's letter reveals some of the pressing questions raised over this issue, as well as solutions drawn from his unique hermeneutic.

Eisenburg's now lost tract presumably rejected outright the possibility of divorce among Anabaptists. Before the discovery of Joris's response, scholars have assumed, from the summary of Joris's letter found in Nicolaas Meyndertsz van Blesdijk's *Historia vitae*, that he replied in favor of polygamy. Since the recent unearthing of the "Response to Hans Eisenburg," the belief that Joris in this work approved of polygamy is no longer tenable. On the other hand, it must not be inferred from this conclusion that Joris necessarily condemned the practice of polygamy.[21] At the most, Joris was indifferent, but not hostile, to polygamy. He had, after all, allowed a group of former Batenburgers who joined him in Delft in 1538 to maintain the practice.

While Joris did not here defend the polygamy of Münster, he did maintain other aspects of the Münsterite program. One of these was Bernhard Rothmann's belief that there was only one reason for sexual relations between husband and wife that was not sinful. This was the production of holy children who would add to the number of saints in the kingdom, the 144,000 of Revelation 7. Another element Joris shared with the Münster heritage was his patriarchal conception of marriage. Joris's repudiation of religious leadership for women flew in the face of the practice of the Strasbourg Melchiorites, who accorded great respect to several female prophets, including Barbara Rebstock and Ursula Jost.

* * * * *

[305ʳ]
This Is Written to the Wise.
Do not let the ignorant know it. Do not give salvation to the dogs, neither cast your pearls and roses before the swine [Matt. 7:6]. Behold.

The Response to Hans Eisenburg, 1537
Chapter 1
It is a matter of great concern for all of us whether or not a holy person or person of God speaks. The men of God or the holy prophets, however, could certainly err. Namely, like the prophet David, who committed adultery and murder [2 Sam. 11]. You therefore must not observe, believe, nor follow after his words or teaching. I am concerned that the words do not stand in vain. The Lord provide that he look into and confess this, that he has spoken them with a simple heart without examination. For I desire this from my heart on his account. For I know that it is not fitting in such a manner, [305ᵛ] nor will it be pardoned by the Lord. Behold. For it was not spoken in a wise but a foolish manner in that portion.

Blessed is the person who has not fallen in his words.[22] Therefore, do not be quick with your mouth, nor let your heart hasten to speak something, not to mention to define something in the Scriptures. If you are quick to speak, then a fool has more hope than you.[23] Whoever is quick of feet stumbles easily.

See, the children of a hundred years will die and the sinners of a hundred years will perish.[24]

Iniquity will be cast into the ashes along with those who do iniquity.[25] If you do not keep yourselves constantly in the fear of God, your house will hasten to be cast there.

If people love righteousness and work for wisdom, they will have great virtue.[26] They learn sobriety, prudence, and righteousness, and complete virtue. They know the indiscretion of speech and the decay of silver. And God loves no one, except those who live with wisdom. Behold.

See the fear of the Lord, that is wisdom.[27] And to reject evil, that is understanding. If you call for understanding, you will then obtain it. If you seek it like silver and seek it like a treasure, then you will understand the fear of the Lord and find the knowledge of God.[28] Where there is humility, there is wisdom.

Where are now the scribes? Where are the questioners or disputers?[29] Where are the chancellors? You will not see the [306ʳ] strong people there, the people of deep speech, whom one cannot understand, nor those of a strange tongue, whom one cannot understand.

See, I will speak of the Lord of hosts to those of you who are poor and simple and who have yielded themselves to the name of the Lord.[30] Behold.

Behold.

See, what God has brought together, no person can separate.[31] Observe this correctly in every way. But what Satan, or the fleshly nature, or the evil world, or human reason brings together, God or his Spirit may indeed separate. Is this not so?[32] Yes, read. There is still the hatred of former times between the serpent's seed and the woman's. Namely, between the flesh and the spirit. This happened through Christ, who came in order to send fire upon the earth [Luke 12:49]. What does he desire of this? That it immediately be kindled or burn. This is the law of the Spirit, his fiery, pure, earnest love, which is as strong as death and his angry love consumes like hell. Its blaze is fiery. This flame of the Lord cannot be extinguished even by much water, nor can the rivers overflow it.[33] Behold. But O unfortunately, not everyone understands this, nor do they have such earnest love. Therefore, they stand in great danger of falling. Yes, they fall frequently, and obtain harm from the world and the flesh. If they have not yet come into the perfect [306ᵛ] level in the holy of holies, that is into the life. And see, only there will be found the correct, true servants of God. Yes, just as is written, they will be like gods and angels.[34] They will also reign as kings and priests. These are also called servants of flames of fire [Heb. 1:7], who are one with the Word of Life (which is compared to fire). These ones will stand and will survive outwardly because of the Word, but all flesh will perish as hay.[35] For they will run like sparks through the reeds [Wis. of Sol. 3:7]. They will judge nations and rule the people, in that great fearful day of the Lord, when the flames and fire will be like an oven, says the Lord Sabaoth, who is a fire to Zion and an oven to Jerusalem.[36] Thus will Jacob's house possess this sanctuary, which it previously had occupied. For the house of Jacob will become a fire and the house of Joseph a flame,[37] but the house of Esau will become straw, which they will kindle and devour.[38] Furthermore, I will make the leaders of Judah like the glowing oven, which, like a burning fire in straw, will consume all people around about, both to the right and to the left, says the Lord. You who are far, see what I have done, and you who are near, mark my writings. The sinners are amazed at Zion; trembling has gripped the godless [Isa. 33:14]. Who among us has lived in the consuming fire?[39] Who among us can remain in the fiery heat? Read and pay attention. For this reason, those who do not allow their eyes to look at evil, even if they are old, they will dwell in the most high and their surety and shelter will be in the rocks. They will certainly receive their bread and water; [307ʳ] their eyes will look at the king's beauty. Behold. Why? Their eyes will be light, innocent as doves and their hearts are pure. Pay attention, for we have to speak about this.

Chapter 2

So understand. The angel Raphael speaks: "Hear me, I will reveal to you who they are, over whom the devil has authority."[40] Those who enter into marriage in this way, who exclude God from their thoughts, and give themselves to lasciviousness, are like a horse or mule which has no understanding. Over these ones the devil has authority.[41] Read. Further, Sarah speaks: "If by chance I am not found worthy, for you have mistaken me for another person." And still the angel spoke. Therefore, she had no other choice, for she was pure of heart [cf. Gen. 18]. Therefore she was protected by the Lord so that she would not be defiled. Although there are teachers, who will say that it is pure (let them dispute among themselves as much as they want) or fitting to remain with the impure. But their childish understanding, will, I hope, be ultimately revealed to them. For they have frequently given this advice, but not from me, says the Lord.

Further, we are children of the holy ones, says the pious Tobias [Tob. 4:12]. We therefore must not [307ᵛ] become joined in this way, like the heathen who do not know God. "And now Lord, you know that I have not taken my sister as a wife on account of unchastity, but only from the love of children."[42] See, these ones are truly brought together by God, and these two are one flesh; they have one will, one spirit, one mind, one heart. Woe to any person who would separate such. Also, one cannot do this. Why not? They are one body.[43] Behold. And there is peace among those whom God calls his own. This is said of Adam in an incorruptible fashion. In particular, that he was a bone of mine, and flesh of my flesh. Understand. "Therefore a man shall leave his father and mother, and cleave to his," etc.[44] Think now in what shape they then stand. In brief. One must not separate such. For God brought Eve to Adam, who was of his own flesh, who was just like him; he gave her to him as a helper, to be joined together. Between these ones I advise no one to come, except between Esau and Jacob, the two kinds of people, the one with his hand on the other's heel [Gen. 25:26]. Do not ask me further about this, for here it is hidden. Pay attention. Look sharply and wake up. For here is the morning star, which separates the night from the day, this world from the future. Praise now the name of the Lord who gives all of this.[45]

Further, one should hold fast to that word which was spoken first in an unpernicious manner, for we need to use it, namely that the two should be one flesh. [308ʳ] In the first place, this was a hidden figure of Christ and his beloved bride, which was flesh of his flesh and bone of his bone. And now God be thanked through Christ Jesus for his grace, which has opened our eyes and has removed our understanding,[46] so that we could comprehend to what end, what will, and of what flesh the Lord spoke, and its ultimate meaning. He meant it about the first human, who, although in the visible flesh, is distinguishable as two; nevertheless, they were one body or flesh. That is, they had one will, one heart, one mind, and one simple, innocent, unroguish spirit. And now, where there is not one will nor one lust or desire among the children of flesh, nor one mind and one heart in them, they are not able to make one body or flesh. But we will pass over this and not think at all about the old world. For it must be so: "The vain remain vain, the full remain full" [Rev. 22:11]. Whoever has been wanting, at a loss and oppressed here are meek and humble in their heart. They will receive the perfection of grace and become exalted. But the proud ones he will drive from their throne and leave them in vanity.

For these are the children of flesh, likened to the hay of this world, born of Esau, Ham's family, Cain's seed, Ishmael's nation. Their hands always seek trouble. They are a people that is proud and armed with spears, a people that is always fighting and desirous of war.[47] When the great ones gather, they are the strongest among the sons of the mighty ones. Like calves they leap after their tails until the time when they are humbled. These will [308ᵛ] all be completely destroyed and perish. For they are the adulterer's seed, from the unchaste bed, born only of the flesh, not from the noble women.[48] Pay close attention.

Chapter 3

Was Jacob not right in separating from Esau? Yes, certainly, indeed. I say this also to the spiritual of heart. Woe to him who tries to prevent this. See, in this same fashion Israel was supposed to separate from the same, to become free from the uncircumcised, without sin, for all manner of reasons. But they were like Asenath, Potiphera the priest's daughter, who was given to Joseph [Gen. 41:45]. Or like Ruth the Moabite [Ruth 1:15-17], and more others, who should not have been so easily adopted into Israel. Nevertheless, Israel did shamefully and appeared as sinners, in spite of the fact that it was their own flesh and bone in their degree. But they abandoned it for all manner of reasons in order that such be allowed, because of the hardness of their hearts.[49] But others kept themselves undefiled from this and they became free from foreign wives.

Further. For this reason was Joseph married in Egypt and had more there. This was, moreover, foreseen in this way [Gen. 41:45]. Though it was such before the law. Or to whom would he have gathered, other than to Ishmael's seed, which is to presume that they were also circumcised?[50] This, however, is good and was decent in this way, for it was ordained by the Lord, as is written.

[309ʳ] Further. Samson took the Philistine daughter. This was also from the Lord, as is written.[51] Furthermore, it was known to the Lord that Moses took the Midianite as a wife [Exod. 2:21]. Nevertheless I am certain that much of it has happened as an image. For the holy, God-fearing men must take no heathenish, uncircumcised wives. They must first be inclined to the saints and find those of good and mature nature. Behold.

Further. It was also written in this way. You must not become indignant about the children of the Edomites and Egyptians who are born and want to come into the fellowship of the Lord.[52] Further. I will remember the Egyptians and the Babylonians who know me. Behold. See now one new thing. The Philistines, Tyrians, and also the Moors will come running, so that the glorious and the famous will be born there [Ps. 87:4].

Further. Can one easily understand all this without that which has been narrated above? Or on this basis judge well, that Israel was not in this way bound to these foreigners? For the Lord forbade such to Israel. And they were warned enough that they not take the heathen to them, nor should they go in to them. Neither give heathen daughters to their sons nor give heathen sons to their daughters. For they will certainly draw your hearts to their gods, says the Lord [Exod. 34:15-16]. Therefore, the word and counsel of God has not been kept in this respect. Through this many have perished and become blind. Yes, even the wise Solomon himself. Behold. For this reason those who love danger will perish by it. This is certain, as is written.[53] For it is not a negligible joining together. [309ʸ] God's wrath, hatred, and curse is over it. Read and see what Esdras said in the book of Nehemiah.⁵⁴

Therefore, when Esau saw that Isaac his father was not pleased with the daughters of Canaan, he went and took a daughter of Ishmael.⁵⁵ Furthermore, seeing how soon the children of God took the daughters of men as their wives, whomever they chose, the Lord said "My Spirit will not always rule in humans, for they are flesh."⁵⁶ Behold.

Chapter 4

Now the difference between the people of God and the heathen, between the flesh and the spirit, has been well enough explained or heard.⁵⁷ For how does the wheat accord with the chaff? The grapes with the brambles? The lies with the truth? Light with darkness? The believers with the unbelievers? The righteous with the unrighteous? Christ with Belial? Therefore, there must be a separation so that the good will not ultimately be expelled by the evil, nor the pure by the impure. Thus the many who are born for sin's sake perish, says the Lord. But my grapes will be saved in my planting. For I have perfected them with much labor.⁵⁸

Furthermore, we know that the wife must be one with her husband and not the husband with the wife. I speak concerning the spiritual, and not of the fleshly; of those who will live, not those who will die.⁵⁹ Therefore, the wife should listen to her husband, and she must follow him. Just like the husband must hear and follow the Lord Christ. [310ʳ] This is God's will. If he follows her, he castrates himself and loses his beard. He thereby dishonors God's glory and despises his order. He becomes effeminate and is called a woman. For he is one with the wife, which is not proper for a true Christian man. This has gone on so long, and still does among most Christians, not to mention those of the world who act like women. But God will not bear this any longer, but desires that they become like men. This will be a new thing upon the earth. As it is written.⁶⁰

So then, as the husband is, even so must his wife be. If he is spirit, namely incorporated into Christ, so she must also be as spiritually minded as he, or she is not one body with her husband. If he is flesh, then so is she. If she is spiritual, she cleaves to him. Similarly the husband, if he is a Christian but cleaves to an unchaste wife or whore, then he is one body with her and not with Christ.⁶¹ For if he is one body with the woman or with the flesh, he then loves and cleaves to her and is not one spirit with Christ. Therefore, he is excluded from such a grade and damned.

Further. What the apostle said to the Corinthians was so that they could better purify and defend themselves, for he could not protect them, nor make them pious. For Paul (so that you can understand me) did not express his words any broader, wider, or higher than as good advice, not as a command [1 Cor. 7:25]. But it was necessary according to their belief or, as he expressed it, according to [310ʳ] the occasion of the time. It was also praiseworthy and commendable in this first instance. It was necessary that he express this indiscreetly because of their tenderness and childishness. He therefore gave milk to each of them and not strong food. For they were not familiar with the Word, not knowing the difference between pure and impure, good and evil. Give good attention to this. And what Paul said in his sermons was spoken prudently so that he could lay the foundation well. He did not want to lose any because of an omission, but desired to win many. Therefore, he appeared to be weak to the weak, not to please himself but the Lord [1 Cor. 9:19-23]. For this reason he humbled and lowered himself, although he was in the form of God, he regarded it not as robbery to be like God, but took our sickness upon himself and became (although he was the Most High and honored one) the lowest or most despised and poorest for us [Phil. 2:5-8]. Behold. Even in this way did Paul act here, and became as a Jew for the Jews. He became as a heathen without the law for the heathen who are without the law, even though he was not without the law of Christ. And although he was free, he made himself to be a slave of all, so that he might win many.

Chapter 5

Christ our Lord said to his [311ʳ] disciples: "I still have much to say to you, but you are not able to bear it" [John 16:12]. Further: "What I do now, you do not know, but you will find out afterward" [John 13:7]. Behold, yes, give careful attention to this. I see of what I speak. In this way Paul dealt with the Corinthians, saying: "Dear brothers, I could not speak with you as with spiritual persons, but as fleshly. Just like infants in Christ I have given you milk to drink and not food, for you did not have the ability for food, and still do not, for you are still fleshly etc." [1 Cor. 3:1-3]. See, Paul gave similar spiritual counsel and advised the same thing in a letter, all just as their need required. This you can easily understand.

Further. Paul at first allowed Timothy to be circumcised; nevertheless, later on he came to forbid it as damnable [Acts 16:3]. Observe this wise procedure. But such hidden wisdom is too lofty for the fools, for it is much too sharp for the unlearned. An ignorant person will not remain in it.

Further. Note that the apostles and all the elders made the law regarding what was necessary to keep themselves from the heathen, in particular: not to eat meat mixed with wood, namely idolatry; nor to eat blood of the strangled; and to keep themselves from all fornication. Now none of these four related necessary things have been maintained by us. Neither were they regarded by Paul or the elders [Acts 15:28-29], [311ʳ] in particular, the first three of these necessary things. The first concerning idolatry: Paul said to the Romans more similar things, saying "I know and am certain in the Lord Jesus that nothing is common or impure of itself, but to he who regards it as impure, to him it is impure" [Romans 14:14]. Further. "It is blessed that no one make these things into a matter of his conscience. For whoever doubts and still eats, he is damned, for he did not do it out of faith. Therefore, whatever does not happen from faith is sin" [1 Cor. 14:20-23]. Behold. Therefore, though it was necessary and needful for the Holy Spirit and the apostles to adopt it as good for the heathen, it has been done away with. The two other things, concerning blood and strangled things, these in the same measure have been ended by faith, which is much longer, mightier, and more living, in which the righteous live. But Paul regarded being contaminated by fornication as abominable. For such will not possess the kingdom of God [1 Cor. 6:9-10]. Pay close attention, my brothers. For in your suffering, you are elected to God's temple. Therefore, be chaste and pure, holy therein. Circumcise yourselves from lusts and from the desires of the stomach and concubines. Do not be overcome[62] but suffer in the flesh. Mortify the old Adam. Keep yourselves from sin. Enter the kingdom of God with simplicity and innocence. Put on the brilliant, snow-white bride's garments [312ʳ] which have been known only by a few among thousands. But now this has been revealed to you. Rejoice and prepare yourselves to enter before it is too late.

Chapter 6

For this reason, my brothers, will you stand firm on the one and not on the other? Here it was explained that the Holy Spirit thought it fit and necessary to maintain it. Therefore, see this through your eyes. Obtain modesty or you will be caught covering your words [1 Cor. 3:19]. This I say to you as certainly as a word from the Lord. You esteemed ones have great gifts. Allow yourselves, however, to be taught by the simple and little ones and do not despise the counsel of the poor.

Furthermore, Paul says: "This I say, not the Lord" [1 Cor. 7:12]. This is always regarded as less than what the Holy Spirit thinks fit to do at the time, and has therefore perished. It stands inferior to the greater. Do not think to follow your own spirit. Do not aim at your own will or knowledge. But see what is said here. For I have knowledge from the Spirit of God. Of this I am certain. Listen to it, for it is better than the fat of rams [1 Sam. 15:22]. For this reason, I say that what was the good advice of Paul was not a command of the Lord in this matter. It was, however, good for the situation at the time. Why? Paul laid the foundation, Christ, as a [312ᵛ] wise carpenter. No one lays this in any other way, nor can preach another gospel than that which was preached there [1 Cor. 3:10-11]. Even if an angel appeared to come from heaven who preached contrary to Christ or the gospel, it must be damned [Gal. 1:8-9]. We have received the same, covered by the blood.[63] We will remain therein until death. But the secrets of God are not locked outside. For the Lord has given knowledge of these things to the small and simple ones who worship him reverentially and who are his beloved. For he has given them the kingdom, hidden as a city and kingdom, so that they will be the true poor in spirit. But the rich he leaves vain, as is written [Luke 1:53]. Also the full money chests will be found empty. And the sown places appear unsown.[64] For they have defiled the holy name of the one who created them. They are not thankful to the one who brought them to life. Therefore, my judgment is now revealed, says the Lord. I have not shown this to everyone, but only to you few. Behold. The future will reveal those who are correctly called wise. Behold.

Furthermore, I mentioned before that Paul said that they were still fleshly children in understanding. They lived in much fornication and whoredom. Against them Paul had the wisdom to proceed with them, as is written.[65] Namely, as with unspiritual people [1 Cor. 3:1-3]. Should this be? For they at that time were a crude or gross people with heathenish understanding. [313ʳ] Many more thousands would have come to the faith if these things were good and needful for their foundation. For if one cried the alarm, others from all lands would have risen up. For this reason it was good and needful for edification at that time, but not now. But Paul permitted it. In particular, that if the unbelieving partner was pleased to live with the believing. Understand that this did not mean the believer with the unbeliever, for the unbeliever would rule or command or forbid what is proper, holy, or edifying for the believer [1 Cor. 7:12-13]. No, not in this way. Therefore watch what you are opposing and what it is that you are commanding. But practice modesty according to the time. Behold.

Chapter 7

Further. I am certain of what I am saying to you. If believers desire to follow the will of the Lord, whether it is to go, to stand, or to pray, they must give themselves to holy things and to necessary practices or to holy concerns. That is, if they desire to bring up their children in the fear of the Lord and implant their faith in them. Also, if they desire to serve the saints, giving liberally according to their ability, joyfully receive and hide them, and not leave the fellowship. I tell you how it should happen that they discharge their promise. This is what Paul wanted, that they never permit this, not that they should never [313ᵛ] be able to separate. Therefore, it is not a matter of conscience. But do not destroy those who are troubled by it by compelling their minds and wills [cf. 1 Cor. 8]. What do you say to this? And what counsel is here? What do you think about it now? Behold. Yes, watch what you do. Do not stand or advise against the Holy Spirit. Do not kill the soul which lives in the Spirit. Neither kill those who live in the Spirit. Guard yourselves from the flesh, O you effeminate hearts. Let your beards grow. Or will you give no more regard to the Lord than you do to the flesh? Will you not fear God more than mortals? Should one not love Christ more than Belial? Can one serve two opposing masters? Will you not hate and leave one or the other [Matt. 6:24]? Will you not regard this word: "Whoever desires to come to me and follow after me, but does not forsake or hate father, mother, wife, child, yes, even his own life, cannot be my disciple" [Luke 14:26]. Further, "if your hand offends you, cut it off; or if your eye offends you, pluck it out and throw it from you" [Matt. 5:29-30]. Now I say to you that such counsel was good, according to Paul's meaning and the condition of the people at the time. For I say that the foundation was laid first. The gospel first appeared among the heathen who had not heard nor been taught everything. Although they did not come to the knowledge in the first month, they perhaps may have understood in the second month. Who then accepted with them the scorn and suffering and submitted to him, should they have been cut off in this way? No. It was not to happen so hastily. To all such hearts I say: Israel did not do this, nor was she able to expel [314ʳ] her foreigners, whether from Egypt or elsewhere, who subjected themselves to her. These were willing to become slaves and to keep themselves with the people of God. These accordingly received great freedom, just like those in Baal and Achior [cf. Hos. 2]. But the Belialish hearts must be cast out of their fellowship. Yes, not only those who are foreigners, but also those of Israel. Now will all people hasten to prepare themselves to build Zion [Zech. 6:12-15 or 2 Esd. 13:33-36]. The Lord comes to his temple, which has been built over for so long [Mal. 3:1]. Although many believe that it will be started only after Babel's fall or destruction, they do not observe that it has been fulfilled in the Spirit. It will be constructed into a temple of living stones and into a spiritual dwelling of God [1 Pet. 2:5]. O if they spoke of and knew the basis of the future Zion and who will be able to inhabit it. And if they would lead the people to the mountain of the Lord, which is now being humbled and tread upon by the feet of the heathen, until the time when they themselves will be humbled and the days for it are fulfilled [Luke 21:24]. After being tread upon and humbled, this mountain of Zion will be highly exalted and lifted up by God in the Spirit [Isa. 2:2]. But the time draws near when the veil will be removed [2 Cor. 3:16], then the people will be stopped. They will see it openly; they will know and confess it. All people will turn themselves to this mountain. For she will be exalted and glorified above all other mountains, namely kings, dukes, counts, princes, and lords. Then the mountain will be visible from the north, for it is a beautiful land. Read.[66] [314ᵛ]

Chapter 8

Therefore, one should follow Solomon's teaching. Be afraid to blaspheme those things which one does not know or when one comprehends them merely as an ignorant beast. Neither lightly oppose nor easily accept something. Instead, fear the Lord and pray. We must be taught by God before we can define something that we do not understand from the secrets of the Scriptures. This is not easily done where there is no true, perfect fear of the Lord. Without this, it is without soul or life, however beautiful it sounds. Yes indeed.

Further. You believe about this that two will be one flesh and, therefore, one should not separate one flesh [Gen. 2:24; Matt. 19:5-6]. But two must be one spirit, therefore, they can indeed be separated. Here you have heard the explanation far enough. This understanding is completely childish. Have you understood me in any other way? Many words are not necessary for you. And if anyone on account of these words supposes that it is no more than the bringing together of a man and a woman, it has its fulfillment and end in that word. Think of the holy fathers and the elect people of God. For if by this nothing more is meant than that a husband is married to one wife, then the fathers were marriage breakers and adulterers. But this was far from them. For this reason, guard yourselves from thinking such things, not to mention saying them. Concerning this I will narrate [315ʳ] more broadly. But I have proclaimed this matter more extensively in another letter which concerns marriage.[67] You could understand it more reasonably there.

For this reason, behold, if you will, that those who are fleshly minded cannot please God. Why not? Because they are not submissive to the law of God. Can such then please us? I say to you that it is certain that such is from the devil, not God. Such godless seed will be cast out. Behold. For their bed is impure and defiled. Read.[68] However, if you, in your ignorance, should say to me, "We and our children were born in sins and came from a defiled bed," I answer that we must be born out of water and out of the Spirit [John 3:5]. Otherwise we will remain lost in sin. Pay careful attention.

Further. You still say, "Two will be one flesh." This is true. But Paul said whoever is fleshly cannot please God. Did he mean by this the flesh of hands, feet, and a body? Behold. Further. Fleshly minded is death. Therefore, the word must be understood according to its spiritual and not fleshly meaning. For we are members of the body of Christ. It is therefore not a physical flesh. Observe here your error, brothers, for not all flesh is the same. All beasts were brought to Adam, but among all of them he could find no helper [Gen. 2:20]. But it must come from his own flesh. When one is unchaste, that is fleshly, dark, and roguish, [315ᵛ] or has been in the devil, then the wife must be one flesh with him and cleave to him. Therefore, they will be judged outside of the house of God with the dogs and beasts.[69] In this way it is written, "What fellowship does the holy man have with the dog?"[70] With these beasts Adam, or the man, could not be joined, but was kept separate from them. For they are different kinds of flesh and cannot be one, but separate. One is rough, the other mild. The one is savage and wild, the other modest and moral. Here human hands must be put between the two, to separate the hand and the heel. So that the upright will not be ruined by the unrighteous, the pure by the impure, the lillies by the thorns [2 Esd. 6:8-10; Gen. 25:26]. For they are hinderers and opponents and prevent believers in the Lord from living to please the Lord and from obeying the will of God our Lord, blessed in eternity. They will be strengthened with might and armed in order to stand against their enemies.[71]

Chapter 9

Now while Christ has proceeded from the Father and is one with the Father,[72] he has, however, shown himself humbly obedient unto death to his Father as his head and Lord. Even so should the husband be humbly obedient unto death to his Lord Christ, in whose image he [316ʳ] must be. Flesh of his flesh and bone of his bone. Third, similarly must the woman or the wife be obedient in everything to the husband, her lord or head [Eph. 5:22-23]. With tolerance and meekness, she should rejoice in his godly, holy nature or life, with whom she is one body. If she is like him, if she is one mind with him and does his will, she will show herself willingly obedient. See, from these will be born pure generations or healthy, timely children.[73] These partners will come together only from their love of children; from the Spirit and not from the flesh. Their seed is holy and blessed by the Lord. For it is then a work of the Lord and not of the devil. Their children are won with simplicity and innocence in the day, that is in the light and not in the darkness or the night. Behold.

Further. Regarding what Christ had spoken concerning the eunuchs.[74] Up to now this has neither been grasped nor understood correctly by us, regardless of how wise or learned in the Scriptures one might be. Christ responded to the apostles' comment, "If the relationship of the husband with his wife is like this, it is better not to marry" [Matt. 19:10]. Behold, is it therefore not good to marry a wife? Jesus said: "All people do not understand this word, except those to whom it is given. For there are some eunuchs who were born that way from their mother's womb. And there are some eunuchs who are made eunuchs by people. There are some who have made themselves eunuchs for the kingdom of heaven. Let he who is able to accept this, [316ᵛ] accept it" [Matt. 19:11-12]. Behold.

But the same passage has been used by all the wise ones, yes, by all the preachers upon the earth, be they pope or monk, yes, even by Hans Eisenburg. Their interpretation can be easily grasped and understood, regardless of how fleshly one is. But it must be otherwise. For the Lord said, "Not all can understand this word." Namely, that "one makes himself a eunuch or pure on account of the kingdom of God, except to whom it is given; only these can accept or understand it." These are the small and simple ones, who will be a poor, simple people. Behold. But even though this passage was used by Hans Eisenburg above, he believes that it strengthens his position. But he puts the last words of Christ in place of the first. Namely, not all will understand this word, but only those to whom it is given. He leaves the first part floating and takes in its place the last of the text. In particular, that there are eunuchs who make themselves eunuchs on account of the kingdom of heaven. Whoever can accept or understand this, let them accept it. Further. When he said this, he did not mean that they must castrate themselves or have violence done to them on account of the kingdom of God. For he says that the word will not be accepted by everyone, except those to whom it is given. He says, therefore, that to remain without a wife and to live in chastity is not to be accepted by everyone, nor does everyone have the strength for it, except those to whom it is given by God; these may do such and maintain it. To this I respond that the one to whom the strength is given, he must not castrate himself nor do violence to himself. For he is already a eunuch. But [317ʳ] the Lord did not speak about this in the sense of not having a wife. For this reason when the apostles spoke those words, that it is therefore not good to marry a wife, they did not comprehend it as he wanted it comprehended. Therefore, understand. But even if these were their words, it is still therefore not the same which was spoken by Christ. For if the word was valid then, it is not so now. For one must beforehand be given power from above. Therefore, I say that according to your opinion or explanation at first he was not different, as you understand it. For I say it would then be good to circumcise him, or to catch him easily without struggle or doing violence. But it is, I say, to be understood differently, as you will hear.

Further. Solomon said, "When I was brave, I entered an undefiled body, but I knew that I," etc.[75] This does not agree at all with your interpretation but is against it and strengthens my interpretation. For he said that he came to an undefiled body, though he came to bravery and understanding after his youth. And Hans said that to become such, one must remain chaste, without a wife. And if one can obtain or have an undefiled body only without having a wife, then even the apostles had not come to such. And what did Solomon do with his thousand wives? What do you allege when he says he came to an undefiled body, when he came to the understanding and correct wisdom? Furthermore, God gave a wife to Adam. Was that done then to defile him? O foolish understanding, what will you [317ᵛ] brew next? O darkened vision, how will you find the way? For the true light does not shine upon it. Pay close attention to this.

Chapter 10

So now, observe well, my brothers, and accept what you understand. The apostles of Jesus Christ have not castrated themselves for the kingdom of heaven, yet were they not chosen to be his witnesses unto the end? Or, was the understanding of the word, according to your interpretation, not given to them? But to them were all things given to know, even concerning the Son of Eternity himself and the hidden things of the kingdom. Were not all twelve of them chosen to become his holy angels or messengers? Of these, one was a son of the devil, namely Judas. Were they not chosen as fathers of the spiritual Israel, sealed in the Spirit [Eph. 1:13]? They will sit upon the twelve thrones and will judge the twelve tribes of Israel according to the flesh [Luke 22:30]. Or did only Paul and Barnabas understand this, and not the other apostles? Is it given to no one else? Are they alone pure in this and found upright? Did they alone grasp and comprehend this and not the others? After all, they had been sent first and were imbued with power from above.

Or do you come to this interpretation from what Paul said: "I would that all men were as I am" [1 Cor. 7:7]. Or from similar statements elsewhere, such as: "Do not Barnabas and I have the right to bring along a sister?" [1 Cor. 9:5] Do you take from these statements [318ʳ] that he and Barnabas never had a wife? This is spoken with too much pride and too quickly, merely from presumption. Remember that the day has twelve hours. Also, one who will still doubt it must say only that it would have been right if he indeed had a wife, as it appears or as one supposes the others had. Otherwise, he was not as free as the apostles had been. And the word "right" is a proof that he also had the ability, as well as Barnabas. But he dared to abstain from such because of much trouble and holy service. For he thought it best to abstain and he wished that all people would desire to do the same. By doing so, each one would not seek fornication nor the lusts of the flesh. Pay attention here. For you too must believe that he did not desire that the human race would ultimately cease and no one else be born. Then he would have misunderstood the phrase of the Lord and our friend would never have been, but only study himself by himself. Therefore let us place the one statement next to the other and see which weighs the heaviest, meditating frequently on what we have said about their meaning. Then it will sound well.

Further. Be that as it may, give attention now to the word that was written by Paul to the Philippians.[76] Namely, "I pray Euodia and I pray Syntyche to be one in the Lord. I certainly admonish you also, my true comrade sister or helpmate, help the women who together with me have come into the gospel." From this it is easy to observe how far [318ᵛ] it extends. For he names no one in this way except the one who carries and bears one yoke with him. For she, a sister, was a true helpmate or comrade. Behold. We should not doubt nor err regarding this.[77] I leave the learned to quarrel about it. I have received this from the Spirit in a living fashion. I therefore know that no one can deny me. The Lord be eternally praised.

Chapter 11

More is said here than can be understood by any of the words, but only those to whom it is given can understand. This was given to me, an unworthy, great sinner and a poor man, only by the grace of God and to his praise. For God has promised to reveal the concealed things only through a great, living, spiritual, clear light. By this the great ones will be humbled by the small ones, to his glory. And his wonderful acts will yet be seen by his almighty, powerful right hand. This must be in this way for a perfect purification. For this will not happen through those who are most respected. Behold.[78] Yes, pay attention to this. For it must happen through those who are as nothing.

Therefore, this must have been the meaning of Christ my Lord. There are some who in this way are born eunuchs inside, but not in the external flesh. But these are castrated in the inward, old roguish being, in its natural, titillating lusts. They have no work or looking to the flesh. Nevertheless, from nature they have food. Understand. For they are not made of wood [319ʳ] and stone. For they too grow and increase in their nature.

The second. Those who are castrated by humans. They have lost their ability or strength in natural lusts, but outwardly, in a nature different from the first. For these are castrated by human hands, and become like the beasts who without difficulty are without strength.[79] These ones are therefore without concern, for they are truly castrated. When a woman comes, they can proceed without struggling. For this reason they are chosen to be the king's bedroom attendants. These ones are also not wood, although they are like wood in that they are immovable and unconcerned. They do have (so that you can understand me without comprehension) nature in their loins and strength in their bones. Namely fatness, so that they are unfruitful and useless to marry. For they are ruined in their reproductive nature and are internally unmoved or unburdened by lusts. But all of this is still without praise and value from the Lord.

But the third are those eunuchs who have castrated themselves from lusts and who withhold from themselves the desires of the flesh. They therefore do not approach or take their wife except for the love of children. Observe that you now understand this well. They go to their wife not from the love of the flesh, nor from the lusts of the flesh, nor from the desires or burning of the flesh, but instead only from the love of the true Spirit, with lust in the Spirit and not a burning spirit; only for the sake of the breeding of healthy, blessed children, who are holy in their nature, just like Samson, Samuel, and John the Baptist.

These otherwise abstain in order to kill the lusts of the flesh, the old being in all its desires. Furthermore, they abstain in order to become completely [319ᵛ] dead in everything, and fight against the sinful lusts in which those who are living remain dead in the flesh. These ones instead purify themselves and become holy. They are the perfect in spirit, soul, and body, without wrinkle or spot. They become sincere virgins, maintained for the Lord. This is not done through the outward flesh, but only through the pure, tested, fiery heart. The Lord describes these ones as virgins or young maidens, as it is written. These are the ones who are not defiled with women, that is with the flesh [Rev. 14:3-4; 2 Cor. 11:2]. These alone will sing the new song. In them will be found no deception, nor will falsehood be found in their mouths. They are, I say, those who become worthy of the Lamb; pure of heart they follow after him. The King God will give the whole world in all its beauty to them, for they are internally pure of heart. Behold. It is uncontrovertible.

Chapter 12

Do you believe this refers to only those who do not have a wife? Where then will you find the 144,000 [Rev. 7:4]? In the entire Scriptures you will hardly find more than five or six, indeed not even that many, who had not been outwardly defiled by women. Behold indeed. For it is otherwise and just as we believe. But this word is not generally comprehended. For it is frequently read or heard only in the general sense and there are few who will accept it. Why? For if the humans or weed accept it, they remain in the life, their true life, [320ʳ] and truly kill lust, evil, and death. Yes, they kill the old being, much more splendidly and more gloriously than if they were physically killed by others, although this certainly costs flesh and blood. Here too their hands grasp their loins in pain on account of the old nature's evil and strife. Therefore, their crowns will be more valuable than those who have been physically killed or those who have not approached or handled women. Yes, in this way many more will be especially blessed above those who are killed, whom the fire has taken away and protected. But those who are left behind, these have the strongest works and faith. For although they are still alive, they are continually dying. By their faith they win over the world, death, the devil, and the flesh [Heb. 11:33]. Yes, make your own reckoning about this. Those who remain behind must fight against death, the last great enemy, which lies concealed in the flesh. It will eternally gnaw away at all those who do not win. Remember, then, what kind of death it will be; to go outside of life or to lose it and be preserved in the victory of the name of Jesus Christ [1 Cor. 15:54-57]. But here, I say, will great violence be done if they are castrated in order to enter the kingdom of God. Therefore, my beloved brothers, I pray, pray, so that you might comprehend and grasp it. The eunuchs in the flesh are an image of this and describe to us where the true basis lies concealed. Yes, these are the elect, spiritual, undefiled people, the new heavenly creature, [320ᵛ] the pure bride, the young children, the simple, innocent, straight, and sincere ones who alone will be found worthy. These will be the beloved ones of the kingdom of God and will possess all things. These will be able to return to the garden through the blood of the innocent Lamb Jesus Christ. Blessed are those who are clothed and whose shame or nakedness is covered [Rev. 3:18]. Behold indeed. For here will those who are the prominent of the Lord God of Hosts have their progress. This has been hindered by the devil from the beginning in Adam and Eve. Behold.

Blessed are those who are barren and undefiled, who have not mingled with sinners. They will have fruit in the presence of the holy souls. Blessed are the purified who have wrought no unrighteousness with their hands.[80] An unrighteous person is a poison to the righteous.[81] Prepare yourselves now to fight Esau or the flesh. Behold, do not oppose Jacob or the Holy Spirit. Judge not according to appearances. The heathen are regarded by the Lord as a drop in a full bucket.[82] Further. Are not all heathen against him? Indeed, he regards them as savages and outsiders.[83] Further. You have chosen Jacob, but Esau you have separated from you.[84] Further. You created the world for us, but the other heathen, born from Adam's seed, they are nothing, for they are likened to spittle.[85] And now, O Lord, behold, the heathen who are before you regarded as nothing (understand) have begun [321ʳ] to rule over and devour us. But we, your people, O Lord, whom you have called your firstborn, your only one, your dearly beloved, we are delivered into your hands. And if the world has been created for us why do we not possess the world as our heritage? How long will these things be?[86] Further. I will make an end of all the heathen, among whom I have scattered you. However, I will not make an end with you, says the Lord.[87] Further. Just like the refining of silver, you have purged all the godless from the portion of humanity upon the earth.[88] And further. The godless you have purged in this way, that no flesh be terrified from fear.[89]

Behold. "See, this is the judgment, that the light has come into the world and people love the darkness more than the light" [John

3:19]. And "behold, God separated the light from the darkness" [Gen. 1:4].

"Whoever does not believe in the Son will not see life, but the wrath of God abides on him" [John 3:36]. Yes, all are damned. "But whoever believes in him, he is not judged. But who does not believe is already judged" [John 3:18].

"Do not leave a wife and good woman who partakes with you in the fear of the Lord. If you have a wife according to your soul, do not cast her out, and do not trust the godless with all your heart."[90]

If I, David, have erred in understanding, or if I have written anything badly against the Spirit, then instruct me where I have done so. And teach me from the Spirit and with better truth, you who are humble and meek, pure of heart, and who have the perfect fear of the Lord.

The Building of the Church, 1537

This important missive from 1537 seems to have been sent to Joris's supporters near Oldenburg, Westphalia.[91] In it he describes how to establish a church, how believers were to love and support each other, and how to deal with several specific problems within the fellowship. These problems included the selection and authority of church leaders, whom he calls ministers, elders, teachers, pastors, and priests. With this letter it becomes evident that in 1537, Joris, along with other Anabaptist leaders, had a plan for church organization. In this issue he was most concerned that ordinary believers become submissive to the ordained leadership. Their other duty was to love and bear with each other.

As a corollary to the topic of mutual love, Joris deals with the question of financially supporting poor believers, and whether this ought to include the practice of community of goods. The original recipients of this letter were evidently in touch with the small remnant of the Münster kingdom which had found refuge in the territory of Oldenburg. One of the marks of the Münster kingdom under Jan van Leiden was of community of goods. It appears that, as in other issues, Joris sought a mediatory position on this topic.

Most interesting are his comments regarding Heinrich Krechting, identified as H.C., and his group of refugee Münsterites in the area. Krechting had been the chancellor of the Münster kingdom, but was one of a small number of Anabaptists who had been allowed to leave the city after it was recaptured by the Bishop of Münster's mercenary forces. For a time these Münsterites continued to plot a revival of the kingdom in the former city of God. Through 1537 Batenburg and Krechting conspired together to reestablish the kingdom in Münster in 1538, but Batenburg's execution in early 1538 put an end to these designs.[92] It is not surprising that Joris should communicate and occasionally cooperate with revolutionary Anabaptist leaders such as Krechting. Joris's main goal, after all, was to bring together the revolutionary and pacifist Melchiorite camps under his inspired leadership.

Possibly at the instigation of some of Joris's Westphalian supporters, a meeting was arranged between Joris and the Münsterite remnant for the spring of 1538. According to the anonymous biographer, before meeting with the Münsterites, Joris conferred with his own supporters in the region, conducting a general discussion of problems which had developed in the post-Münster Melchiorite community, especially regarding marriage.[93] Joris appears, therefore, to have been dealing with some of these same problems by missive even before he arrived in the region. While the discussion with the Münsterites proved only to provide a temporary agreement, it illustrates again Joris's widespread influence, which reached beyond the Dutch provinces and into Northern Westphalia.

○ ○ ○ ○ ○

[331ʳ]   # The Building of the Church
Chapter 1

The construction of the house of God, built on Mt. Zion, does not happen quickly, nor will it happen quickly. For the final house, temple, mountain, or city of God will be erected in honor, it will remain glorious, and nevermore be broken down nor destroyed. Observe it. For this reason it will happen in an amazing fashion, concealed from all flesh. For this construction and preparation will occur without the clanging noise of ax or hammer [1 Kings 6:7]. For it is to be done in the Spirit, which is opposed to the work of the flesh, world, devil, and death. So therefore it must happen shrewdly, concealed from the world and all flesh. Therefore, the Behemoth, the Leviathan, Satan, the devil, in whatever form, must be captured with his own eyes. His jawbone must be pierced with an awl, his nose bored through, and his tongue bound with a noose [Job 41:2]. Therefore, everyone who works on this house must make sure that they are wise, subtle, and shrewd, or understanding. For these are the favored ones who will have a part therein, who are not imprudent nor a hindrance through their lack of prudence. [331ʳ] Whether it is with words or works, let everyone watch their mouth and guard their tongue from questioning or saying anything to another which is not for instruction and improvement for the fear of the Lord. And allow them to know whatever is done is for their instruction, according to the will of the Lord. Everyone, moreover, be careful to do the will of God. For it has been written not just to know, but to do it.

So I command, that everyone be obedient and faithful to their Lord. Never, by lack of foresight or through lukewarmness, stop or hinder the work or will of God. Everyone apply themselves to quietness, morality, courtesy, modesty, and humility. Always look first to the Lord. Let your heart desire wisdom, and covet to know the best counsel, the best thing to do and when best to be silent, when to question or speak. Desire to do well, whether by remaining here or going there, according to the ordinance of God. So that we will not in any way remain in our egotistical pride and bring pain to the Lord. So that we will not transgress against the Lord, our Master or Teacher, whom we must hear or question. And in this way must all the elders teach their children, not doing it from themselves, but questioning first.[94]

Much blood has likewise been shed through lack of foresight, where one person has been guilty to another. Whether it is in words [332ʳ] or by unthought things, whatever has happened through egotism must happen no longer. For as in all other things, we must become prudent, perfect, faultless, and understanding. Do not remain like children, which only brings great sadness to the Lord or the Spirit and his servants. Do not keep running against each other. Do not call unnecessary meetings in which you have nothing to do. Do not be a burden to the others. Maintain yourselves in quietness and in a firm hope. Pray and watch always.

Chapter 2
So prepare your stones, namely, make your hearts level and straight. Become square and leveled, without flaws, without crack or blemish. Pay attention to this first. For when someone builds a house from expensive, hewn stone, one does not first build the stone walls or the framework. But first they are prepared, cut straight, planed level, prepared so that they will fit. Whatever does not fit must be removed before one can bring together the pieces so that they can be butted together. Pay attention.

Now therefore, O you stones, you believing hearts, allow your-

selves to be well hewn, cleansed, leveled and made fitting and square
by the masons. Behold, if you do not do this, then you will not be able
to have or maintain a place in the house of the Lord. [332ʳ] If you
were in the city of God, then you must leave it. If you do not arrange
yourselves next to the foundation stone, cornerstone, proofstone, and
valuable, elect cornerstone [1 Pet. 2:4-8], then you will have no place
in the pure, valuable work of God. Take notice of what you are hearing, therefore, and how you are progressing. Allow yourselves to be
constructed by the wise, without any murmuring. But pray for and
love them as you love yourselves, so that you will always obtain more
and more understanding, which will stick to you. Make sure that you
learn obedience, humility, and meekness. In this way they will be able
to administer their office with joy and not sighs [Heb. 13:17]. The
greatest honor which we can show to the others is obedience, humility, and meekness. All of you submit yourselves like children. If you desire to become adults, mature and grayheaded in the mind of God,
then heed what I say to you and let the elders who govern you well
look to you even more closely and more lovingly. If you have understanding, then you will receive their chastisement with joy, that is, if
you desire to become understanding, chosen and alive, pay attention
to what I am saying. Fulfill it in the fear of the Lord and do the best.
Submit to them and pray for them, this is the will of God. If you are to
submit yourselves under him, blessed, then you must honor his servants and ministers (who have been made priests or elders by the
Lord). If you believe God, then believe also his prophets, so that it be
well with you. Fear God with all your soul and keep his ministers in
great worth [1 Tim. 5:17]. Therefore, love with all your strength those
[333ʳ] who have made you, and do not abandon his ministers. Fear the
Lord with all your heart and soul, and honor the priests, and purify
yourselves with the poor.

Chapter 3

Furthermore, always make peace, maintain unity, and seek love.
For this is the fulfillment of the law and the prophets [cf. Matt. 22:39-
40; Rom. 13:8,10; Gal. 5:13-14]. Bear the burden or sickness of each
other and fulfill the law of Christ, for therein is hidden strength [Gal.
6:2]. Pay close attention to this. Always take care that you are found in
love, or you will not be able to stand in the great day of the Lord. If
your heart believes in God and if you love him, then you must also
love what God has created and what he desires to be done, especially
that love be perfected. People of the world love according to the

flesh, on account of their lusts, like whores and villains and thieves. While they love well, it is not a real work, for they still prefer to love those who love them, not in the manner here. For if it is to be correct, our lust must be transformed in the Spirit into love for the Lord, with all our heart and mind [Matt. 22:37]. This will produce fruit in our brothers. Again, not only for those who love us, for we must feel love for our enemies, those who contradict or oppose us [Matt. 5:43-44]. This must be fulfilled by those who believe and boast that they know God. Those who [333^v] have not done this from their hearts, who have not prayed thoroughly for our enemies (understand), have neither seen nor known him. For this reason become perfect in everything, including distribution of charity with a voluntary heart and an affectionate spirit. For God loves a cheerful giver [2 Cor. 9:7]. For this reason make your countenance joyful in all your gifts, and joyfully bless the Lord with your tithes. This must be fulfilled first. But after this each one will reap as he has sown [Gal. 6:7; cf. 2 Cor. 5]. For love is not based or hidden in kisses, nor in any external work, but in the heart. For such cannot be contained, but must radiate and shine. For what love does is completely pure, and acceptable, even when there are no gifts, for it is powerful [1 Cor. 13:8]. Stand in this and let it take you the right way.

Now you should give from a liberal and trustworthy heart, according to the ability of your heart. For in this you will be judged. Not that you should give nothing out of caution or miserliness. For now it is evident that all individual Christians bring together[95] their property and goods [Act 2:44-45]. But here you do evil when you think, "Here are enough goods, I want to have as much property as any other." In this way the flesh proceeds further, when you think "What if everyone who was in a bad state and in poverty should come?" Here comes pride, when you then think that it is not good, but of the devil. Those who have had such a miserly, avaricious, cautious, false self-love will thereafter not be seen with all [334^r] their possessions in the arrival[96] of the saints and the eternal, undefiled love of God. Therefore, give now before this time, and appear faithful and of a sincere nature. If you become poor on account of Jesus or righteousness, you will therefore be helped by the others. And if it should come to this, you will first receive by pieces and parts, such as one or two loaves of bread, one or a half cheese, two or three double stuivers.[97] Accept the gifts just as they are given; do not divide them. It is not to be given in any other way except through examination which is currently necessary, so that we will maintain ourselves much better. But our Lord and King of all kings, God himself, whose possession is the whole earth with all that is in it, wants us to support each other and be at peace. Put them aside. But it is not good if any have money or possessions and know that their brothers are in need, yet close their heart and do not do this out of love or with unconcerned desire [1 John 3:17]. Your heart must first be purified (to question, find, seek, and not to flee from each other), completely cleansed, and renewed in this. Thereafter will the poor be completely assembled and come to one heart, become like David's heart which was found to be according to God's heart [1 Sam. 13:14; Acts 13:22]. Namely, become humble, meek, and patient toward each other. Bear and suffer with each other. Love each other with your whole heart and spirit which will be given to you. What you would do to the Lord, even so [334ʳ] do this to your brothers in everything [Matt. 25:40]. Each one be brought to unity, like one person, one holy temple, one dwelling or crown of God. For they must be constructed upon the old capital city, which was founded at the beginning of the world according to the image of God. In this will stand the temple of the Spirit, as it ought to stand, and this city will never be torn down, which is prepared and constructed in this way [Rev. 21:2-3]. This is a certain, true word from the Lord through his Spirit, and given to you as a sign. For this reason all of you hasten and prepare yourselves, all who have given themselves up to the obedience of faith. Woe to those who do not desire this, for they will remain bastards and not children, being without chastisement or the instruction of wisdom [Heb. 12:5-8]. They will moreover be reckoned with the dead church [Rev. 3:1]. Take heed.

Chapter 4

O all of you become understanding and sincere in yourselves, and do everything for the Lord. Become modest, brave, and wise in everything. Do not follow anyone else's faith if you are not able to perfect it in your heart. But live your faith, whether it is strong or sick, little or much. Understand yourselves; be brave, strong and certain. Neither fight nor corrupt yourselves with [335ʳ] the others. Do not corrupt the Lord your God through your sin, but walk in love and in the fear of the Lord, with chastity and meekness [Eph. 5:2].

It is still the Lord's pleasure that everyone submit themselves and stand in obedience. Do nothing except by the approval and consent of those who are lords, heads, and patrons. Let no one remain any longer dissolute in the devil's cares. For if you submit yourselves in humility and place yourselves under the obedience, then you will be able to win your own soul. Pay attention to this. For to this were you called, chosen, made free. Furthermore, examine those among you, so that those who are the best, fittest, and strongest will be selected as your ministers, according to the ordinance of Paul [cf. 1 Tim. 3:1-10; Tit. 1:5-9] and with the advice of our brother, H.C.

Let this happen peacefully, and be ordained by the faithful pastors and not by the congregation[98] because of roguishness. Do you hear this well? It must be in this fashion. Woe to him who contradicts this, he will lament it. Do it in this way among you, you men and pastors. You women who have not been examined in the approved deed, keep quiet, for you do not know how or what [1 Cor. 14:34-35; 1 Tim. 2:11-12]. But admonish everyone to progress in the fear of God, and to abide in peace, so that they will not question or speak, as was written before of this.

Hereafter, you who are competent and chosen, do everything to become pure, to be brought to unity according to the will of God. And then [335ᵛ] the mountain of the Lord will be established by God at his time, and the city of God will stand as a praise and laud upon the earth [Isa. 2:2-3]. See, the beloved shall surely come out into the garden to look at the blossoms of the shrubs and to see if the vines bloom and if the pomegranates are growing [Song of Sol. 6:11; 7:12]. Yes, it will come quickly upon those who are not found ready, and they will never be found prepared or fit in eternity. O pay close attention. The time of the sinners draws near. Therefore, seek humility and righteousness, being protected from harm and shame. Seek, seek, yes, seek while he can still be found and call upon him while he is nearby [Isa. 55:6]. Remember this. In particular, that no one continue or begin with the children or youths without first asking the elders, who have the wisdom, understanding, and the trained senses. Therefore, you subjects must pray eagerly for your pastors and teachers. And you who have been called or led as elders and pastors, do not be proud, but fear the Lord. Answer the inquiry of your neighbor or others, if you have the knowledge. But if not, put your hand upon your mouth. Do not be ashamed of this. Furthermore, let the Lord have all the honor and praise, for he alone is wise. And make use of the wisdom, knowledge and understanding of his true ministers, in order to instruct, rule, or serve his people. Whoever prays for this without doubting will receive it, and know what he should do or answer. Do it now in this way. It is God's will. Pay close attention.

Through Krefting, in the year 1537,
from Delft.[99]

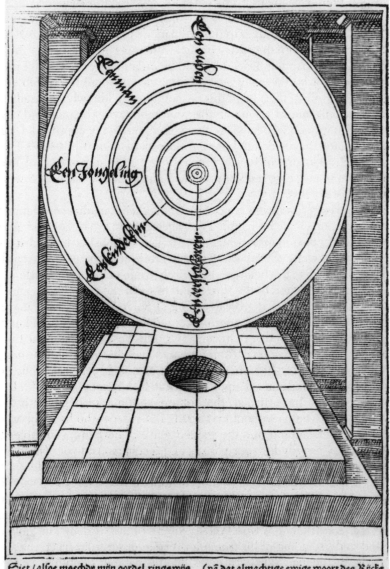

David Joris, "How One Can Perceive the Spirit's Mind,"
The Wonder Book, Part II, fol. 196r.
Courtesy of the Mennonite Library, University of Amsterdam

7

The Strasbourg Disputation, 1538

As seen in the "Response to Johannes Eisenburg," there were major differences of opinion between Joris and the Melchiorite leadership in Strasbourg. Attempts to resolve these by letter or by the mediation of others had ended in failure, so an official debate was called for Strasbourg shortly after Pentecost (June), 1538. The record of the debate, known as the "Disputation" ("Twistreden"), survives in manuscript form in the Basel *Jorislade*. It may have been published or intended for publication, although no example of a printed version has survived. Even as a manuscript, however, it is one of the most important documents for understanding the mental state of Dutch Anabaptists in general and Joris in particular in the crucial years 1537 and 1538. Its importance was noted by Roland Bainton, who excerpted portions of it in his 1937 study of Joris.[1] Fortunately for the researcher, and this translator, the full document has recently been edited as part of the Strasbourg Anabaptist sources.[2] The translation here is based on this modern critical edition and follows its pagination.

The "Disputation" was originally edited by one of the more important Strasbourg Melchiorites, Peter Tasch, based on the notes of the meeting transcribed by Leonard van Dam for the Davidites and Paulus Goldsmith for the Strasbourg leaders. Some parts were added afterwards from memory by Tasch. While not completely happy with the finished product, Joris added his signature to those of the other participants. The document is therefore considered generally reliable, although Joris's later critical comments are discovered in the margins of this manuscript version, copied from the original by Joris's secretary, Henrich van Schor around 1543.[3]

The vigorous give and take of the discussion reveals more clearly than any other source not only Joris's conception of himself, but also Melchiorite reaction to his ideas. Participants in the debate itself included on one side the educated Melchiorites such as Tasch (van Geyen) and Johannes Eisenburg (Jan Pont or Pontmacher), and the prophets Leonard Jost and Barbara Rebstock. On the other side were Joris and his traveling companions who included Leonard van Dam and Jorien Ketel. Peter (Petrus) Glassmaker and Jan Matthijs van Middelburg (leader of the Dutch Melchiorite refugees in England), who had earlier attempted to mediate an agreement, were also present. While the main issue to be discussed concerned the leadership claims of Joris, the discussions that followed (the debate itself lasted three days) touched also on the questions concerning spiritual perfection, confession of sins and marriage. Evidently Joris fully expected all Dutch Anabaptists to submit to his religious authority and to gather around him in building the kingdom of God. In his opening remarks he affirmed that he had made the difficult journey only to warn the conference participants that "the day of the Lord is very near" and that they must heed his teaching before the final judgment. It seems evident that, among other things, Joris sought the stamp of approval for his leadership claims from the Strasbourg Melchiorites, assuming that their approval would provide him with the authority of the imprisoned Melchior Hoffman himself.

✿ ✿ ✿ ✿ ✿

Disputation

[162] How David Joris proceeded with Melchior Hoffman[4] and others at Strasbourg.

Foreword of the Dispute.

Foreword to the proceedings of the meeting which occurred at Strasbourg between David Joris and Jan Pont, Peter van Geyen, Peter Glassmaker,[5] Paulus Goldsmith,[6] Hendric in Flanders[7] and many others. [163]

In order that a little of the following meaning be better understood, I will briefly set forth for the Christian reader the basis or reason for these events.

It happened that at the end of 1536, about three or four weeks before Christmas, David Joris received a revelation from the Spirit above. And in the revelation he received the basis, doctrine and instruction by which to come to the perfection and maturity of the Spirit. Above all, to the edification of the church which is the good and holy purpose, just as is known by many. This doctrine and admonition he had to proclaim in Germany, England and Frisia, to the three regions. This must proceed more and more as an admonition to everyone who desires their salvation and the way of life of the perfection or maturity in the Spirit.

And see, it happened, that I, David, sent two letters here to Strasbourg in the beginning of 1537 where they were a little corrected and improved.[8] But they regarded them as false and devilish because their understanding and Barbara's were opposed to them.[9] This was said through a woman Barbara, who in her dreams, visions and words they hear and believe as they do God. But I did not know this at the time, for they gave me no answer.

After this they received two or three printed booklets, also a long letter on marriage, and a booklet written on marriage against a booklet of Hans Eisenburg, made by Melchior Hoffman.[10] This and more other things they received through Petrus Glassmaker and Jan Matthijs.[11] Quickly many complaints and lies spread about, although I received no answer for all my letters and books. So much so, that Peter believed that if I were to go to them in Strasbourg, or they to me, then they would proceed with and instruct me in such a way that I would indeed find it differently and I would be able to speak just as I have proclaimed. They said more similar words. This soon expired, and I believed that if they were earnest, then they would have instead come to me to correct any errors I may have made, since I had written and admonished them so strongly.

In summary, Peter finally had done so much, that although anyone could have come to me from them, such did not happen. But Jan Matthijs was finally sent to me, or he came on his own, however it may be. This one wanted to dispute with me and set the matters straight, but he was either not able to do such or was not allowed to level the high matters of God. He regarded the differences between us two as insignificant. I regarded him too small and too hasty and too fast of feet, not wise enough for it.

Thus I have written you that I am prepared to come personally and to respond or testify before all the teachers and wise ones about the things which I have written. But, when I wrote before, I indicated how those who desire to be able to judge God's matters must be fit.

In this way I required of them all, yes, swore them to it in Jesus (which they did not allow), that if they loved the church,[12] to show me the truth from the Spirit or [165] from above, about those things which were false or devilish or any doctrine which was misleading and impure. But they did not agree to come to me, although such a meeting would have happened much better than rashly bidding others to gather together. I would prefer that they meet alone and then write me a short answer or five or six letters, about what they desired to do. But this did not happen, but they returned and transmitted everything to me without giving me an answer.

And so I complained about this, that it was of little worth, it was not proper, etc. See, finally Peter let me know that if I would travel to Strasbourg, they would request all the others to meet there. They hoped perhaps even Melchior Hoffman would attend also. It was said to me in this way at someplace.

In summary, I have for this reason traveled to you not without danger and at great expense, although I had little mind for it. All in order that I might know further, if you stood upon Melchior and desired to do nothing apart from him. In summary, the Lord impelled me to it in the midst of a vision, in which I saw that the end and the Day of the Lord is very close. See, I must therefore come here to testify with my mouth and admonish them still once more, so that they will be without innocence. See, I have come here with them this afternoon, and you have received me and the two who are with me, Leonard and Jorien, with a friendly hand. From this time you began to speak with us, as has been heard in part here.

But these words, which were spoken in the afternoon, were not written down, except those written from memory as Peter van Geyen could remember some days later. I was not completely at peace about this, but they desired that one should indeed write them down. Moreso, after it had been written down from memory, they desired that it should remain so, with or without my agreement. One may hear about this, for more should have been written between or in the lines. But in the middle of the last section, during which I had carried much [of the discussion], I sought only to have an end. I allowed their claims and did their will, but as something irksome. For it could not be otherwise, whether it had only a partial beginning or a conclusion, or none at all. So it has happened, I do not lie to you.

The contents of our proceedings are briefly summarized here, regarding what they desired to hear from me, why I came and what I had to say to them [166] in chastisement. I answered briefly with this meaning, along with other long speeches.

I have come, so that one may teach and say to me, where I am in evil or error. And this was written to me by Berent van Deventer[13] who said through others that I should come and teach. Had I done so at that time, then there would not have been half as many words (I believe) as now. But I had known the basis of their spirit, love and statements. I was not pleased that they would be shamed by me before the others. I had intended to capture them in their own bravery and ingenuity. But I did not do this because of true love. For I desired to show them the kind of heart necessary for us to come together, before they can judge or ridicule the aforementioned. For they must know and feel their age, their ways, their spirit, work and understanding; only then could the business proceed better, without fighting or quarreling. I thought this, that the matter would happen in a very pure, fine, and right way. But with such wisdom I knew well, that one must receive much knowledge and understanding from above. But alas, it would not be according to my wish, will, spirit and pleasure. Satan had too great a hearing; there was so little simplicity and unity or good faith, that good was received as bad. Because of this they raised many questions and reasons, but only to interrogate me, not to give answers. I was forced to maintain their first answers and teaching in the things which I still did not understand. Nevertheless, they did not receive or touch the teaching, for they did not regard or believe me to be sincere. Therefore I could not speak with them. For this reason the long matter came, yes, through this. For I spoke or taught them, but they did not believe me. I questioned them, but they did not answer me, but neither would they let me go freely from here.

It therefore happened like this, it truly occurred without error. Now believe most of all the Spirit over both sides, whoever has desire to read.

Dispute at Strasbourg.

Peter van Geyen first wrote and let know the following in brief:[14] [167] In the first place, Jan Pont thanked God about his coming, namely of David's coming. He then related how he promised several times in his writings, books, letters and through good friends, to come to us, and that he professed to desire our judgment and would be pleased to hear it. Thereafter Jan Pont answered that the idea of responding in writing was not actually his, but it came to him first through these friends, namely Paulus and Peter, that one should write David himself. To our knowledge this is how it happened, otherwise we would have done as little or much with the gifts of God given to us, by God's grace, and not to be silent on the smallest point. Brothers,

188 / *The Anabaptist Writings of David Joris*

Jan Pont said further,[15] since this is the situation, it is therefore much better to hear you in person than in many writings. Therefore it is our desire, that you will briefly relate again the summary which was composed in books. Then fraternally instruct us or speak to us in those things which you have higher gifts than us, and lead us by this way to our need. We will hear it thankfully and deliberate to our best ability, by God's grace, and even to receive it.[16] Above this, Peter van Geyen and Jan Pont asked David what moved him or was laid upon him to come such a long way to us. Or to what end he himself reckoned it.

David answered: You ask me the reason why I came to you. You must already know what kind of spirit it is, that it is clearly a great love that took up such a long, arduous journey to you here. Consider this among yourselves. But see, I had to come here because of the fear of the Lord as well as on account of love for you. So much so, that even if it cost a hundred guilders, and I did not have it, I would have produced or raised it by some means so that I could come to you unhindered and not stay behind. For I have to fulfill the cause of my [168] Lord to you and the office of my God wherein I stand, according to my ability and to the best that I know. For the end of all perishable things and the great terrible day has come near, yes nearer than anyone thinks or believes. So I must warn you fraternally, whether you believe me or not. Yes, believe me, brothers, that I would not take even ten times 100,000 guilders of gold, yes the whole world's treasure, in place of this thing, or before I would forego the time which I journeyed. This is how valuable I regard the time at hand, which now exists just as I, and indeed we all, have observed it. For to me and to all the righteous, one year has become one month, day, yes one hour. In this way one can pray for and receive from the Father as much in one hour than what we before could obtain in one year, therefore observe the time truly.[17]

Brothers, do you think it is appropriate, that one should begin so bluntly in handling such great matters of God? For is it not proper, that in order to prepare us for it (since you are all brothers), we should first meet together with a good mind and will in prayer, and earnestly call and cry from our hearts to God our Father, that he might open your eyes to the Spirit or to understanding, so that you can understand me with meekness?

Do you think this is right and good, or not?

Though even before this can occur correctly, you must first know how you can become fit and predisposed to prayer in order correctly to find or understand the fear of the Lord in its beauty. Without this we will receive nothing from the Lord, nor will he hear us. For I know, that not only do you not have it all, but even what you have, you do not know it correctly. See, I know what I say and I am certain. Pay attention. For I know where you stand, for I previously stood there also. Therefore I know now from the Spirit, who has given me to see.[18]

O brothers, I know indeed that you do not yet understand me. [169] What I have to say to you concerns the fear of God. The Spirit has blessed it. O, would that you not become embittered with me, nor wrathful, nor despise my youth nor harden your hearts. For I speak to you from love and from the fear of the Lord, my God.

O, if you would bear it. See, I would gladly (believe me) bow to you, if only you had clear eyes and the fatherly understanding. For my eyes are not able to see lofty things, nor is my heart proud, but I am small of strength [Ps. 131:1]. But first it must be called for in prayer and obtained with a humble, fallen, mournful heart, as from those who are poor of spirit [Matt. 5:3], and found as nothing.

Jan Pont: Yes, we are without doubt inclined of heart to cry to the Lord, and we daily seek to do it, and having previously and currently done so, we desire to do so still. We observe that you also have done so. But we are not agreed that doing so again here is good.

David: O, I wish that you were like this, although I know that you have prayed and also cried many times. But I know also that you have not prayed correctly, in the way that it must be among us. For you still do not know what I know, and I say it to you freely out of brotherly love. You must examine your hearts to your own profit; not from pride, as if I would know of it. No, that is far. Pay attention.

It is true that you have cried, just like you said, but have you prayed with tears to the Lord because of your damnation? And have you become anxious in such a way, that when you sought the Lord from your hearts your blood turned to water? Have you let go of your own well-being, just as it is fitting? O dear brothers, is it not necessary for us to bear such suffering, until our hands shall come upon our loins and to nothing? Yes, to dust, earth and ashes, or become entirely crushed in the flesh before one can or shall receive the fear of the Lord in its power? This relates to those who incline their eyes and heart to understanding, and struggle to become foresighted. Who in this way, on account of wisdom, I say, call and seek God's knowledge, just like one would for silver and gold. They work in this way to perfection, hungering and thirsting to righteousness [Matt. 5:6]. They shall find it first and be worthy to receive it.

Now I know well, what you might say to me: Do we not seek wisdom more than silver and gold, have we not let go of all that? O, you dear people, I know and confess all of this well, how it has happened. I know [170] what I say to you, but still you do not understand me, this I must say. But do not embitter yourselves against me, on your own account. For you do not understand, since I know, of what I speak and mean.

Peter van Geyen: Now you say you know that we do not understand and therefore must first pray for understanding. Further you say that before the true prayer to God can occur, we must first learn better what the fear of the Lord is. That is, to learn knowledge and understanding in its beauty, so that our prayer will go before God in a pleasing fashion, and be truly received. Let us say this is the case, that we do not know fundamentally any of this, just like many other things that we do not understand, for our understanding is still small. Therefore we desire that you will teach us the knowledge of the things which you understand better than us. For we are prepared to listen diligently and to learn submissively.

David: Berent and others have informed me that I should come and I would be allowed to instruct and teach. Therefore I will instruct you out of love for you. But before this can happen, there are conditions to be met, since my teaching is said to be of the devil. In order that you not judge lightly, I have desired to open your hearts before you, so that you can perceive the way in which you still stand, forgetting your age, however old, and be thoroughly examined. You should know that a child has a child's mind [1 Cor. 13:11] to judge lofty things and hence does not understand. And therefore heed what I say to you. It is better to think, not that you will teach and thus refuse to listen, but that you will pray to God that your mind be opened. For I say to you, that you must also know how one is able to go to God in prayer, before it can be done. This I say to you as a precaution, so that we can be better united. This does not mean that I will teach you the knowledge of truth and the fear of the Lord before you are able, even if you will trust me as a servant of the Lord. Is this possible? If this is true, I will speak, otherwise, not. For if you do not believe me, how can I then teach you?[19] [171]

O, how am I able to speak to you all? To relate the fear of the Lord with all its branches and sprouts, which sprout forth in such manifold and innumerable ways? But I may, however, by the grace of the Lord, speak of it incompletely, as is given to me to do. For the Lord has taught me therein. I am daily still more and more richly instructed in the Spirit of power with understanding, so I know how I should proclaim to you with my tongue. How can I do this? For I know that you will not understand me in the things in which I am able, not to mention those things in which I do not have the ability. For example, you must remove your own wisdom and set it completely in the dust, become nothing and perceive yourselves to be poor of spirit. For I know that you are rich and your heart is still proud. Therefore, in order for me to speak in a fundamental fashion concerning the fear of the Lord in measure and grace, I must be given the complete freedom to speak to you.

(Here rests the meaning.) I must put forth my spirit so deep and high, and speak forth with words so wide, that you will just think it foolishness. It will be as if I have become childish on account of the words, as has happened often to me. For I have sometimes spoken in half words, although I took them entirely seriously. I thought they had understood me well, because it was so clear and living to me. O, if all grass and leaves upon the earth had eyes and hearts, mouths and tongues, and could praise and testify with me of the Lord's grace which is given to me [Ps. 96:11-12]. I speak as the Lord impels me to speak and I desire indeed that all of my words be written down just as they come forth. For I know that I will stand before the Lord, to account for whether I have spoken them correctly to you. But it is not I, but the Lord who works in me. I regard myself as a black earth through which runs a clear fountain.[20]

Brothers, do you think it right as I do, for I too must endure this, that our bodies be given rest until morning? For our bodies are fatigued with travel, to such an extent that the spirit is hindered and we might speak hastily of the high matters of God. It is true that we do not have much time; you know better what our situation is here. This is truly our desire. If, however, you do not agree, we will do it to the best of our ability.

There was generally this response: Yes, since the matter and opportunity was requested in this way, so we will not refuse it, etc.[21] [172]

In this way the meeting was adjourned to the following morning, when they were to come together again after reminders to diligence, in order to further the proceedings.

The First Day.

Jan Pont: In the name of the Lord and to his praise, please continue where we left off yesterday, in order to speak with even more words.

David: Have you, brothers, considered well and thought over my words of last night, whether they were from the Spirit of God or from the devil? For I am not of a mind to dispute with you, nor have I come for this, but to admonish you and to set before you as correct what I have written to you. That is, as far as they have been correctly printed, for in the books and letters some things may have been missed by the printer or writer. But if you have anything from me which is against God and the truth, then reveal it to me.

Jan Pont: You ask us, if we have considered well the words of yesterday. We believe yes, that we have taken them to heart. For we desire to know what is necessary for us, if the same spirit is from God. Therefore the first point is justified. Whatever serves the common admonition, whatever may lead to wisdom, chastity and the fear of God, this we confess to be right. For this is the approved spirit of the apostles and prophets, as is revealed. But that we, as a result of these words or principles concerning discipleship which you have explained, must give an answer before we have even heard them correctly, this we cannot do. For examination must proceed.

David: I mean, that if you had understood the spirit of my words correctly, then you would have answered easily. But now I know that you have not truly grasped it, nor understood it even basically. I know what I say, for the same Spirit who impels, disciplines, teaches and leads me to the perfection of God is not confessed nor grasped by you in everything. How can you then understand me? For you first must let yourselves be instructed like children by the spirit of lowliness and simplicity (understand) in the fear of God, letting your own spirit depart, before you can correctly understand the words of the Spirit or God, [173] not to mention to receive the kingdom of God.

(At this the people answered, do you think you have it all?) David answered: See, I proclaim here the Spirit and testify it to be from God. To him be praise for his grace. Therefore you people have heard God's voice. Observe that you do not harden your hearts, nor that you become embittered against me through the evil inspiration of Satan.

Therefore I admonish you to hear his voice. Do not let your hearts become embittered. Hear what I say to you and behold what you now do.

Jan Pont: That we must first let ourselves stand under examination we do not find nor consider correct. It is therefore a long fight now. And because we have not yet understood it to be right (as you say), so it is our need to know what you mean by it. Furthermore, we require the same Spirit's clarification, for do you mean, that we must let go of all the understanding that we have learned through the Scriptures, or through Melchior Hoffman or others, that we must let all of that fall? We do not know what your meaning is concerning this.

David spoke to Leonard Jost, who sat next to him: The Lord gives wisdom to the little ones and understanding to the innocent or simple ones (not to those who are double or egotistical of heart) [Matt. 18:4].

Leonard Jost: This is true. The Lord has given me much, which I understood little at the time. But through the help of the brothers it has been opened or released to me, and the Lord gives me daily still more.[22]

David spoke to Jan Pont: Do you allow me to answer? I say this, that yesterday you made a bad decision about him (there was much that happened that remained unwritten) and this must offend the Lord. Lord, be not moved to wrath, for when anyone offends him [i.e., Jost], it is only through childish thinking. I will not amuse you, my brothers, about him. That is far from me. But this I say to you, that God's Word, the fountain of wisdom, does not lie in the literal letter, but in the deed and power; this Word is fiery, eternal and living. It is not to be understood by anyone except those who have cast away their own wisdom and are poor of spirit, [174] for the Word of God is given to the little ones, understanding to the innocent, and to no one else. Is this not so?

Jan Pont answered: Yes.

David: So David desires, as does Leonard Jost, to hear about what he did not understand, that they would explain it to him, so that he, who has the Spirit of God, might know what was said of him on the first day at noon.

Jan Pont said to Leonard Jost: Our brother David said, that we had spoken unwisely of you yesterday, as if you did not have enough clear understanding or wisdom, and so could not judge in our matter, as a result of education in the Scriptures or of intelligence.

So this was the matter why we explained that you have the gift of God of prophecy and the fear of God and love (also more than all of us), but you do not have the gift of speech, nor of interpreting differences or contradictions in the Scriptures, nor in understanding the meaning of the language. This is what we said about you yesterday, simply put, not to despise you, but to do justice to your submissiveness[23] of spirit. Therefore whatever happened afterwards was in good intention, and so it has proceeded in love.

David spoke to Leonard Jost: I said yesterday, that my spirit and your spirit gloried at the first witness. Therefore I desired to speak with you. For I know that you have the fear of the Lord, and wisdom and understanding, so that they also should not be tempted (even though they remain therein), just like I also asked them. This was my word and meaning, why I came to you, because I had desired to speak with you and suspected that you, more than all of them, could understand me, because you did not have knowledge in the letter. For I have also given up the letter, I have felt the Spirit of truth in my hands, now that I have found God's grace. For the Spirit alone shall abide, lead and teach me well in all truth.

(Here was a little more spoken, but it was not written).

David spoke further to Jan and Peter, who had said that they understood him well. He asked: Then it is my desire that you briefly recount my position for a little, to see if you have understood me, as you say, and then I will answer you. For I suspect, that you have not understood it as well as you say you do. In particular, you have not understood my basis nor the foundation of my meaning, even though you have prayed over it, yet you still err.

To this they gave no answer, but questioned and spoke quietly to each other, and did other things not to be mentioned here.

David spoke: You are not of the meaning, I mark well, if your [175] spirit brings nothing forth. Therefore I have proven that you have not understood my spirit, I give you up to ignorance.

See, this is the meaning of the Spirit, who teaches and impels me, about what you must do first. If you want to speak of God's Word, so you must know, what God's Word, wisdom and understanding are. You must know your age and birth, see where you stand, and understand how far you have gone and have yet to go. This same you must know, for you certainly know that a person is not born first as an adult, but as a child; this child enters into the first schooling. But the child must improve and leave behind the childish understanding, as is written [1 Cor. 13:11]. For to him, there is no difference between good and evil, light and darkness, pure and impure. Therefore he must let himself be taught by his elders, to forgo this childish nature. Otherwise he cannot please the Lord. For it must die, even if it were a hundred years old, as far as the time is given that they might come to perfection, ascending from the one virtue to the next, from the one clarity to the next, until the perfect full-grown maturity of Christ. Yes, this shall and must be so. You cannot remain in the forecourt of the fight, or our teaching shall err. If you have now understood me, then you will be able to answer me with only a few words. But many stories from the letter do not help, for there are many meanings therein, pay attention to this. For these words are not from me, but were spoken from the Spirit of my Lord, who impels me. Behold.

Jan Pont: Ascending and progressing are nothing new for us to hear about, but we have been taught well and understood them from the old foundation of the prophets and apostles. But what is your meaning about the means of progression, how one is to progress? This let us know.

David: Hear, brothers. Some had written to me that I should come here to Strasbourg where I would be allowed to instruct, along with other similar words; now I am here, so I speak freely, as the Lord gives me to speak.

Since you here then are the elders in Israel, so I believe, if you understand me, you should instead instruct me in those things in which I have spoken badly. For you do not do such, following daily usage or doctrine, but you question me. See, in the godless thoughts shall the questioning be [Wis. of Sol. 1:9]. And since you are always questioning me, so it seems modest to me to ask you now, [176] if what I have spoken to you (I say) up to now, both yesterday and today, is from God or from the devil, or if there is anything that I have handled unreasonably with you. For what I have written to you, you have not heard nor will you receive it as good, but you regard it as from the devil.

Jan Pont: Have you let go of the letter? From where do you speak the word then, "the inquiry shall be in the godless thoughts"?

David: Have you grasped well the word, my brothers? This word is my escape.

Jan Pont: How do you then understand the word, namely, "in the godless thoughts," etc., in the spirit or letter? For sometimes the God-fearing are questioned sharply with diligence. Also the word of Wisdom of Solomon 1[:9] does not maintain your meaning, that one is therefore godless if one asks many questions, but that God shall interrogate the thoughts of the godless in order to judge them.

David: I speak from the Spirit, which I have. Read Malachi in the second and third chapters, how the Lord afterwards was questioned.[24]

For you must find this same mind, just as I have spoken it. But you have no intention of answering, for you, above all, insist on being right. Therefore, however you understand it, I must affirm that you will receive all my words with a false meaning. I have not said that you are godless, but that things are not as they ought to be with you. That is my meaning and admonition.

Jan Pont: We will not dispute on account of the letter. For the word of Wisdom of Solomon is not so understood.

David: The Lord gives fatherly understanding.

Jan Pont: I repeat, by witnesses shall such words stand. We will answer from the common admonition and Scriptures, and if you are happy to give weight to the words of the Spirit, then allow us the balance in the words of Scripture. You said, we should answer or teach you. It [177] was concluded previously by you that we do not understand. We therefore desire to be enlightened on all things. But you alienated us, since you regard us as fools in need of interrogation. We therefore desire to hear from you, and then we will rest. Thus, we desire humbly an answer from your spirit. For we hope to have no disunity in the Christian life. But we do not have understanding in everything that is in your books, letters and words.

David: If you understood me and knew this voice, then I could have said it to you briefly. Or, if I were strong enough to discuss it with many words. But because of imperfection I cannot easily express the words fluently or without stumbling.[25] Although it was made possible for me to do it, you, however, required me to speak with a mouthful of Scriptures, because you speak out of the letter and I out of the Spirit.

How then can I speak to you and you to me (since you do not believe me), so that we understand each other? But now I ask you, do you know well what the fear of the Lord is? I desire indeed that you answer me with a summary.

Jan Pont: I do not know what this turning and turning again means. Why do you not tell us what it is that you say we do not understand? For we desire to know what the fear of the Lord is, and how one should pray, and what is the way of the Lord.[26]

David: Why do you not answer me? See, this is my foundation. I rejoice in the words that you spoke, that you are humble and desire to hear me. If I then ask you, will you accept me as a servant of the Lord, just as I must regard you, will you hear and learn as one who stands outside the covenant? If you will believe me in this, then I will speak to you as the Lord, not any person or letter, has taught me. For these words will not nor cannot be confirmed by external things. For these same things which were revealed to me will be revealed afterwards. If, however, you will gladly hear what I say to you, then I know you will come to perfection. Pay attention.

Therefore I ask you, brothers, that you take to heart the foregoing, which you confess to be the truth, about how one who goes to the Lord [178] to pray can know the fear of the Lord. If you demand to know such from me, then you must believe me, and say so. But since you have the reputation, then you give me an answer, so that I may believe. For I say to you, the knowledge of what to say was given to me, by grace, for the hungering or needy souls.

Jan Pont: All faith stands on truth and reason. Therefore prove your pretensions, then we will believe. But faith without reasonableness merely falls to the ground. We have previously accepted Melchior Hoffman and several others only after examination. If we are now to believe you, you must instruct us more reasonably in the truth, as previously all truthful spirits have done. Those things which you have brought forth from other sources, of which we have not heard, must stand upon reasonableness, so that we might ascend higher with you.

David: You should know that I have a great burden to bring you, for I see your innermost thoughts and what it is you seek with me. You know that a child never understands his elders. For this reason, how can I give the judgment of those things about which I must speak to you? For if it is neither understood nor believed, then how can I speak with you? Therefore I do not know how I should begin to instruct you. The Lord must give you great perception and understanding. I ask you first, since you are teachers, have you fulfilled or kept Christ's promises? Or are you proceeding on the road, having taken and eaten your daily bread [Matt. 7:3]?

Jan Pont: The question requires not only a general, but also a specific answer. For as we have the ability, we have followed after. But when, because of the weakness of the flesh and the deceitful serpent, there has occurred anything to our harm, then we have an advocate, Christ Jesus. Though I say in general, that of all things known and certain to us, human shortcomings have done us much harm.

David: Brothers, there is much to say about this, yes, as much as the Spirit gives me, more than anyone is able to write with the pen. See, in his principle Christ counselled us to leave ourselves [John 3:3]. Understand that we must learn from him humility, meekness, obedience, lowliness or nothingness. Now I ask, have you taught and understood all of this well? If not, then learn from me in his name. For you know, that there is no other wisdom than humility, and no other understanding than meekness and patience. And see, if you have or desire this, then I can speak with you. All people must always confess this principle to be true. Do you desire that I speak further? [179]

(As there was silence, David spoke further):

See, this much will I say to you, that you are not able to have this except through much suffering, strife and ordeal. But these things are not with you, as you are still blind and ignorant before God and grope about with your hands just like those who stumble in midday [Isa. 59:10]. For I say to you, sin is the means which separates us from our God, so that he cannot hear us, regardless of how much we pray and call to him with beautiful sounds.

(For this reason—if you desire to learn from me—I will hold up the mirror before your eyes, look at it. For otherwise in three days my meaning and word will not be answered by you.)

I therefore will ask: Do you now know well the fear of the Lord—humility, meekness, longsuffering, friendliness, mercy, chastity, truth, simplicity and innocence? Even more, do you have them? Give me now an answer.

After they had been silent for a long time, Barbara interrupted, which caused a disorder. She prevented the answer which they were now supposed to give. But she began to speak in this fashion, that we will indeed stand before the Lord, and that the brothers or church must not allow anything to be written down here unless it will be to their honor. It was their desire that she be allowed to speak. She asked: Might I too speak a word? For my spirit impels me.

Jan Pont: Yes, since the Spirit impels you, why should you not speak?[27]

Barbara spoke: I will proceed as the Lord has uttered to me. I think that some who are here desire to pluck the fruits of our tree before they are ripe. Therefore the Lord warns us that no one speak further, for they will account for it. [180]

David: Do you speak this by the Lord?

Barbara: I am compelled to do so.

David spoke to the brothers: I ask you if I have spoken against the truth. Give me an answer. I ask you, Barbara, if you know indeed what I have said and if you understand me.

Barbara: No, I firmly believe that it is still necessary to talk further about it. For we have been of the fear of the Lord for over ten years, do you believe that we are godless?

David: Now I can say that you have not spoken from the Lord, but from the devil. For you have interrupted our speeches here and have thus disturbed the Spirit (by hindering the answer). For in this manner good has not spoken to good, on account of those who sit next to her.

Jan Pont: At this point Jan Pont spoke again: But she is of such a mind that it is necessary to speak of this matter. For she has been of the fear of the Lord for many years. Therefore she has not needed such rebuke.

David stood right up and spoke to the brothers: I say to you, that you are not small nor poor, but your understanding is veiled, so that you do not see. I would be pleased to let you know how you might serve God further. But the will of Satan has its way, for he comes to disturb the Spirit and to plug the ears of the oppressed by the serpent's deception. Now I say to you, furthermore, since you have believed her, then I will cease to speak any longer. And I, as a servant of the Lord, warn you all, proclaiming to you the Day of the Lord, that you beware, for he is near and I am free of you. For I was prepared to instruct and also to correct you, as the Lord has given me ability, so that you will not be surprised on that day. For it will come as a thief in the night before you know it [Rev. 3:3]. Pay attention. And as long as you think of yourselves as something and are not humbled any further, then you will find yourselves deceived. See, I warn you that you not let yourselves be misled. Men, regard yourselves above the women, then you will not be deceived. Understand correctly.

Jan Pont: David, you speak and judge too hastily, for you perhaps do not understand her speech. For she admonishes us all, that we should watch where we are going.

The speeches remained stuck here, and the morning continued without anyone sitting down. For David had no intention or desire to speak further with the people. But they remained with the subject until noon, as is related here.

Afternoon of the First Day.

In the afternoon it happened that Jan Pont and Peter van Geyen, [181] together with the others, greatly desired to speak with and question David Joris again. And so, after some time, they went to David in a friendly fashion and spoke pleasantly about some things, such as prophecy and the promised David, and they proceeded to speak with and to question him in a friendly manner concerning the name of God and the misuse of confession.[28]

The brothers Jan Pont, Peter, and Petrus and Paulus asked: We ask you, brother, how did you receive the aforementioned articles? Did they proceed from the Scriptures, or from visions or other inspirations?

David: The Lord give you a simple eye and fiery faith, an innocent, clear understanding, so that you can question me only to understand the fear of the Lord. This I would grant you very well.

Jan Pont: Amen.

David: See, I cannot now relate to you in much detail how these things were given to me. But this I will say to you, that the Lord gave me inward seeing eyes to observe how Israel and the whole world have used the names of God. How that the worthy holy command has been tread upon and not esteemed. I made this known through writings and words; to this I have been awakened. How that no people can become healthy in spirit, soul and body, unless they confess this and are purified therein. Understand. See, in this the Lord has increasingly instructed me daily, and to no person more than I. Although these words seem lofty, yet you must realize that they have been spoken to me in power, so that I can write such high, mighty things. Whoever knows these things, must testify [182] that I am not proud of heart. Therefore do not consider me proud.[29]

For I wish that you would perceive the good, just as you always desire to do so. For in this I have received many daily gifts and clarifications in the Scriptures, being compelled to write down some of the words. Hasten, hasten, I will go before you in a friendly fashion. For if it is true that you desire to run, as you know and say yourselves, then I am far in front of you. See, you cannot understand me further, despite all of my speaking and calling to you. For I, by God's grace, have obtained much progression in the Spirit, just as it has happened to me, unworthy, up to now. And see, this amazed even me.

At this time, or afterwards, a letter came to me from a sister, concerning what office I held, or should hold.[30]

I am not able to express all of it now.

And the appearance of the Lord shone about and shook me for eight or ten days thereafter, but where I was or how I was placed there I do not know. For a great light or brightness shone in my eyes. Not an external light, for I cannot express in words where it came from. For I did not observe things at the time in any external, physical manner; it was as if I had no outward eyes at all. But I saw with an internal vision the children of God come as shining [183] young children. And the whole world fell down before them, as well as before you and me. I saw all the godless lords and authorities fall down terrified before them, and there occurred great misery when I and the children of God were announced. This was so amazing to see, I cannot describe it all.

And then I came to my senses and looked around with my physical eyes. I discovered that I was still standing upright on my feet. I was filled with breath, and when I saw another vision, in which when I saw around the walls all manner of naked persons, I was forced to shout out in this way, "Lord, I may see all." For hours I had to write quickly, so quickly that I could scarcely move the pen fast enough. For my mind overflowed with so many words, that I spoke three or four times faster with my mouth than I could write with the pen. When I wrote one word, three more came out with it, and it had to happen in this way. How could I prevent it? Although this is ridiculed by some, the Lord has heard and seen it. But when this was done, I sang out in verse form the whole meaning.[31] [184]

And see, the Lord, in a illumination or vision, gave me the knowledge of how one can become just like a child here in this end time. I furthermore received many dreams and many inward visions after this, which might be revealed at this time, if it is indeed the Lord's will.

After I had lain in bed for three or four days, I fell onto my knees and grasped the writing instruments and from morning to evening I wrote down, without ceasing and with a fast running pen, those things which were inspired to me. In this was contained the whole clarification of the foregoing.[32] Furthermore, for a long time after this there were still many more verbal inspirations, dreams and visions, which will also become well known, if the Lord allows. See, in this way did the Spirit first come to me, not from the old fathers or literal Scriptures, although one indeed will find their meaning contained therein. Thus, I could not conceal it, but had to speak to you through a simple spirit, without evil doubts, and it will stand through all contradictions or differences. I am pleased to be regarded as the least, for I live in lowliness.

Thus I received understanding concerning the confession of sin, purification, chastity, and the angelic marriage, as it is called [Mark 12:25], as well as of the simple and innocent in Christ. I did not write of these things first from the Scriptures, but afterwards I wrote down the texts of the Scriptures, from both the Old and New Testaments. I did this by the command of the Lord for the unbelievers and scribes, but not for the simple, God-fearing, believing, lowly hearts.

Jan Pont: Since this confession is the true foundation by which to know and come to God's grace, we are amazed that you do not base your foundation on the prophets nor on the apostles. The reason for this we still do not understand at this time. Nor are we able to clearly observe if there might exist somewhere a clear example of your proposal given previously by you. We are not able to agree in our conscience that the Scriptures which you use support all your words.

David: This you do with your own wisdom and intelligence, which keeps you from the simple understanding. My heart is very troubled for you about this, and is surrounded by anxiety in this, as it now goes. I indeed previously thought (do not be offended) that here I would deal with high mountains, namely with high, proud hearts. I have to deal with the small ones, who are entirely poor [Isa. 45:2]. Therefore, turn your eyes and give your heart to lowliness and faith, then you will then understand the meaning of the Spirit, otherwise (I know well) it is impossible for you to live. [185] I believe indeed, that previously confession of sins from our youth until now was not as general or important as it must be for us. (For the fall or darkness has never been as great as now.) Think of how much longer, how more exalted in an inward fashion the Spirit will be at the Last Day. Nevertheless, we must truly repent from the sins and lament their evil in this way, knowing them and confessing them, if we desire to be released, delivered and freed from them, as the Scriptures show well enough.

But the Lord gave me further knowledge, on account of our blindness and the desires of youth, regarding the kind of burdens and needs we bear because of sins and the previous iniquity from which we die. For we must feel or examine their harm or burden, so that, now perceiving their ugliness, we may feel their burden. For it was on account of this sin, burden, and need that Christ was sent to release us from them or to help us from them. Whoever is without guilt or need, does not require it. We must, therefore, not be ashamed to spit out our sin, nor be restrained from confessing our guilt and from confessing our transgressions. Otherwise, I say to you, you will still remain in sin and the old being. Yes, struggle therefore to be released from the devil, namely from shame. I say this—not I, but the Lord. And see, is it true that you are not able to believe that the sin of your youth must be confessed and penitently proclaimed because it does not stand clear enough in the letter? Yet it has been most clearly written and shown to you in the letter. For where have the prophecies of Leonard Jost, Barbara and Melchior Hoffman, and several others, been preserved in writing? When the prophecies were first spoken, where were they confirmed with Scripture? Where is all that was written and spoken by the fathers, patriarchs, apostles and saints, confirmed by Scripture? Brothers, examine what is being said to you at this time, it too is not found written down, nevertheless you are compelled or admonished to believe it, if you desire to be one with them and with us, however far we have come to it. See, I have my knowledge from Christ. Those who fear the Lord and are in darkness, who hear his servant's voice, the light and understanding shall come to them indeed. Take heed. I will testify to this with my blood. Believe God and his prophets or his

Spirit's voice, which does not speak its own but the Lord's words. Then it will go well with you. And the same will proceed and be found just as true as those spoken through his saints, apostles and prophets. Bide the time and behold, pay attention.

Jan Pont: You speak in this fashion: If we would believe it, then we can do it if we will. You are certain of it, but we still remain uncertain of your foundation. Moreover, [186] we would like to hear if you are willing to delay[33] in order to reveal the matter to us. For since we have seen and heard so much, we have much to examine. We do not want to adopt something because it is easy to believe. For in this way it may be easily taken away from us again.[34]

For since you confess that it was not previously exhorted as strongly as now, but now the Spirit promises it and speaks in this way, why should we believe you so easily, since we accepted Leonard Jost and Melchior Hoffman? Is everything you have said based on the Scriptures? See, this is our reply. Regarding Leonard Jost, he has proven his teaching to us on the testimony of Scripture. And Melchior Hoffman did not introduce anything new which was not proven with the clear testimony of Scripture. He also commanded us: "Do not let yourselves be driven away from the Scriptures."[35] And at the time of the faith of the apostles, their new doctrine was introduced at the time with signs and wonders and all things were changed from letter into spirit, but now Christ's teaching abides forever.[36]

David: I have a great affectionate love for you; I will therefore answer you insofar as the Lord has given me. For I hope that you seek nothing more than understanding and truth, and to do the same. But I truly know that such is not the case, and I should really have no desire to answer you; this I say to you. Concerning this, one will observe that when a person is guilty, he does not confess things of which he is ignorant, but those from his experience. And since now, in the Last Day, some who are remaining will not sleep nor perish, namely die [1 Cor. 15:51-52], nevertheless it must come in the Spirit to the old being. So think, how can this begin and end? See, for this reason was this doctrine sent. And we who maintain a real love know that the Father has long suffered and borne with us up to the Last Day. But if we despise it, then he will so utterly forget us that we will die just like cattle which have no more thought. [187] Whoever prays with a good, sincere heart, just as I have told you before, will come to understand. For you know well, that if you desire to come to the forgiveness of your guilt, then you must first know and confess it, be entirely inclined to stand away from it, and then you will have the Lord in this way.

Therefore I say, do not oppose God proudly or contumaciously, nor oppose the truth. For your sins, whatever their nature, will be revealed before God and people or angels. Watch out, that you do not fight on behalf of the old being and Satan, for I fight for the honor of the Lord. Those who do not believe what I say to you, they shall miss it (they who do not see the morning light proceed with difficulty). But I do so, just as I say. How I am thankful, that I can crush and shame the old being (which is against the Lord and my blessedness), without my own activity, and take off my vile rags when I have nothing beautiful nor new [Eph. 4:22-24]. I could not otherwise learn or know from anyone else, how we can come to the victory and final maturity of Christ without becoming like dust, earth and ashes. This does not happen outwardly with those who desire to remain with the evidence of Scripture.[37]

For this reason the Lord admonishes you, which I tell you as a command, that we should wake up and hear what he teaches and commands (for he alone is wise and knows what is necessary for our good) so that we can please him. Is this not so? For if it is not so, then I must be punished. At this may the Lord open your mouth and make me dumb before you, outwardly and inwardly. Yes, so that only God's Word and truth be revealed and fulfilled in strength. See, I have not only once or twice confessed my iniquity, but indeed six or eight times, and I am not ashamed to do so even more. During this confession I realized that I, because of my flesh, am minded solely to unrighteousness or evil; from top to bottom there is nothing but sin. For in this separation we must change from flesh into spirit. I have spoken this to those who must ascend quickly to the victory, to the praise of my God. Lord, you know. The Lord give you a meek spirit, so that you will not promote yourselves, for all of you are struggling to injure me. Instead, prefer to write of my childishness and ignorance and pray with me to the Lord from your hearts, so that we will do such according to his will. Do not be so strange, for it will be so wonderful, yes more than flesh can believe and see, before the [188] Last Day will come. Therefore brothers, do not push against me, I say, or you will all sound foolish. I speak just as the Lord, who knows all of our desires, for he knows what we seek and do.

Second Day.

David: May I speak first, brothers? See, I always desire that before we speak, you will remember the Word. Or, if I, up to now, have not correctly spoken to you (what I have explained to you), then give me an answer. Or, is there anything to which you do not agree? Speak to me then, why you are making such a fuss and trouble against those things which I have spoken to you in meekness and simplicity, which is in Christ Jesus.[38]

For this reason I desire that you will answer me with a pure conscience, if I have spoken or written anything which is not right, so that we can make an end of this. For in this is my meaning understood, and I will not speak in any other fashion, however much you prod, request and grant.

(Here they secretly counselled among themselves or they asked each other and spoke to each other, as they frequently did. At this I spoke in this manner:)

I can judge this easily, that you speak with flesh and blood, about how and what you will answer me. But I say to you, this is not right, especially because each of you is a head or teacher.

(Here they made a noise together, and did this most of the time).

Jan Pont: The same is still in need of judgment, if conferring with the saints is the same as speaking with flesh and blood [Gal. 1:16]. This also needs a judgment among the brothers. But tell us whether we should respond to the first speeches, or not?

David: Yes, this is my desire.

Peter van Geyen: It is amazing to me and a concern of my heart about you, that you tell us that we should remember well and correctly examine your words and answer you patiently, and that [189] you advise us that you will not do the same. And then you judge us because we speak together, before you know what or how we will respond.

David: To clarify this will result in too many words. But I will speak as much as the Lord gives me, as much as the Lord, the teacher, desires to teach me as I stand before him. Thus I have spoken truly, for my answers are from his own heart, according to his meaning or basis, without asking you. But I grant this to you all, on account of your rudeness and ignorance, that I would gladly be abused by you as a deceiver. But that is an evil inspiration, which you do not know, but you will soon know better.

Jan Pont: This must still be judged by the brothers.

David: I have spoken by the moving of the Lord. In particular, about first consulting with one another before you answer me. For since we teachers will have to give an account for the brothers, we ourselves should possess the wisdom, according to the voice of the Spirit which speaks inwardly to us. For this has been your meaning, as you say, but it was my meaning that you should answer first, then let all the other brothers judge.

Jan Pont: God grant that it be so.

David: Yes, that is true.

Jan Pont: There are some things, about which we had spoken yesterday, in which we have not yet reached a full or true, basic agreement, such as concerning the name of God and now concerning confession. For in some things we are one, in others, still divided.[39]

David: I believed that you were as good as your word, that your tongue spoke the truth, that you explained the truth with a simple spirit. But now I find that this is not the case. For you had rejoiced greatly from your hearts when I presented my reports, and you confessed that I had spoken well before all of you regarding the fear of the Lord, how to pray, and the way of the Lord. And also about the [190] Hebrew word for God, which again sounds better than the word Lord. This was disputed, and now I confirm and confess it again.

For the Hebrew should not be taken literally, as I have been told it was previously. I have written about this, that such should not be. For when we discussed this issue I thought we had agreed. But since you have asked me about this again, know that the Lord himself will respond to it, or I will keep silent. Is this not right?

Jan Pont: Yes, so that it not become false. But when I asked you if it is not good to recount first what was said yesterday, it was for the benefit of those who were not present yesterday, so that they too can know the matter which we are now handling.

David: Yes, it is indeed necessary and good that they also know. But I advise you, as submissive little ones, that you do not stumble against the Word of God in this way, nor be timid in this, nor belittle his glorious majesty in it. Instead, we desire to keep honorable that which remains from the prophets and apostles. And the unbelieving, blind Jews do not believe in it, for they have already kept it this way now for over six or eight hundred years, esteeming more highly the word "Lord" above "God," so I regard their meaning not to be the best.[40] I believe he be named God, as one is able.

Jan Pont: We must become convinced by you with reasonable proofs, or otherwise we would make useless disciples for you. Surely you do not desire that we believe you without reasonable proofs, for that belief has no endurance.

David: Let it not be otherwise. But I will stand on my word which I have spoken, and I have believed that God is also a Lord, before whom I stand, as also before the Lord. I seek his honor and speak his word. He desires indeed that all my words be written in their hearts.

Jan Pont: In order that you not be tempted, you are able to understand your words and understanding well. But tell us if we should let fall all the words and understanding which we have learned from Melchior Hoffman, the apostles and the whole Scriptures? But do you mean, as you say, that we should lay aside all intelligence, letter and human understanding?

David: I do not say this, that you should regard the good doctrine as evil. I desire instead that you fulfill it; I speak therefore of your own understanding. Otherwise, tell me what is the letter-learning which will then be brought to shame? Or what is the wisdom which will become captured in their mind [2 Cor. 10:5]?

Jan Pont: That is all the wisdom which lies in the schools, which has been taught out of the ABC books, and from those who [191] abandon themselves to human wisdom and their own intelligence without God's fear or without improvement from their sin. For not all letter-learning is to be cast out in this way. For Christ himself spoke of letter-learning in the kingdom of heaven [Matt. 13:52], as did Paul [Acts 13:1] and Apollos [Acts 18:24] and in this way stands also Ecclesiasticus [38:24], that God will place his honor upon the letter-learned. Therefore the Jews were not condemned on account of the Scriptures, but on account of their misuse of them, which they falsified to their own harm and to that of others.

David: Yes, that is right. Blessed is he who is taught from the Spirit about the heavenly kingdom. But to all who are taught from the letter, they draw near to the Lord with their lips but their hearts are far from him [Isa. 29:13; Matt. 15:8; Mark 7:6]. They say much, but they have not done anything about it, and they shall be brought to harm. But the small, lowly ones have left themselves. They are the poor of spirit, who are oppressed and terrified of heart wherever they go. They stand under the obedience of faith and desire to fulfill all of this truth. God will therefore give understanding to them; he will let them serve the Most High in his majesty, and they will speak only from him and to him. But all who do not leave themselves, who proceed only in the intelligence, tongue, pride and cleverness of humanity, are therefore scribes and Pharisees, for they have more regard for the writing than for the rule of truth. They will not be placed among the small and humble ones to the glory of God, nor will they proceed with them. They will not know the mind of God to the truth. For only the humble have understanding and only they proclaim the Word of God. These are the ones, I say, who have abandoned all carnal and human wisdom, who have not dared to presume or to understand on their own, but from God's Spirit. They are like the poor spirits, hungering souls, who are thirsting for the righteousness [Matt. 5:3-6]. These ones, I say, have put to death their own wisdom and intelligence; in this way they will know much and know it correctly out of their ignorance; they will rightly divide the Scriptures [2 Tim. 2:15]; they will find life out of death. For although you have heard the word from Melchior Hoffman, you have not yet understood it all. And if you have understood it all, you have not fulfilled it completely. For this reason, I must tell you what you still need to leave, die to, and live for, if you desire to become a disciple of Christ in the truth. What do you say to this?

Jan Pont: God alone knows our hearts. But concerning what you say here, we are at peace, for what we still have to do in this way, we must also do. For before I knew Melchior Hoffman, I thought that I had it all. And when I first heard them, I thought that they were fools. But then I began to observe, I must let large horns run me down and through the fear of God bow myself under a poor furrier[11] and other servants of God, and learn again the a.b.c.'s from the ground up. [192] I have confessed myself as such. So I know now that we must no longer refuse to hear the things which we have learned in this way, for we have put on the armor of God [Eph. 6:11], which the Lord has given us through his saints, in order to stand strong against the antichrist which now runs about everywhere, as you have said. Therefore to ascend is correct. However, are you completely perfect?

David: I may speak just as Paul did, although he was not yet perfect, nevertheless he had received the Spirit of perfection out of grace, in order to teach the people about perfection [Phil. 3:12]. I too am like this. Therefore I admonish you before the great Day of the Lord, in which everything which exists in the flesh shall perish, behold that you deliberate on this day and night. For the Spirit warns you to fulfill the word of Christ in its true sense. For many glory in Christ, but they nevertheless remain in the first schooling, contrary to the Holy Spirit of truth and the holy doctrine, that is, those who do not let go of their understanding. I therefore speak to you in the name of Jesus Christ. I will no longer warn you except this one time. Therefore observe that you take off the old being and put on Christ Jesus [Eph. 4:22-24], in truly sincere righteousness and sanctity. For your old flesh (if you boast in it) must rot in the earth, and you must hate yourselves. O, if you understood this and had the wisdom to come to it. But you refuse to come to it. Yes, you will not know the way as long as you despise the counsel of the poor [Ps. 14:6]. This I will testify to you to be the truth. It shall be found so.

Furthermore, although I stand here to reply to those things which I have written to you, whether or not they are from the devil, I nevertheless must continue now with disputation. But I am willing to hear if you can correct any errors in my writings. I stand here at this moment to hear and to explain the truth, I say, and for you to confess that it has been written correctly in my meaning. Hear or allow it.

And at this there was silence.[42]

I ask you, does not what I have said to you agree with the saints and prophets? Is it good or evil? Is what I say to you from the Spirit and not from the letter? I desire, therefore, that you open the book, although you confess orally that you are still children, small in understanding and still desire to be taught by me; this I desire indeed to hear. If this is not the case, then I will [193] show how you still do not have a complete understanding of it, and that because of this you will not follow the counsel of the Holy Spirit, for you will not listen a little to me.

Jan Pont: If these words were explained with modesty, then they would be good, and we would be able to reply before the Lord, placing before him the judgment of your and our conscience. For we will not allow ourselves to take the praise, truly this was shown with words. You should like to have such disciples who might remain with you. For whoever will easily join you, might just as easily turn away from you.

David: Yes, that is true. But you do not understand me. I have confirmed all of this in the book on Perfection (which is called the *Book of Prophecies* and which they have had long enough to read); the book (I say) was written from the Spirit of God without textual or literal scriptures.[43] Now do not tempt the Lord about this, by relating it all again unnecessarily. Though I will indeed read it to you, so that you might be able to report or answer concerning what is not right in it. Do not ask of me anything further, because you do not grasp the foundation of a heavenly person, neither the way to it or how far you have come and how much you know. And you do not understand or perceive the Spirit, who speaks out of you or to you. I therefore advise you now, do not judge lightly. What more can I say?

At first I said to you, that we were first born as a child. After this follows the youth, then the old age.[44] We cannot know or understand how to leave this childhood without leaving behind ourselves, this is right and certain with God. Therefore as long as you do not see this, you will never come to an understanding with me. It is therefore useless for us to answer you. For you do not grasp the meaning of the Spirit, nor do you fear this. But if you do understand me well in this and say or report that you want to come to the holy place, then I will hear you. But before this is the case, that you know it, I must be able to hear it in what you say. Therefore observe the gift which was given me by grace to know such, yes, in order that we might progress from grade to grade in life. Therefore I say, watch what you say and what you judge. I would gladly excuse you and not offend or shame you, if you will believe me.

At this they were silent.

If you will now believe me and give yourselves to fulfill it, [194] then you could understand the Spirit, without which you cannot understand me. But how can you understand me, when you refuse to believe me, and when you do not perceive yourselves or Satan who inspires you and is preventing this. I will indeed be punished if I speak in an evil or incorrect fashion before the Lord. If you will say to me, "you speak too high, how can we believe you?" Then remember and perceive, who believed Christ and Paul? Who believed Noah? Who believed Lot and more others?

Therefore I know well, that few will hear and believe me. For it is written, "when the Son of Man shall come, do you believe he will also find faith upon the earth" [Luke 18:8]?

Jan Pont: What shall correct our words, since you say we do not know your Spirit? These words contradict each other.

Peter van Geyen: We sit in order to hear and to learn.

David: O brothers, if you knew what you said. If only you spoke it from living power with truth in good intention, namely, "we sit in order to hear and to learn." Then you would easily understand me. For I say to you as a word from the Lord, that all brothers must bow themselves under the Spirit, whoever desires to come to the perfection in the kingdom of God. I therefore admonish you heartily that you not repudiate the Spirit. And if you do not repudiate the word and are well disposed to hear and learn, then I must ask you Peter, do you believe me and will you answer as a servant of the Lord? Then I will teach or question you. Give me an answer. I had not wanted to question you because of your love and honor, before I had first pointed out to you when, and when not, to judge, while, by the Lord's grace, I stood before you in this place where you stand. In order that you know whether my messages for you are correct or not. So let it happen now. Remember this well. For I say to you, that much diligence has been practiced among us and there is still much more to come, which we have not done or known before. The days are now not as they used to be when they were easy. You deliberate on this.

Peter van Geyen: I cannot believe you without either proof or hearing the truth, then I will give an answer about you, which was not in our first response. For as we have said, we are prepared to learn, and if the doctrine is reasonably explained to us and we still do not believe it, then will we be guilty in this matter.

But these spirits came to us with even greater words, and they were better in speech than you, and they too had a holy appearance. They highly boasted of having much from the Spirit and from the Lord's Word, and presented themselves as the two witnesses [Rev. 11], as the angel of Revelation 10, and as Elijah and as Enoch, etc. They said many times [195] to us, "I speak this from the Spirit and as a word of the Lord." In particular, there was Hans van Rottenburg,[45] Heinrich Shoemaker,[46] Claes Elser,[47] Jan Batenburg[48] and the Greek from Macedonia,[49] and other women, whom we ourselves have seen and heard, and they said, that they spoke from the Holy Spirit. Should we have believed all of them, who have spoken in this way from the Spirit? Do not regard us as evil nor become burdened by it, because we do not hastily believe you. Would you believe me? Or how would you answer me if I stood in your place and you in mine, where you now regard me as standing?

David: If you stood in appearance where I stand and I stood in this way where I see you stand, then I would answer you, just as I would like you to answer now. I would gladly inquire of and examine myself, to see where I am in the progression. I would not sit in order to comprehend you. My word is none other than that I desire to ask you to examine what you mean. And this is my word: If you will first believe me, then I will speak to you. But if my doctrine is condemned out of hand as from the devil, how can I then speak with you?

Peter van Geyen: Whether your words are from the devil or from God, this I cannot yet know; tell us the difference, for I must examine it with discernment. [196]

David: So now I say, as I was responsible to do, if you could clearly show me that my understanding was childish, then in modesty I would have to allow you to teach me, and with a God-fearing heart I would bow to you and humble myself in this. When I sought the kingdom of God and the truth, I had to examine whether I was fit or immature in the true knowledge, and if I understood the mind of the Lord; then it would belong for me to speak. This may not be countered. For a rich person thinks that he is wise, but a poor person examines himself [Prov. 28:11]. Remember the word in your hearts and thoroughly examine yourselves. Do not proudly esteem yourselves. Do not think yourselves to be wise, but pray with me for the understanding from the Lord. My answer is that I would examine myself in light of your comments, to see if I have sought the fear of the Lord as silver and gold, I say, and the understanding. Had I done this, I would rejoice; had I not, I would have to confess that I did not have it, and let myself be corrected by you in the truth. I would then listen to you without resisting, as you must now do to me, as much as you can listen, and fulfill it with meekness.

Peter van Geyen: This is my answer, we must believe the words which are from the Spirit. For this point is only partially answered; for we sit here only to learn. For the master-teacher, who teaches the children, knows how to teach the children, for he must teach them with regard to their condition. And if you are the same, why have you not therefore done this for us?

David: Yesterday and the day before I sought only to ask and have an answer from you, about what I have spoken and written to you, but I did not obtain this. See, grasp understanding alone, and acquire that single eye, this I ask you. Watch what you say. Soul and Spirit, who impels and teaches me in the truth to the life (although there is not yet one person, I believe, who has come to it), seeks nothing else in you, but that you daily fulfill the Word of the Lord, to become flesh of his flesh and bone of his bone [Eph. 5:30]. And that will not happen except you leave the old being or life and become circumcised in your hearts [cf. Deut. 10:16]. You have begun well in your faith, but you have not daily perfected it. I know what I have experienced, heard and seen in the Spirit. This is why I said, "will you believe me?" For this reason it must come to this. Behold, your hearts will be given into your hands.

Therefore I must ask you first, before proceeding, whether you have kept yourselves innocent in the things you have received. For how can I speak with you, if you are still carnal or proud? Or if you still prefer the works of the flesh, seeing what the Lord said: [197] "Behold, a person must completely leave himself, hate himself, take up his cross daily, otherwise he will not be his disciple" [Matt. 10:37-39]. Understand.

And therefore I boast that the Spirit impels me to admonition, so that no one who does not desire to be lost will remain lost. Why then do you not hear or believe me? Now no one is worthy of the teaching of the Lord, or is able to enter life, except he hate himself and leave his own wisdom. It is in this sense that I now speak to and question you. For I now seek to give your hearts into your own hands, in order to make you know and see where you stand in light and darkness, in life and death.

So I ask you, is it not right, that one ought to confess what one is? Furthermore, that one ought to shame the old being, just like he were in the place of public sinners [Luke 18:10-14]. Otherwise we will remain as conceited as the scribes and Pharisees. We, I say, who boast that we walk in the temple, who call to God in heaven in the Spirit and claim to serve him.

Jan Pont: I will respond. This indeed is right and good and pleases God, being taught by Jesus Christ himself: to take off the old being, to shame it with zeal and desire and not to be proud or exalted, as the scribes were who did not confess their sins. And to be humble, to confess with public sinners, this I say is correct. But that from this teaching it is proper that one should confess one's sin from one's youth up with words, works and thoughts, in front of the church or brothers or the world, this I do not know if it is from Christ and the apostles. Neither do I know if this is what they intended to say about public sinners, that public sinners are an example of this. I desire to hear and to learn more of this.

David: I say to you in the name of my Lord Jesus, that the same must indeed be found among us. Namely, that all of us must become just like the public sinners of the world. Are we not required to recognize, speak out, and confess our sins, especially those since our youth? What we are will certainly be revealed before the Lord and his angels, along with our faithful church. What we have been since our youth, which we have previously concealed before people, was not concealed before God and still remains known to his angels. This is what is given for us to do, in order to come better to humility, meekness and lowliness. We therefore prefer that to be clothed with repentance and mourning, we seriously seek to remember well how we have lived during the days of our lives. This serves to show us, and is necessary to know, how much we have missed heeding the Spirit. For the parable [Luke 18:9-14] is, I say, a figure of this, that we confess what we know ourselves to be: earth and ash. You say no, I say yes, watch what you do. [198]

Peter van Geyen: From where do you say this?

David: From the leading of the good Spirit. Should it not be viewed as correct, I have indicated the texts for this. It is, however, not necessary for me, but I have done this by grace for your good, so that you perhaps might receive the texts for a better examination.

Peter van Geyen: About this last word, that we have had little of the Spirit, and that you say we have been in the covenant for so long and have not matured. I am ashamed that I have been so long on this earth and have been a brother in this way for a long time and yet have not progressed further. Also, that I still am not better clothed with the garment of Jesus Christ, namely, with humility, meekness, lowliness and simplicity [Col. 3:12]. That is my sorrow.

But that the parable of Luke [18:9-14] should be construed as a figure of this aforementioned confession, we contend that the parable has a contrary meaning. If you base it upon your visions, then we will examine the spirit of the same, or if it exists upon the Scriptures, then will we examine those passages, to see if it is contained in them. We do not understand what you said, and you cut us off with few words in this way. You must show us and make known to us, how we might know who this Spirit is, so that we might know him.

David: If it is true, that you have correctly learned humility, meekness, simplicity, lowliness and friendliness from Christ Jesus, our Lord and Master, then you should be able to understand by the Spirit, what our Lord said there in a hidden fashion because of the natural being. For a natural, conceited person does not understand what is from the Spirit of God. If you are not learned in this, or poor of Spirit, hungering and thirsting to righteousness [Matt. 5:6], moaning and crying to the Lord on account of your iniquity, so that you can become a new creature, then you are not able to understand this. But you now boast that you are learned in it, and if this is true, then I must now be shamed by you. I, nevertheless, will not be shamed, for you have confessed to not understand it.

Peter van Geyen: Brother, you have asked it, therefore I have answered you at least three or four times. And now you ask again concerning the Spirit, namely, what Christ said concerning humility, meekness, simplicity and lowliness. We do not boast, except diligently in our weakness, as it should be. But we do not have your understanding.

We have received the Spirit of Jesus Christ in the childhood, but we do not [199] have your glory with God in full power. Since this is still necessary for our perfection, we desire to learn your Spirit.

David: If I teach you further, then you must believe me, if you desire to learn from me.

Peter van Geyen: What should we believe about you?

David: To be a servant of the Most High, as you also regard yourselves, who will teach one another.[50]

Peter van Geyen: From what should we confess it?

David: From the word of simplicity and lowliness, which is the one Spirit's living word. For I am now compelled to boast before you, that I have received this according to the measure of God's grace, more clearly and living than you. In order to examine with proof of truth, what you must come to understand through tongues or understanding, although I am not able to drive it forcefully enough to you. You must yet receive it with humility, as the Lord had desired of the Jews. But if you desire to correct my lies, and say it is not so, then the matter between me and you remains just as it did before.

Yes, whether or not I have received wisdom above all of you, or by grace have received or felt these gifts firmly, shall be revealed in its time. But you do not hear or believe me, instead you desire to understand everything, as if you had the wisdom. Now I tell you, if you do not have it, then will I teach you. What more can I do? Blessed is he who hears me.

Peter van Geyen: That last word, that we must learn and hear, since we are ignorant, we desire to hear clearly. Otherwise I am not able to reply again, for we have heard many commands since you say that we do not know. But that we should believe this word about you, namely, that you are a servant of the Lord, this I have not yet understood. Nor have I heard where this comes from. Should I believe that you have more wisdom simply because you say so? This is an amazing faith to me, that we should believe such. If so, we should previously also have believed others who spoke in this way from the Spirit's inspiration. We had as little proof.

David: You could easily judge this from the words which you have heard if you desired to seek after wisdom or understanding. That is, if you have it deep in your heart. [200] For since you look only upon God's wisdom, you should receive and see this. That is, if you have his nature and if you stand properly as his child or servant and do his teaching, as you have previously heard from us.

But if you have not felt or done the same, then you do not yet have the Spirit or gifts. The first must perish, in order that you might come to perfection. It is fitting that you perceive or see yourselves as you are. Allow yourselves to be instructed. Hear and believe the voice which tells you what you are and must become to please God. Namely, take off the first old being and put on the new pure one. But you will not do this, desiring instead to be masters of the Scriptures and of everyone. However, you confess with your mouths, even against yourselves, that you are still children and ignorant. See, how can we then ask or judge much deeper matters? I would be happy indeed, if there was one person on the earth who came to me to be taught to perfection. I find in the Scriptures indeed that one is to become just like a child [Matt. 18:3], but I have not yet heard nor explained it. Nor will you receive the ability to do it except through many prayers, fasts and watchings.[51] One must first come to know oneself. See, then will you be able to judge and know me and what I have received above you. But you do not yet understand me; I will therefore teach you. For if you had the gift to see how far you have come, then you could better examine my words and, hearing me well, believe. And if you do not have this, then I must first teach you, until you are prepared to perceive what the gifts are. To examine a person's heart to see how far it stands is not possible for any mortal. But see, this is what I would do to you by God's grace, if you will confess yourselves poor of spirit and blind. If you still desire to find the truth and what it does, then I can speak with you in order to come to further understanding; otherwise not.

I have more to say to you, but you are not able to bear all things, for you are still carnal and roguish of eye as Paul [1 Cor. 3:3] and Christ [Matt. 6:23] said. You still do not see it. But nonetheless, you should know what you have done. This I received over a year ago and wrote to you. But you have despised the teaching with the work that I have shown to you. This you will confess in the great day, when all hearts are revealed and all your flesh shall burn. But whatever is gold, silver and precious stones, shall in that time be able to endure and remain within the consuming fire. But before this day everything [201] must be first tested and cleansed through the many kinds of instruments which serve to it. Concerning this you are amazed on account of the wisdom which is in it. In this no manner of evil, whether unrighteousness, cunning, roguishness, unchastity, avariciousness and whoredom will remain, neither hypocrisy nor shame. For these believers will stand in the light and live in the life. The Lord has called his bride to make her prepared daily to his praise [Rev. 21:2, 9]. But in order to perceive this way, do not neglect to eat the provided daily bread. For understand that this bread which we are brought up on is our Father. Now, is our Father or the Father of us all correctly observed day to day in your hearts? Occupy yourselves in it. If I have now answered poorly, give witness. O brothers, your stony, proud hearts must bow down [Ezek. 11:19] and be crushed to ashes, before God's Word can cleave to you. Do not resist this. For this barking of a dog might help you, the dumb, who cannot bark and who will be cast out [Isa. 56:10].

I continue to admonish you in the name of my Lord and I say to you that the Day of the Lord is near. He will come upon you before you believe it. For he comes like a thief in the night [Rev. 3:3]. If you do not watch and pray, then you will be shown that I, a small one, must speak this correction to you. Do not therefore become embittered against me, for it comes for your improvement. If I have spoken poorly, then correct me.

Peter van Geyen: I conclude in this way about whether or not you have answered correctly: Your speech is not just an answer, but also a proof of my earlier question. But our question is this, why should we believe you? From where should one know? From where was the Spirit? Then you replied, because of the wisdom, of which you have received more than we, for this reason should we observe it. To this is our reply, that such spirits were previously among us, with all manner of boastings. Should we therefore have believed them? For they were certainly still deceived in the faith. These others said to believe David, because he alone among us has become the same form and nature as the only God and Christ in humility, meekness, simplicity and lowliness.

Now answer still further: The ones who previously came to us defended themselves and boasted that they brought the Lord's Word and that they spoke this from the Spirit as it was given to them. They said: "I am certain and will also always stand on this" and similar words. These too have shown the one true God. They also held a part of the truth of Christ just like we, and perhaps also like you.[52] [202]

They were also impelled to the perfection with complete diligence and submissiveness and their words had also been of mortification, purification, patience, mercy, love, etc. And they were similarly found to have a false spirit, although such salvation had been evidenced in submissiveness and also with works. And this should not have been completely strange to us, for such was testified of God's servants. For if Satan could change himself into an angel, much more could his servants be changed into apostles of righteousness [2 Cor. 11:14]. This is found not only in the words about the servants of God, but much has been found in the deeds from the Old and New Testaments, which are written for our teaching. An examination has shown this to be true many times. Our masters, the apostles, therefore taught us to guard ourselves from adopting new doctrines because they can be mixed with the truth [Col. 2:2; 2 John 7-8]. For from the evil spirits

218 / *The Anabaptist Writings of David Joris*

the evil teachers seasoned their doctrine with truth [Col. 4:6], so that they would appear acceptable and good. The teaching of Christ and the apostles is full of such admonition. Guard yourselves from false prophets who come clothed in sheep's clothing [Matt. 7:15]. Guard yourselves from adopting new teaching. Further, some will come in the form of angels which they have never seen. When they at that time brought in new evil things with the good, it was very ruinous, and about this they complained. Therefore it is necessary for us to have further proofs, in order to perceive the spirit. The second thing you said, that we should examine ourselves, this we accept as an admonition.[53]

David answered: These are words which pleased me well, sounding valuable against those things which are done in a false appearance from the inside or which come in this way. But I have demanded an answer from you. That is, have I spoken against the truth or against the Holy Spirit? You should testify about it, whether no or yes. And I ask further for an answer about what I had previously explained and said concerning what we must do. Is this not right?

Peter van Geyen: We gave an answer in the beginning about your words of proof, as much as your remarks and questions desired. Now, if this is not good enough for you, here is our answer as given at the beginning: concerning humility, meekness, lowliness, and fear of God, we always confess these to be good. [203]

But those intermingled things concerning confession have not been explained well enough to us. We desire more explanation of them before we will answer further. For examination must come first, otherwise we are not able to give either yes or no.

David: I have said this will be moored here a long time, for you have all sprung upon me and have not examined the words which I held up before you. In particular, what must be done first before anyone can be Christ's disciple and be able to learn from him. You confess indeed that you are still far from it, nor have you done it as it must be done.

Wherefore I say to you, you do not have the most basic thing which begins the schooling, since you refuse to become like children, not with the mouth but with the heart. Therefore I cannot speak further with you, especially concerning the things that go higher than you are able to understand. For no natural human, I say once more, can grasp what is contained in the wisdom of God.

Therefore I must cease and leave the matter as it stands. I admonish you to show great affliction and mourning, placing yourselves in the dust and dusting yourselves with ashes. Further, that you will do this, calling and weeping with sorrowful, oppressed hearts and desiring that God by his grace will overlook your time of sin and great transgression. Observe that you have not walked properly in the ways of God from your childish days up to this hour. If it is otherwise, correct me. If it is just as I have said, then accept what I have said and do it. Make yourselves like children and become poor of spirit, bearing penance, weeping and crying. Yes, this you should and must do freely. Also fulfill the word of Christ. Desire the kingdom of God and his righteousness, so that there may be peace between brother and brother [Matt. 5:23]. Seek righteousness, hunger and thirst for it [Matt. 5:6]. But if you did not have this when you began it, then do it first. Stand in the good will, perfect in everything, submissive according to the Word of our Lord, without regard to the person. Only then will I be able to speak further with you. Only with such a spirit will you understand me well and be able to speak with me, otherwise never. I have not encouraged nor compelled you to do anything else than to come to the true understanding of the perfection and clarity of Christ. To do such is a true understanding of God which stands in a living power and vision of truth, not in any dead letter. If you would accept this as satisfactory, then I am at peace. But if you think that I have spoken with you unwisely or without experience or strength or in an ungodly fashion, then pray for me, and I will be mindful of such love. Only fulfill or remember the words which have been said to you. And let us (if it is possible) separate as brothers, since I too seek God, who is my Father, with my whole heart. [204] I exist only for his praise. I also despise, shame and remove the old being, hating it, and loving the new. This is my work in the Spirit. He has taught me in this fashion, and has provided me with the words to speak to you.

Peter van Geyen: In this speech is understood that we are not perfect nor have we done faithfully. This we freely confess, for it is true. But that because of this you will end our discussion and speak no more, this is a miserable trick. For you have journeyed too far to stop speaking. You yourself said that you knew our position well before. We also desire to hear indeed, if you will tell us, how well you have done all this or if those who are with you have done it also.

David: Remember that the Lord does not lie and we humans must remain as liars before him [Rom. 3:4]. But if we have called correctly to the Lord, if we have observed well our daily bread, then we should experience an increasing maturity in the more advanced understanding of the Spirit. This is not to be found in the letter, but in an obedient, simple spirit of humility, which is given above all to the small and hungering, not to the proud of heart or mind. Therefore, we listened and examined that such had not been done by us. Instead, we had remained ignorant as children, who will only die if they remain so ignorant. But now we have, by God's grace, come to the understanding that it is a process of growing up. Furthermore, there had not been any growing up among us in power, truth and deed, nor in obedience and listening (keep your eyes sharply on it), but that the time in between had been wasted. The Lord, however, is gracious, longsuffering and merciful to those who (through hearing about the misuse) are fearful, oppressed and anxious of heart. He suffered a long time with the childishness of the ignorant and until now he has turned a blind eye to it. But now, in the last days before it is completely lost, he has let us be warned. We should make certain that in the time left we show humility and mourning on account of our previous iniquity, confess our sin and become poor of spirit. This is daily found among us as has been testified.

So we found from this, that whoever has received his word, feared from his heart and earnestly mourned and lamented, etc. This is given to me. I, above all, desire to be obedient and God-fearing to the Lord in everything. We have taken up the performance of the rudiments. You have disdained this, but you will soon lament, since you struggle on behalf of this world and the old being. You have not entirely removed it from your heart. [205] Your heart therefore remains stony, without help or counsel, for as long as you remain proud. All because you do not look into the preceeding nor do you examine it or accept my teaching, as was said before.

The Third Day.

David: Now you humbly desire for me to show you the scriptural proofs and you will not cease requesting that I relate again the Scriptures to you. To this I answer, that I am not able to arrange this. You now have the texts which the Spirit made known to me at the time. These are set down in the *Booklet on Confession*.[54] Do you still desire that I read these to you? I will listen to whatever you might have to say against me on these.

Jan Pont answered: And the first to be read is Ezekiel 37 and 36.

Peter van Geyen: First, one should read the passages, and if they serve the point, then we will follow it.

David: See, these are merely an aid for the one who understands the Spirit.

David read Ezekiel. "First the Lord of Hosts spoke to his people Israel saying: 'They will no longer defile themselves with their images and abominable things and all manner of sins. But I will help them and they will become pure.' "[55] This cannot be said, until they stand in it and see or find the same.

(He read further). Furthermore, the Lord said: "I will pour clean water over you, so that you will become clean from all your impurities. From all your idols will I purify you, and I will give you a new heart and a new Spirit, and I will take away the stony heart from out of your flesh" [Ezek. 36:25f.].

(Read). "Then you will remember your evil ways and your past intentions which were not good, and then you will mourn for your sin and idolatry. Such will I do, but not for your sake, says the Lord God, let it be known to you. You must shame yourselves, oh you of the house of Israel, because of your ways."[56]

The Lord God speaks again in this way: "At the time when I will cleanse you from your sins, then will I cause these cities to be inhabited again, and the dwellings will be rebuilt, the desolate land be cultivated again" [Ezek. 36:33-34].

Jan Pont: As far as we can see, these passages do not refer at all to confession. [205]

David: I would not be able to understand the passages either if I did not have the revelation from the Spirit.

Jan Pont: We understand these to be about the restitution, not about confession. For he will deliver them out of prison again, where they have been imprisoned [Isa. 42:7].

David: When you seal the external imprisonment in the Spirit over the inward, and perceive the inward as the outward, then it will be as obvious to you as the light of day. But those of you or us who have not yet been proven or examined, cannot perceive it. For we are flesh, and we must be sealed before we can understand God's Word according to the Spirit. Only in this way will you understand this and the other passages. For these passages and others contain so much in them, that they reveal, indicate and force the meaning, although it is not clearly explained. Nevertheless I could not have understood them on this basis at the first, if I had not received a revelation apart from the texts. I mean, I received clarity from the Spirit.

Peter van Geyen: Beloved, I am perplexed about where these other brothers received their faith, since you have believed or received it in revelations. We desire indeed to know this, how your brothers have come to their faith, so that we might understand it.

What if I too believed this because David said it is from the Spirit? Then another might also come to me and tell me the same thing. I would make it an insignificant work to confess sins. Yes, I would do it so easily, just like taking off my belt, if the Lord truly willed it.[57]

David: See that you neither regard such too lightly nor neglect to walk according to the Spirit. For you know that he, God, will pour out his Spirit upon all flesh [Joel 3:1].

Leonard asked David: Will you allow me to speak about this?

David: Yes.

Leonard: There is still much difference between the confession of which you speak and that which we have confessed. For you have not yet felt the pain of it. It does not occur as easily as you have said, namely, as easy as untying your belt.

Peter van Geyen: I ask you, from which basis is this revealed? Is it from the words which David provides as having been revealed to him from the Spirit, or is it from the proof of Scripture? [207]

Jorien spoke similarly: Will you let me speak?

David: Yes.

Jorien: See, I had also opposed this position, as you do. At the first I had opposed Batenburg's position or teaching, which in part also immodestly opposed his position. But it was revealed to me afterwards while I was in great turmoil from the fire of unchastity: "behold, this is the thing which you oppose," and I was forced to confess and to regard it as correct. I also recalled the passage of James, which convinced my conscience. Pray now in this way for the same Spirit who has led me to understanding. It is a sufficient witness for me, let it be a satisfactory witness to you also.[58]

Peter van Geyen: It was seen very well before, that one has made small, insignificant matters like bearing a sword into a matter of conscience.

David: Let us read further. These serve the matter at hand.

And he read Jeremiah 17:9: "See, among all things which live, humanity has the most roguish and cunning heart (understand). Who then will understand it? I, the Lord, can search the heart and test the kidneys (these are the thoughts) and I give to each one according to his ways and the fruits of his works, says the Lord of Hosts."

Understand further, what Esdras has described and left behind. Namely, "he has created humanity and set his heart in the middle of his body, and given him spirit, life and understanding. But see, the breath of the Almighty God, who has made all things, examines all things in the hidden places of the earth."[59]

(Pay attention well). For this one knows your font and every sin that you think in your heart. You therefore cannot conceal your sin. For this reason the Lord has examined all your works, and he will incriminate all of you. Yes, you will be ashamed when your sins appear before people, and all the unrighteous heathen will see them (behold), and they will all stand as incriminators in that day. Take heed.

Therefore spit out and confess it, do not be ashamed of it. Instead purify yourselves, [208] become holy and pure of heart in this time, before it is too late. Furthermore, the Psalmist speaks in this way: "You have placed our sins right before you, O Lord; sins which we had thought to be secret and which we had committed in our youth. But in your sight they are much clearer than the day" [Ps. 90:8].

Do these basic texts not move you?

Peter van Geyen: According to us these do not serve the issue, but they imply only that one ought to lament one's iniquity before God.

David: Have you indeed lamented them? This you must know.

Jan Pont: Yes, we certainly do lament, but not in your fashion, as you decree.

David: If it is true that you have done this correctly, then it will proceed well with you.

At this Jan Pont answered again, but it was not written clear enough for him and he desired that I not set it down. The general intent of what he said was that the Zwinglian Psalter[60] was correct and Campanus's[61] was incorrect. He also believed and interpreted the text according to his meaning, namely, that they understood it to pertain to lamentation but not to confession. Thereupon David's answer was this:

David: That you hold your translation alone as correct, I do not take it to heart. For I let the learned quarrel while I follow my Lord's good Spirit who inspires me, whether it is written down or not. Therefore I say only that the passage is not to be understood as you interpret it, but that it now goes to us. For my spirit is also for the truth and is not opposed to it. Just like the sayings of the apostles, who did not always speak from the Scriptures, nor were they founded in the letter. In this way I have now also dared to sever myself or cease from the literal words of the books, but not from the meaning as it must come to pass through the Spirit. I much prefer to follow his meaning, rather than the dissimilar books of Scripture. For I believe they erred, and contradict each other at many points, especially in the words. [209]

I am therefore free before the Lord God before whom I stand;

for we found that we stood in the same freedom experienced by the apostles. For the kingdom of God exists not in any particular words. But the Lord be praised that we do not judge lightly before we are certain (in the Spirit) of it. Therefore you watch out, that you do not judge badly, being found to be fighting against the truth.

Peter van Geyen: This passage serves well to penitence, and not to confession.

David: This is what you say, but I understand it better.

Much more was discussed at this point, but it was not written down.

And they read these passages: "The sins, which I have done in my youth and the iniquity, which has followed after, O Lord, do not remember any longer. But deal with me according to your goodness, for your goodness sake."[62]

Furthermore, David, the man of the Lord, spoke in this way: "I had indeed spoken because of fear. For I have had to suffer beatings and on account of them I must bear my wounds always (understand) with me" [Ps. 38:4,17]. "This is the great wound of my heart, that I confess my evil just when I remember it and in the remembrance of my sins (understand) let me not forget the pain."[63]

Further: "My evil deeds go out above my head and have become troublesome to me to such an extent that I cannot bear them. My sores stink and have become filthy because of my great evil" [Ps. 38:4-5].[64] "By the heaviness of the sins I am oppressed to the point that I am humbled beyond measure and go about sorrowfully the whole day in mourning clothes" [Ps. 38:6]. "When I come to myself, then I confess my sins, and my sins stand always before my eyes."[65] "I beg you, turn your face away from my sins and remember not all my iniquity" [Ps. 51:9]. "I turn myself in sickness (towards you) and speak: O Lord, be merciful to me, make my soul healthy, for it is sick" [Ps. 41:4].

Furthermore Ezra, the priest, said when they were brought again out of captivity: "Realize that you have been unfaithful and you have taken strange wives, [210] thereby increasing the guilt of Israel. Thus proclaims the Lord, your fathers' God."[66]

(He read there) "in the 24th day of this month the children of Israel came together fasting with sackcloth and dirt upon them, and they separated the seed of Israel from the foreign children. They went about and confessed their sins, also their fathers' iniquity."[67]

Furthermore Christ said: "When your brother comes to you and confesses his sin, you should forgive him" [Luke 17:3-4]. "And when you offer your gifts upon the altar, and you remember that your brother still has something outstanding against you, then leave your offering by the altar and go first and be reconciled with your brother, and then come and offer your gifts" [Matt. 5:23-24]. "The whole Jewish land and those from Jerusalem went out to John and they let themselves be baptized by him in the Jordan and they confessed their sins" [Matt. 3:5-6].

Further: "Confess your sins to one another and pray for the others" [James 5:16].

From these preceeding passages and counter passages it is neglected and omitted in the writings.

David: Read further James the fifth chapter.

Peter van Geyen: James's passage is not dissimilar to that of Christ. Namely, that one will be punished because of sin and anyone who is sick in the flesh, as from pestilence or whatever may happen, or from other illnesses of the flesh, then he should call the elders of the church to himself, and let them pray for him [James 5:14]. Also, he must give information about the sin and about the burdens which oppress him. Because of disunity among his brothers he should also confess and give knowledge of the reason why he is punished in this manner. Briefly, this still happens among us, and in this way let them pray for him.

David: I ask, since you know the passage of James, does this signify a person who has become sick because of sin only in his flesh? Or do you mean that the passage signifies no more than a plague in the body, such as pestilence and other illnesses? And what if he does not speak of such sickness or illness, as David said in the thirty-eighth Psalm [Ps. 38:3ff.]? Or had David no sickness as a result of the sin of his youth?

Jan Pont: On account of what sin of his youth should he be sick, since he had not sinned except with Bathsheba [2 Sam. 11:1-5]?[68] [211]

David: Why did he speak then so much of it? Such as in this way: "Do not remember any longer the sin which I have committed in my youth and the iniquity which has followed thereafter, but handle me with your goodness" [Ps. 25:7]. If it is spoken neither of him nor us, what does Psalm 25 therefore mean?

Dare you say so freely before the Lord, that James signifies no more than what Christ said concerning a speech between brother and brother?

Peter van Geyen: The same is tied and bound together by both Christ and James the Apostle. We therefore do not make a differentiation between them.

David: I ask you, are you saying that the meaning of James and David is that the sickness is one merely of the flesh?

Jan Pont: Yes, no more. James spoke of outward sickness, but David of the oppression of the heart. The apostles had blessed the sick with external oil through the command. Such as Paul, who speaks of the sickness in the flesh. Read 1 Cor. 11[:30].

David: This is still my question. Is it no further?

Jan Pont: No, not further.

David: How proud you are, when you say that James speaks of physical sickness only. I say, however, that it refers to spiritual sickness as well. How will we separate?

Peter van Geyen: This interpretation that it is a spiritual sickness is indeed in need of proof.

David: You seek many detours and turnings. But you will not confess it. I confess and testify that we have become or must become sick of heart and the flesh with a heavy spirit or mind because of sin, until we are salved with spiritual oil, which does not wear out. And I ask if this foundation, which I laid before, may not stand in this way? Give me an answer.

Jan Pont: We do not agree that this can be regarded as a general rule or law, for there is no example of it. For those that have been given above, one is a confession before the Lord and the other before the brother against whom we have sinned. Of this we have examples, but not of your confession. [212]

David: See, if this is so, then the saints and forefathers had erred and have left behind a bad example, because they so freely confessed and expressed their sin, and left this behind in the Scriptures. Watch what you say. We sit in the presence of the Lord, and your words will also be written in the highest. The Lord sits to judge over us, in order to perform an examination of his saints. You sit to defend the old being, I sit to defend the Lord. Therefore I testify from the Spirit about what was given to me from the Scriptures. You profess not to be against this, but you surely are. For you deny what the Lord promises in this way, and because of your disbelief you will also reject us. Lie as much as you want; I offered you some Scriptures which you should observe. The meaning of these is not to be held as completely strange.

Jan Pont: You must still prove this. Or tell us why Christ said, "first secretly," [Matt. 18:15] and Paul said: "punish them publicly before them" [1 Tim. 5:20]. There must be a difference here.

David: Dear worthy people who are with us, if you will hear me, realize that it is a good rule among us, how one should daily proceed.

Since we have once confessed our sin, are we not further required to do such daily? That is, if the heart is not faint, to be against them indeed. Furthermore, you would not find such havoc or rebellion as there is now. Thus, I conclude by the Spirit that such must now occur. Yes, it should be done, if we seek to shame the old being and if we desire to mortify it, to be against it and kill it. You know, however, that you do not have all the writings, which have been written and taught by the prophets, from Christ and his apostles. Therefore beware that you do not continue too long with the old being. For with it everything will perish, as you believe.

Jan Pont: We say that the words of Christ at the first and second admonition speak of secret correction. Furthermore, Paul said, correct them before all. Speak to us the words by which we may be able to distinguish these.

David: When we have mournfully confessed from our hearts from our youth, then we proceed in a different way because of the rule of the teaching of Christ, that anyone who publicly has given pain to someone, that one must be punished publicly according to the Scriptures. But I ask you, does James not refer to the confession of sins, and also from the youth up? Speak and give me an answer.

Jan Pont: James speaks to the brothers, who have come to harm in this way. But in Ecclesiasticus it states, "if you have sinned, reveal it not" [Ecclus. 19:8].

David: Ecclesiasticus also says contrary to this: "Do not be ashamed to confess [213] your sins or errors" [Ecclus. 5:6-7]. Those who hide their sins, it will not go well with them, but those who confess them and relieve themselves of them, they shall find mercy.

In this way one must observe the differences in your allegations. Otherwise it will be against either Christ or Paul.

Jan Pont: Observe, Christ desires that all people be saved, yet "many are called, few chosen" [Matt. 22:14]. This appears to be a contradiction, nevertheless the one passage does not truly contradict the other.

David: Yes, I understand well this means of distinguishing. The meaning of the passage of Ecclesiasticus presented to you is that we should not confess our sins before our enemies. This was indeed not what was taught, but instead to confess before the brothers. I warn you that the time is coming when all of your hearts and thoughts will be examined by the Lord. They will be made public and will be brought into the daylight. Things which you now intend to conceal, and over which you have not previously cried or lamented according to his admonition, these will certainly be revealed. Therefore behold the things which are right and good, which I have written to you, before it is too late. Now do as you will.

I know and am in good faith certain that you are not able to see, grasp and taste it first, but instead you must believe. Because of this you will rejoice, as is written, over what the Lord has begun in us who fear him for our purification.

Jan Pont: What the Lord does to us, we will suffer patiently. What he has commanded us, we will do faithfully. Whatever one can prove to us with truth, we will not neglect it, by his grace.

David: If so, then you would not be found guilty by your own words, when all hearts are revealed. So believe the message which he has sent to you. You do not perceive him, so pray that he be made known to you. O, if I had a thousand necks, I would stick them all out by God's grace,[69] so certain is it in my heart, that it is right and good.

Jan Pont: No, no, do not stick out any necks, no one persecutes here. For the papacy is full of that. But that you say we should pray, this we will do and have done. But our proposal does not have this in it. We say concerning the passage of Ecclesiasticus, that it says not to reveal your sins neither to your enemy, and see, nor to your friends.

David: Yes, but what do you mean by your friend?

Jan: Indeed just as it stands written there.

Peter van Geyen: Now, it goes just like this. If I do not believe that he is my friend, then I do not regard him as one. But on account of the deceiver is it mostly said, to regard the one indeed as a friend. [214]

David: How is it then that you say it does not serve at all, for then all the others must fall and not be right. But I will let the wise ones judge this, and if you will remain with your interpretation that one should not confess one's sin according to this passage, and continue to distinguish between them, then both they and you, I say, are against Christ's and James's teachings and against all who have done such.

Jan: See, it is said in this way. I am unable to describe it without distinguishing, as the brothers have heard. It is not contradictory, for Christ's and Paul's words do not contradict each other. For the one says: "Correct the sins before them all," the other says: "Correct him between he and you alone." There must certainly be a difference here.

David: Since you understand better than I about what you have answered, therefore enlighten me. For these 'friends' and the others, namely the brothers, are not to be compared. For the one deals with a

Christian, and you confess yourselves to be responsible to do this. The other was to conceal your sin from one called a friend, before whom one does not do this, but regard him as one among the deceivers.

But so that the speeches be kept brief, it is therefore concluded. No and yes is a long struggle, and our long speeches will not be of much benefit. I will therefore leave it as it stands for you.

Jan Pont: The text says yes. Why should it then be no?

David: I let you win. For you desire only to be right.

Jan Pont: I do not desire to be right if it is not truly in this way.

David: You desire to have the last word, but the truth will judge us, whoever has put forth the right teaching.

Jan Pont: I speak on all their behalf for truth and righteousness.

Paulus: Therefore we sit here to listen.

David: How then will you have it? If it is not just as I but as you have said, is it not a contradiction? Do we not then believe, as you say, the Spirit of wisdom of either Christ or James?

Jan Pont: We deny it no more than the two passages: "correct them in front of everyone" and the passage of Christ, "correct him secretly." Furthermore, if a Christian is burdened, then he has the passage of James in large pieces. But if it is not heavy enough to burden his conscience, then he does not have to confess it.

Peter van Geyen: Let us not dispute about this passage, let him remain where he is. But there is still the passage of Christ: "correct him secretly," and the passage of Paul, "correct him publicly," these are not yet distinguished. There must of necessity be a difference between them. On this I desire an answer.

David: Paul says this of the elders who rule, that one [215] should not receive a complaint against them, except through two or three witnesses [1 Tim. 5:19]. But when someone is a sinner, he should be corrected in front of everyone. But it is true that this does not mean that his matter be revealed before the brothers of the congregation.[70] With these he must proceed according to the teaching of Christ. He does not exclude the public correction, but merely desires that a brother first be warned once or twice in secret. So far there is a difference between here and there, for Paul discusses the correction of elders who have sinned. Those who have a double honor, must have a double shame as an example before the others. But nevertheless he does not call them cut off. But Christ corrected these common, hardened, disobedient sinners here and cut them off as public sinners, or regarded them as the heathen.

There you have my discernment of it now, as I have understood you. But now you should understand that our basis is like a father and his household, who is free to correct the one or the other without regard.

Peter van Geyen: That Paul in 1 Tim. 5:20 spoke of the elder in reference to public correction, this we do not deny. But it is also understood that it is quite similar in word and is not different nor done away with by the passage of Christ concerning secret admonishment. If we do not make such a distinction, then the confession must happen publicly; then the secret correction occurs in vain. All Christians have, without a doubt, followed after this secret admonition.[71]

David: Well, I have not then accomplished your goal. I must therefore cease. For I cannot answer further. But I say to you, that from henceforth it must happen in this way, if we are to come to one body [Rom. 12:5]. For the one must not feign, be ashamed of or shun confessing his sins before the others as one body. It certainly happened previously in this way in the Old or New Testament, and does it not concern the last times? Therefore Ecclesiasticus states that one, I say, should first know and distinguish well the friend [Ecclus. 6:7]. This must be so now, [216] for he says that if you have sinned he will have heard and watched you. But he will act just as if you protected your sin and he will then hate you, if by chance he finds out [Ecclus. 19:7-9]. Therefore it is good to hear from this, that these friends and the brothers are not to be compared, since the latter are become like brothers in one body in Christ Jesus.

Here was read Psalm 32 with its explanation.

David: Do now as David, who spoke in this way to our instruction. Namely, "I have become of one counsel and have agreed not to hide my sins any longer, but to confess to you the evil which I have done" [Ps. 32:5].

See here, some will believe that they know certainly that it is still necessary to come to understand your evil. They will not once observe that the person of God knows indeed that all his sins are naked and public. Yes, not only that, but he knows well that he (blessed) has supplied his thoughts long before they would come into his heart. Know this, just as is written in Psalm 139[:1-16]. Read. In this way he knew better than to keep them silent and to speak them only secretly in his heart to the Lord. But because of his guilt he had to confess them with the tongue or keep silent. No, he did not think this, for one deprives the Lord when one does not speak with the mouth. This he certainly knew well. Yes, all things, however hidden, are known to him, and it was therefore not necessary to say it only secretly to the Lord, but also with the tongue. No, that continued to pull and disturb him, to suffer such a burden, but only, I say, because he did such secretly. Believe not, that he desired to keep it silent, or we must regard him as a fool and as completely ignorant. Instead, he brought it publicly into the daylight before the Lord, who (for the one who keeps it silent and will not do it) day and night beats and robs him of such strength until he is compelled to confess freely his shame in case he might bear them again. For it is right to confess publicly, or one will always carry with him his sins and vileness before his eyes, as one who esteems the great, significant, and important ones. For these ones are humbled and shamed of face and humble of heart, the poor of spirit.[72]

That was what vexed and severely oppressed David. Nevertheless, as long as he kept quiet, his strength faded away (understand). This thing constrained him strongly to exclaim them, weeping like something that bursts from splitting and cannot remain concealed or be held in. Pay attention. But hasten in this way as I did; for he says, take away the evil of my sins [Ps. 32:5].[73] [217]

Read and see, what then followed next.

I speak from the inspiration of the Spirit and that must not be looked to as incorrect. I will, however, confirm it with Scriptures, those which I have noted down by God's grace in the *Booklet of the Confession*. So good is the Father, who has allowed me to note these down because of the opponents. Nevertheless it is not necessary on its own account, but it was done from mercy by divine grace. Now tell me, if it is not right in this fashion?

Jan Pont: What David the prophet has spoken, that is without doubt correct. But that this be understood to mean publicly confessing sins, this we do not understand. For there were no brothers present, but only the Lord. For the Lord is not a human, and a human is not the Lord. Is this not so?

David: Does the Lord speak or his servants?

Jan Pont: The Lord speaks and his servants, or the Lord speaks through his servants.

David: That is what I desire to say. So then, whoever is the Lord's servant will hear his servants' confessions. He is there to hear the confessions for the Lord who has sent him in his name. Therefore whatever one does to these, he does to the Lord [Matt. 25:40]. Is this not so?

Jan Pont: Yes, in his grade it is so. But that this is the Spirit's meaning here, we do not believe this.

David: But we believe it indeed. Therefore the matter must remain quiet with us, until that day when all things will be revealed, and seen whether we are correct or you. Do you desire to proceed now, or have you more to say?

Jan Pont: We have said that we do not believe it is so, nor have we been impressed. For there is no teaching nor example of any of your understanding. For if indeed it is true that one honors the Lord when he honors his servants, yet he does not desire to have done to them what belongs solely to him. Otherwise one must fall before the servants and worship them. This passage, "that what one does to my servants or the least, he does to me," does not relate to those things shown to him by angels and people.

David: It will happen, however, that they will also inherit God's honor, praise and worthiness. For the name of God will be written upon them, which you still do not yet see [Rev. 3:12]. Therefore I say that you said yesterday that there was a difference in the Scriptures, and that no one is given a clear explanation of this differentiation except the one who has the wisdom of God or perception of the truth. But those who will not enter, are those in whom there is still an evil will or hypocrisy. They do not live in a body that has subjected sin. [218] But David says it of those who are the true worshippers, who are resolved to worship God in the Spirit and truth. But that because David kept spiritually silent before the Lord and such pain and hurt caused him to confess spiritually or inwardly, to this I respond that it is far from David's meaning and spirit. Now must the Spirit of God be a judge here between me and you. Whoever has been given the same can speak proudly indeed.

Jan Pont: We gladly confess differences in the Scriptures. That the same must be taught through God's grace, we are at peace. But we dispute that it must be a humble and earnest person who has sought the wisdom of God as silver and gold, who must have all gifts and discernment of Scripture, who must be found above all others in gifts and spirits. Moreover, the Spirit distributes them, to whom he will, according to measure [1 Cor. 12:11]. Further, what you said, that it must then remain standing between us until that day, the same neither God nor we desire. For it is now necessary to examine this teaching at this time since we seek the Lord. And the last word that you said, that David said that his sins had been such a burden that he had to confess, this we understand not. Also the words of this passage do not confirm it so far. For the text goes in this way: "For when I kept silent, my bones grew old, as I cried the whole day. For day and night is your hand heavy upon me. I am turned to misery, since . . ."[74] the thorns stick me, my sins I have confessed and I have not concealed my un-righteousness. I have said, I will confess to the Lord my unrighteous-ness contrary to myself and you have forgiven me the godlessness of my heart" [Ps. 32:3-5].

Therefore we do not understand that David had been so bur-dened in himself that he had to pour out his heart before God. Instead David sinned without looking to or remembering God, and thereafter he became darkened or stupid through the sin. He had gone a long time without true penance, humility or lamenting before God, before Nathan came to him. He was like one who stupidly ran away from God's judgment and neither regarded it nor believed it. He was not trying to conceal a heavily laden heart. He sometimes had experi-enced the oppression of anxiety, feeling that he would as a result fade away, but he did not come to a true humbling for a long time.

Afterwards, seeing that he must be ruined under the burden and stupidity, he grasped his heart and poured himself out before God and made himself [219] guilty with anxious cries for his mercy. This is our first interpretation, to which we stick.

Your second interpretation is that the man of God easily knew that all sin is revealed before God and it was not necessary for him to conceal it before God and to keep silent. We answer, that in this same passage, he also knew well or should have known that he should not commit adultery nor murder, and that such sinners must be cast out of Israel and have no part in the Lord's house. He, without a doubt, did not know this at the time, that is, he had not considered it. Otherwise the remembrance of the heart and of external things and the fear of God would have driven the sin far from him. Because this did not hap-pen, as we see, then the beggarliness of sin became like a cloak and fog covering his eyes. That is, his understanding was darkened at the time, and in this way and at this time he was damned by the sin. For the Holy Spirit spoke, that sin makes a person stupid and rude [Heb. 3:13]. But David in his sin had forgotten God's judgment and stupidly continued to conceal it from the Lord according to his stupid belief, just like the passages of Ecclesiasticus 16:11, 17, 21, Psalm 94:7, Jeremiah and Esdra had said [Jer. 23:24, 2 Esd. 16:63-66], that when people conceal sin from God and believe God does not regard it, or that it will not go badly, these ones therefore bear neither anxiety nor pain nor suffering, where there is no pain and suffering. Pay atten-tion.[75]

Peter: To speak further on this (that it is not necessary to confess in this way to the Lord, for he knows it well): In such a practice, therefore, must all the saints have kept silent, and not lamented their failings in words of prayer before God, since God already knew well what was lacking in them. But nevertheless they exclaimed such oppression and confession before the Lord with words, from their needful and burdened hearts, as there are many examples of it in the Bible and written for us to our instruction. Just as we too must conduct ourselves in our need and also to trust, so that we know how and when we should seek help and expect faithfully. In this way is David's speech and his lamentation of sins written down here now for us in such a form, for an example and an admonition.

David: You have made your reply so long, that I have now forgotten everything that went before, to which I must reply. However, I must reply briefly, not to all your words, but to the meaning. [220]

First, concerning the humble and God-fearing, who have called, wept and sought for wisdom and understanding as gold. You said that these ones do not have understanding of all parts of the Scriptures. To this I reply, that the truly humble and God-fearing ones have grasped God's wisdom and God's understanding and know the meaning of the teaching of Christ and the Holy Spirit. They know how to distinguish between good and evil, light and darkness, between letter and spirit; whatever is necessary for us to know for our salvation at the right time. It is written.

Furthermore, that for as long as he did not regard or sense God's judgment, that God regarded it not. Why then did he go about the whole day sorrowful, anxious and oppressed concerning those things which languished inside him in his silence? But the text of these Psalms, which you regard more reliable than Campanus's which I have read and written to you, I cannot doubt, since you have more ability in Latin, but he had more ability in the Hebrew and I in the Spirit. I, however, remain in the same meaning as I have written to you. Now if you had David's heart and mind, spirit or understanding, then I will fail in that day before the Lord and before you and I will come to shame in this, but God never wills this. My spirit does not think it good to say more words about it, except to say, read the text aloud and be mindful of my spirit and inspiration and to what end I have written and now speak to you. I would then have much more to say about it, but the words will have no end for as long as both you and I desire to be right. For my spirit, which leads to simplicity and the fear of God, forbids me to dispute with the scribes, except to admonish them well so that they cease from it and make captive their understanding under the obedience of the faith of Christ [2 Cor. 10:5]. This must happen for those who desire to be found among the small and humble ones, to whom the hiddenness of the kingdom will be given (as also happened previously in the time of the prophets and apostles) and will proclaim the wisdom and will of God above the great ones. Just like also Leonard Jost, whom you believe to be a prophet of God, has said, that the divine truth should be proclaimed by the least without any literal writing. He spoke particularly in this way: "I have let out my breath among them, and they illuminate my sheep. I have bound[76] my sheep in their work and in the houses and in the hedges or thornbushes or shrubs, so that they will speak my divine truth without any Scripture and should confess me from the least to the greatest." [221]

Further Leonard Jost spoke in the eighteenth chapter of the confession[77] in this way: "Now I will make my confession as a public sinner in the house of God and will make public all my secret sins before all the world, etc." With this I have ended my speech.

Jan Pont: You have repeated at the beginning of your speech that the God-fearing, the small and humble ones, who have diligently sought wisdom in this way, will therefore be able to distinguish all that is necessary to know for salvation. To this is our straight reply, that such is distinguishable in this way. Nevertheless, not every God-fearing one has the gift of explaining all the Scriptures or all passages which serve to salvation or the instruction of everyone. Just like you yourself should not be so bold to say that you have an explanation of all the necessary and blessed Scriptures.

Further, that you will not fight over the meaning of David, which we believe is explained from the letter better than your meaning from the Spirit. We let each one go his own way. We ask, are you certain from the Spirit, that your explanations or texts are given from the Spirit to understand, and that you have their proper meaning? Yes, this we desire to know, if the first text of Campanus is correct according to the Spirit, and if those later ones properly contain the profession which your printed book explained concerning this article. See, this is our position. Do you desire to answer it or will it remain here? We therefore leave it with you, saying that our interpretation is not undone in our minds and that the bringing in of wrong Scriptures does not apply to us. For we do not follow the carnal meaning of those ones who do not fear, seek or follow God. Therefore the speaking of the truth is not against us. But we ascend in the knowledge of the rule of Christ, in which is complete perfection, only with those Scriptures which are not against other Scriptures but are in accordance with the Scriptures.

We also have something to say concerning Leonard Jost's confession, as it needs a reply. First, we say, that it is partly contrary to your own statement when you say, not to confess the sins before the world or the godless, but before the brothers. But Leonard is, on the other hand, concerned with the confession of the priests and monks about their secret sins committed under the appearance of service to God, who speak these before the whole world.

David: I will answer this thing which you have said to or asked me, that I should not nor must not confess myself to be able to understand or to explain all necessary, blessed holy Scriptures. To this I say, you attack me so strongly and harshly and believe to capture me in these words. I respond in this way: See, there are many Scriptures written, spoken and taught, which we do not now have in written form. [222] Second, many writings in the Old and New Testament have occurred which served in a literal fashion to the temporal situation of people, according to their nature.

Third, there are yet many Scriptures which shall or must occur (whether we have them or not) at the time of the seventh trumpet [Rev. 11:15], when the hiddeness of God will be finished. Then all hidden things will be revealed through that most clear sevenfold light. But the Scriptures, which serve us now at this time, are necessary in order to know what to do. I basically confess that I have received understanding daily from the Lord. Moreover, I am still receiving daily more and more understanding according to the mind of my Lord, through God's grace. Praised be my heavenly Father concerning his goodness, that he has served up his word and light to me, so I can perceive his will.

Further, if the text of Campanus, of which you speak, is according to the sense of the Holy Spirit, as David had written or spoken from word to word, is unknown to me, just like I supposed that it was also unknown from the Zwinglian or other texts, whether it should be written formally in this way according to your words and sense. Nevertheless, if the words stand here and if you find them here in the text, then I will regard them as good in themselves. For they move my spirit as serving my proposal, while you say no. So then this must remain as it stands and be given over for judgment to the spiritual people or to those who fear God—the believing, lowly hearts. They best judge the meaning of what the Lord has spoken.

(Furthermore, what you said concerning Leonard Jost, that he said to confess in the house of God; are they not the believing or true Christians? Although it is written regarding the priests, teachers or leaders, do not forget that they also included the members, their followers.)

Jan Pont: It will be enough for us to respond to the principle of your answer. For you know or confess that you are still daily receiving understanding of necessary things from the Lord. From this then it should be easy to truly understand that one does not have all knowledge nor can have it all. For Paul too desired that the door of the word be opened further to him through the intercession of the saints [Col. 4:3-4].

Furthermore, concerning Campanus's translation, our examination was not a dispute in the word, but a inquiry about the meaning, if it were to be understood in this fashion. If it was, then it must have been practiced in this way also in the time of Israel. This is what we heard until yesterday. For we believed that such a broad way which you now describe is not true. Also if this is obligatory, then there must always, as we believe, be a command or law concerning it. But since there is none, and the promise[78] was horrible to them, we can therefore not regard it in this way. [223]

David: This is indeed a puny defence. Just because there has been no previous law for confession in this way, as you say, you will therefore not receive it as good or to be kept. You cannot make yourselves innocent. For this is now another time and there is a stronger or greater word or teaching. But since I cannot fulfill your meaning well enough with all of this, so I must keep quiet. I must, however, point out about your answer, that the Holy Spirit in the last days, which was promised through his prophets, will be poured out on all flesh, as it is written, then also sons and daughters will proclaim God's Word as prophets through the Spirit [Joel 3:1]. This was not described correctly in former times when it was comprehended in the letter. Is it therefore less important which Spirit or understanding of God each one has received according to the measure of their faith?

Jan Pont: If this is so, then let one leave behind the introduction of the law and prove the matter through the new inspiration of the Spirit. For the Spirit has been shown trustworthy before. As Leonard Jost says, his testimony directs along with the Holy Scriptures and not contrary to or against them. Therefore we were warned by Christ and his apostles not to go above the image of Christ. For each disciple is fully able if he is like his master [Matt. 10:24-25].

David: Be quiet and let it now be enough, the Lord will yet make you know indeed.

The afternoon (of the third day) they desired to speak further.

David: Do you now think it good that we cease, so that you will then be right and help the others? Therefore if you cannot conduct it to wisdom or instruction, then I do not know how to answer you further. It is furthermore not allowed for me to speak much further with all your disputing.[79]

David: Even if many people are found to be long unbelieving, untrue and slothful, the Lord (behold) still proceeds just as well with his work. This is just like the word of Christ and the apostles which was little believed and despised by the proud and those who followed after their own spirits. [224] Therefore, if all of you too do not believe the Spirit and say that you do not understand it, then know that such was prophesied by Leonard Jost: "Many will hear you and not hear, many will see you and not see. Many will hear you, but not see. Many will see you, but will not hear." Chapter 6.[80] And as long as you look to the letter and not to the Spirit, it will be found among you that the book remains closed. For this Spirit does not teach your heart to madness or to disunity. You proudly speak against this, but you will still mourn, when you see the morningstar descending on the simple ones. God will dwell with the despised souls. This will be found true, whether you believe it or not. Therefore I desire indeed that we cease and that one compile what has already been written, along with the others. Let this then be sufficient. Seeing that you still stand upon Melchior Hoffman, then it is my desire that you transmit this to him just as it has happened and been written. With this I will let all things stand. And see that you do it well. I have warned you. I am therefore free of you. You cannot make me responsible, for I have not withheld anything from you. If you had believed me and had received as good the Spirit with which I speak, then you would truly not be witnesses against God and his Christ. If you have lied, then watch what you do. You can truly know your meaning only through an examined, innocent, holy understanding; otherwise not. If you are now willing to do such, then let it happen with you. For if you did this, we indeed could sit seven days and the last should be the first and the first, last [Matt. 19:30; 20:16].

Jan Pont: See, all that is fitting and reasonable we would gladly do. What is diligently copied from our sitting together, shall not be neglected. But you complain that we opposed you and would not receive your spirit in everything. The Almighty is our witness, that we have been strongly moved to do so. What it was that stopped us was mentioned previously and is not necessary to repeat. You said that we will not truthfully profess that your basis and spirit is against God and Christ, but the same is not sufficient to us, or it is not enough to us. For other teaching or inspiration is forbidden just as well to us and we are commanded not to be wise above our heads, nor to receive things which are openly contrary. Therefore it was necessary on our part to still have at this point a proof of these things of the image of the rule of Christ. Therefore it is our rule, that the matter be understood through the testimony of the Spirit or Scriptures in the teaching of Christ. Therefore we do not want to stop, for we have not spoken about these articles and the passages which are noted with them. For even though we remain stuck in one article, we desire to discover [225] if we might come together in others. In this way we could come together in the others and help each other and read through the booklets, for this is your and our intention.

Peter van Geyen: I also desire that the speeches not be ended here, but that we hear them again so we can respond. If we were already recalcitrant, although such is not the case, even then not all would be lost. For when these writings come to us or to your brothers, they then might be observed out of your strong witness and through our ignorance. For there is not a priest, monk nor teacher who does not also have the same proof-texts. They also say the same and they have said it before; they still have fallen into error. So we desire a further answer and we also will give an answer, as much as we are able.

David: (You will not be able to obtain any further answer because the word must be believed. This first thing has not been shown as it should be, you have therefore lost through his power. Remember the command of the Lord through the archangel who is predicted to come at the Last Day [cf. Rev. 7:2-3]. What is his command, other than what he has previously commanded and taught for a long time. You should fill your mouths with silence).

Further, I am indeed certain that it is not necessary to make a longer period of speeches on account of our brothers. For these small, humble hearts are able to comprehend and understand me much more easily, with only a third of the difficulty, because of their faith and trust in God. And as you have not believed me here, as I say, on the things which are easily understood, how will you believe me concerning those which I have held back? In particular, about the meaning of the texts that I have held up before you. There is therefore no use in speaking further about them. It is just as I have written to you; all is straight. This is true, judge it well. This you cannot do until you have become circumcised of heart, simple of eyes and God-fearing.

I have said enough to you, so that you could understand that the child stands under the youth and the youth must bow under the adult and under the grey-haired, that is under the spirit of maturity. As long as this is not understood nor done, many errors will occur. As is written, the correct understanding and the pure, naked truth is regarded as incorrect and as lies by the proud.[81]

Remember Judas and Theudas [cf. Acts 5:36-7] who, as you said, are a warning [226] not to believe others easily. So behold that you not be found like the scribes and the Jews who laid hands upon Christ and upon those who follow him. Desire instead to examine this.

Peter van Geyen: We will leave this speech alone. This was said as an admonition that we should not be proud and as a warning that we, by the grace of God, not become like the scribes or Pharisees, who treated Christ in a depraved manner. We, of course, do not desire to oppose Christ and the truth. Judas and Theudas, however, did not have this same basis. But those who approached us who generally had the same basis as you have described, we are still doubtful of them. But these speeches do not serve us at all to the basis. But concerning what hinders us, we desire you to give us a basic answer. But we beg that you give to us the basis of the matter for you and our brothers.

David: As you have not understood nor received as good the least of my professions, namely confession, I therefore cannot speak with you again of the greater or more heavenly things [cf. John 3:12]. Therefore do not regard me as evil if my mouth is now closed. But it remains between you and me until it is revealed to either you or me. Those of you who can, pray, for I say to you, it is more than time.

Jan Pont: With this we are not served. For the speeches are nevertheless not finished or ended, because they still remain dark. We will not accept them, because there is no law or command.

David: Dare you say that? See, on the contrary, the Holy Spirit witnessed to me of humility, meekness, simplicity and innocence and they are certainly in our hearts. You will not come to the perfection until you begin as a youth and become like a child. This is revealed by Christ through his Spirit to us all by grace. Behold. Should I now speak further against you, contrary to my conscience and the truth? For I cannot give you that understanding, if you do not believe me. I desire to be instructed by you, but you do not dare it. Though if you still desire such, then do so, but our mind is certain. For the Spirit of Emmanuel (this I say to you) is in the daylight. He examines the hearts and can perceive evil. He will correctly prove and judge all things. Let it also be enough here. Do you know otherwise how to make people wise? If so, then you have better instruction than I do in teaching by God's grace. Thus it will no more be possible.

Words of Conclusion.

At the end of the proceedings Peter van Geyen spoke as a conclusion of the matter.

My brothers, have I permission to speak some words about our proceedings?

See, dear brothers and friends, who you are. For I see that our [227] speeches are summarized in writing and for the most part are set down with a broken sense and jotted down to read with an improper understanding. Or some were remembered afterwards which were not noted down at the time but were mixed in at some places. Similarly, your words were expanded and changed at some places, or were afterwards improperly brought in and written out from our brief notes.[82] But you yourself must permit this as I myself. For I have heard from your mouth, David, that you have charged Leonard to listen especially and particularly sharply to your words and that he should diligently note them down. We (so to speak) have also shortened our recording to some degree. At the last, however, the truth will be protected and made clear. Although Leonard has received your word as most diligently true, he himself has confessed above that he has not understood well my speech. Therefore not all of my words have been written and those that were written have been shortened or mixed by ignorance, to such an extent that he himself, yes all of us, frequently cannot receive an understanding from them; although we have spoken them ourselves and you all have heard it. Concerning these, our brother Paulus has been too slow in recording them to such an extent that he sometimes did not grasp the meaning of neither your nor our speeches. Nor has he very well summarized completely, properly or entirely your speeches, half as well as Leonard, or at some places not as much. On the other hand, he at times had some words on both sides which Leonard did not have. These speeches are signed in Leonard's and Paulus's handwriting, from which you, David, have written this according to their best meaning and content.

Also know that those who were here at the end were David, Leonard Jost, Jan Pont, Peter van Geyen, Peter Glassmaker, Paul Goldsmith, and Hendric van Ghent.[83] And above all of this there are many things which were spoken in our proceedings which were not written down, for example, concerning the name of God and also some things on the confession. [228] Afterwards a few words were inserted in the margins which also exist because of the recording of our side-remarks. Although one has mentioned to him afterwards that the speeches have been set down in such a form that those who read them quickly might not understand what was asked and answered on account of the previous speaker's style. Also there has been a detour of some days long, as one may hear, before one came to the matter. And so when one begins to touch upon some long speeches, one necessarily loses the flow again and again through a detour. Therefore we and especially I myself have frequently complained in the speeches and have advised just as was added to the writing. Many words on this account also have disappeared which we both agreed to leave out of the writing for the purpose of brevity. And although afterwards the writing needed some correction, it might have been better improved in its meaning if we all agreed, according to the requirement of the matter, either by shortening or lengthening, or by clarification of the meaning. It is true, however, that sometimes it was needed and done. Nevertheless, in this understanding I considered that David was perhaps not as long-suffering in the meaning nor as patient in the speech as it was often required. But it appeared, dear David, that you became angry whenever someone began to correct those of your words which we heard as good or evil. I have diligently provided such observations of correction, but I spoke only as little as possible, as you must know. To the end that we not be aroused against God in a great dispute, nor become angry or despising the one against the other without reason. For then we would be consumed by God. We had much better let it remain as it is, whether or not it makes sense or whether it has a conclusion or an answer or not. You must answer to your conscience concerning the things about which you enquired the meaning. For it is certainly thick enough and you too also believed that enough had been said. All the long speeches and those things which are transcribed must, however, be concluded with short replies or answered or replied to in very few words. You felt or you wanted this, that it might afterwards by God's grace find a place, and then we could expect your answer. It is understood in the disputation that you came here in order to admonish us before the Day of the Lord and to stand and to testify that the [229] things which you have written in your books are right and have been produced from the Spirit. We, without a doubt, have spoken against much in them. But for these brothers who desired to hear about our disagreement on marriage, whether to keep many wives or possessions at this time, do you now believe that we can proceed about this? If it is not so, then I will let you speak and thereafter proceed from here. I desire to write it down first, and after writing about it I will explain it, so that it would not be shortened or altered like the first, as is written before. If you also want to do it in this way, then I am at peace.

David: The writings which you have composed about our business according to your own meaning, two or three days after the discussion of the book had ended, you have written in this way according to your own spirit, concept and right, as you have believed. I partly understand that I then should give an answer so that my signing would then be certain; the Lord does not permit me. Behold to what end you have written such. If it has happened to the Lord's praise, then I let the Lord judge. He will enable you to see your own hastiness, wrath and obstruction against me. Also he will reveal clearly your understanding where you sought to capture me in delusions. Nor would you permit me, as I have warned you, to proclaim and to write this. Yes, I have allowed you to speak together, among your brothers and to allow you to write your speeches, sometimes from the mouth of the one or the other, sometimes two alike. Thereafter were both my and your speeches compared by the others and after one had written this, they were added by the others and corrected, yes sometimes twice. Now you come to all of this and still make long involved complaints about it. I did not think this was proper for a wise person as you are regarded, nor especially for a Christian. In spite of this I allowed you to write it as correct and right, spoken behind my back. Write after this matter from the question and answer of the book, as beautiful, wide and broad as you will. You seek in this merely your own honor and to be right. Only allow me to do the same, for I will reply before the Lord concerning what has happened.

Furthermore, you have written this not from my mouth nor in my presence but in my absence. Instead, it is mostly from your memory, according to your understanding or from what you have remembered about each speech or where you simply have questioned me about what I thought, or just as it seemed. I first desire indeed to examine the same, to check my own words and meaning, so that no one will understand anything from my words [230] which are against the Lord, or judged badly, when you do not accept the guilt. If you will not do it, then I must endure this myself and take the matter to the Lord, before whom I stand.

Peter van Geyen: The things that I have spoken or written there, I have been motivated by necessity or love, the necessity of truth and love of the brothers. This I have done as David said, after the conversation, but not after the end when the transcript was read over. But I had not desired that anyone who reads our proceedings be more confused, but instead be improved through it. This alone has moved me to speak as I have.

Furthermore, to reply to all your speeches would be done or conducted unfruitfully. But if the thing is not true, then one can ask or read the testimonies of it while one is here present and is still among the others, for both your signatures and those who are named have been involved in the correcting and proceedings. I have therefore produced this so that I, by means of them, might cut off the false backbiting from which David also one time had admonished us not to say anything behind his back. With God's help we will keep this.

Concerning my anger or interruptions in these proceedings, I have absolutely no knowledge. I believe also not anyone of these others did this. We desired to make few words of these things, so that we not write it to our honor, but to protect God's honor. And we will also now let all such things proceed further, as much as concerns us and is possible. We will allow them to remain unchanged so that we might handle the foundational things of faith or doctrine in a brief manner, and let the Lord be judge about the detours.

Further, that David desired us to examine our memorial, we desire from whole hearts to do so gladly. Also, in order that we provide an answer to all the things that he furthermore asked or desired from us in friendly love, in order to allow to happen all that is possible in this way. I desire from you the same. Here also be remembered the speeches about marriage.

Furthermore, we regard the time to have run long enough to set forth these our proceedings any wider, broader or more beautiful, as you allow us and desire the same yourself. It stands as it stands and it remains now as it remains until our God gives you or us another mind.

David: Well then, I desire just as you desire in this part.

Peter: Furthermore, we have discussed marriage, where we had some writings of David concerning it. Upon this we thought it good to say much about [231] them or to write to him. But as he was present with us we have given to him these our writings after which he testified to us his basis in them, that he has written them correctly and regards them good as read, or how we have interpreted them. After the end David had responded to our speeches, the sense of which sounded like this:[84]

See, there is much for me to reply to. But since (as it pleases you) the time has expired and we must board the ship, it is our desire indeed that you would send the book to us so that I may answer you from it. If you are not at peace with it then I will arrange to do it now at this time before I leave you. The time runs on as it will. I will give an answer to you as much as the Lord gives me something to say about it. But if you will allow me to journey as I desire, then you, Paulus, Petrus, and Hendric, will also write down what to say. Then if any of the brothers might question them thereafter, they will not answer it any further except in this way as it actually happened. In this way, yes, one leaves them the answer before their eyes. . . .[85]

David Joris, "The Fountain of Life," *The Wonder Book*, fol. iiiv.
Courtesy of the Mennonite Library, University of Amsterdam

8

A Blessed Instruction for the Hungering, Burdened Souls (c. 1538)

This remarkable tract has never been cataloged and only briefly analyzed. It was recently rediscovered in a bound volume of tracts in the Mennonite Library, University of Amsterdam. While this volume was printed in 1616, all of the dated tracts were composed before 1547, with two dated to 1539, and it appears that all of the works were composed in the late 1530s or 1540s.[1] A quick glance at the contents of *A Blessed Instruction for the Hungering, Burdened Souls* suggests a relatively early date also for this tract.

An estimation of the date of this tract can be made by reference to its contents. In it Joris criticizes Martinians, Evangelicals and Covenanters; the first was a common self-designation of the followers of Martin Luther (their opponents called them Lutherans), while the last was what Melchior Hoffman's Dutch followers, the Melchiorites, called themselves during the mid-1530s. What he meant by Evangelicals is not altogether clear, but probably refers to those reformers in the Low Countries commonly called Sacramentarians. All of these groups were prominent in the 1530s. What is even more telling, however, is the lack of any reference to Menno Simons or to his supporters, the Mennonites. Were the tract composed in the early 1540s or later, there is little doubt that Menno would have been included in Joris's list of sinfully proud reformers. Beginning in 1539, in fact, Joris and Menno crossed swords in an often vehement disputation, both by missive and by verbal debates.[2]

Also providing clues to the dating of *A Blessed Instruction* is

Joris's blistering criticism of Hoffman's heirs who had turned to the letter of the Scriptures, ignoring their truer, spiritual meaning. This critique is best understood as Joris's response to his meeting with the Strasbourg Melchiorites in the summer of 1538. Here Joris had faced the followers of Hoffman and found them to be biblical literalists, caught up in their own education and wisdom and refusing to bow to his spiritual interpretation.

The work translated here stands out among Joris's tracts also because in it he openly presents his view of church history. Had Joris been influenced in this by world histories such as Sebastian Franck's popular *Chronica*, published in 1531?[3] What we can discern from this work concerning Joris's interpretation of history compares favorably with Franck's approach. As part of his historical overview, Joris criticizes in turn the Jews of the Old Testament, the early Christians, monks and priests, Lutherans, and Melchiorite Anabaptists. Each group, Joris affirms, held a measure of the truth, but all eventually fell into the pitfall of pride. They would not have done so, he suggests, if they had been aware of their proper place in the apocalyptic scheme, and that they would be succeeded by a seventh trumpet or angel, presumably signifying his own teaching. What is surprisingly missing from this tract is any reference to the third David. If the work were composed with the Strasbourg Melchiorites in mind, this omission becomes more comprehensible. For this audience Joris diminished the more esoteric elements of his thought in order to convince them of his essential leadership role. If the tone of this work is any indication, any hopes that Joris may have entertained about converting the "Elders in Israel" to his position had become slim indeed.

❖ ❖ ❖ ❖ ❖

[111ᵛ]
A Blessed Instruction for the Hungering, Burdened Souls

Behold.

"Just like a rosebud or flower among the thorns, so my lady friend, the beloved woman, is despised, ridiculed, and hated among the evil women" [Song of Sol. 2:2]. "Just like a sweet apple tree among the wild savage trees, so is my friend, the most beautiful, among the sons of the mighty, the evil men of Belial" [Song of Sol. 2:3]. They have rejected and opposed him, they have done evil for good, they have given hate for love. Finally they murdered the innocent Lamb and have not willed his will.

See, all of this is happening to the Beloved, the Dove, the Elect Woman, the Mother of Zion and the Bride of Christ. She must drink the wine of bitterness from the same cup. With this same drink and through the suffering and terror of the bitterness of death, she must be dipped or plunged under the baptism [Mark 10:38-39]. Here her Lord and Master (the Head) has walked before her. Regardless of how many opponents, enemies, and corrupters rebel against him, he still breaks forth like a shining light while she is perishing in her blindness. He has risen in life from the dead, manifesting triumph over all. [112ʳ]

Therefore the ploughmen, the workers of evil, the enemies of the truth have ploughed up Zion's rye [cf. Jer. 26:18]. They have made many deep furrows [Ps. 129:3] in order to oppress her. See, in spite of this they still are not more powerful than she. Yet they cast falsehood, deception, lies, and envy before her and smite her in the face, in order to make her black, unseemly, despised, abominated, and to make people adverse to her. It will not help them at all, but she will come forth glorious and shining and be exalted above all mountains and hills [cf. Isa. 51, 52]. She will be beautiful and pure as the moon, pure as the sun and as terrifying as a judge.[4]

In this way the truth must break through the lies. For they are the enemy of the truth and will be defeated and brought to shame by the same. However, lies with their seed have the prominence for a time. But just as quickly the truth will overhaul them, just like the day and light breaks through the night and darkness. Or just as the brightness of the sun appears, piercing the haze or mist and all dark clouds (driven by the wind) [Jude 12]. For she is stronger than all that. Behold, all you who have understanding, you people of God who bear the law of God in your hearts [Ps. 37:31, 40:8, etc.]. And do not cause offense in this, even if people scorn, slander, and tell lies or scandals about you, regarding you as an abomination, turning away their faces from you. It must happen in this way, just as it [112ᵛ] is happening. Woe to you who value and highly esteem humans, for that is horrible and objectionable before God. Remember the words of the prophets and of your Lord, rejoice when the Scriptures are fulfilled in you [Rom. 8:4]. For in this be certain that when the Lord chastises you, he loves you and desires to teach you. When he visits you to test your heart and thoughts, and sets you in lowliness and misery, it is to purify you, to make you elect. He will exalt and bring you to honor [Heb. 12:4-11].

It is time that the judgment begin at the house of God, that the adulterers be punished [1 Pet. 4:17]. However, blessed are those who are found sincere and faithful, patient in tribulation or temptation and testing. For they will receive from God at the right time the unfading crown of righteousness, the glory of his inheritance, the joy of his glorious riches in all fullness [2 Tim. 4:8]. Blessed is he who overcomes.

For this reason, O you God-fearing, believing, lowly hearts, be of good cheer. You militant giants, do not let your hands grow weary, nor let your spirit decrease. Instead, hold up your hands [cf. Exod. 17:12]. Pray that you gain the understanding of the gray-headed, that the light of your eyes becomes clearer, your heart more pure, your soul more watchful, and that your work prosper. All so that you will be steadfast in your faith and might be found faithful to the end as a sincere Christian or member of the body of Christ. For there is no spot, nor is there any wrinkle [113ʳ] in this body or the holy true church. With this alone do the Father and the Son have fellowship [Eph. 5:27]. The same will be found as a dwelling of God in the Spirit, but no one else. O you good-hearted, hungering, righteous souls, exult in your living God, your fortress, your strength, your protector, shield, and blockhouse [Ps. 144:2]. Through hope lift up your courage or horns into the pure truth and repel the horns of the evil one [Ps. 75:10]. For once he sees your great perfection and your resistance against the devil, he (who is the head or wisdom of the old Adam) will flee from you. In his flight he will be turned to horror and terror. Hold out your hands only to God (your surety and help). Namely, pray with all your strength and without ceasing. Understand. And let not your heart slacken nor rest, neither close your eyes nor cease praying to the Lord, until the time when he is merciful and gracious to your great desire, hunger, and thirst. And let your desire be to see your enemies, namely, to hastily abandon all the hellish, evil spirits—sin, death, the devil, hell, and world. You must completely and forcefully oppose and assault them from your heart, in order to enter the kingdom of God, that is, to obtain the mature perfection of the new creature in Christ through faith by grace [2 Cor. 5:17]. This you will receive as a result of your strong, continuous and diligent desires. Believe and trust God. [113ᵛ] You have power, if you receive it, to defeat the world, namely to bring under you the kingdom of Satan, just as Christ and the apostle John have spoken [cf. Acts 26:18; 1 John 3:8].

This is now so much. But if you desire to do God's work and to enter the kingdom of God, which in the beginning was robbed from you by the devil, the old serpent Satan [cf. Gen. 3], then you must seek to earnestly and diligently fulfill the word of the kingdom and his righteousness. Namely, to stand under the obedience of the truth in the Spirit of Christ and fulfill his commandments and teaching. That is, become meek and humble, even to nothing. And love the Most High above all other things, and then our brother or neighbor as ourselves [Matt. 22:37-39]. Pay close attention to this and make sure that you will not be punishable in this. If so, you will live and you will see your soul's desire in rest. Only fulfill the word which you have believed; it is not far away or high above you, but is nearby, in you and in your hearts. There it works mightily, but not on the outside. Take heed, yes, pay close attention.

Follow my advice and teaching in the Lord which I counsel you, if you do not wish to err. O those who wish to be blessed, hear and do this. Yes, behold the late and early rains [James 5:7]. Become filled by them, O you beloved, and become drunk, fiery, and soaked; sprout and grow well. And produce living, sweet fruit from your heather, through the power and the breath of God, at the prepared time to his praise.

How long will you be unmoving, slow or fainthearted? Instead, progress, do not stand still, but increase your work, quicken your pace, and you will rejoice. Delight more and more in your work, not tiring on the path, but be strengthened in the battle. For the lust of the Spirit will illuminate and sweeten for you all things which previously were bitter or sour. Things that were heavy or a burden for you will become light. What was unbelievable or invisible to you, you will see face-to-face with truth in the Spirit. Indeed you will taste and feel when previously you were too weak. You will become strong from this, for where you were once dead, you will become living.

See, this you will meet with, and so you will be changed and quickened through the clarity of Christ. All of you who are sustaining struggle, suffering, and defeat, will, according to your wish, defeat the evil with the good, which you love or take pride in, and possess the kingdom of God. Therefore, hasten, hasten, to come to the rest in the garden of Eden, into the life. O all of you, the children of truth, sons and daughters of Abraham, of the almighty Father, who desire to escape the wrath and the great anger of God, know your visitation and behold your valuable time. Look in the mirror of the animals, O Israel, and do not be blind or disobedient. See, the owl knows its time, the swallow [114ʳ] knows its time, the cuckoo knows its time, the finch and the herring know their time [Jer. 8:7]. But if the fishermen or seamen do not perceive or observe these times, then they will catch nothing. If the finch-catcher does not closely observe the finch, it will fly away from him. It is the same for you. If you do not seek the Lord while he is to be found, then you will lose him. If you do not call out to him while he is nearby, then he will leave your sight. Behold, the Lord has for a long time stood in front of your door and knocked [Rev. 3:20]. O you disobedient, lewd, hardened hearts, remember what I previously said to you, that he will leave you and go to another. But when you see this, then you will for the first time know and feel what you have done. Therefore, listen and be awake. Put your pound⁵ to work and serve your neighbor with whatever you have, according to your ability, to the praise of your Lord. But if such oil of mercy and love does not burn in you, then you will remain outside [cf. Matt. 25].

Hear, O you fruitful good trees of righteousness planted at the flowing waters. These were meant to divide up into many lovely rivers, in order to moisten all lovely places (understand).⁶ And to gladden, I say, the thorny, dry places. Namely, the thirsty, believing hearts, which cry and weep for the quiet, running, clear water, which flows under the threshold of God. It flows out of the sides into all the larger waters, in order to make healthy all living animals therein [Song of Sol. 4:12-15]. [115ʳ]

Blessed are you, O you of the earth, rejoice in the heavens which pour out their riches and fullness upon you, to the help and trust, to the glory and joy of the burdened who dwell therein. For they who have lain alone in the long desert will yet appear pleasant, verdant, and joyful. The field will blossom just like a lily and open like a rose [Isa. 35:1-2]. And it will smell of the sweetness of pleasant-smelling herbs and overflowing blossoms, just like the powder of an apothecary's fire. The mandrake (understand) and all the good, holy fruits will grow to overflowing and increase upon the earth, which will be renewed and refreshed in mercy [Song of Sol. 7:12-13]. This is what the earnest love, truth, and righteousness of God will do. He will certainly dwell therein and remain eternally unchanged. Pay attention, the mouth of the Lord has spoken it.

All who have certain faith and are now born of God will win, since they are of his divine nature—humble, meek, long-suffering, friendly, merciful and true, simple and right, pure and perfect, full of righteousness. These gifts [cf. Gal. 5:22-23] have strength against the contrary things. Therefore, those in whom these things are found, will receive the inheritance of the kingdom. For they are God's children in deed and power. These ones will not remain outside, nor will they be harmed.

God is truth. His children [115ᵛ] of divine nature must likewise be truthful and not liars. For just as he is, so should they be, and they must not be seen in any other form than his [Col. 3:9-10]. All people must examine themselves closely to see just how close to God's nature they are. For you will not have any honor from God before this, nor will the Father be able to correctly name you [John 10:3], until you are of his nature and are hungering and thirsting after these gifts, being clothed with their deeds. You cannot know this except through the testing. In this examination, one must evidence patience or endurance before anyone may have the honor of the love, truth, and living hope. This is certain, that we must be compared to God's Word, which is seven times purer. Nevertheless, we must be found fully sufficient in all things. Those, then, who do not keep the word of patience, or who do not let themselves be reproved or chastised without words of complaint or evil or roguish murmuring, will be brought to shame. Behold, my sheep know me, and I know them.[7] These cannot be deceived, for they know the truth from the lies and are able to separate the chaff from the wheat, the good from the evil [Matt. 3:12]. For just so is Emmanuel and his justice born from God, without doubts or error.

However, the egotistical and witty are blind and proud and become increasingly blind and hardened in their ignorance because of their opposition to and blaspheming of [116ʳ] the truth. In this way too the Jews and blind scribes also thought that they could protect themselves from temptation and remained (or so they thought) with the Scriptures. But they did not understand what the Scriptures are and how they are. In particular, that they stand not in the letter, but in the Spirit, power, and wisdom, and those serving the Scriptures, whom God has also inspired. Regardless of what kind of persons they are, learned or unlearned, these ones correctly divide the Scriptures [2 Tim. 2:15], bringing it forth in whatever form. And they are necessary to instruction, for they bind and give power and life [cf. Matt. 16:19], seeing that they are breathed into and given the ability by the Spirit. If it is for chastisement, then it happens to our improvement; if it is for instruction, then such happens for righteousness and places the person perfectly in Christ, completely alive, understanding, and healthy.

See, these Scriptures will not be forgotten if they are sown, received, and written in the heart, just as people do the letter. But whatever all such people produce, this is certainly the Holy Scripture or God's Word, which is written in the heart. And this God's Word is not torn into pieces or cast into the water or burned, as is easily done with paper and parchment. Neither does it rot, for it cannot be destroyed, but remains living, fiery, and even powerful into eternity. So do not fulfill the paper letter which people learn externally and remember through a good memory. Such will remain [116ᵛ] lost if it is lost and it will not return if it is destroyed. They cripple, change, and remove parts. For the one text maintains this, another maintains the opposite. Yes, some places contradict others. Are they both God's Word? Therefore, grasp understanding and become truly seeing and understanding.[8]

Here it is. They are always teaching but the people never become any wiser in divine understanding. Nor can they come to the true knowledge of the truth of Christ in its power. Instead, they are hardened and blinded through their own fancy and the knowledge of the letter. Look thoroughly at all the nations of the world. Most of them use the complete Scriptures, Bible and the New Testament, with many other books. Yes, look at all those among us, the Jews, monks, priests, the Martinians, the Evangelicals, and the Covenanters. Each of these helps and teaches the other from the written Scriptures. They pull and bend the Scriptures according to their own will and believe that they have the best interpretation. Everyone uses them and tastes from them as they will. But unfortunately we are not any more pious, but instead we have become even more evil! Each one opposes, devour or treads upon the others. First the Jews thought or believed that they were sharp. However, the Christians (which are now called Christian men) desired to have a better and greater wisdom than the Jews, as they certainly had at the first. [117ʳ] But having destroyed the Jews, they also became vain in their minds. After this came Martin [Luther] who despised all of these, revealing their foolishness and driving out the monks. He and those with him were highly regarded. For at the start he too (this I say to you) had received many great gifts. But he also finally became vain and inflated in his own estimation. After him arose Melchior Hoffman in our own time. He, with his followers, have run over the Scriptures with their feet, climbing well above these aforementioned ones, regarding them as fools and vain. But at the last he himself has become vain and corrupted through his understanding. They also thought too highly of themselves. Furthermore, the one in front, the other behind (although each began in the first level of piety) have, through the deception of the devil, become proud and evil in their self-esteem or highness. Yes, those who came and stood up later worst of all. O if only they had remained in their piety, if only they had observed their time and had not stood up against each other (like the land against the sea and the sea against the land)!

O if they only understood that there are seven lighters,[9] seven stars, seven lamps, seven seals, seven trumpets or angels, and seven levels [cf. Rev. 3:1; 4:5; 5:1; 8:2], and that each one must complete one's own work. O that each one would keep himself quietly submissive under the others, according to [117^v] the ordinance of God. If each one had only kept himself unchanged in his lowliness! But no. Each wanted to be the master over the others and revile the others as rogues and evil doers, as heretics and deceivers. All of this the Lord has clearly seen and it has not pleased him at all. Especially that each one places himself so high in his own estimation and sets the others in contempt. I too believed many twisted falsehoods until I listened closely. Therefore, I, as well as all these others, must descend to the lowest and be regarded as the least. O if only some of them recorded and confessed to have erred!

See, all these have been masters, doctors, and great scribes, and still are. But the word of Isaiah will take away the courage of all those who proceed in their seductive high-mighty proud mind.[10]

They have all of this, yet they do not understand God's Word, all who have the letter or know the languages. No. If so, the Jewish or Hebrew, the Greek and Latin masters would have had the wisdom, instead of the other unlearned or simple poor Netherlanders. But God our heavenly Father be thanked, who through his Son Christ, allowed the Holy Spirit to appear to us, as well as upon the apostles and disciples of Christ, along with those with them. This Spirit of God [118^r] is understood or comprehended just as well in one language as in the others. For each one heard or understood his language and instruction in his own tongue [Acts 2:6]. In this way the Spirit is not bound to the tongue or letter.[11] But those who find themselves sitting in darkness and blindness and cry out in fear to the Lord, if they hear the word, they will receive the light of his clarity, the power of his Holy Spirit and the mind of God. But the seeing will become blind in this [John 12:40]. Pay attention. Earlier Melchior Hoffman had said and written the same thing many times, but afterward he thought little of it.

For this reason I say that all who can externally cut and fit the Scriptures are not able to perceive or have God's Word or Spirit. For they interpret, propose, and teach only according to these doctors and great masters. No, they do not perceive, neither do they have

God's Word, says the Lord. Whoever rejects or perverts God's Word rejects the greatest love. But how is each one able to learn the understanding of God's Word through the mind of the Spirit alone, namely, to have God's mind and the fear of the Lord, and lead an undefiled life? This understanding is neither granted nor given to anyone except to those who have completely put outside their own reason and bravery, their own wisdom, spirit, or understanding. And they must hate their own life, regarding it as nothing, as dust and ash [Gen. 18:27]. Namely, they must become like a small, young [118ᵛ] infant, in humility, simplicity, and innocence, without roguishness or cunning, as we must become.

Question: But what if someone thinks, "What kind of life is one like an infant's, for it is neither wise nor brave?" What kind of prudence and knowledge does it have? One is able to deceive and attract it with an egg or an apple and take it away from its father and mother and thus mislead it. Therefore, we must be as cunning as serpents [Matt. 10:16].

Answer: See, I say to you through the Holy Spirit that you must in any case become like an infant. Your own wisdom must depart and you must become a fool, or you will not be able to enter the kingdom of God. Nor will you be able to become cunning and crafty or prudent as a serpent. For understanding comes from God's Spirit, and prudence from the perception of the eyes, but the sight or the perception of the eyes comes from light, and the light comes from God, the life [1 John 1:5]. Therefore, do God's will, fulfill his Word. Be his servants and become like young infants. Abandon your proud heart and bow under the rod. Abandon your own wisdom and become a fool. Put aside your own understanding or spirit, do not follow it. Allow yourselves to be instructed by the little ones, who do such as God's servants. And become poor of spirit [Matt. 5:3]. But listen to the kingdom of heaven. Then the Father will accept you as his true children under his protection. And [119ʳ] he will watch them whither they go, in or out. The angel of the Lord has been commanded to protect these ones (without consuming)¹² in all their ways and to bear them up in their hands, so that they do not strike their feet against a stone [Ps. 91:11-12]. Namely, that they should not think badly or err. For they are the chosen and called.

Therefore, these little or simple ones will not be led into evil. For on account of the great struggle, temptation, lying, and deception (in this present time), this would happen easily, were it possible. But the Lord directs, leads, teaches, guards, and delivers them. For they are sheep. They know his name and listen to him [John 10:27-28]. When they (who are such) call to the Lord and he (blessed) hears that it comes from their hearts, then he heeds their situation immediately and is with them in their need and helps them out of it. And he does not give them over to damnation, nor does he let them get so far that their enemies are able to fulfill their desires against them. Instead he leads them so that they will see much honor, just as they will truly see with their eyes the reward of punishment for the godless who will be tread to dirt and ashes under their feet.[13] The mouth of the Lord has spoken it through his servants.

I also believe that we who proceed in the fear of the Lord will soon see that those who have laid the net of destruction around us, in order to capture us and who have dug the pit of death in front of us, will themselves [119ᵛ] fall into it and be captured [Ps. 35:7-8]. For those who do evil must be brought to harm, and not us. They must be found as the shameful ones and as liars, and not us. Lord, you are with us and give us the knowledge to speak the truth in good faith to all our neighbors, and to seek the salvation of all people who desire and wish for such from their hearts. Our mouths are full of your praise (O Lord) when you look upon us. But outside of you our ability is nothing. I am set like an infant. The Lord allows me and all God-fearing, simple hearts to win the righteousness in Christ Jesus and to obtain the divine perfection. It must be so.

See, in this way is the true knowledge and the hiddeness of the kingdom of God with these ones.[14] For God is their instructor who gives them who desire the ability to know all his heavenly secrets in the ground of their hearts. And he is their eyes, their care, and their protector. I say, they who are the poor of spirit do not have enough understanding by themselves. He satiates or fills these ones with overflowing goods. But the rich he leaves in vanity [Luke 1:53]. Yes, the full treasure chests will be found empty and the scribes and disputers will come to shame. This word is true into eternity, and this is what the Spirit of God says to you. Listen to him.

Therefore, these ones are truly able to do this, I say, and not to be deceived. For they dwell [120ʳ] with the wisdom of God. Who can oppose him? Who can separate them from God, who leads them by their hands [Rom. 8:35]? For their protector is greater, stronger, and more cunning than anything. He (blessed) watches over them and neither sleeps nor slumbers [Ps. 121:3-4]. He does not leave them in hunger or parched with thirst. Nor does he leave them without trust. For they are of his own nature and flesh; children of the truth, light, and life.

They will not come to shame, but will be victorious in all things according to the promises. They will inherit and peacefully possess all things always and eternally.

For this reason I give this advice to all willing, sincere hearts who desire not to be found in the ashes between two stools.[15] Sample the Spirit and cease from carnal reason, human wisdom, and your own understanding. Bow under this Spirit which all flesh and blood hate extremely and oppose in envy, regarding it as an abomination. For the Spirit of truth comes without deception and with the power of deeds to disgrace and shame the evil one. Without averting he will cast his honor and life into the abyss. Therefore, learn what is true wisdom, knowledge, and correct understanding. And do not wander about with the will and knowledge of those who follow their own wisdom, regardless of how beautiful they speak. We do not follow our own wisdom, but God's wisdom and Word. And we abide with the teaching of the apostles and Holy Scriptures. Now the Jews said the same thing and gloried even more in the Scriptures. But they nevertheless did not have the fear of God nor his knowledge or faith. All they had was the letter and the glory in the flesh. Similarly, the monks and priests also have the Holy Scriptures, but look at their righteousness and faith. The Martinians and all those who boast themselves as Evangelical say that they have the faith, but look at their fruit. The Covenanters are supposed to be the most pious, maintaining that they meet together in Christ in a special way, but one can also easily perceive their words and circumcised hearts. For the mouth speaks from the overflowing of the heart [Matt. 12:34]. How dare the godless speak so proudly of God's Word and take the covenant into their vile mouths [Ps. 50:16]? Note how they hate or are angered by the chastisement or reproof and reject the word of the humiliation and insignificance of the saints in Israel. Therefore, observe how well these scribes clap and snap with God's Word, but in reality they remain with their shameful thoughts; with the old tipsy, riotous, false senses; with the crafty, carnal, avaricious, evil heart; with the roguish eye, the false mouth, the vain words, and lying tongue; the evildoing, impure hands, and the vile feet. How can these blind ones show anyone the way? Or what kind of truth can these liars speak? When they say [121ʳ] that they have God's Word, they are liars. God's Word is living, fiery, and powerful [Heb. 4:12]. They are not sent. They run but they have no office. They promote the letter. They serve to point out the first school instruction of the childish nature. But we must leave this instruction along the way and proceed to perfection. For the kingdom of God does not exist in any special words, but in the power of God.[16] Nor does it exist in human wisdom, but in God's wisdom. At this all proud hearts are disgraced and all flesh is foolishness. Therefore, I warn you all in the name of my Lord about these teachers, for they are proud toward the Lord. They do not have God's living Word, but only the dead letter. Do not listen to them in their pretensions, nor believe their beautiful words, nor receive their cushions or bolsters. They say blessed are you, but they deceive you. Therefore, do not bring yourselves relief with their slanderous speeches, for they neither live nor bind. Do not fear the fifty who stood proudly against Elijah.[17] For they are the proud saints, who deceive you and who will be swept outside like filth or dirt and be cut off on account of righteousness and the kingdom of our Lord. They will come to shame and perish like grass in their mind and beauty. But from these you must be cleansed and purified. Take heed. Therefore, suffer all of this. Endure all and hope all, you children of Jacob. You anointed of the Lord will not perish. I mean, according to the outward person. The Lord perceives and knows it.

[121ᵛ] Therefore, be understanding. Know your blessed teaching and the hiddenness of the kingdom. For when it appears that your wisdom, understanding, and spirit have been lost, by such faith in the promises of God you will receive again the imperishable for the perishable [1 Cor. 15:53], the heavenly in place of the earthly, light for darkness, good for evil, truth for lies. Otherwise, people are led into deception. When it appears you have lost your life or yourself, you will be preserved. When it appears you are dishonored, he brings you to honor. When you appear to become sick and weak, you will become strong. When you appear poor of spirit or understanding, behold, you will become rich therein. You appear to become foolish and childish, but you become wise and a truly perfect person in Christ Jesus. In him our wisdom, salvation, righteousness, and victory is completely concealed.

This is the true Holy Spirit, God's testimony, in which all things will be restored correctly. Hear and follow his teaching, his advice and testimony, so that you will be blessed. O pay attention and observe closely what is written or spoken to you from this Spirit. Beloved, take to heart and grasp the meaning and basis. Then do it, yes, do what he says to you, without neglect or delay. Do not become fatigued or tired in your hands. But hold them up with Moses and you will defeat the Amalekites [Exod. 17:11-12]. The persecutors and opponents, God's enemies, Pharaoh or Satan, will have no ability against you. [122ʳ] Merely bend your knees, namely, your heart, and become humble in your countenance. Then you will receive what you desire. It is certain.

How long will the people err and the doubting hearts hate and leave God's wisdom and truth! Where are your eyes? Where is your mind? On what does your glory stand? Beloved, look up and behold what the Spirit of God says to you for your instruction through a strong love. Where has God's Word or his commands gone? Why was his law or teaching given, and why were all the things set down in the written Scriptures? Did it not happen for our instruction? So that the unwise should learn wisdom, and the ignorant or those who do not understand should receive knowledge? So that they would know what God has done and might experience together that there is only one God, one Lord and one Spirit of the good? So that God will be truly found in each one's heart with a clarity and likeness of the truth, a similarity of the mind or will of God's image? So that they should seek God from the testimony of the Scriptures, receiving trust and hope in their misery and infirmity?

Furthermore, the Scriptures were breathed into the authors through the Spirit and were given for service, to bring the needy to trust [2 Tim. 3:16]. This does not refer to teaching the letter or exterior of God's Word. No. For the [122ᵛ] mind of God or Christ is not in them. Therefore, I do not know them any longer in this manner, in the manner according to the flesh in the letter. For it is not the letter, but spirit. He wills that we should fulfill, yes, fulfill what he has called us to do and not merely to remember the external words or to leave them empty. Instead we are to gladly and willingly fulfill them, having received them with power. For all those who receive the Word of God in this fashion are protected, but not the others who reject it. For it is not taken by the hands or in the mouth. No. But it is received into a believing, willing, humble heart. Only then will it rise up, working in a mighty and living fashion.

Do the Scriptures serve in any other way? Or do they advise us differently? Do they not reveal that we must remove all unrighteousness or roguishness, the old nature with all its works, and become renewed in the Spirit of faith, so that we might become holy?[18] For this reason they tell us to wash and purify ourselves, to put away from us the evil nature. To hate the evil and love the good. Like children of righteousness and truth who are obedient to or of the same nature as their Lord and Father, we are to love, hear, and follow him above any other. Is this not so? Do not those who in this way walk in love and abide in righteousness fulfill the law and prophets? Look up. Is it possible for anyone to maintain that this can be done through the knowledge of the letter or of the exterior of the Scriptures? Who will maintain [123ʳ] that the wisdom and fulfillment of the law and commands of God are in such? But now an abbreviated word and a new command is committed to us. Namely, love which is the law of Christ, written by the finger of God onto the believing, God-fearing, humble hearts [Matt. 22:37-40; Exod. 31:18]. In these the testament or the promise of the inheritance of God exists or is concluded.

Who preaches this gospel? Who speaks the truth from the heart and not the heart from the mouth? Yes, who perceives the truth? Who has the mind of Christ in this? Who correctly divides the Scriptures [cf. 2 Tim. 2:15]? Who binds their words in heaven [cf. Matt. 16:19]? Who has the understanding to judge? None except the spiritual person or a new creature, who is truly the enemy or contrary to the old nature of sin. For those who have mixed their speech and work in grace with salt are acceptable before God [Col. 4:6]. These ones' heart is firmly founded on the instruction of their God. They are preserved from the fall and their tongue always speaks correctly. For their heart proceeds with wisdom. Then these humble hearts exist as examples and judgments, lights or stars in the earth [Dan. 12:3]. These are the living fountains. Blessed are they who are planted along their sides [Ps. 1:3]. For here there will be no lack of bread or water, but people will find good meadows. Here they can go in and out, grow and increase. And like the sucking of the fattened calves, they will have all they want. These ones can be questioned, for the mouth of the Lord is in their hearts, and his wisdom [123ᵛ] is on their tongues. Who contradicts this? Do they require any human teaching or letter? Do they not speak from the truth through the Spirit just as well as the other saints? Will not the Scriptures be truly and unmistakably fulfilled through such ones? Must they know the literal Scriptures or be skilled in the external letters? As if they existed in particular words. Do you not know the Spirit and power of God any better than that? If you esteem the person because one wears silk, colored, or velvet cloth, then you honor the clothing.[19] Yes, these are well known among you. But you do not thereby honor what is concealed under them. O you evil, proud shepherds, desist. Perceive your lack of wisdom, or the sword of God will come upon your arm and your right eye will be blinded [Zech. 11:17].

Remember the previous people and teachers. They had to admit and confess (although they said such with their mouths, their deeds were otherwise) that they were still children in understanding. They regarded Melchior Hoffman above all others as a servant of the Lord, filled with the Holy Spirit and with all the riches of the truth and knowledge of God. Namely, as the true Elijah, Michael,[20] promised David, the mighty angel from heaven, whom people must hear and follow. Yes, that the one who was joined with him, namely Enoch,[21] stood far behind him, and would not come nearly as far in the splendor as he. And nevertheless, they have presumed and pretended that they announced the letter to him (Melchior Hoffman) [124ʳ] while he announced the spirit to them. Is this not an abomination and shame? Indeed, is it not a great slander by the saints in Israel that the earthly, reasoning, cunning human should teach the perfection or quality of the letter to the Holy Spirit and protect him from error? O how they have made each other blind and false! Although I have said and written this to them often enough, and have pointed out their error to them, yet they refuse to believe me. Instead (being filled with anger and envy) they give honor to themselves and revile me with slander. By this they display their ignorance as unreasoning beasts, into which they have made themselves. O if they only saw how I detest dullness and proud thinking. O if only they were wise, then they would hear me!

Now I will tell you so that everyone can identify those who truly have God's Word and teaching. Namely, I say, those who do God's Word and live the Word of Christ. Those who have his Spirit and mind and who speak what is right and good from their heart and through their mouth. They flow like a running fountain, where there is no need for water or teaching of wisdom [cf. Isa. 65:17ff.]. But according to these scribes, God should no longer speak. They believe that his hand has been shortened [cf. Isa. 50:2 or 51:9] and that the fountain of wisdom stands still. That people should be compelled to examine if they have the language and the letter. But they will very shortly discover the truth when they see the little and simple ones, the humble hearts, [124ᵛ] shining in the kingdom of their Father. They will find themselves in shame and disgrace. O you dear people, wake up, if you happen to read this! But I fear that they instead will oppress the mountain of God and injure the ark of the Lord. Each one take an example from this.

Behold the Spirit of truth. See, the Scriptures will be fulfilled and perfected through the power of the Holy Spirit. Then the books will be publicly opened and inside them there will be found: "**The spirit discloses the letter, the invisible the visible; but not the visible the invisible**."[22]

The multitude of Israel and the worm of Jacob [Isa. 41:14] will be small, poor, and few. They will endure perfectly and receive the kingdom of God. For they are the few who will accept and perform the baptism of suffering and terror and drink the cup of bitterness. They are able to bear willingly the woe or pain in the stomach as well as the misery and grief as something good or the best. So they will have a little faith or a little of God's fear before their eyes. But many find this a mockery or too hard and heavy for them. For they must give no room for the flesh and oppose its lust and desire. They must not allow it to remain living. But it must be completely crucified, killed and buried, rotted and forgotten [cf. Rom. 7]. Only [125ʳ] the earnest lovers of the truth, the lowly, mourning, anxious hearts lust for this food and desire to drink of such drink. These are the hungry and thirsty for righteousness [Matt. 5:6] who confess from their insignificance that the old must be completely done away with and perish. And they fulfill the Word with obedience to the death of the cross. I write to all such as these, to pursue and drive them forward, so that they will not be overtaken and surprised by the terrifying day of the Lord, which will ignite and burn over all unbelieving and disobedient flesh [Mal. 4:1]. Therefore, hasten, hasten, and be purified in this while there is time. I proclaim, I proclaim the great day of God's strict judgment. Who is able to endure it? FINIS

9

Joris's Letter Concerning Martyrdom, 1539

This missive, published as part of the *Last Testament* of Anna Jans in 1539, is one of only a handful of Joris's writings which have been edited and published in the twentieth century.[1] It is noteworthy for its frank discussion of the martyrdom of some one hundred of his followers in 1539, including twenty-seven in his home city of Delft. Among those slain were two women very close to David. Anna Jans, an important associate, met her demise on January 24, 1539, at Rotterdam.[2] Joris's own mother was also put to death on February 21, 1539, in Delft, while his wife, Dirkgen, barely escaped execution in Utrecht. How Joris privately handled the trauma of these great losses is a matter for speculation. What we have here, however, is a missive which provides some insight into how Joris publicly dealt with the issue of martyrdom, and how he encouraged his followers to maintain their faith in the light of the horrendous persecution which they were witnessing. Karel Vos, who edited this letter in 1917, accused Joris of hypocrisy at this point. Yet it must be remembered that Joris had already experienced imprisonment and torture for his beliefs in 1528. It is moreover clear from the anonymous account that at the time of the executions Joris himself was in extreme danger of capture, and several times escaped only by the courage of his devotees.[3] It was not until the late summer of 1539 that Joris and his family found a relatively secure refuge in Antwerp, and even there an investigation of the magistrates into the presence of heretics in the city forced Joris's final move to Basel in 1544. Joris therefore knew the effects of persecution first-hand, even though, to the delight of his followers, he avoided martyrdom itself.

Joris treated the theme of martyrdom in several other works. The most notable of these is *The Eight Blessings*, written in September 1539.[4] Joris, in relative security in Antwerp, was able to reflect more thoroughly on the ramifications of the persecutions of his followers. He affirmed that such tribulation was another sign of the nearness of the end, and acted as the "baptism of fire," bringing believers fully into the body of Christ. While the letter translated here is meant for a private readership, *The Eight Blessings* decries the persecution of innocent religious dissenters to a wider audience. Selected passages from this tract will be included in the relevant notes to illuminate Joris's comments translated here.

✺ ✺ ✺ ✺ ✺

Letter of David Joris, 1539.

The following is to praise the witnesses of Jesus,
sacrificed at Delft.
To a brother in his fear,
written for belief and awakening.
The Lord is with us, let us be with him,
cast away the evil and cling to the good.

Greet my beloved brother Jor.[5] I have been very apprehensive over you, and Jac.,[6] the beloved in the Lord. But now I rejoice in this, now that I know how it is with you. The Lord our God and mother of faith, who has guarded and delivered us, be thanked. To him alone (blessed) be fear, honor, and glory in all his great love toward us.

Beloved brother, what do you say about this? About the orchard and garden, about the righteous trees and plants of the Lord, which will bring forth their fruits and blossoms in their time, namely, the word of the Spirit which they have believed. Yes, what will still be heard and seen from this? I am certain that the work of God will yet be revealed at its time, for it is truly not a human work or power. Where has the world heard or seen such, that an entire fellowship has remained steadfast and that so many are the men who stand under the Lord our King Christ, so that the women will follow? Yes, they have gone with joyful spirit, desire, mind, heart, and ability, as a true seed of Abraham. They are the sons of truth, children of the living God, having not fulfilled in name, but in deeds [1 John 3:18].[7] Is this not pleasing to hear? Yes, there was not one solitary forsaker, from the smallest to the greatest. Risking all, they have been as strong as David. This was written in particular of the prophet David. You people should be willing in the days of your strength, or at the time when you your-selves shall be shown all power, this is now evident.[8]

Furthermore, "smoke comes from the middle of the night or from the north, and there is no straggler among them" [Isa. 14:31]. What will the ambassadors of the heathens say between both parties? In particular, that the Lord has upheld Zion. This is light that rises out of the darkness, which shall be seen overall [Ps. 112:4; cf. John 1:5]. Yes, let them do what they will, the Lord will be a surety and shelter for his people in the time of need [Ps. 46:1]. And he (blessed) gives them strength in their heart and strengthens their weakness. A heart will not become faint when it is strengthened in the midst of the fight. It is in necessity that the supply appears, so that the holy faith and the kingdom are upheld, for it must be full of temptation and distur-bances. Also, it is for our God's praise and wonder. Yes, I know what I see and confess, regarding all such power and life. For I advise no one that he seek to keep his own life here, or that he run from or be fright-ened of death or his enemy, but that he willingly come against it. Yes, wake up, for this is the basis of the Spirit, for the Lord desires that we be submissive in this manner, completely trustworthy, and stand pre-pared, according to the will of God, ready to be delivered up as sheep to the slaughter.

Also, I am able to testify of this deed because it is known well to me, beloved. See it and believe in the name of our Lord, in his saints and great works of love. Pray and be awake, suffer and fight and win, so that you might sit and reign, from eternity to eternity with Christ our Lord Jesus, eternally blessed [Rev. 5:10; 22:5, etc]. Amen.

Sarah is a prefigure of Zion, when her glory and strength was gone. For though like a forsaken one, she yet rejoiced [Gen. 18]. In the midst of anxiety and trembling, when those of us who remain ap-pear forsaken, standing in the midst of need and oppression, with tears in our eyes, then our deliverance and the strengthening of the Lord comes from heaven. Therefore, be not dismayed or murmuring, for the Lord is wonderful in his works. He protects those who cling firmly to him, he gives them power and might as young lions [cf. Prov. 28:1]. For this reason, let us give praise to the Lord, and give up the vengeance to our Father [Rom. 12:19]. It is written therefore that "vengeance belongs to me, I shall repay. In their time their feet shall slip, and their hope fail, and their future hastens. Look, the Lord shall judge his people and have mercy upon his servants. For he sees that their strength is weak, and that the resolve of those who remain is nearly finished" [Deut. 32:35-36]. Pay attention to this, for it is good to hear that Zion on the last day will appear to have the freedom to say, "The Lord has delivered me, the Lord has not forgotten me" or "Truly he has done no work for his people except that he has borne a great esteem and a careful attention and concern for them. He has granted that his faithful house be well guarded from the thieves and robbers" [Song of Sol. 3:7]. Eternal praise be to the Lord for his grace.

The number must be fulfilled, before the end is [Rev. 6:11]. The one who is last, God knows him, but it appears to me that he must be a faithful witness [cf. Revelation 11]. Who, just like Zechariah, a peaceful man and conciliator, was nevertheless killed standing between the temple and altar [Matt. 23:35]. It must end and cease, for there will be a final accounting of the number [cf. Rev. 7]. And it is also written that from Abel to the blood of Zechariah, who came before me, that, from the first to the last, beginning from Christ Jesus, the Lamb which was slain from the beginning, we must suffer, as Abel by Cain, the righteous by the unrighteous [Matt. 23:35]. Abel is an image of Christ; Zechariah, of the faithful witness of the truth of God, a plain, simple and innocent man in the Spirit, who shall be betrayed or killed by the deceptive nature of Belial, by the abusive Cain and Esau, whose seed shall be clearly revealed. These are the brothers among the others, who have willed this and would have done it themselves [Jude 11]. Namely, those who despise and deliver up the others, mark the time.[9] This tribulation, however, will not endure forever. The testing of the faith, courage, and spirit of the saints must appear now to the praise of God who has prepared us for his praise, halleluia.[10] Admonish everyone to a courageous spirit. Yes, to those who regard their weakness as strength, they shall have strength through faith and grace. And be faithful, and maintain the love, and make peace between brother and brother, and in this praise the Lord. Greet the faithful for me, and let them pray also for me. Each be quiet, and be full of hope and supplications and tears, unto imprisonment, the torture bench,[11] to the death. In everything persevere, with joyful willingness.

Title Page, *The Wonder Book* (Deventer: Dirck von Borne, c. 1543)
Courtesy of the Mennonite Library, University of Amsterdam

10

The Apology to Countess Anna of Oldenburg, 1540-43[1]

As a representative of Joris's early Spiritualist (or late Anabaptist) works, we present here the published defense of his teaching which was addressed to the Countess Anna of Oldenburg. One of several works written by Joris to governmental authorities,[2] the *Apology* serves as an example of Joris's public ideology, lacking the more esoteric elements reserved for tracts written to his followers. While frequently evasive, the *Apology* is written uncharacteristically in a fairly lucid and unencumbered style, providing readers with an unusually clear glimpse into how Joris responded to negative assessments of his teaching.

Joris could not have addressed his *Apology* to a more tolerant ruler. Under the rule of Anna of Oldenburg, East Frisia had become a haven for Anabaptists from the Netherlands.[3] In 1543 she appointed John a Lasco as Reformed superintendent and allowed the establishment of the Reformed Church in her territory. Anabaptists of many persuasions—including Mennonites and Davidites, but excluding the radical Batenburgers—found a degree of toleration in East Frisia, and public disputations between Reformed and Anabaptist were commonplace here.[4]

Joris produced the *Apology* primarily as a response to a twenty-four point summary of his doctrine composed (according to Blesdijk) by Menno Simons's associate, Adam Pastor.[5] Unfortunately, despite the popularity of Pastor's work, a copy has not survived.[6] It was apparently spread throughout the Netherlands, England, and Germany, and was known in Wittenberg. For example, it seems that Pastor's work formed the basis for the "Artikel der Joristen" (Articles of the Jorists) which the magistrates of Strasbourg had originally received from the Deventer city council and which they subsequently sent to the Basel magistrates on December 15, 1544, as a warning against Joris's teachings. Although there are only twenty-two articles in this list compared to the twenty-five of Joris's response, the specific charges of the two documents are very close in language, and presumably emanated from a common source.[7] Joris, then, was responding to a widely popular presentation of his teaching.

A major problem with identifying Pastor as Joris's literary opponent arises when the date of composition is taken into consideration. While the *Apology* is dated 1540, Pastor did not write his list until 1542. The date on Joris's tract is therefore presumed to be mistaken, for as a response to Pastor it could not have been composed before 1542.[8] This work can be safely assigned to around 1543, the same time period when *The Wonder Book* first appeared in print. Although written in the necessarily defensive and evasive tone of an apology, on the whole this text is a fairly reliable presentation of Joris's teaching as it had developed by the early 1540s.

*   *   *   *   *

[Title page]
APOLOGY OF DAVID JORIS COMPLETED
and presented to the Highborn
Lady, Lady Anna, born Countess of Oldenburg, etc.,
Countess at Emden etc., in the year 1540.
Against the mistaken false articles
written and spoken about everywhere.

Deut. 27:24:
Cursed is he who smites his neighbor secretly.
And all the people shall say, Amen.
Ecclus. 28:18:
A deceitful tongue is like the bite of the serpent:
Many perish with swords,
many more through the tongue.

[2ʳ]   APOLOGY OF DAVID JORIS.
Completed and presented to the Highborn Lady, Lady Anna, born

Countess of Oldenburg, etc., Countess at Emden, etc. Against the
mistaken articles written in enmity toward him and repeated everywhere.

Hear Now the Charges
and the Answers.

HIGHBORN Gracious Lady, together with your most wise coun-
cillors: Through the prayer of the little ones and through the entreaty
and desire of the weak, I humbly ask that Your Grace would graciously hear me in this matter, as one who is poor, reviled, [2ʸ] everywhere greatly despised, and the least worthy, and that you will carefully examine my answers. Should Your Grace consider it too long, remember please that I consider it far too short, and that a modest answer is only as brief as the question. The apology cannot be any
shorter than the accusation.

For I have kept partially silent for a long time, ignoring all insinu-
ations and suffering the stinking foul stream coming from the old Serpent and Red Dragon [Rev. 12] (vomiting out to me, just as he is zealous against all the saints). Namely, I have suffered all roguishness,
cunning, lying and deception, foul, unsubstantiated, murderous words
[3ʳ] and perverted, slanderous, deadly utterances against me alone.
Again, I have borne this patiently and alone. This anger has made me
frightened and alarmed in my own territory (for the reason that all
people are restless and all lands and people are stirred up against
me—the innocent one—and in this way have incited the lower orders,
frightening and alarming them with my most monstrous name). Nevertheless, I thought it good to present this reply to Your Grace (who is
not unfamiliar with such matters and to whom a part of this matter is
well known). Furthermore (I hope) Your Grace will believe the good,
so that everyone here and there will recognize my innocence
(through experience) in the answer of truth, and be reassured and put
to rest. [3ʸ] The others damage and harm themselves, when my enviers without reason and through their evil anger untruthfully make me
out to be an insurrectionist. May my enviers be still awakened by
grace, so that (even though they would like to forbid and hinder me)
they will toil and hear and might obtain friendship and peace in the
world. I half believe that, being patient, I will overcome in this. For
(though they regard themselves as holy and will not hear me in the
truth, refusing me a fair answer, unreasonable beasts, blaspheming
and making me to be an abomination) I am not saying this from my

opinion, for I am certain of it, that they shall come to naught in the judgment of God. For as God is my witness, they will not be able to oppose the eternal light and the heavenly truth, neither extinguish nor suppress it. Nor will they be able to oppose the wisdom (which has been placed into my heart and mouth by God's grace to be proclaimed). This is well known and apparent to those people. Although they (as the unashamed) do not concede to me (being abandoned of all human help), but instead by Your Grace proudly and above all in my absence, they seek my harm, to make me vile and despised by all sorts of evil speaking and imposing shame on me. They appeal [4ᵛ] to the apostolic teaching (as one may see over one's shoulder), in which these people also boast. Which I (the accused, who shall be triumphant through the blood of the Lamb, knowing his unborn nature) have borne and overheard heretofore with much patience. For herein I now have freed myself (not for myself), to let you know my innocence in these articles, with God's and Your Grace's pleasure. Moreover, in order not to make it too long, I shall give Your Grace and everyone (who may read or hear these my written articles) a short and true answer, without craft or cunning, and what I believe in these matters. [5ʳ]

I. The First: That I, David Joris, proclaimed myself to be the third David and made myself to be like Christ. This is a lie, I deny it vigorously: I know better than that (thank God). I know well that Christ is God's Son in eternity, but not Joris's son,[9] who was born of the blood of a woman. I, however, pursue with my whole heart this Christ in the second birth of the faith of the Spirit, in order to become like Christ in all my desires and manners. To become flesh of his flesh and bone of his bone, in order to be one body with him, so as to declare our calling. For I do not boast of having obtained the complete perfection and maturity of Christ in its power. Although I, as anyone on earth, will boast and try on his eternal heavenly knowledge in the truth of God's [5ᵛ] grace. Thereupon I appeal to all who have life and understanding on the earth, to examine themselves before the face of the firmament, in order to improve the body of Christ.

II. The Second: That everyone should be called literalists (as they all have copied me) who would defend and protect themselves with the Holy Scriptures. I deny this totally also. For I also do the same. I too will make use of the Holy Scriptures in everything which I believe, do, or accept. Because in this manner I have indeed spoken or written and still say again that, even though they all read and learn (just as it is written there), they do not understand. Therefore, these same people are only literally but not spiritually wise, whoever does not recognize the Scripture's power and nature according to the Spirit and truth.[10]

[6[^r]] **III.** The Third: That one must confess or profess all sins, iniquities, or guilt in person, publicly in the church. I have not written thus, except that I confess through scriptural and reasonable argument that this is indeed partly right and good. When people recognize their sin, guilt, or iniquity, they then release the aforementioned, forsake themselves, desiring to leave and resist the devil or the sinful flesh. At no time must they seek to excuse, conceal, or stand on the path of the old being of sin, but instead freely admit it to be vile and ugly. Remove its garments and freely confess what it is that oppresses them in front of an sincere, spiritual person. They are not to feel ashamed before such a one, who intends to do no less. In this way have the Holy Spirit, the Scriptures, and the Lord together with his disciples testified thereof.[11] [6[^v]]

IV. The Fourth: That there are no angels, but only pleasing[12] people. This I also say no to. I have never let such leave my mouth nor writings. Of this I maintain in brief, only as the Holy Spirit and the Scriptures testify.[13]

V. The Fifth: That there are no visible or real devils. I have not said this. For I know that the Lord Jesus himself called Peter a Satan and Judas a devil. For I confess that my understanding of the devils has been also held, meant, and described by many for a long time, but now is not so held. That they, without me, by themselves alone, can do nothing. For that reason do I challenge all these devils (however many there might be evermore in hell). For they, in their own strength, outside of God, on their own without me, are unable to manifest themselves to me. [7[^r]] But (after the Word has become flesh, God has made his angels into spirits, his servants into flames of fire [Heb. 1:7]) if there are any who remain who are of its blood or race, they must give answer before him. I, David, say to them in the new testament that they (as the people think) are nothing, without any ability of their own, outside of humanity, I say, and of God's wrath. People are an enemy and devil to themselves; they have to guard themselves from no one more than from themselves. It is found similarly in the 110th Psalm [Ps. 109], also of the enemy.

VI. The Sixth: That Christ will not return himself for judgment, just as he has ascended. I have not said, but profess to the contrary, such will always happen. Namely, that he should in this fashion return, just as he ascended. [7[^v]] And of that say few, as it is written. But I say for this reason that everyone should cease indeed from their evil, that they might watch and pray; for he will truly come as a thief in the night, when the world least expects or thinks of him.[14]

VII. The Seventh: That the last judgment shall take place in the righteous through David Joris and his equals. To this I answer in this fashion, that the righteous or saints will not only judge the world, but even more the angels (as Paul and the Scriptures openly testify). But that it shall occur through David Joris, much more must be said and written to prove that statement. But one part of it is true, namely, that it is through the righteous, according to the Scriptures, among whom I, in my rebirth, [8ʳ] hope and seek to be found. That it shall occur through David Joris is not my word; I have not made such a clumsy proclamation, nor would I leave the Scriptures whole and unbroken. Know well what is written, which I also in eternity will not be against.[15]

VIII. The Eighth: That one should now regard Joris as the third David upon the earth. I have never thought, said, nor written in this fashion. But that one should now observe the third David (of whom the Scriptures I believe speak as I have noted and confessed in the Spirit and truth), namely, the Spirit of the eternal truth.[16] For I have not spoken of David Joris, but of the anointed David. I say, I meant the one of whom the Scriptures have testified so richly by name, [8ᵛ] the one who is expected in the last days, his coming is foreseen. Read.

IX. The Ninth: That Christ is none but David Joris, the person whose voice all who want to be saved must hear. To this I say many times no. For I regard the same, namely Christ, as my Head and Lord. Listen not to me, but to his voice. How I should best believe and follow after the eternal almighty Word of the Spirit and of power, without ceasing, and I counsel the same to others as well as myself.

X. The Tenth: That all of those who are found outside of David Joris's fellowship are cats and dogs. I have neither spoken nor written this. They have falsely imagined these words out of their own heads like many others in order to oppress me. For, above all, the [9ʳ] Scriptures speak of those who are found outside the true community of Christ as outside the ark.[17] The same voice says I judge myself as another. But not that I have pronounced anyone to be saved or unsaved, because they do or do not hold fellowship with David Joris. For our fellowship is with the Father and his Son Jesus Christ, according to the Spirit and truth. There is outside of that nothing else.[18]

XI. The Eleventh: That my teaching contains that we are free to murder, steal, slay, lie, and deceive against those who are not of the same mind with me. Look, they spin such great nonsense, that I will leave it at that. Just the opposite is true of me. What else can I say to this but that I now must be like a dove and like a speechless person who does not open his mouth. [9ᵛ] I must cling fast to my God and leave the matter to him, hoping that they will tire of it and learn to be ashamed. What others do (who boldly use my name without giving credit) I do not take to heart; for it is so far from my heart as heaven is from the earth—examine all my writings.[19]

XII. The Twelfth: That one no longer marry any women, but have them in common. No one will be able to find that I have written such or taught this to anyone. It is far from me, I myself would in the first place not tolerate such. How then could I counsel or teach the same to others? Instead, I indeed have maintained the Lord's Word, believed and rightly confessed it. Who foresaw such and testified against the Sadducees, saying: The children of this world marry and let themselves be married, but the worthy shall inherit [10ʳ] the coming world and the resurrection of the dead; they shall not marry, neither the man nor the woman.[20] For they will no longer die, they will be like the angels and children of God, for they are children of the resurrection. I admit to having written about this, but not that one may therefore have women in common.[21] All my preaching and sayings are against it. Namely, that one put to death the sinful flesh, the old being (which lusts after such things) and tear out its evil lusts and put on the new being. How are these reconciled together? But this I have indeed said, how we all, together alike, must be one body in Christ. I confess furthermore that just as we are called, everyone must be baptized thereto or quenched with one Spirit. And that is the teaching of Christ and Paul. But if there are any who walk improperly according to the flesh, [10ᵛ] using their freedom (in which we stand united in Christ) as an occasion or cause thereto, in order to ignore the pure teaching, they are far from us (if they do not turn nor better themselves, heartily repenting and proving it with their life). For I know indeed that those who do not walk or live according to the Spirit, but according to the flesh, must die, just as it is written. Also is our manner and walk before the Lord according to the truth and in the light.[22] Would to God that all people were angels, that they say and know certainly.

XIII. The Thirteenth: That one should leave unfit wives. Although it is different in this matter (just as our writings on marriage have proclaimed) and greater mercy is found among us. It is nevertheless stated with humility that this is not so amazing, nor against the

Scriptures. [11ʳ] For Ecclesiasticus, that open letter, and Paul allow this also. Just as Christ says that one may do so also in the case of adultery. But if we have encountered an eternal love, which the Lord himself has not lightly denied us, then as much as is possible for us, are we not also to forgive? Should we do other than he? This is not to mean, that one may do just as anyone else does.

XIV. The Fourteenth: That the resurrection of the dead has already occurred. To this I answer in this fashion, that it is a complete misunderstanding and has been written about me out of enmity. For I am, in all modesty, clearly against those who say this. Where (since I seek to stand before God's truth, and seek to protect his majesty) have arisen more enemies or opponents against me. For the scorning of those who scorn his Word (which all flesh [11ᵛ] is against) falls therefore upon my neck and upon all who favor such. But in this fashion I am being falsely accused. I comfort myself with all the saints, clinging to the Scriptures which witness excellently thereof, by chance perhaps above all my accusers.

XV. The Fifteenth: That the kingdom of Christ shall be visible upon the earth. This I hold truly with humility. For Daniel alone proclaims enough about it even if the rest of the Scriptures were silent. But I confess also that it shall be heavenly and eternal, according to the Scriptures, which speak of another world, of a new heaven and earth, upon which our faith stands. I hold to a future time or world and to the eternal life.[23] Which new world, new heaven and new earth, will not be seen or understood except by those of a faithful, believing heart. [12ʳ] Thus the Scriptures testify richly thereof, let each believe who will. And see, herein (whoever has believed the Lord) shall the righteousness dwell. As Peter has proclaimed of the same [2 Pet. 3:13]. Above all, the kingdom of God is internal; a spiritual, hidden heavenly kingdom. Which only the reborn in the Spirit and truth see, perceive, and know. And these receive it (being like children) with mighty hearts against the devil or sinful flesh. The kingdom of Christ (or the anointed) is, above all, not only spiritual, internal, unseen, but also visible. For he is not only divine, but human, namely, he is God and man. Therefore, those who do not hold to or believe in a visible kingdom, they neither hold nor believe in a physical resurrection, nor in a new heaven and new earth, nor in the [12ᵛ] coming world, in which righteousness shall dwell. And they also deny the humanity of Christ. Therefore, let no one be surprised if there is an outward resurrection; then there is also irrefutably an outward kingdom, joy, love, and peace.

XVI. The Sixteenth: That David Joris shall be a king in the kingdom of Christ. I desire this to be true. Namely, that I may sit with the Lord upon his throne, and at his right side. To be before him as a king and priest, according to the Scriptures. Just as he has promised to all the overcomers in the faith and to all the children of God.[24] That I should have spoken it about my own person, I beg that one should convince me or prove such. For my calling is only in the Lord. Whatever he pleases, that shall I be. But I raise not my eyes to that which is high, [13ʳ] my heart is not so proud; God keep me from that. I will not exalt myself against my God, to be this or that, other than a good servant of the Lord and, out of my faith and trust, a son of the Most High. I have also called God my Father, just as the whole of Christendom does. And to be and to remain perfect is my daily supplication and bidding. For that reason I have also spoken that people are blessed or damned only as they stand in the living or death-giving Word. Furthermore, I have neither received nor cast out anyone, because for that purpose the Lord returns. Nevertheless, I confess and know firmly, that he has given his true servants the ability to bind and to loose, as it is written.[25] Also, I expect my honor or crown, the rewards of the kingdom, with all the true saints, not given by mortals, but only by the Lord [13ᵛ] and through the Lord. Which furthermore, like God himself, is preserved in heaven and which he has promised to give all believers. For those who praise themselves with the mouth are not wise, rich, blessed, nor healthy. Instead, only those who are convinced of the wisdom, riches and blessedness will be proven to be healthy.

XVII. The Seventeenth: That the heavens and clouds are to be understood spiritually. See, the same I truly confess according to the Scriptures correctly spoken in its place with modesty.[26] In particular, that they are being used by the Spirit in figures in another tongue, so that they should not hear me, says the Lord. Also, no one knows these heavens and clouds of witnesses, of which the Spirit of truth speaks, other than those who are themselves one.[27] In particular, those who have God in them, namely, love; and who are a [14ʳ] wagon, seat, tool, or cloud of the Lord; from whose mouth the rain of righteousness showers upon the dry earth to moisten or empower it and make it fruitful. That this is true, testifies alone the word of the Spirit through the mouth of David, where he said: "I will open my mouth in parables (the foregoing) and proclaim the concealed things which are from the beginning of the world."[28] Who is he who refutes this? See, the Lord shall (says Paul) come down with a shout of the archangels or earthly angels. Be constantly on guard, that you perceive therein the word of eternal truth. So that your vision according to the figurative heaven be not found outwardly in error or reproach (when he appears in the heart).[29] [14ᵛ]

XVIII. The Eighteenth: That the property of the heathen shall be given to Christians and that they may take it freely whenever possible. This is attributed to me like all the others. But this is far from me, that I teach, counsel, or do such. But it is testified with blood by some of our people that we teach and counsel to the contrary. Namely, that they should seek the kingdom of God and his righteousness. Whatever else is necessary shall be added to them, according to the Lord's Word. If any therefore lack something, they themselves are witness that they do not stand for the kingdom of God and his righteousness (to obtain thereto). For they have missed the promise of truth, so that it misses them. Which would otherwise be impossible (if they meant it and sought it in their heart), unless they could take or steal it out of want since the mouth of truth has said it. [15ʳ] Here I remain fast: Were this not the case, then some (so inclined) would not so hate and be against me. They should not lay their guilt upon me.

XIX. The Nineteenth: That child baptism is free, unnecessary, and all ended. To that I say once more, both yes and no, that it is free to me. For such is unnecessary, not only for children, but also for adults, who receive such without the Lord's command (unsent) outside the power of the Holy Spirit. For it is children's and not adults' work, and makes no one pure and free by means of the water alone, but in the holy faith and the Spirit of truth.[30] In which faith no one may boast without certain penance and true repentance (through which must be received another heart, mind, and spirit), understand, without also another baptism of the Spirit. Which speaks better than [15ᵛ] figurative water. This has been shown by the Lord Jesus himself, who had affirmed and spoken of another baptism, saying: "I must be baptized with a baptism, and how anxious I am as the time for it draws near" [Luke 12:50]. Few come to this baptism of truth, for it is that baptism of the Spirit which comes through the same person who comes after John (who nevertheless had been before him) who must also baptize, as it is written.[31] This is what is meant by "through the water" and what its function and ministry is at present in its righteous and true substance. But when this is fulfilled, the image, figure, shadow, and the letter will cease, just as the child is superseded by the adult, John by Jesus, and Christ after the flesh by the spiritual, just as the light of mortals is superseded by the sun, which for the present must first shine before that other may cease. [16ʳ] Otherwise, the baptism of water would be able to make each person's conscience pure, holy, and righteous. Otherwise, Simon Magus and everyone who is baptized in this world would have been Christ's. But it is otherwise and is not so.

XX. The Twentieth: That all may freely go into any church without causing the sin of idolatry. See, herein has my accuser trapped himself. For he holds no outward places as good nor capable of purifying or sanctifying anyone; nevertheless, he scolds and judges me concerning this matter, as if they were impure to me. I confess these to be free places, which are no more impure than any other. For had the places been able to make anyone holy or good, Adam would not have fallen, the angels would not have lost their dwelling, and Christ would have remained captive in hell. Therefore, to the pure all things are pure. What can be [16ᵛ] said against this? Idolatry, above all, must be far from us, together with avarice, which is also called idolatry, that everything in all manners and places may take place in the heart. But we believe in the one glorious God, who has created and made heaven and earth, visible and invisible things, and in Jesus Christ, etc., according to the Articles of the Holy Faith.

XXI. The Twenty-first: That permitting children to be baptized is like bringing them before the idols and holding the Lord's Supper with heathen. See, these words I also deny completely; also, this has never been my interpretation or way of speaking, although about this interpretation (so as not to be too long) I have said more than enough.

[17ʳ] **XXII.** The Twenty-second: That the teachings of Paul are a work of little worth compared to David's teaching. I have not said this. But Paul also says himself that his knowledge and prophecy is only a partial work and that it shall cease before the perfect. I therefore also have the right to say that. But that word, piece-work, was notorious to the people. "A work of little worth" is, above all, a scornful word, and that they do lay upon me. Would to God that they would for once shut up and keep their jawbone quiet, that they may no more slay anyone in secret (as Cain did his brother Abel). Above all, I highly praise the word of the high knowledge of God (which has been revealed to me and made known to me), which I have said is no piece-work (as Paul confessed of himself). For I will come before the presence of the firmament (where the gentle ones receive a hearing), and come into the open, [17ᵛ] against all the learned and wise of this world. Not in order to confound or to put them to shame (although it is in my power to do so against the self-wise, I say), but to exalt the eternal wisdom and truth. They should give me a small, gentle hearing and find out by means of the truth whether they confessed the Father and the Son; or if I and my word, teaching, and understanding go too high; or if the time (of which I testified) shall not surpass the former, to our glory. See, they interpret my words or speeches on their own, as happened to Moses by Jannes and Jambres [2 Tim. 3:8]. What value have their speeches, they shall all be swallowed by mine.

XXIII. The Twenty-third: That telling lies and forsaking the truth are not sins and that one may let the Articles of Faith, which are too high, go by the wayside. Concerning the first, forsaking and lying I have neither spoken, thought, nor written. The other, concerning letting go of the Articles which are too high, I also have not stirred up, but cling to the word of Christ Jesus, saying, "Be not concerned about what you should say, etc."[32] I will also do according to his saying, counsel, and inspiration, expect in that hour to speak (as in every other time) as my Father shall give me. That and nothing else is my word, counsel, and teaching, that is how it shall be so found.

XXIV. The Twenty-fourth: That the world will perish spiritually. This I confess to be right and true in part, but also the outer with its sinful nature. But my meaning is not as the common person believes, who knows nothing of God, neither of right nor left, light nor darkness, pure nor impure, flesh nor spirit, according to [18ᵛ] the knowledge of the truth. For wood and stone, etc., will perish in a different way than normally seen. But therein is not the world, for it is in humanity, and humanity in the world. Together they make and are a world full of evil deeds. For that reason it is denounced much longer. To which world God will return with wrath and without mercy, upon which he nevertheless has first conferred such love. Not, I say, upon stone and wood, but upon humanity, as it is written. And that not all shall sleep, many fewer shall perish, testifies Paul openly to the Corinthians, in addition to all the other testimonies,[33] which are too long for me to relate here, as in the Psalms, Isaiah, Jeremiah, and in Ezekiel, etc. These stand sufficiently expressed in many places. In this manner hear you that such is right, as is well understood. But as the world is [19ʳ] wood and stone, so shall it perish as well. But these words which you have heard signify something else, but not all people know this.

XXV. The Twenty-fifth: That the salvation of the saints will not be in heaven, but upon the earth. This I have never said nor willed in any fashion except as the Scriptures testify. Also, this speech has a double meaning. Therefore, I cannot explain it with few words. Since one might say that it was spoken of those who place their salvation in mere earthly things and the lust of the flesh, who have their stomach for their god. But they are the enemies of the cross of Christ, those who covet earthly things. The others might say, it is spoken of those who have salvation and resurrection, who will have their walk and conversation [19ᵛ] upon the earth, not in heaven. Whereupon I briefly answer and say that they think of the bodily resurrection, and see where it shall occur: Upon the earth or in heaven? If it is then to be upon the earth (where the graves are, for where the graves are, there is the resurrection), so one should not think that we are thereby being relegated to a lesser conversation, desire, joy, and life in such a heavenly existence. As if we mortals alone were being deified, by means of the kingdom of God which we have in us. As we would all be in heaven, even if we were physical. For the Lord from heaven himself had done such before and after his resurrection. Yes, he ate and drank. What is that saying? This is not to mean that there is no question among us; there are few words among us. Blessedness shall be in [20ʳ] God and in his Son in eternity. So if he did not come to make our unblessedness blessed (just as he said), living and walking among us upon the earth, according to his promise, to give the earth to us to possess, then so would I, with those who think thus, have erred.[34] Moreover, all flesh is depraved and diminished. But, above all, the Word of our God abides in eternity. Blessed are they who are found therein according to the truth.

See, this is briefly the summary and the conclusion of my small answer and apology to Your Grace to this and similar seditious articles, which in various manners have gone out over all, here and there. And whose immodest, stinking speech has, above all, accused me (and such as me, who are in agreement with the eternal truth of God). [20ᵛ] Which I have borne patiently by God's grace and have suffered for a long time. Yes, I have carried it and still desire to do so. For I remember that old proverb, namely, "when the lies are swift, the truth will stand its ground." Although I have commended my cause to God and to Your Grace to judge these speeches, I beg likewise that Your Grace will come to rest and peace with these answers and report, in the tender hearing of the truth, and through such a means the evil and proud hearts will be restrained. As also has been brought forth through some writings under my name according to my manner and customary words (by some adventurers who boast themselves to be ours, without my knowledge, who, to be shunned, are in part also a reason for it).[35] Moreover, that in some places where the articles have been sent [21ʳ] people mistakenly think that we intended to capture

Emden and other similar cities.[36] Therefore, the entire world must be silent, there is nothing but lies found in such reports. Just as they would neither let themselves be found by us, whoever our accuser and envier is, whose feet run to shed the blood of the innocent. Because of whom God's wrath is aroused over the entire land, as Your Grace knows, and everyone who reads this writing confesses, that I have also been against such perverted meaning. I wish all the land much good and no suffering, that the sword be put down and the shedding of blood be avoided. Rather, I have encouraged them to hold a different sword of the Spirit in their hands (against the same) and thereby do away with great bloodshed, murder and fire, which are the fruits of perdition. If given the benefit of the doubt, it will be known in its own time. [21ᵛ]

"The innocent I will not slay, for I do not justify the godless, says the Lord."[37]

"You shall be an intercessor yourself even before the court. Speak out the words on behalf of all the dumb and orphans, who have been forsaken by all human help."[38] Protect with your mouth the just and right cause of the poor and wretched.

"Deliver those who are in agony of death, hide not yourself from those whom they would strangle, do not spare yourself."[39]

"Speak to him who permits wrong, to the hand who oppresses them."[40] Be not fainthearted in your soul to stand before him, for the Lord hates such, that the evildoers are allowed to [22ʳ] go unpunished when they condemn and fight the innocent.[41]

NOW CAN YOUR GRACE, Highborn Lady, and your respectable lords no longer say that we did not know. Think not that he who has made the hearts, does not know such, or that he who has made your conscience cannot look into it.[42]

Published in the year 1540.

[22ᵛ] A THOROUGH ACCOUNTING of our understanding and Christian faith. Couched in writing and also briefly in summary.

OUR FAITH and teaching is of, on, and in the one eternal, almighty God the Father, Son, and Holy Spirit; through the same Lord has our understanding been opened. Here, as far as possible, we give a short description in a literal fashion, for it is given to everyone who wants to investigate and test it. Whatever is not perfect, God will give us in Christ (with which we, in spite of ourselves, through his light and understanding, forevermore will attune ourselves and confess him to be our Lord and Master according to the Spirit in truth), according to the promises. For we always gladly hear his word willingly [23ʳ] (it is through them who will it) and do his will according to our ability.

We believe in God the Father Almighty, creator of the heavens and the earth and all that is therein. And in Jesus Christ, his only born Son. Furthermore, all that he has taught, spoken, suffered, and done. How he came from above, received of the Holy Spirit, born of Mary into the world; crucified under the reign of Pontius Pilate, died and buried; descended into hell; rose again on the third day; thereafter ascended up to heaven; now sitting or standing at the right hand in the power of his heavenly Father; and shall return on the last day, according to his word, to judge the living and the dead.

We believe in the Holy Spirit; [23ᵛ] in one community of the saints; in the forgiveness of sins; the resurrection of the body (flesh); and after this life, another eternal life in truth. Amen.

Furthermore, we also teach our children how that the holy church of Christ (God's holy believing community) does not mistake the outward-speaking faith of words for the right, true faith of the power according to the Spirit. Therefore, one must make sharp and prepared different eyes, ears, and understanding or sense of the heart; then this faith can be perceived and understood with conscious comprehension and understanding. So we teach them that they do not have certainly the ability to think, if they have not felt faith in, out or through a different heart, sense, will, and mind to God, other than that according to the flesh, out of their human birth.[43]

[24ʳ] Further, we teach them to understand the words of Christ (according to our best understanding). Similarly, we teach according to the gospel, written in the holy biblical Scriptures, how that we may not, according to our understanding, human sense or self will, pull, bend, or understand them, but instead according to the meaning and will of Christ's Spirit. For the same Spirit is in every way completely against our human or fleshly sense and will, to such an extent that it never rests at all (to those who hear and believe). For those who bring themselves under instruction, through much punishment, reproof, and chastisement, and guard themselves and us from that eternal corruption, have been freed from sins, death, the devil, and hell.

Here also we teach and counsel them to pray the prayer of Christ frequently every day. [24ᵛ] To grow in the holy faith, according to the Spirit, and not to live in vices according to the flesh.[44] If they do otherwise, they will die, and may not be united to or please God and his Christ; yes, they cannot and may not. The flesh will always lust and act against the Spirit. It is contumacious against the law of God. Therefore, lay aside such ways and make an end of displeasure daily according to the time, by beholding and considering the purity of the Holy Spirit and the virtue of God.

Again, we counsel and teach them that they remove from their hearts all vanity, evil, guile and roguishness, yes, every vice. They should watch and wait, so that they thereby will walk desirably in the light of the holy, heavenly understanding, that they may be pure just as he is pure. Then in him and through him, we will and must be [25ʳ] washed, cleansed free, and pure in our souls from all impurity and dead works, through the blood of his cross and the love of his true friendship. To which we (who will have fellowship and unity with him) might come.

Here too we teach and counsel them that they themselves must depart out of the old sinful nature and must enter Christ's one eternal, heavenly, righteous, virtuous nature. That they otherwise will learn nothing from him and will not be his disciples, children or youths. They will otherwise not enjoy truly or profitably his holy sacraments; neither will they participate in his death and resurrection, nor may they be called faithful, demonstrating that with many similar things. Also that we ourselves in baptism are indebted to keep our children even in the same [25ᵛ] and therein to bring them up, according to our ability from God's grace. That they were born in blessedness and not in damnation (as is written of the godless, who have their part in the curse).

Further, we so counsel and teach them that they are not to be here impotent, giddy, slothful, and immoderate. But to be always awake and praying, honoring their elders, that they should love, honor, and fear God according to his command, in all things, from full hearts and souls, to all our power and ability. Thereafter, that they love their neighbor as themselves [Matt. 22:39]. Further, that they respect, be polite and peaceful (as far as is possible for them) toward all people. That they, in order to advance according to the Lord's command, also ought to do good to those who do evil to them; from their hearts love those who hate them; [26ʳ] and bless or speak well of those who speak evil of them [Luke 6:27-28]. They should pray for those who cause them suffering. Therewith that we might entirely defeat our old nature and keep our feet from treading or walking in or doing its evil, unbelieving, roguish ways, with the time; so that the rest and peace (given in Christ) might come.

Further, we so counsel and teach them that they are to honor their authorities on God's account; to pray to God for them, that they will always proceed well in goodness, be long-suffering, and that their servants serve according to his pleasure. So they will protect the true poor, widows, orphans, and the foreigners of the earth, distinguish the good from the evil, and preserve peace, love, and unity, so that no one be withheld from living righteously and piously but splendidly and joyously. To God always [26ᵛ] they should be firmly betrothed and thankful. Summary: We teach them that they ought to live, confess, know, and understand their faith from the heart. And that they prove themselves in divine, true power throughout the day, not to let anything stand on the spoken Word alone, since they are therein not Christians under the fellowship of the saints; but they should appear according to the truth in the righteous Spirit of the perfection; to be with God and his eternal Word in truth, always and forever, even to the death and blood. Thereto help and strengthen us all, God, through Jesus Christ. AMEN. [27ʳ]

THE GLORY OF OUR HOPE
in all such ground is this:

NAMELY, ONLY upon a gracious, certain God of eternal peace, love, and righteousness. So what we have obtained, we obtained with him and in all things, namely, to have need of nothing here. Whether we are then (named, in the eyes of people) rich or poor, so would we be well satisfied there. It is more than enough to be over richly favored with God and in God. Since we believe and know that in him is all fullness of life, light and understanding, [27ᵛ] rest, joy, and peace. In such a way that we neither trust in, be quiet or at peace in, nor rejoice in anything else. Neither glory in opinions, but in the unity of the love of Christ and in the perfection of the true knowledge of God. There the ground and basis of our rejoicing stands eternally fixed; outside of that everything perishes.

THE LOVE WHEREIN WE NOW stand,
or in such faith and hope began, is this:

TO KNOW THAT WE all mutually take the other to heart; [28ʳ] that we grant to others, as ourselves, the good and not the evil. No one, by our knowledge or ability, is left in need or let down. We forget none of them, according to the measure of each one's faith, to demonstrate love from our faith, with heart, sense, and mind. Not only concerning the outward needs of their body, but to the inward soul, for which benefit we must diligently seek. "For physical exercise profits little, while the service of God profits much" [1 Tim. 4:8]. For the

Lord Christ Jesus was sent, crucified, died, and rose only for this purpose. So any here who are not found upright [28ᵛ] must be reproved and punished, and we bear mourning and suffering over them. So those who do this not, they are cast out and are godless and a devil. Then they fall into the wrath of GOD in eternity, whoever, I say, will not better themselves. Above all, we cut off no one who stands in love, for we pray instead of cursing. Since we hope to win over the evil with the good, we do not become tired in love. For God protects us, through his Christ, judge, king, and lord, he provides for those who are his forever. See, this is in summary our faith and teaching, just as with the apostolic [29ʳ] Christian church overall, whether near or far.

THE END

Appendix 1
Joris's Hymns on the Dutch Language

Two songs which Joris composed apparently around the middle of the 1540s are included here because they are perhaps among the most fascinating of Joris's compositions.[1] These texts are among a cluster of works in which Joris promotes the Dutch vernacular over against the classical and biblical languages, as well as proclaims the lowly Netherlands as the site for the kingdom of God. They are important as among the earliest manifestations of Dutch patriotism and of the movement to purify Dutch which increasingly preoccupied Dutch writers after the middle of the sixteenth century.[2]

The first song, "To the Praise of the Netherlands and of the Dutch Language," uses the parable of the sower (Matt. 13:1-23) to show how God had sown the seed of his Word to first the Hebrew, then Greek, and then Latin peoples, but each in turn failed to produce the requisite fruits. All have since been rejected, but now the sower has given the seed to the Netherlands, and there it will blossom as "a beautiful garden" into which all people will come. Joris elaborated on these points in the second song, "On the Clear Dutch Language." Here the Dutch chauvinism is clearly pronounced. According to Joris, just as with the Netherlands as a whole, the Dutch language would likewise rise up from its humble beginnings to become the dominant tongue for the world.

Apart from their subject matter, these texts are quite distinct from the other songs in Joris's *Songbook* for another reason. They are composed in the style common to songs and refrains of the Chambers of Rhetoric. Although he was not a known member of a rhetorician chamber, these poetic works show Joris was at the least very interested in and influenced by rhetorician drama and other cultural aspects of his society.[3] Evidently he hoped to use these interests in the service of the spiritual well-being of his homeland.

◦ ◦ ◦ ◦ ◦

Refrain to the Praise of the Netherlands and of the Dutch Language

Ever lowly Netherlands, you shall be highly exalted,
above all the fixed mountains which span the crown;
for the Sowers have given the seed to you,
all will finally come to live in you.
Therefore, you shall appear as a beautiful garden,
so that the people will come to you from every province;
the vintner himself shall come in human form,
he will plant in you all manner of trees of the Spirit.
He had indeed sent his sowers or ambassadors
in former times and in diverse languages;
but now he himself comes against the great giants
with his consuming fire and blazing flame,
so that he will destroy all thistles and thorns.
Stone houses and homes will tremble at his word,
those who have forsaken him will be lost,
although they carry the law outside of her borders.
But a new rising appears to us from the north.

....

Previously the day first appeared from the East,
then those in the South rejoiced even more.
But it finally vanished completely in the West,
thus with full rejoicing a new day comes to us from the North.
Through Moses, God wrote his law
in Hebrew upon the Hebrew youth.
He sowed a good seed tending to virtue;
but it fell by the way, it could not stick,
for the destructive birds would not leave it there.
O it was tred upon by their impure feet
and it was therefore erased from their hearts.
Disbelief kept them out of the land of peace,
they perished on the way and remain beneath
in the earthly health, which they followed after.

So that they have collapsed, with all their cities;
most of all their learned scribes have smothered in sin.
But a new rising appears to us from the North.

....

Then the sun rose even higher in the South,
it seemed to appear for both Jews and Greeks.
There it was sown in Greek by the Greek people,
the apostle Peter was one of these sowers.
But alas, the seed fell upon the hard rocks,
so that it was not able to grow deep roots.
The Greeks sought wisdom and found none,
like the Jews who sought after signs.
Through their egotism they rejected God's wisdom,
therefore, most of them perished in shame,
believing the lies, they abandoned the truth.
For when the sun's heat began to burn,
the apostasy came into many lands.
The wise withered completely in their wisdom,
with the results of rebellion, persecution, and imprisonment.
On all sides they do evil to the cross.
But a new rising appears to us from the North.

....

Thereafter came the exalted apostle Paul,
but his planting was also not fortunate;
he sowed the seed among the Latins in Rome,
many fell among the thorns, where they were entirely overgrown.
And although he was enraptured in the third heaven,
yet he testified of the apostasy of another day.
Yes, he regarded his knowledge and prophecy as fragmentary,
so that he could not obtain the perfection;
but when the perfect comes, then nothing carnal remains,
all piecework and tongues will cease.
Thus Jews, Greeks, Latins must surely fall away,
for they must age before the new.
Yes, in teaching and love they became utterly cold,
as one will now hear things which no one has heard before.
Where then will those who oppress the pious remain?

O their egotism will murder their souls.
But a new rising appears to us from the North.

Prince[4]

Away, you Hebrews who did not believe the truth,
you Greeks and Latins must finally yield;
your title of derision stands over Christ's head,
therefore, everything that you have built will be torn down.
But the Dutch sower comes to instruct us,
namely the Spirit of Truth, who exists eternally;
for the daylight overcomes all previous lights,
for he has come from the Father and the Son.
Through these shall the good earth become fruitful,
it shall increase manifold.
The antichrist will be overcome by him,
then shall the people be converted to God.
He shall clear the way and repair the dunes.
Those who have angered the peaceful ones shall flee;
no one can avert the intention of God,
not even the snake who charmed Eve.
But a new rising appears to us out of the North.

Prince

Now at hand comes our Prince, the Dutch sower.
Quickly, all you lands, receive his word now,
let the heat of your love burn to this captain.
O, you enemies, think of what you have done
to your shame; you will find yourselves standing at the title,
when you look to the cross above.
But if you still do not believe,
then you will perish in the oven's heat,
just like weeds.

Refrain and Ballad of the Plain Dutch Language.

Alike East, West, South and North,
are the Hebrew, Greek, Latin, and Dutch words.
From these the Southeast, Southwest, Northwest, Northeast
have names, work, power, and faith.
All the other languages have come
from these four which I have named,

and it is therefore also good to understand,
which of them is superior.
Of all of these one may know the best,
truly the Spirit has appeared upon the last.
Greek, Hebrew, Latin—both people and language,
have merited the wrath of God.
Through guilt, which they began at the cross,
the sign on the cross confuses them;
they have perished in their own lands.
But the Dutch people, land, and language exist still;
they have been lifted up out of the sea,
(for Christ must suffer from the way of the sea).
Many will be of that fourth kingdom,
their feet are now from sea and mud.

For the rising in the East,
when God gave the Hebrews the first faith,
has since given way to the rising in the South,
through the apostles in the Greek words.
This again gave way in the West,
to the Latin which came next.
So stand ready to expect out of the North,
a rising in the Dutch tongue.
The eternal gift shall appear,
Dutch must now be firmly believed!

Ballad

The humbled Netherlands will rise from the lowliness,
the clear Dutch language will rise above all languages.
Therefore, I must highly praise the Netherlands and Dutch,
for God desires to make the world's wisdom into nothing.
Yes, all tongues which have forsaken the Spirit of truth
will cease, and perish everywhere.
Now people will taste the spiritual gifts
which are given to us in Dutch words,
for the Spirit of the Lord rests here in the North.

Appendix 2
Articles of the Jorists, 1544 [1]

The following list of Joris's teachings was apparently first sent from the magistrates of Deventer to their counterparts in Zutphen sometime before December 1544. It was likely composed for the Deventer authorities at the time of the arrest and interrogation of Jorien Ketel in the summer of 1544. On the fifteenth of December, the Strasbourg authorities sent a copy of the "Articles" to the Basel magistrates to warn them of the teachings of David Joris and his followers. The list is very similar in language to the charges against which Joris was responding in his *Apology to Countess Anna*, and seems to rely on the work presumably composed by Adam Pastor in 1542. Although cast in a rather negative light, this list reveals the public and official perception of Joris's teachings by the early 1540s.

❖ ❖ ❖ ❖ ❖

Articles of the Jorists
New heretical teachings, which the Deventer council wrote to the magistrates of Zutphen in this fashion:[2]

1. They are Lutheran clerics, who prove their matters with Scriptures and who will not believe any articles which are not proven with biblical Scriptures.

2. That one should confess all sins, with the deed and the persons, before the people.

3. That there are no angels, only physical people.

4. That there is no real devil.

5. That Christ will not come personally for judgment.

6. That the last judgment will occur in the spirit through the third David.

7. That the third David should now be perceived on earth.

8. That Christ is not the person whom all the blessed must hear.

9. That the resurrection of the dead has already occurred.

10. That one should no longer marry a woman, but have wives in common.

11. That one may leave unfit wives.

12. That the heaven and clouds, wherein the Lord shall be seen to return, are spiritual heaven and clouds.

13. That the kingdom of Christ will now be externally upon the earth.

14. That this third David will be a king in the kingdom of Christ.

15. That the brothers should rob the godless with the external sword.

16. That the goods of the heathen belong to the Christians; they can take them, where they are able.

17. That the baptism is not necessary and is ended.

18. That one may allow infant baptism, bow before idols, and hold the Lord's Supper with heathen.

19. That the teaching of Paul is a piece-work next to the teaching of this David.

20. That faith and denial of this faith in articles, which are too high, is not a sin.

21. That the world will perish only spiritually, and not in reality.

22. That the salvation of the saints will not be in the heavens, but on the earth.

Notes

Chapter 1

1. The major studies of Joris in the nineteenth and twentieth centuries were composed by non-Mennonite scholars. These include the critical study by Friedrich Nippold (Nippold 1863) and the somewhat overly generous account by Roland Bainton (Bainton 1937; the original English manuscript is also in MFCL 392-A/1). Recent studies have corrected the extremes of Nippold's and Bainton's works. See Zijlstra 1983; Stayer 1985; Waite 1990.

2. For more on the Batenburgers, see Jansma 1988, and Waite 1989a.

3. See Boon 1988.

4. For Hoffman, see Deppermann 1987.

5. Joris *Ordeninge* (vdL 99; MFCL 400). See Waite 1990, 89-106.

6. See his "Confession" in *SAW*, 204-25.

7. The count was made by reference to the standard bibliographies of Joris's works: vdL; HBA; Cramer 1844; Rogge 1894; Bainton 1937; and NKNB. I have recently rediscovered several published works which have not been cataloged. See Waite 1991a. S. Zijlstra has rightly pointed out that the *Jorislade*, a fifteen-volume collection of manuscripts in the University of Basel, has also never been cataloged.

8. See Waite 1990, esp. 113-22; and Zijlstra 1983, 19.

9. The martyrdom of a few of these were originally included in the *Martyrs Mirror*, the most famous case being that of Anna Jans. See Packull 1987a.

10. He had earlier sought refuge in Strasbourg, England, Overijsel, and perhaps Friesland.

11. This doctrine was maintained also by Menno. See Voolstra 1982.

12. Waite 1990, 117-18, Zijlstra 1983, 7-9, and Deppermann 1987, 359-61, discuss this conference. Hoffman had taught that sin after baptism could not be forgiven.

13. See Packull 1988.

14. See Waite 1987, 46-57. Karel Vos (in Stayer/Packull 1980, 91) remarked, "But a slain Jan Matthijs is worthy of respect in comparison with a soft-living David Joris who saved his skin at the right moment and lived luxuriously at the expense of those whom he misled."

15. In 1539 Joris wrote a scathing missive to the Court of Holland at The Hague in which he, by the authority of God, ordered them to stop "the great bullying persecution of his companions and not to join with the Roman Antichrist in the shedding of innocent blood." The unfortunate courier of this letter was caught and executed in Leiden. A summary of the letter is found in Blesdijk *Historia*, 81-84. For the possibility that Joris had written this letter, or another like it, in the spring of 1534, see Waite/Zijlstra 1992.

16. Edited, translated, and discussed in Bainton 1935, 305-309. The letter dates

from September 1553. The original is in Joris *Sendbrieuen* I, part IV, letter 9.

17. Dirk Philips (1504-68), Menno's associate, had been a monk.

18. See Bergsma/Voolstra 1986, 25-35.

19. See Stayer 1984, 459-76, and Zijlstra 1988, 249-56. Menno called Joris a hypo-crite and an antichrist, while Joris repaid the compliment by describing Menno as a mere scribe, unillumined by the Spirit (Zijlstra 1988, 253).

20. Zijlstra 1988, 253-56, notes that on most issues, Joris and Menno were not that far apart. The published records of the discussions revolved around Joris's view that infant baptism was allowable as well as his practice of Nicodemism or outward conformity to mainstream religion and society.

21. Some of his followers, however, continued the polygamy of the radicals. See Waite 1990, 104-106, 148-49.

22. See "The Response to Eisenburg" below.

23. Public confession was an important topic at both the Strasbourg and Olden-burg Colloquiums in 1538, and the sexual ethic at the latter. Blesdijk *Historia*, 75-77, noted that after Joris had returned from the Strasbourg disputation, a delegation of the Oldenburg Münsterites approached him with a list of disputed points, objecting, among other things, to his view that nakedness and the expulsion of shame were useful for obtaining perfection and that one must confess all sins publicly in the fellowship.

24. Menno too had received the patronage, albeit in a more limited fashion, of some of the nobility. Marshall 1984, 280-81, notes the noble Ulrich von Dornum's spon-sorship of Menno. For noble support of Anabaptism in the Low Countries, see Waite 1992b.

25. See Joris *Berichtinge* of 1543 (vdL 17, no MFCL), 97[v]. A copy is in MLA no. MA 376, in a 1614 reprint.

26. The Evangelical Rentmeester of Groningen, Hieronymus Wilhelmi, writing to the former Stadholder of Groningen Karel van Guelders after the latter had sent him a copy of Joris's *Twonder Boeck*. The letter is found in Blesdijk *Billijcke*, 102[v]. In Joris "Hydeckel," 454[r]-456[v] is a letter sent by Joris to Dr. Hieronymus in 1543.

27. See Zijlstra 1983, 62.

28. See Mellink 1963, 155-68.

29. For the resettlement, see Bainton 1937, 58-59; Burckhardt 1949, 21.

30. See Joris *Twonder Boeck* 1551, part I, 58[r].

31. With the master dead, Blesdijk's doubts about Joris's teaching and criticism of Davidite practices were set in writing. He returned to the Low Countries and eventual-ly became Joris's staunchest critic.

32. The events surrounding the "Joris trial" are covered by Bainton 1937, 98-107, 122-222.

33. Nippold 1863, 627.

34. See Waite 1991c.

35. Droz 1965, 154-162. Many more of Joris's works were reprinted in the first three decades of the seventeenth century. For Joris' printers, see Blouw 1991.

36. Nippold 1863, 626. See also Waite 1991c.

37. Joris *Liedt-Boecxken*. An attempt to provide modern harmonies for the songs is made by Hoogewerff 1930. Those songs that are dated fall between 1529 and 1536. For an analysis of the music of the hymns, see Johnston 1990, 113-34.

38. The court record relating to Joris's trial in 1528 indicates that he had com-posed and distributed an anticlerical broadsheet, although only brief excerpts survive in this account (*CDIN* IV, 349).

39. There is at least one known instance where he toned down radical vocabulary in a song text. This case involved the song of Anna Jans (1509/10-39), a wealthy and zealous supporter of Joris who wrote her song in 1536, probably with Joris's help. Pack-ull 1987a, 159, n.62.

40. The main source for Münster Anabaptism is the collection of the tracts of the Münster propagandist Bernhard Rothmann (c.1495-1535?). These are in Stupperich

1970. Unfortunately, few works written by Dutch Anabaptists during this critical time survive. For another example, see Waite/Zijlstra 1992.

41. While van der Linde managed to catalog ten writings from this period, for three of these van der Linde relied on Cramer's list.

42. Joris *Onderwysinge* (vdL 1, MFCL 400, but mistakenly listed as vdL 167 in MFCL).

43. Joris *Vianden* (vdL 3, no MFCL), available in MLA no. 2494 B18.

44. Joris *Lyeffde* (vdL 166, MFCL 400, but mistakenly listed there as vdL 1).

45. Joris *Wtroepinge* (vdL 2, no MFCL), available in MLA no. 2497 B19, in a 1616 edition.

46. "Neemt waer/ ende waeckt op myne Kinderen," Joris *Hand-Boecxken* III (vdL 222, 1).

47. "Neemt waer een Gesicht, van eenen die de Waerheyt ende dat recht Godts lieft, openbaer by dage" (vdL 4), available only in Lebensbeschreibung, 730-31. The vision was actually experienced by one of Joris's closest associates, Leonard van Dam, but was probably written or at least edited by Joris.

48. Joris *Wijsheit* (vdL 167, MFCL 400).

49. Joris *Salicheden* (no vdL nor HBA; Cramer 1844, no.3). Available in MLA no. 2497 B19.

50. Joris *Ehestands* (no vdL nor HBA; no MFCL), MLA no. 2497 B19. It can be set to the early period by Joris's instruction to his readers, the "oppressed, poor, abandoned people" (24ʳ) to come to the "glorious freedom of the children of God" (24ʳ); the first phrase referring to a period of intense persecution and the second is a nearly verbatim citation from Rothmann, "Verborgenheit" (Stupperich 1970, 296-7).

51. Joris *Eynde Coemt* (vdL 165, MFCL 400, mistakenly listed there as vdL 166). Again, the nature of the apocalyptic message here confirms an early date.

52. Joris *Zielen* (no vdL nor HBA; no MFCL), MLA no. 2497 B19.

53. Joris *Gelouighe* (no vdL; no MFCL; HBA 2926a), MLA no. 2494 B18. See Rogge 1894, 10.

54. See below, p. 245.

55. The other major contemporary account of Joris's life is by Blesdijk (Blesdijk *Historia*). This biography, written after Joris's death and Blesdijk's defection from the movement, is discussed in Zijlstra 1983, 165-71, and Stayer 1985, 358. The critical *Historia vitae* provides a necessary corrective to the often uncritical anonymous account.

56. See below, p. 201.

57. It is not surprising considering the apocalyptic emphasis of the Melchiorite tradition, that a high proportion of scriptural references were from the prophets and apocrypha. Using his "Response to Johannes Eisenburg" as an example, of a total of 178 identified references, 45 were from the prophets; 47 from the remainder of the Old Testament; 57 from the New Testament (five from Revelation) and 29 from the Apocrypha.

58. "Response to Eisenburg," below, p. 165.

Chapter 2

1. See Waite 1990, esp. 49-87. For example, its story about Joris's trip to England c.1520 to install some windows in the manor chapel of Henry VIII's Treasurer, William Sandys, has received confirmation in the research of art historians. See Koegler 1928, 157-201; Boon 1988, 117-37.

2. Lebensbeschreibung, in Arnold 1729, 703-37.

3. Blesdijk "Oorspronck." This important work was only recently rediscovered by S. Zijlstra (Zijlstra 1983, 147-65) who suggests it was composed after 1559.

4. See, for recent examples, Packull 1987a; Waite 1990, 59 n.2.

5. Blesdijk *Historia*.

6. While Arnold has included marginal notations in his translation, they do not

appear to have been original to the document. In his translation of Joris's other works, Arnold added marginal comments which do not appear in the originals. They therefore had not been included here. It seems also that Arnold has added verse references to the Scripture citations. They are used here.

7. Maritje Jans de Gortersdochter (d. 1539) was originally from Delft, Holland.

8. Joris's father was a Joris de Koman or Joris van Amersfoort, a lesser merchant from Amersfoort. He was probably a member of a Chamber of Rhetoric and the part of the Israelite king was a common one in late medieval scripts. See Waite 1990, 61, n.20.

9. *Bunds-genossen* (i.e., *bondgenoten*, the early followers of Hoffman).

10. This trip occurred in the summer of 1544 after Joris and his followers had been compromised by the testimony of Jorien Ketel in May of that year. Joris's name Johan von Brugge (Bruges) may indicate that Bruges had been the city of his birth.

11. The story of a particularly severe childhood leading to uncommon religious devotion was a common one in biographies of this type. See the account of the childhood of Hendrik Niclaes (1502-80) in the "Chronica," *DAN* VI, 9ff. The more famous story of Luther's childhood is another example.

12. The "small schools" were elementary vernacular schools and the "large schools" were secondary institutions teaching Latin literature and grammar. Classes in the Latin schools began with the eighth or ninth and concluded with the first grade, although most schools finished at the third grade, considered sufficient preparation for the pupil to attend university. Most students quit at the fourth grade. The curriculum of Latin schools concentrated on the learning of Latin grammar, although usually including some study of hymns and music, readings in the catechism and Gospels, and perhaps a little logic and arithmetic.

13. Possibly the Court of Holland in The Hague.

14. An enormous sum for any early sixteenth-century merchant. As a comparison, the total income of the city of Amsterdam was only 56,310 pounds sterling in 1531 (Tracy 1985, 16). Expressed in practical terms, 2,000 pounds sterling would buy a house on one of the best streets in Amsterdam or between 3,000 and 4,000 bushels of rye (Tracy 1985, 224). There were six florins or guilders to the Holland pounds sterling.

15. If Joris's family had moved back to Delft after his father's death, Joris's acquaintance with a prominent citizen and mayor of that city would go a long way in explaining his relatively light sentence in 1528 and ability to remain in the city while he was one of the most wanted heretics in the empire. Unfortunately, neither the identity of this rich merchant nor the city in which he resided can be identified.

16. It was common for aspiring master craftsmen to embark on a journeyman's tour before establishing their own master shop. Where Joris was trained is unknown; his name is not inscribed in the membership book of the St. Lucas guild of artists in Antwerp. See Rombouts/Lerius 1864.

17. Lord William Sandys (d. 1540), Henry VIII's treasurer and commander of the city of Calais.

18. Basingstoke is actually about twenty-five miles from the heart of London. The house has been identified as the Chapel called "The Vyne," part of Sandys's manor. According to Boon 1988, 117, this window was designed by Bernard van Orley (c.1488-1551), a prominent glasspainter from Brussels. If so, Joris may have been an apprentice under van Orley and may therefore have received part of his training in Brussels, not far from Antwerp. The window, still extant, depicts the suffering, crucifixion, and resurrection of Christ.

19. Probably a reference to the renewal of hostilities in 1522 between France on the one side and the Empire and England on the other, which was the reason for Charles V's visit to London in that year.

20. Joris had evidently returned to the Netherlands by 1522, for he was commissioned in that year to paint several windows in a church at Enkhuizen. See Koegler 1928, 169.

21. He married Dirkgen Willem (d.1556), about whose past little else is known.

22. Scheffer 1873, 356-7, suggests that one of these teachers was the "Lutheran Monk," the ex-Dominican Wouter of Utrecht, who became a leader of the evangelical movement in Delft.

23. Several iconoclasts were arrested in Delft in the years 1526-28, including two weavers who had destroyed a monstrance in 1526; Jan Joestez, a bookbinder and his apprentice, Adriaan Jansz van Blenckvliet in 1527; and Jan van Haestrecht, Jan van Schoonhoven and Gijsbrecht Aelbrechtsz, a tailor, in 1528. See Waite 1990, 53.

24. The account of Joris' trial on July 30, 1528, includes brief excerpts of a broadsheet which the court officials regarded as his. About the use of images in the church, Joris apparently had written: "These false hypocrites, monks and priests, have made us believe, that [images] were the books of the unlearned, but the Spirit of the Lord says, that they are snares to the falling of the unlearned and are tempters of their souls." Joris had also castigated the religious professions, writing that "the religious, having preached that the images were the books of the unlearned, are themselves false hypocrites, and set against . . . the holy Scriptures, for the people, seeing the images of the saints, are moved to suffer a similar life." The broadsheet also decried religious persecution, identified the old church with the Babylonian whore and the papacy with the antichrist, and denied transubstantiation. See *CDIN* IV, 349; Waite 1990, 53-54.

25. Joris's initial sentence, passed by the Delft city council after his arrest in May, was quite lenient. The Prosecutor-General forced a more severe sentence which included a severe whipping, the boring of his tongue, and a three-year period of banishment. As best as can be determined, Joris traveled from Delft to East Frisia.

26. Presumably the execution of Hoffman's apostle to Holland, Jan Volkertsz Trijpmaker, who returned to Amsterdam from East Frisia in late 1530. Trijpmaker and nine other Anabaptists were burned at the stake on December 5, 1531, in The Hague. For the names of the other martyrs, see Waite 1990, 63, n.57.

27. A reference to the Great Trek of March 1534, during which thousands of Anabaptists traveled by land and water to reach the designated gathering spot in Overijsel before proceeding in relief of Münster. Most, however, were turned back by the authorities and the leaders executed. See Mellink 1988, 211-20; Stayer 1986, 261-88.

28. Nothing else is known of her.

29. Did this debate concern Hoffman's incarnation doctrine? If so, a song from November 1536 illustrates that Joris too adopted it. In this composition, he wrote that Christ

became flesh and for us has suffered,
The Son of Man Named.
His flesh has come from heaven. (Joris *Liedt-Boecxken*, 46ᵛ-47ʳ).

30. Mandates against the Anabaptists were issued almost yearly by the emperor and the regional authorities. Examples are found in *DAN* I-III, V. See also Tracy 1982. The authorities had tried a period of grace extending from February 13 to 26, 1535, but cracked down with increased severity after its expiry. The harsh measures came into effect in Delft by March of that year. By April Joris was absent from Delft looking for a more tolerant residence, and on April 17 his absence from the city was noted by the sheriff. See Waite 1990, 66-67.

31. Leonard Jost, a major prophet of the Strasbourg Melchiorites, was a butcher by trade and seems to have been the Leonard mentioned here. Strasbourg had been regarded as one of three cities which God had intended to give to the Anabaptists. But, because of its maltreatment of Hoffman, still in the city jail, Strasbourg soon received the brunt of pessimistic prophecies. Deppermann 1987, 349-58.

32. *gemein*, used elsewhere to refer to the church, hence this could be a reference to what Joris regarded as the poor state of the church in Strasbourg.

33. "O Christen Gheesten wilt hier op achten," in Joris *Liedt-Boecxken*, 41ʳ-43ᵛ. The song is translated below.

34. "Die Heer is Coninck in Israel," Joris *Liedt-Boecxken*, 58ᵛ-60ʳ. The tune reference is to Luther's more famous hymn.

35. *roste*, the exact meaning of which is uncertain.

36. Horst 1972, 77, remarks that this negative report was greatly exaggerated, although twenty-five Anabaptists were arrested in England in the late spring of 1535, and over half of them were executed.

37. Nothing else is known of this Martin.

38. *Haefersou*, a village just a few miles northeast of Delft, where, under the leadership of Pieter van den Binchorst (d.1536), the noble Bailiff of the Gravenzande, some Anabaptists had attempted to reestablish the kingdom of God by force of arms. In the ensuing melee, ten of the Anabaptists were killed and several arrested, while others managed to escape. Batenburg had made plans to join in the enterprise, and we know that he purchased weapons for the attempt, but there is no evidence that he actually was in Hazerswoude at the time of the uprising. See Waite 1989a, 176-80.

39. Most likely Damas van Hoorn, a revolutionary Melchiorite who supported Münster and preached throughout Holland.

40. Obbe Philips (c.1500-68). Philips confirms his involvement in his "Confession," *SAW*, 223. Obbe Philips was in Delft during the fall to early winter 1534 and Damas van Hoorn may have been in the city on his way from Monnickedam to Middelburg, where he proclaimed the Münsterite message around Christmas, 1534. See Mellink 1981, 165, 168.

41. These included Bernhard Rothmann's "On the Restitution," "On Vengeance," and "Concerning the Hiddenness of the Word of God," which were spread throughout Westphalia and the Netherlands by Münsterite emissaries in the winter of 1534/35. See Stupperich 1970.

42. This conference, which took place before the Anabaptist attack on the Amsterdam city hall in May, 1535, was dominated by those like Damas who supported the Münsterite program. Aside from this account, little information about the meeting has survived. The Waterland is the region north of Amsterdam and was the home of the later Mennonite Waterlanders.

43. Presumably Damas van Hoorn.

44. A reference perhaps to the Spaarndam meeting later in the year which Joris did not attend. See Deppermann 1987, 342.

45. In February 1536 Adriaen Adriaens van Hazerswoude, a survivor of the Hazerswoude debacle, proclaimed himself the king of Israel and set up his reign in Poeldijk, just northwest of Delft. In the following month he collected around himself forty followers, including several other Hazerswoude veterans, presumably to avenge the defeat at Hazerswoude. According to the testimony of two of his followers, Adriaens "was to receive out of heaven a horse, crown, and a sword in order to punish the unrighteous" and to "smite all those who were not elected by God." See Mellink 1981, 218-9. The group was again defeated by the authorities.

46. Unfortunately this correspondence is not extant, nor is there any external confirmation for the veracity of this dialogue between Joris and the Poeldijk radicals.

47. Jan Matthijs van Middelburg (d.1538), one of the Melchiorite refugee leaders in England. Although residing in England, Matthijs spent considerable time on the continent between 1536 and 1538 seeking to reunify the Melchiorites. Maastricht and Schoonhofen were Melchiorites from Holland. It appears that along with Joris these leaders were opposed to the Münsterite position. Blesdijk *Historia*, 14-15, provides a more complete list of those who attended the conference.

48. These would have been the refugees from Münster who had gathered in Oldenburg around Heinrich Krechting (1501-80), the former royal chancellor of the kingdom.

49. Horst 1972, 79, suggests that this may have been the prominent and wealthy English religious dissenter Henry Hart. Annette Gottwaldt ("Twistreden," QGTElsass3, 163, n.4), however, more plausibly identifies this Henry with the Hendrik van Ghent (Hendric in Vlaenderen) who later attended the Strasbourg disputation. If this is the case, then Henry was like van Jan Matthijs van Middelburg a Dutch refugee in England.

50. Joris's successful mediation of an agreement and authorship of the now lost protocol is confirmed by Blesdijk *Historia*, 14-15.

51. Unidentified, except that the later reference to the fire in the city suggests that this was another name for Delft.

52. I.e., from one of the homes adjacent to the city wall. This story shows similarities with the story of the apostle Paul's escape from Damascus related in Acts 9:24-29.

53. Presumably the terrible fire which destroyed the greater part of Delft on May 3, 1536.

54. Probably Den Brill. See Packull 1987a, 153-54.

55. This woman is presumed to be Anna Jans, a prosperous woman living in Den Brill. See Packull 1987a.

56. Presumably the barber/physician Arent Jans who had been in refuge in England.

57. In the sixteenth century Den Brill was on an island. If this was Joris's hiding place, he therefore had to cross what is now the Maas (although it was much wider then) and then travel by wagon to Delft, a trip which exactly fits the description here. Packull 1987a, 153-54, suggests that because Joris and his companions wanted to arrive in Delft at 4 a.m., but instead arrived at the gates after the sun had arisen at 5 a.m., that this must have taken place in late April or early August.

58. "Onse Handen wy mit onschult wasschen," Joris *Liedt-Boexcken*, 44^r. Johnston 1990, 130-34, suggests that the music for this hymn was not suited for vocal performance and that Joris purposely sought to create a new musical style to promote his concept of true spiritual singing. Joris also included a discussion of spiritual singing in Joris *Twonder Boeck* 1542, 193^r-194^v.

59. The identity of Anthon cannot be established.

60. Joris's thoughts about blaspheming God are seen in other works, such as Joris *Onderwysinge*, and was a question for debate at the Strasbourg disputation.

61. Joris's vision here is reminiscent of those of the Strasbourg Anabaptist prophet Ursula Jost (d. by 1531). See Deppermann 1987, 206-210.

62. The author at this point quotes verbatim from Joris *Hoert*, 1^r-2^v. Because a translation of the original text is found below, it is not included here.

63. This translation is from Stayer 1985, 355. The version in Joris *Liedt-Boecxken* is "Myn ooren hebben van bouen ghehoort," 71^r, and dated December, 1536. Another translation is provided in Deppermann 1987, 362.

64. Large sheets of parchment, probably of the size used to keep accounts.

65. This publisher was probably the prominent Deventer printer Albert Pafraet (1512-50). In 1544 Pafraet confessed before the Deventer city council that in 1539, at the instigation of Jorien Ketel (a native of Deventer), he had produced three Davidite tracts, two of which he identified as Joris *Vianden* and Joris *Lyeffde*. He is known to have published several other Davidite works, although he acknowledged to the authorities that he did not know what the contents of the works were. See Hullu 1897, 321-24.

66. By 1543 Joris had quite a number of associates who acted as messengers. Over a dozen are identified by name in Joris "Hydeckel."

67. The Münsterite goal of an earthly kingdom and of sharing the spoils did not die with the fall of Münster in June, 1535. Instead, the group of Münsterites around Heinrich Krechting in Oldenburg and the Batenburgers continued to make plans to take Münster in 1538/39 and to capture other cities. They also continued community of goods.

68. *gantz gelassen.* The theme of "resignation" or "submission" (*Gelassenheit*) was a commonplace of the Radical Reformation.

69. The large number of executions of Anabaptists and the unclear time frame for this promise makes identification of this particular group difficult. Obviously some of Joris's spiritual compatriots had offered to support him financially. The authorities normally confiscated a large portion of executed Anabaptists' estates.

70. Joris was in The Hague in 1531 after the expiry of his banishment from Delft.

71. The biographer may be referring to hearsay such as that reported to the Delft authorities by Dirck Vincent, a local brewer, who supposedly overheard a glasspainter by the name of Laurenz Rykertszoon claim that Joris had said to him, "We see that the clergy are in brave business, and get a deal of money with little pains. We have read the Scripture as well as they. Let us likewise undertake something about Religion. And if we can get so far, that people will believe all we tell them, we shall get far, and be rich enough" (Brandt 1720, 75-76).

72. Presumably after the expiration of his ban in 1531.

73. Joris and Dirkgen eventually had ten children, several of whom would have been born by this time (the early to mid 1530s). George (Joris), the eldest, was born in 1525.

74. I.e., just before his visions of December 1536.

75. Jan van Batenburg (1495-1538) was the bastard son of one of Duke Karel van Guelders's captains, Dirck van Batenburg. He had lost his position as mayor of the Overijsel town of Steenwijk over a dispute with the Habsburg government early in 1535. At a meeting in Groningen province in 1535, he was persuaded by a group of dissatisfied Münsterites to replace Jan Boeckelsz van Leiden (d.1536) as the new David. He took leadership over a group of revolutionary Dutch Anabaptists to punish the government and the Catholic Church. See *DAN* I, 147; Waite 1989a.

76. Absalom had plotted against King David. Like Boeckelsz before them, both Batenburg and Joris regarded themselves as the successor to the Israelite king. There could be no room for two such royal figures. It is also noteworthy that in his confession to the authorities in 1538, Batenburg called Joris the head of the Anabaptist movement. See Hullu 1897, 252; *DAN* I, 144f.

77. Batenburg apparently believed that only those of his followers who were baptized before 1536 could be true Christians, while those who joined later could aspire only to mere servanthood in the kingdom. Water baptism, therefore, was ended at Batenburg's command, for he believed that the number of elect was fulfilled. See Jansma 1984, 56.

78. Batenburgers most frequently targeted the property of the religious estate.

79. This accusation that the followers of Menno Simons had threatened to murder Joris is incredible. While many of the followers of Menno bore an ill will toward Joris, it is hard to believe that any of them had actually made such a threat.

80. For Batenburgers who joined Joris, see Waite 1990, 145-57; for the Mennonites, see Zijlstra 1988.

81. *grott oder stuiver*. There were twenty stuivers and forty groats to the Holland pound of Charles V (the *Karolus gulden*).

82. *Weisspfenning*, probably in Dutch a *Witpenninc*, a small silver coin.

83. *angelotten*, probably the *Karolus gulden*.

84. The most prominent forms of execution for heresy in the sixteenth century were buring at the stake, drowning, and beheading.

85. It seems that Joris had earlier attended dramatic performances such as those put on by the Chambers of Rhetoric.

86. Cleves is on the Rhine in Westphalia, just across the border from Nijmegen and west of Bocholt, while Oldenburg is over 200 kilometers northeast of Cleves. It is probable that Joris was asked to stop in the region of Cleves to meet with some of his supporters, particularly those in the household of Gossen van Raesfeld (d. 1567). See n. 90 below.

87. *rotte ruhr*.

88. Presumably Zwolle in Overijsel.

89. It seems the highwayman was accompanying the group on the pretext that he would protect them. If this was true, he may have expected money for his services. In any case, Joris and his companions believed that he intended either to rob them or to turn in Joris for the reward.

90. Raesfeld is about fifteen kilometers southeast of Bocholt. Count Barent van

Hackfort was another of Duke Karel van Guelders's captains. His son-in-law, who was later to inherit the Count's office and holdings, was Gossen van Raesfeld. While van Raesfeld's later career as the Twenthe bailiff indicates he was no friend of Anabaptists, he may have been more open-minded before receiving his office in 1539. Joris later corresponded with van Raesfeld's wife. See Waite 1992b.

91. It was common for Batenburgers to abduct women. The person identified as "N." here was possibly Gerdt Eilkeman (Geert van Coevorden), d. 1544, a sailor who resided for a time in the region of Raesfeld. He had been baptized by Obbe Philips but was converted to the Batenburgers. He used as a pseudonym Peter van Noerich (*DAN* I, 167). According to the testimony of the Batenburger Dirick Schomecker in 1546, Merieke Steinmetzer, presumed to be the woman in question, had been abducted by Eilkeman after he had killed her husband. Eilkeman then forced her to marry Gerdt van Zwolle, a fellow Batenburger. When this husband was himself killed, she was given to his brother, Hensselin. She then escaped to Joris (*DAN* I, 175).

92. Kaal was a grain merchant and mercenary and a known associate of Batenburg. He joined Joris's group in Delft, but was executed in 1539 along with some two dozen of his associates.

93. Presumably Tecklenburg, north of Münster on the way to Oldenburg.

94. The refugees from Münster had found a home in Oldenburg because the Duke of Oldenburg and the Bishop of Münster were then at war and the Duke saw in these refugees potential supporters in his campaign against the Bishop. See Kirchhoff 1963, 43.

95. It is likely that this companion who was summoned by the duke was one of the Oldenburg Anabaptists who had persuaded Joris to embark on the journey in the first place.

96. Foot washing, based on John 13:5-12, was practiced as a rite by many Anabaptist groups, including, it appears, the Davidites.

97. It is not certain if Heinrich Krechting was present at the meeting.

98. For specifics, see Blesdijk *Historia*, 75-77.

99. The authorities often hired ex-Anabaptists to infiltrate Anabaptist groups. There were also "bounty-hunters" after the one-hundred pound reward on Joris's head.

100. I.e., the woman who had escaped from the Batenburgers.

101. This appears to have been Heinrich Kaal.

102. They presumably followed the Rhine to Strasbourg.

103. The identity of this man is unknown. Both of Joris's main lieutenants, Jorien Ketel and Leonard van Dam, completed the trip to Strasbourg. Hans de Wael, Deventer's paymaster (*Busmeester*), was another well educated supporter of Joris who could possibly have been on the trip. He was a skilled linguist and would have been an invaluable aid in Joris's discussions with the Strasbourg leaders. The delivery of a letter ordering the man's return makes sense if the man was a city official. See Waite 1990, 153.

104. The conference coincided with a major Strasbourg market, thus making it easier to avoid detection from the authorities. The "other" may have been Jan Matthijs van Middelburg, who was a prominent figure in arranging the meeting and in convincing Joris to attend.

105. These included Johannes Eisenburg (d.1541) and Peter Tasch (d. after 1560).

106. This would be the "Disputation" or "Twistreden."

107. Johannes Campanus (c.1500-75) was a radical reformer from Jülich, whose writings condemned the Catholic practices of the mass and infant baptism. See *ME* I, 499-500.

108. Melchior Rinck (1494-after 1545) was an important leader of the Anabaptists in Hesse, Germany. He had had an excellent education, being nicknamed "the Greek" presumably for his mastery of that language. *ME* IV, 337.

109. Presumably Jan Matthijs of Haarlem, the former prophet of Münster.

110. Batenburg, recently executed, had been viewed by some of the Dutch Melchiorites as the true Elijah.

111. By 1538 Eisenburg and Tasch were visiting Hoffman in the hopes of winning his assent to a proposal which would not only release him from prison, but bring an agreement between the Melchiorites and the Strasbourg Reformed leaders.

112. This letter is not known to be extant.

113. Moordtjou could not be identified.

114. Because of his success in winning over several radical Anabaptists to his side, it was easy for his uninformed critics to associate Joris with the criminal activities of the Batenburgers. There was a report that before the fall of Münster, Jan van Leiden had given Joris some money in order to raise forces in Friesland and elsewhere for the relief of Münster (Brandt 1720, 76). There is no evidence to support this contention.

115. These associates would have included Jorien Ketel, who was known to have disputed with some Batenburgers, as well as Joris's ex-Batenburger associates who were also prominent in attempting to convert their former cohorts. See Waite 1990, 145-57.

116. Batenburgers tended to implicate Joris in their own designs. In 1546 a Diderich Shoemecker confessed that, "David Joris's opinion and teaching is that he is the Promised David, and that all who believe on him shall reign with him here on earth, and that he shall root out, exterminate, and kill all princes, lords and kings" (Stayer 1976, 298).

117. I.e., that Joris had consistently opposed the use of violence on the part of Anabaptists, and that the charge that he encouraged such was therefore false.

118. An example of this is found in the undated Joris *Eynde Coemt*, 146ʳ, where he writes to believers: "Be foresighted and watch and guard your house well with every weapon. Sharpen your sword, burnish and wipe it until it glistens. And gird it onto your side, because of the terrors of the night. And guard the bed of Solomon well. Keep robbers from the house, so that tormenting spirits will no longer come in and out or run through it. And be of good courage, oh you strong ones in Israel."

119. The event obviously occurred during spring or summer for there to be flowers drying in the attic. It must also have taken place sometime between the spring of 1535, when Batenburger joined the Anabaptist movement, and the end of 1537, when he was arrested. A letter to Batenburg could not be found among Joris's known works.

120. In his confession, Batenburg claimed that he had refused to support the Anabaptist attacks on Emden, Amsterdam, and Groningen (*DAN* I, 149f). The extant confession also makes no reference to any pledge by Batenburg to act as a spy for the authorities. The only comment about Joris recorded from Batenburg's mouth was that "Joris was the head" of the movement.

121. Possibly Batenburg's successor, Cornelius Appelman (d.1545), who had some discussions with Jorien Ketel.

122. Who this convert was is not clear. Several revolutionary Anabaptists joined Joris, including Adriaen van Benscop, Hans Scheerer (Hans van Leeuwarden), Andreis Droochscheerder, and Meynart van Emden. See Waite 1990, 149-53.

123. Jan de Heuter.

124. Most Holland towns resisted outside interference in their judicial domain. See Tracy 1982.

125. Reference to the period of grace enacted by Heuter in December, 1538.

126. The booklet is not extant, although the writing out of dreams was a common practice among Anabaptists.

127. Kaal and several of his supporters were arrested and executed in Delft in January and February 1539. The account of their confessions and executions (in Brandt 1720, I, 75) reveals that these people had come out of a Batenburger background. They had retained the practice of polygamy and practiced a form of communal nudity as proof of their spirituality. They all affirmed, however, that they regarded Joris as their prophet and most had been earlier baptized.

128. Bloodletting involved the slashing of the victim's wrists. Few, if any other Anabaptists were given the choice of their execution.

129. She was executed on Feb. 21, 1539, in a cloister of the Cellebroeders. Apparently this tertiary order tended the sick and buried the dead for the city. The cloister itself was situated in the middle of the city until its destruction in 1578. The sisters of Magdalene were likewise not a true order, but a group of sisters united by the loose bond of a common lifestyle, according to the third order of the Franciscans. Most were connected to hospitals and guesthouses, to help travelers and the sick. See Brouwer 1981, 55-56.

130. David and Dirkgen therefore had at least eight children by early 1539, most of them quite young. The oldest could not have been more than fourteen or fifteen years old.

131. On January 2, 1539, a placard was issued in Holland forbidding anyone to harbor Joris and another former radical who had become a Davidite, Meynart van Emden, on the pain of being hung in front of their own door. The placard was renewed on February 27, 1539. A price of 100 florins was placed on the heads of these two leaders, while the capture of other Anabaptist teachers garnered 40 florins and ordinary Anabaptists 20 florins. See Brandt 1720, I, 75.

132. This vision account is not known to be extant.

133. That Joris was in Haarlem at this time is indicated by a letter which he wrote from the city in March 1539. Joris "Hydeckel," 135'.

134. The renewal of the five senses became a major theme of Joris's writings. He called the true, internal restitution the "renewal of the five senses." See Waite 1990, 211-12.

135. Joris's exact location at this point is unknown, but it may have been the city of Groningen. See *DAN* I, 163-64, n.8; Zijlstra 1983, 18.

136. Joris *Twonder Boeck* 1542, 85'-85' (chapter 130): "What kind of punishment it will be, the Lord has revealed and given knowledge to me, through his Holy Spirit, early Easter morning 1539. And it spoke to me in this way: 'Write what you hear said.' Yes, I was impelled inwardly thereto. And behold, I wrote, how and what. It will at its time be well revealed, it will now, however, be received with derision."

137. Apparently, this section is taken from a published account of the vision that is no longer extant.

138. Van Dam is obviously referring to the danger of detection if he went into the main part of the house.

139. Although Joris's name is not mentioned, his identity as the man in the vision is evident from this description, for Joris was distinguished by a long, red beard.

140. It is difficult to ascertain exactly where the tract ends and the anonymous biography continues, but at this point it appears that Leonard van Dam is no longer the narrator and anonymous author has taken up his story again.

141. The specific work to which the author is referring is unclear, for the humbling of the authorities was a common theme in Joris's writings.

142. The authorities used the infiltrator Adriaen Ariaensz van Dordrecht in this case. Ariaensz had been arrested as an Anabaptist in March of 1534, but was released so that he could aid the government in capturing other Anabaptists. Five years later he was brought into Haarlem by the sheriff of that city and placed into a prison cell containing several Davidites. He managed to win their confidence and the incriminating statements he garnered were used to hasten guilty pleas. Among those arrested in Haarlem was a thirteen-year-old youth by the name of Aelbrecht van Breuchel. Under torture Aelbrecht allegedly confessed the names of several Davidites. See Hulshof 1920, 208-10 & 217-8; also Mellink 1981, 184.

143. Presumably in Utrecht.

144. On April 1541 a suspected Batenburger, Frans Jansz, confessed to his actions of a couple of years earlier: "With his accomplices he had broken open the prison in Leiden, where some Anabaptists were imprisoned, and released these same prisoners, and had kept them in his house for some time" (Mellink 1981, 204-5).

145. Presumably Jan Jansz van den Berch.

146. Delfgauw, now a suburb of Delft.

147. I.e., he was able to pass himself off as an Anabaptist. It is possible that he had been a believer at one time and used his inside information to win Jansz's confidence.

148. Amsterdam in 1539 had four burgomasters, Claes Loen Fransz, Claes Gherritsz Deyman, Claes Doedensz, and Mr. Henrick Dirckxz. After the Anabaptist attack on the city hall in 1535, the imperial authorities had removed the tolerant mayors and had replaced them with more orthodox officials.

149. The record of Jansz's trial and execution is found in *DAN* II, 13. Jansz had been baptized the previous year by a "Claes with a lame hand."

150. There were a total of fourteen Davidites arrested in Utrecht in June 1539. These also included Jorien Ketel's wife, Elsken, who was drowned with the other female Davidites in Utrecht. See Hullu 1897, 276.

151. There are several sections in the *The Wonder Book* regarding the heavenly stream, beginning with the introduction.

152. Presumably Jorien Ketel who was from Deventer. The identity of the other companion is unknown. It is important to note that Ketel in his youth had spent some time as a personal attendant to the Duchess of Buren, mother of the stadholder Maximiliaan Egmont, Duke of Buren, who was noted for his relative tolerance of religious dissent. The willingness of noblemen, particularly in Overijsel, to harbor and patronize radical religious reformers is discussed by Waite 1992b. See also Marshall 1987, 85.

153. Reynier Brunt (d.1539), prosecutor-general of the Court at the Hague.

154. The sheriff of Utrecht.

155. Brunt died on October 15, 1539, hence his death could have had little to do with Dirkgen's release, although he may have fallen ill during the proceedings. For Brunt's enthusiastic persecution of Anabaptists, see Eeghen 1986.

156. The capital sentences of pregnant women were usually delayed until the child had been born. Dirkgen was released on June 18. See Hullu 1897, 276.

157. It appears that it was at this time that he wrote a scolding letter to the Court of Holland at The Hague. In this missive Joris admonished the Court "to cease from the great bullying persecution of his companions and not to join with the Roman antichrist in the shedding of innocent blood." The letter is full of apocalyptical foreboding with respect to the authorities. See Blesdijk *Historia*, 81-4. The missive was to be delivered to The Hague by an unfortunate courier who was caught and executed by the magistrates in Leiden. See Nippold 1863, 117.

158. These news sheets were published on a regular basis and sold cheaply, much like the modern newspaper.

159. The identity of this self-acclaimed prophet is unknown.

160. Presumably the Lübeck merchant Hendrik van Hasselt. According to a report from the Deventer city council in 1544, Hasselt believed that he had been sent from God to reveal the hiddenness of the Scriptures, that the Holy Spirit was nothing more than the mind of God, and that Jesus and Christ were two different persons. Nippold 1863, 524.

161. These letters are not known to be extant, although missives to other religious radicals, such as Hendrik Niclaes and the Antwerp radical Loy de Schaliedecker (d.1544), appear in Joris's correspondence.

162. Probably Leonard van Dam.

163. Leiden's magistrates had placed extra guards over the city's main gates between December 30, 1538, and June 6, 1539, and their plan to capture Anabaptists was probably the reason why Joris showed great reluctance to enter that city. See Mellink 1981, 182-3.

164. There seems to have been a harvest or religious festival in the region.

165. She is otherwise unknown.

166. I.e., he had been a mercenary in the service of the Bishop of Münster, Franz von Waldeck.

167. A Passport involved the examination of persons entering a city.

Chapter 3
1. For the evidence in favor of Canin as its publisher, see Waite 1991c.
2. Packull 1987a, 159 n.62, notes one example of Joris rephrasing a line in Anna Jans's "trumpet song" to tone down its radical message. Yet, as seen in the anonymous biography, Joris was extremely reluctant to revise his own works, for fear of hindering the Spirit's inspiration.
3. Joris *Liedt-Boecxken*, "Ick hoorden huyden wayen," 24ᵛ-26ᵛ.
4. The canopy over the altar.
5. Joris *Liedt-Boecxken*, "O Christen Gheesten," 41ʳ-43ᵛ.

Chapter 4
1. Joris *Ordeninge* (vdL 99; MFCL 400, missing 78ᵛ-79ʳ), MLA no. MA 376. For a discussion of this work, see Waite 1988b, 296-317.
2. Samme Zijlstra suggests that the work reflects some later revisions on Joris's part. Personal correspondence, February 8, 1990.
3. Joris *Hoert*, 30ʳ.
4. "hebben oock die van Munster / dien een groot licht ende vreughde omscheuen was . . ." (Joris *Ordeninge*, 83ʳ).
5. In the tract Joris seems to use the terms *restitution* and *wederbrenginge* interchangeably. We will translate these as "restitution."
6. This seem to be a reference to Hoffman's doctrine of the heavenly flesh of Christ.
7. Here Joris refers to the earlier Münsterite call to believers in the Netherlands and Westphalia to gather under the banners of righteousness before traveling to Münster. In March of 1534 thousands of Anabaptists set out to assemble under the raised banners erected in Overijsel. The call to these banners can be seen in one of Rothmann's comments: "Hyrumme wat sick van Broderen her by dat Panier Gades maken kan vnde lust hefft an der gerecticheit Gades, de willen nicht zumen. Want wanner dat feinlyn gerichtet ys vnd de Basune angehet, wilt volle vngelouige gelouich werden vnde hertho treden" (Stupperich 1970, 293).
8. Here Joris presumably refers to the alchemists' attempt to transmute base metals into gold.
9. Joris here opposes the Münsterites' rationalization for using the sword to defend themselves against oppression. See Stupperich 1970, 282.
10. At this point Joris seems to be addressing his male readers. He then gives different advice to women.
11. The grandson of Aaron who turned back the wrath of God and stopped the plague by killing an Israelite who had taken a Midianite woman, Num. 25:6-8.
12. The left-handed Benjamite who killed Eglon, the king of Moab and delivered Israel from idolatry and the Moabites, Judg. 3:15-29.
13. The wife of Heber the Kenite who killed Sisera, the military commander of the Canaanites, and helped route the oppressors of Israel, Judg. 4:17-22.
14. Late medieval thought was preoccupied with the number seven. The "seven Spirits of God" presumably refer to the seven gifts of the Spirit.
15. Joris evidently practiced what he preached at this point; one of his distinctive features was a long, red beard. Not only was this a matter of comment for those who met him, but when Joris's remains were disinterred in 1559, his corpse was still identifiable because of his beard.
16. *tooverische*, having to do with witchcraft and magic.
17. The reference to "one runs south and the other north" may refer to the supporters of Hoffman who were in Strasbourg on the one side and, on the other, the Münsterite remnant who fled north to Oldenburg.
18. In margin, **the first restitution**.
19. This view had been promulgated by the Wassenberger preachers, especially

through Johann Campanus's work on the Restitution. In a modified form it became the basis for Hoffman's "apostolic community," called out by the apostolic messenger to become the pure bride of Christ. See Deppermann 1987, 245-56.

20. In margin, **the second restitution**.

21. In margin, **the third restitution**.

22. The threefold nature of history and earthly life as a sign of the trinity was a preoccupation of many medieval writers, such as Joachim of Fiore. See McGinn 1985, 161.

23. Here Joris counters the Münsterites' attempt to exactly replicate the social and political structures of the Israelites. For Rothmann, the images of the Old Testament kingdom contained in themselves hidden truth which would be restored literally at the last day. See Stupperich 1970, 223.

24. Hoffman wrote extensively on the bride's wedding garments. See his "Ordinance of God," *SAW*, 191.

25. This command to fill and rule the earth had been an important justification for Münsterite polygamy. Joris's use of "the city of God" vocabulary would naturally have found deep resonance among Anabaptists after Münster.

26. In margin, **Psalm, Dan. 2,7,11**.

Chapter 5

1. Joris *Hoert* (vdL 163; MFCL 400), MLA no. II 1976a. This edition has at the end "uitgegheven 1539," which is incorrect as a date of composition. It may, however, be the date of its publication, or more likely a reissue, for a seventeenth-century version (MLA no. 2494 B18) has a different title page, beginning with "Hoort die stemme des Heeren/ die voor dat aenghesicht des Heeren wtgaet." Van der Linde consulted either this later edition or another from 1610.

2. Joris *Boeck* (vdL 177), 2ʳ-3ʳ. See also vdL 163.

3. See above, pp. 53-54. Joris, during the Strasbourg disputation, dated the vision experience to "about three or four weeks before Christmas" (see below, p. 184).

4. The Song of Songs with its bride imagery for the church was an important source for Melchior Hoffman's writings. See "The Ordinance of God," *SAW*, 184-203.

5. For Joris and spiritual singing, see Joris *Twonder Boeck* 1542, 191ʳ-193ʳ; also Johnston 1990, 130-34.

6. *Parck*.

7. I.e., at the Creation.

8. Literally "between both posts [*stylle*]."

9. Some early Anabaptists, such as Hans Hut, practiced baptism by making the sign of "Tau" on the initiate's forehead. See Packull 1987b.

10. The meaning of this passage is unclear, although Joris seems to be suggesting that believers were to obey the Lord through following the teachings of his anointed servant.

11. *Rentemeyster*, an official in charge of finances, usually ecclesiastical.

12. Joris's word choice is ironic. It was the procurator-general of the Court of Holland who was in charge of the judicial proceedings against Anabaptists.

13. Cf. the 144,000 saints of Rev. 7. While Joris evidently did not believe that the number had been completed, the Batenburgers argued that it had, and therefore, there could be no new members in the community of God.

14. For the "key of David" motif in Dutch Anabaptist thought, see Waite 1990, 90-94.

15. Unlike many of Joris's other works, this tract has no marginal biblical notations.

Chapter 6

1. Joris *Sendbrieuen* I (vdL 225) contains letters from 1546 to 1556; Joris *Sendbrieuen* II (vdL 226) contains letters from 1549 to 1556; and Joris *Sendbrieuen* III (vdL 227) contains letters from 1551-1556, with one from 1539 and another from 1543.

2. The "Hydeckel" is found in vol. 9 (Sendbriefe) of the *Jorislade* collection, Uni-

versity of Basel. The work was recently rediscovered by Zijlstra. Fols. 7ʳ-126ʳ are missing from the manuscript. See Zijlstra 1983, 26.

3. Since 1541 van Schor, a native of Limburg, had been a tutor in the van Berchem household to which Joris had attached himself.

4. I am indebted to Samme Zijlstra for his assistance in the breaking of the code.

5. For Niclaes, see Joris *Sendbrieuen* I, part 1, 92ʳ-96ᵛ; for Schwenckfeld, Joris *Sendbrieuen* I, part 3, 54ʳ⁻ᵛ; for Luther, Joris *Sendbrieuen* III, part 4, 99ʳ; for Agnes of Limburg, see Joris "Hydeckel," 173ᵛ-180ʳ; 346ᵛ-354ᵛ, and Joris *Sendbrieuen* III, part 2, 4ᵛ-7ᵛ; for Wilhelmi, see Joris "Hydeckel," 454ʳ-456ᵛ (1543).

6. "Tot lof ons Heeren vnde stichtinge zeins volx. Neemt waer," Joris "Hydeckel," 291ᵛ-94ᵛ.

7. *ontsich*, literally "fear."

8. Joris elsewhere used the term *voghelkens* to refer to those who were interested in the faith but who required more instruction before joining. For example, in Joris *Salicheden*, 6ᵛ, Joris wrote, "The young birds who are the pious *amateurs* [*liefhebbers*] come as close to heaven as they are able. But they still fly well under it, but not into it. In this way these ones have not come far enough under the oath of the covenant of God, nor are they prepared in the true understanding to the death of the cross."

9. What Joris means by Edomites or *Ee.* is not clear; obviously his supporters used the term to describe some of their contemporaries. The Edomites were the supposed descendents of Esau who sold his birthright (Gen. 25:30). The Edomites were enemies of Israel, although the Israelites were commanded not to hate them (Deut. 23:7). Joris seems also to be referring to the wise men of Edom of Obad. 8. The discussion leads to the possibility that Joris is writing about Batenburgers or other radicals who wanted to join his fellowship.

10. From the discussion here and in the next section, Joris appears to be writing about a specific problem concerning a man who was mistreating a mother and daughter. Or he may be talking about a potential Batenburger recruit who had two wives.

11. Most of the title is in code. Again Joris seems to be giving advice about a specific situation concerning the treatment of a woman and her daughter. If the man had come out of a Batenburger group, he may have been treating them both as wives, hence the reference to his "fleshly freedom."

12. *aanmerken*. The verb has been added later in the margin and is difficult to read through a combination of small print and shortform. Perhaps instead *aannemen*.

13. The meaning here is not clear. Perhaps he must abide with the last decision, or with his last wife?

14. *uutgedaen*, perhaps "put off." There were four known merchants who were close to Joris, including Jorien Ketel, a silk merchant. See Waite 1990, 150.

15. In margin, Heb. 11:25-26.

16. "Antwoort vp Hans Eysenbürchs vorreden," Joris "Hydeckel," 305ʳ-21ʳ. An earlier edition of this translation was published as Waite 1989b.

17. Blesdijk *Historia*, 20-26, entitled Joris's reply as "Responsum Davidis Georgii ad libellum Joannem Eisenburch." Zijlstra 1984, 134, identified Eisenburg's work as probably "Ein kurze erclerung von der waren gotlichen Ordnung des eelichen Standes." This tract is presumed lost.

18. Recorded on a rag that Hoffman used to write on when paper was forbidden to him in jail. See QGTElsass3, 116-17; Deppermann 1987, 354-5.

19. For the possibility that Hoffman was eventually released from prison, see Packull 1983.

20. Deppermann 1987, 369. For Tasch's role in this development, see Packull 1988.

21. In a letter written sixteen years after ours, Joris complained, "O if only those who have taken one or two [wives] had done so in true faith. . . . As far as I am concerned it is all the same whether you have one, two, or four so long as you obey God and the truth," as cited by Bainton 1937, 67.

22. In margin, **Ecclus. 25:8.**
23. In margin, **Prov.**
24. In margin, **Isa. 75 [65:20].**
25. In margin, **Ecclus. 24:8.**
26. In margin, **Wis. of Sol. 7, 8.**
27. In margin, **Prov. 2 [1:7?].**
28. In margin, **Prov.**
29. In margin, **Isa. 33.**
30. In margin, **Wis. of Sol. 3; Isa. 15, 25; Psa. 119.**
31. In margin, **Matt. 19:6.**
32. In margin, **Luke 13, 18; Matt. 10; 1 Cor. 7; Gen. 3.**
33. In margin, **Song of Sol. 8:6-7.**
34. In margin, **Ps. 82; Isa. 70, 71; Pss. 18, 37, 57, 125.**
35. In margin, **Jer. 22; Deut. 33; 2 Esd. 13.**
36. In margin, **Wis. of Sol. 3; Zech. 13; Mal. 3, 4; Isa. 10, 31.**
37. In margin, **Obad. 16.**
38. In margin, **Mic. 5.**
39. In margin, **Isa. 33:10ff.**
40. In margin, **Tob. 6.**
41. In margin, **Ps. 31 [32:9].**
42. In margin, **Tob. 8:7.**
43. In margin, **1 Cor. 7.**
44. In margin, **Gen. 2:22-24.**
45. In margin, **1 Esd. 6:7-10.**
46. In margin, **Eph. 5.**
47. In margin, **Ps. 68:30.**
48. *niet vander vrier vrouwen*, literally "not from the free women." In the sixteenth century, the word "free" was synonymous with "noble."
49. In margin, **Deut. 31.**
50. In margin, **Gen. 45.**
51. In margin, **Judg. 14:3-4.**
52. In margin, **Deut. 25; Isa. 19:17-25; Zech. 9—10; Ps. 87.**
53. In margin, **Ecclus. 3:26.**
54. In margin, **Neh. 8—9.**
55. In margin, **Gen. 28:8-9.**
56. In margin, **Gen. 6:2-3.**
57. In margin, **Jer. 23.**
58. In margin, **2 Esd. 9:22.**
59. In margin, **Rom. 8:13.**
60. In margin, **Jer. 31:22.**
61. In margin, **1 Cor. 6:15-17.**
62. Either *ombeuangen* (overcome), or *onbevangen* (unconcerned).
63. In margin, **Pss. 25, 50; Prov. 3.**
64. In margin, **2 Esd. 6:22; Ecclus. 8.**
65. In margin, **Ecclus. 38.**
66. In margin, **Ps. 48:1-3; Zech. 6:8; Isa. 41:25.**
67. Presumed lost. Joris refers to it and to this "Response to Johannes Eisenburg" in his opening remarks at the conference with the Strasbourg Melchiorites.
68. In margin, **Pss. 21, 37, 101, 105; Wis. of Sol. 3, 4; Ecclus. 16, 41.**
69. In margin, **Rev. 22:15.** This may have been the source for the charge that Joris taught "that all of those, who are found outside of David Joris's fellowship, are cats and dogs." See point 10 of Joris's "Apology," below p. 275.
70. In margin, **Ecclus. 13:15-18.**
71. In margin, **Ps. 80.**
72. Cf. the Apostles' Creed, which Joris quoted nearly verbatim in the *Apology*. See below, pp. 285-286.

73. In margin, **Gen. 1; Isa. 27; 44:2-3; 61:9 [appears to be noted twice], 65:23; Jer. 30, 31; Wis. of Sol. 4:3-6; Tob. 6.**

74. Literally, the "castrated." In margin, **Matt. 19:11-12.**

75. In margin, **Wis. of Sol. 8:20-21.**

76. In margin, **Phil. 4:2-3.**

77. Joris infers from this passage that Paul was writing to his wife.

78. In margin, **1 Cor. 1; Job 5:11-16; Isa. 28, 29.**

79. I.e., they can resist temptation without any struggle.

80. In margin, **Wis. of Sol. 3:10ff.**

81. In margin, **Prov. 29[:27?].**

82. In margin, **Isa. 40:15.**

83. In margin, **Obad.**

84. In margin, **Mal. 1:2-3.**

85. In margin, **Gen. 25:23ff.; 2 Esd. 3.**

86. In margin, **2 Esd. 6:55-59.**

87. In margin, **Jer. 30:11; Ezek. 25, 46.**

88. In margin, **Isa. 4; 46; Mal. 3:3.**

89. In margin, **Ps. 119.**

90. In margin, **Ecclus. 7:26.**

91. "Uprechtinge der Gemeinten," Joris "Hydeckel," 331ʳ-335ᵛ. It is known that Joris sent several letters to supporters in Westphalia. References to H.C. and "Krefting" in the work most likely refer to Heinrich Krechting, who was residing in the region of Oldenburg, Westphalia. See Zijlstra 1984, 132.

92. Jansma 1984, 54-55. See also Blesdijk, *Historia*, 15. It does not seem that at the time of writing this letter Joris was aware of these plans.

93. See above, p. 68.

94. Joris apparently is affirming the catechetical approach of question and answer as the best method of teaching.

95. *Tesamenleden.*

96. *Anual*, perhaps "delivery" or "attack."

97. This discussion is reminiscent of Joris's own experience when he was forced by illness to rely on the gifts of his supporters. See above, pp. 58-60, 63.

98. *Gemeinten*, perhaps "fellowship" or the "common members." It seems that like that of the Münsterites, Joris's form of church order was not democratic.

99. In code. Krefting delivered the letter. It is likely that "Krefting" is a variant of "Krechting." It is quite possible that Joris first sent the letter to Krechting who then delivered it, along with his own advice (noted above), to Joris's group in Westphalia.

Chapter 7

1. Bainton 1937, 43-46, 185-91.

2. QGTElsass3, 162-231.

3. QGTElsass3, 157.

4. Hoffman himself did not participate; he was being detained in the Strasbourg prison.

5. Peter Glassmaker (d.1538) was a former revolutionary Anabaptist preacher in Oldenburg and Appingedam. He seems to have been at the very least sympathetic to Joris.

6. Paulus Goldsmith has not been identified.

7. It is not certain who this Hendric from Flanders (later identified as Hendric van Ghent) is. Gottwaldt (QGTElsass3, 163, n. 4) identifies him as the "Henry from England" who financed the meeting of Anabaptist leaders in Bocholt, August 1536. Several Dutch Melchiorites had found refuge in England.

8. One of these letters may have been "Een Elenden Roepe," which follows the "Response to Johannes Eisenburg" in the "Hydeckel," 330ᵛ-35ʳ, and like the "Response" is without the usual address or date at the end of the missive.

9. Barbara Rebstock was, after the death of Ursula Jost, Hoffman's chief prophet.

10. The "Response to Johannes Eisenburg." The reference to "made by Melchior Hoffman" may refer to Hoffman's approval of the pamphlet written by Eisenburg.

11. Jan Matthijs van Middelburg. Matthijs and Glassmaker evidently acted as mediators between Joris and the Strasbourg Melchiorites. In 1539 Matthijs was caught and executed during one of the few active campaigns conducted against Anabaptists in England by King Henry VIII. See Horst 1972, 74.

12. *die gemeinte lief*, perhaps "church love," or "common love."

13. Berent van Deventer could not be identified.

14. In margin, This is what exists recorded in the foreword, which Peter van Geyen after some days had written from his memory. David was not very happy about it, but he had to let it stand so, if he was to have rest.

15. In margin, These words had fallen on the first afternoon.

16. In margin, These words were not preserved in this way from the spoken form, but written afterward out of the head for their profit.

17. In margin, See, between these words much was spoken among their members, and at all other places, but they have not written these words; why they let me alone speak, this the Lord knows.

18. In margin, There were no other words or replies, besides those which exist here, but I (so that we could have come away from it without a quarrel) had to write it so clumsily or coarsely to my ugliness, and I did it in this way.

19. In margin, Much was said after my answer was given, but they would not set down any more of what I said. They desired instead that it remain this crude, as it had been written from memory, saying, it is concluded enough.

20. In margin, Here they spoke up, but it was not written down.

21. In margin, Here were still some words produced on both sides which were not written down.

22. Jost had relied on his and his wife's visions for religious knowledge. It seems that the better educated Strasbourg leaders had since helped to interpret those visions for him. For examples of these visions, see Fast 1962.

23. *gelosenhet.*

24. In margin, But see, I have answered this above, that I did not speak this way the first time (which remains unwritten) concerning Malachi. But since now they wanted an answer here of my understanding, so I have now answered, just as the Lord has given into my mind above suspicion. They did much like this, but I must write this afterward, so that one should know.

25. Perhaps a result of having his tongue bored in 1528.

26. In margin, David spoke here of the fear of the Lord and how one should pray and of the way of the Lord, what it is, namely straight and true. This they neglected to write, but it was pleasing and receptive for them to hear, as they confessed.

27. In margin, Consider the meaning. They asked if I would like to have a report of this. Had they not said so I would have filled her mouth with silence; her hand which opposed me in the truth I would have placed over her mouth. But they regarded her spirit to such an extent that she hindered their response.

28. In margin, What was dealt with here was the name of God, or the pamphlet that concerned it, and also touching confession.

29. In margin, See they did not let it be agreed upon in a very friendly fashion, so that David, who had not suspected this, had to narrate all of it.

30. This is assumed to have been a letter from Anna Jans which provoked Joris's visions in December 1536. See Packull 1987a, 160-64, for a translation of a similar letter from Jans to Joris.

31. In margin, The song runs in this manner, to the tune [*die vois*] "A Mighty Fortress":

My ears have heard from above,
my eyes have seen far in the forest.

> The innocent ones understand the word,
> quickly consider the sheep of Christ,
> Although they hop, they go a straight way,
> totally sincere.
> In evil they are pure,
> as children are without spot, [Eph. 5:27]
> without shame or any hypocrisy,
> just as Adam and Eve were in the beginning,
> they are at the end.

This was sung followed by others.

This version is virtually identical to the one in Joris *Liedt-boecxken*, 71ʳ, except that in the latter version the "children" of line eight have become "doves."

32. The resulting tract was Joris *Hoert*.

33. *vernieten*, to nullify or reverse.

34. In margin, **This was inserted afterwards. I would have had much to say about it were I given the opportunity.**

35. In a letter written by Hoffman from Wittenberg on June 22, 1525. See QGTElass3, 186, n.25. For a translation of this letter, see Packull 1990, 151, where Packull translates Hoffman's admonition here as "permit not yourselves to be driven about by strange teachings that do not lead to Christ."

36. In margin, **What they sought of David and why they were pleased to hear him and why he had journeyed to speak to them was therefore experienced close at hand.**

37. In margin, 1 Cor. 15:51-52; 1 Thess. 5:10.

38. In margin, **David meant at this point those things which he had said or explained to them concerning the need to show honor to the name of God in every manner and the misuse of it; further, concerning the fear of the Lord; further, how one must pray or how it must occur for the one who goes to pray; and concerning the way of the Lord, which is straight and true; concerning humility, meekness, and lowliness, and more other holy things.**

39. In margin, **David became disturbed in the spirit and angry over these comments, for he believed that they had been quite finished and from their hearts had concluded enough about it, since the previous evening had ended friendly enough. But now this was begun anew, as if it had never happened, and he spoke in this way.**

40. Joris is probably referring to traditional Jewish avoidance of pronouncing the Hebrew *Yahweh* when speaking of God, prefering the other names, such as *El, Elah, Elohim*, etc.

41. Hoffman was a furrier by trade.

42. In margin, **They gave David no answer according to his desire. Instead they merely sought to know and to inquire by all means.**

43. Evidently one of the books Joris had sent to them. According to Blesdijk *Historia*, 19, Joris's entire teaching was summarized in the *Book of Perfection*. Cramer 1844, no. 9, lists a *Profetie of Boek der Volmaaktheid* as published in 1542. No extant version is known.

44. Joris likened the progress to spiritual perfection to the physical development of an infant to old age. See Joris *Twonder Boeck*, 195ᵛ.

45. Hans van Rottenburg could not be identified.

46. Apparently Heinrich Shoemaker was regarded by the Melchiorites as Enoch. See the December 1537 report on the fourteen Anabaptist writings sent from Speyer to Strasbourg, QGTElsass3, 114. Several other candidates for these eschatalogical offices are recorded in this report. Nothing else is known of Shoemaker.

47. Identified as possibly the priest Claes van der Elst, who had been a student of Luther's in Wittenberg before surfacing as a reformer in the Netherlands in 1524. See QGTElsass3, 195, n.30.

48. Batenburg had made a trip to Strasbourg to convince the Melchiorites there to

accept his leadership. According to the Speyer authorities, Batenburg had written a booklet on marriage (QGTElsass3, 108).

49. Possibly Melchior Rinck (1493-1545), an associate of Thomas Müntzer and a participant in the Peasants' War of 1525, who became a Spiritualist. See QGTElsass 3, 195, n.30.

50. In margin, **We are able to say that all of us indeed are children of the Most High, that God is our Father, therefore no one resisted my answer here.**

51. In margin, **No outward fasts or watchings are meant.**

52. In margin, **These words were spoken without being written down, that one should easily conform thereby, as they did. For he was not attracted to it, because the words were against the good.**

53. In margin, **Nota**, [Note].

54. This work has not, to date, been discovered.

55. In margin, **Ezek. 37:23.**

56. In margin, **Ezek. 36:31-34.**

57. In margin, **The fools despise sin, but the wise despise it unmeasurably. A wise person fears and abominates sin, but a fool goes proudly further through it. P[eter?] ouerk[ent?] [Peter convinced?].** Cf. Prov. 14:9.

58. In margin, **James 5[:16]: Confess one to the other.**

59. In margin, **2 Esd. 16:61-2.**

60. In Z XIII, pp. 819-827. This Latin Psalter was first published in 1532.

61. In 1534 a Dutch edition of the Latin Psalter of Johann Campanus (1500-75), *Den Psalter mit verklaringen*, was printed in Delft. This was most likely the version that Joris had access to. Several more editions were printed in Leiden between 1534 and 1538. See NKNB, nos. 1206-1210, 0683-0686.

62. In margin, **Psalm 25:6[7].**

63. In margin, **Psalm 38 verses 17 and 18.**

64. In margin, **Nota bene**, [Note well].

65. In margin, **Psalm 51, verses 3 and 9.**

66. In margin, **Ezra 10:10-11.**

67. In margin, **Neh. 9:1-2; Dan. 9:3.**

68. In margin, **At this David refused to answer, namely to their word that David had not sinned any more. He reserved the reply to a more appropriate time and desired to relate it later.**

69. An obvious reference to the threat of execution which constantly faced Joris as one of the most wanted Anabaptists in the Empire.

70. *gemein broederen*, or "church brothers."

71. In margin, **David and Peter van Geyen had discussed this subject alone, and much deeper than the meaning has been clarified here. Only as far as Peter van Geyen permitted the matter. But because of the danger of disturbing the others, he believed one should allow it and stop only until they were one people who were thoroughly cleansed, and more such things. Upon this David gave a good answer, but Peter desired that one should not write it down.**

72. In margin, **Nota bene**, [Note well].

73. In margin, **Here something was said, but they did not write it down nor did they desire to write it. Neither did they allow David to conclude or to stop the proceedings, as you may read.**

74. The author has skipped over a portion of the passage.

75. In margin, **Why did he then go about all the day sorrowful and oppressed, if he regarded not God's judgment, will he have kept his iniquities silent?**

76. *verstrict*.

77. Probably in the presumed lost *Book of the VII Prophecies of Leonard Jost* (*buch von den VII prophetien Lienhard Jostenn*) published by Melchior Hoffman. See QGTElsass2, 186, and QGTElsass3, 221, n.38.

78. Original is *toesettinge*, corrected in the margin to *toesegginge*.

79. In margin, **To this was answered: then why has it not been produced, for they possibly still might come to know. I fear, that they sought means to make David's speech appear foolish. Therefore, David twice interrupted speeches here.**

80. See n. 77 above.

81. In margin, **Nota.**

82. At this point the text becomes cluttered with slashes (/). For purposes of clarity, they are not included here.

83. Hendric van Ghent. Rebstock does not appear to have stayed until the end of the meeting.

84. In margin, **This David had said but Peter narrated it.**

85. Although the pages continue blank to 110ʳ, the account ends here.

Chapter 8

1. Joris *Salighe Leeringe* (no vdL nor HBA; no MFCL; in MLA no. 2497 B19). For a brief discussion of this work and a listing of the other eleven tracts in this volume, see Waite 1991a.

2. See Zijlstra 1988, 249-56.

3. Franck's *Chronica* received wide circulation throughout Europe, and appears to have been used by Menno shortly after its publication. See Bergsma/Voolstra 1986, 26.

4. In margin, **Song of Sol. 6:10.**

5. *Pont,* money.

6. In margin, **Places which are good, believing hearts.**

7. In margin, **John 10:27.**

8. Joris's discussion at this point may have been influenced by Sebastian Franck's *Paradoxa,* which collected such contradictory statements. The *Paradoxa* is known to have been published in the Netherlands *circa* 1540 (NKNB, no. 948). For a translation of Franck, see Furcha 1986. For Joris and Franck, see Waite 1990, 168.

9. *Lichters,* perhaps "lights."

10. In margin, **Isa. 33; Jer. 8; Ps. 50.**

11. For a study of Joris's promotion of Dutch and denegration of the classical languages, see Waite 1992a.

12. *omschrantsende,* literally, "without gorging."

13. In margin, **Psalm, Mich. [Mal. 4:3].**

14. The phrase *verborgentheyt des Rijcks Godes* is reminiscent of Rothmann's tract "Van Verborgenheit der Schrifft des Rykes Christi vnde van dem Daghe des Heren," in Stupperich 1970, 299-372.

15. The meaning of this phrase is unclear.

16. In margin, **1 Cor. 2:5; Heb. 6:1.**

17. In margin, **2 Kings 1:10.**

18. In margin, **Nota.**

19. Silk and velvet were generally worn only by the social elite—royalty, nobles, and urban patricians.

20. Presumably Michael the archangel.

21. In Melchiorite apocalyptic thought, Elijah and Enoch were to appear at the last day as the two great witnesses. See Rev. 11 and Mal. 4:5.

22. This does not appear to be a biblical reference.

Chapter 9

1. [Joris] *Testament* (vdL 228; no MFCL). Only one example of this edition is known to have survived, housed in the City Library of Hamburg. For an edition and discussion of this work, see Vos 1917b, 163-7; see also Packull 1987a, 155. The present translation is based on the Vos edition and follows its pagination.

2. See Packull 1987a.

3. See Waite 1987.

4. Joris *Salicheden* (no vdL, no HBA, Cramer 1844, no.3; no MFCL), MLA no. 2497 B19.

5. Possibly Jorien Ketel. Jorien's home was in Deventer, where this letter, along with Anna Jans's *Testament*, was published.

6. Not identified.

7. In *The Eight Blessings*, Joris wrote, "Do not be amazed of the fire or heat of the day of testing, as if what happened to your brothers was something new. Do not regard it as a plague or abandonment, as I have written, but glory and exalt the Lord God in your hearts" (Joris *Salicheden*, 20ʳ).

8. In *The Eight Blessings*, Joris wrote: "O the blessed, holy, yes, most holy people, the believing, good natured generation! Who have so liberally offered up to God their sacrifice as a sweet odor, to the exaltation of his most holy name and the eternal truth! O how glorious they are, who have whitened their clothes, who have washed their garments pure and beautiful in the water and blood! . . . What a delightfully pure song of glory shall be sung, and what a joy to hear! Yes, no one will be able to hear it expressed or sing along with it (a wonderful thing) except those who are written in the number of 144,000" (Joris *Salicheden*, 10ᵛ-11ʳ).

9. Joris is presumably referring to the false brethren who turned in the true believers.

10. In *The Eight Blessings*, Joris remarked that "you must be in the place of your Lord and Master, so that dying with him in the likeness of his death, we might be resurrected with him. It is not foreseen nor willed by God in any other way, except through the suffering and death of the cross, to save the believers and make them into the image of Christ. Therefore, all who desire to live like the God-fearing or the blessed in Christ Jesus must suffer persecution" (Joris *Salicheden*, 4ᵛ).

11. A wooden bench on which the bones of the accused were individually broken with a hammer, starting with the extremities.

Chapter 10

1. Joris *Onschuldt* (vdL 9). Used here was the edition in MFCL 360. Another edition of this work is in MFCL 361. Possibly from the same press, this edition differs from MFCL 360 only in the number of folio pages (twenty-two) and in some minor variations in spelling and biblical references. An earlier version of this translation was published as Waite 1988a.

2. Others include a scathing letter to the Court of Holland at The Hague, 1539 (available only in Blesdijk *Historia*, 81-84); a conciliatory missive to Landgrave Philip of Hesse (in Blesdijk *Historia*, 85-87); and several letters and tracts to the Reformed superintendent of East Frisia, John a Lasco, in 1544, including Joris *Cort Bericht*.

3. The Habsburgs were applying heavy pressure on the countess for her to resort to persecution. See *DAN* I, xv and esp. 185, where one finds a letter from the Emperor to Emden (Countess Anna), October 12, 1543.

4. See Krahn 1981, 245.

5. Blesdijk *Christelijcke*, 29ᵛ-30ʳ: "Deur wien van den onsen sijn sulcke loghenen vervreydt? Antwoort. Deur die versierde logenachtige vierentwintich Articule/ die sijn Mededooper of broeder Roelof (welck sich Adam noemen laet) gedicht/ ende den gront der Leere Dauidts tot een tytel gegeuen heeft." And Blesdijk *Billijcke*, 66ᵛ "die xxv. Articulen van D.J. Ontschult/ by hem aen die Gravinne van Embden in't Jaer 1540 gepresenteert/ tegens die verkeerde valsche Articulen by Hieronimi Apostel (Rulof of Adam genoemt) ghecolligeert ende te samen ghedraghen."

6. Entitled (according to Zijstra 1983, 37), *Dit zijn de articulen van David Joris leer*.

7. See QGTElsass4, 120-21, also Zijlstra 1983, 38-39 and esp. 247. For a translation of this list, see Appendix 2.

8. Zijlstra 1983, 40. It is conceivable that the date 1540 included in the title (22ʳ) could instead refer to the year Countess Anna was widowed (from Count Enno of East

Frisia) and became ruler of East Frisia. It could then have become accidentally transposed into the date of publication.

9. David's father was Joris (George); therefore, Joris Senior's son was David Jorisson.

10. In margin, Isa. 33; Matt. 22; Mark 12; 1 Cor. 14.

11. In margin, Ps. [32]; Isa. 29; Job 31; 2 Esd. 16; Prov. 18; Matt. 5; Mark 1; Luke 17; James 5.

12. *lustelijcke*. The Strasbourg list of Joris's teaching has at this point the German *leipliche*, which means "physical" (see Appendix 2, point 3). It is possible that *lustelijcke* is a misprint for the middle Dutch *lijflijc* ("physical"). However, in responding to the following charge, Joris uses *sichtbaerlijcke* and *weselijcke* to denote the meaning of "physical." It seems, therefore, that the later list made a misreading of the original Dutch.

13. In margin, Gen. 18; Isa. 40; Daniel 4; Mal. 2; 2 Esd. 1; Mark 1; Pss. 96, 103; Heb. 1; Rev. 19.

14. In margin, Matt. [24:33]; Mark; Luke [12:39]; 1 Thess. [5:2]; 2 Peter [3:10].

15. In margin, Isa. 3; Ps.; Ecclus.; Wis. of Sol. 3; Mark [Matt.] 12, 19; 1 Cor. 9; 2 Thess. 2; Jude 1.

16. In margin, Ps. 89; Isa. 55; Jer. 23, 30, 33; Ezek. 34, 37; Hos. 3; Zech. 12.

17. In margin, Rev. 21.

18. In margin, John 1.

19. A reference perhaps to some who reinterpreted his teachings for their own purposes; a common practice among Batenburgers, such as Johan Morveldinck, who claimed to be a member of "David Joris's people," who, according to Morveldinck, "believed not in the worthy sacrament but only in the Son of God sitting at the right hand of his heavenly Father, and that our teaching is that men may damage churches and keep all church goods in common" (Hullu 1897, 264; also Stayer 1976, 299).

20. In margin, Matt. 22:30; Luke 20:34-36.

21. In margin, Men or women, that is. Neither are to be united other than with God by the Spirit.

22. In margin, Gal. 5.

23. In margin, Isa. 43, 65, 66; Dan. 7, 12; Matt. 22; Mark 10; Luke 8; 1 Cor. 3; Heb. 2; 2 Pet. 3; Rev. 3, 20, 21; Ps. 90.

24. In margin, Exod. 19; Lev. 11, 20; Deut. 18; Isa. 66; Hos. 4; 1 Peter 2; Rev. 3, 20; Esd.

25. In margin, Exod.; Matt. 12:12.

26. In margin, Isa. 29; 1 Cor. 14.

27. In margin, Deut.; Isa. 65; Joel 3; Ps.

28. In margin, Ps. [78:2].

29. In margin, At midnight a shout is heard, go out to meet your Bridegroom. Etc. [Matt. 25:6]; Song of Sol.; Acts 1.

30. In margin, It is blessed, says the apostle, that no one force his conscience over the things that he receives. Rom. 14.

31. In margin, Matt. 1; Luke 3:16.

32. In margin, Matt. 10:19-20.

33. In margin, 1 Cor. 15; Isa. 51; Jer. 3 [33]; Mal. 3; Ps. 90.

34. In margin, Ps.; Ezek.; Zech. 2; John 14; 2 Cor. 6.

35. Zijlstra 1983, 41, suggests this refers to Pastor's *Articulen*, which was frequently mistaken for Joris's own work. Considering the frequent confusion between Batenburg's and Joris's teaching, it may refer instead to Batenburgers, who, having acquired some of Joris's writings, propagated their version of his teaching in writing. It may have been for this reason that Joris turned down the Batenburger Cornelius Appelman's request for a copy of *The Wonder Book*. See Hullu 1897, 278.

36. In a letter of October 12, 1543, the emperor warned Countess Anna that an attack on Emden had been devised by some Anabaptists, implicating Joris as the head of

the movement. The following month the Court of Frisia responded that they had expelled some Anabaptists from their territory in order to foil this plot. *DAN* I, 185-186. This incident reaffirms Zijlstra's contention that the *Apology* was published around 1543.

37. In margin, **Deut. [possibly 19:10].**
38. In margin, **Prov. 31:8-9.**
39. In margin, **Prov. 24[:11]; Ps. 82[:3-4]; Isa. 2.**
40. In margin, **Ecclus. 4:1.**
41. In margin, **Prov. 17:15.**
42. In margin, **Prov. 24:12.**
43. In margin, **Faith is a work and power of God.**
44. In margin, **In vices, that is, in things evil and pernicious to our soul.**

Appendix 1
1. "Refereyn tot Lof des Nederlandts unde der Duytscher Spraecke / met sijn Liedeken" and "Van die duydelijcke Duytsche Spraecke," in Joris *Liedt-Boecxken*, 85ʳ-92ʳ. The repetitive refrains of the songs are not included here.
2. See Waite 1992a.
3. See Waite 1991b.
4. The "Prince" referred to in rhetorician refrains was the prince or symbolic head of each rhetorician chamber.

Appendix 2
1. From QGTElsass4, 119-21; also Zijlstra 1983, 247.
2. This sentence is in Latin.

Bibliography

Sources Cited Only by Initials

ARG   *Archiv für Reformationsgeschichte / Archive for Reformation History.*

CDIN   Paul Fredericq, ed. *Corpus documentorum Inquisitionis Haereticae Pravitatis Neerlandicae.* vol.1-5. Ghent and The Hague: Martinus Nijhoff, 1889-1900.

DAN   *Documenta Anabaptistica Neerlandica,* Albert F. Mellink, ed. - vol. I: *Friesland en Groningen (1530-1550).* Leiden: E. J. Brill, 1975; vol. II: *Amsterdam, 1536-1578.* Leiden: E. J. Brill, 1980; vol. V: *Amsterdam, 1531-1536.* Leiden: E. J. Brill, 1985; vol. VI: Alastair Hamilton, ed., *Chronica, Ordo Sacerdotis, Acta HN. Three Texts on the Family of Love.* Leiden: E. J. Brill, 1988.

DB   *Doopsgezinde Bijdragen.*

HBA   Hans J. Hillerbrand, ed., *A Bibliography of Anabaptism, 1520-1630* Elkhart: Institute of Mennonite Studies, 1962.

ME   *Mennonite Encyclopedia,* vol. 1-5.

MFCL   The Radical Reformation Microfiche Project, Section I, Mennonite and Related Sources up to 1600. Leiden, The Netherlands: Inter Documentation Company.

MG   *Mennonitische Geschichtsblätter.*

MLA   Mennonite Library, University of Amsterdam.

MQR   *Mennonite Quarterly Review.*

NKNB   Wouter Nijhoff & M.E. Kronenberg, eds. *Nederlandsche Bibliographie van 1500 tot 1540.* The Hague: Martinus Nijhoff, 1923.

QGTElsass2 Manfred Krebs and Hans Georg Rott, eds. *Quellen zur Geschichte der Täufer,* vol. 8, *Elsass* II, *Stadt Straßburg 1533-1535.* Gütersloh: Gerd Mohn, 1960.

QGTElsass3   Marc Lienhard, Stephen F. Nelson and Hans Georg Rott, eds. *Quellen zur Geschichte der Täufer*, vol. 15, *Elsass* III, *Stadt Straßburg 1536-1542*. Gutersloh: Gerd Mohn, 1986.

QGTElsass4   Marc Lienhard, Stephen F. Nelson and Hans Georg Rott, eds. *Quellen zur Geschichte der Täufer*, vol. 16, *Elsass* IV, *Stadt Straßburg 1543-1552*. Gutersloh: Gerd Mohn, 1988.

SAW   George H. Williams and Angel M. Mergal, eds. *Spiritual and Anabaptist Writers*. Philadelphia: The Westminster Press, 1957.

SCJ   *Sixteenth Century Journal*.

vdL   A. van der Linde, ed. *David Joris. Bibliografie*. The Hague, 1867.

Z   *Huldreich Zwinglis Sämtliche Werke*. Edited by Emil Egli, et al. *Corpus Reformatorum*, vols. 88ff. Reprint: Zurich: Theologischer Verlag Zurich, 1983ff.

Works Cited by Author and Short Title

Blesdijk *Billijcke*   Nicolaas Meyndertsz van Blesdijk, *Billijcke Verantwoordinge ende eenvoldighe wederlegginghe Nicolaes Meynertsz. van Blesdijck op eenen scheltlasterighen brief door doctorem Hieronimum Wilhelmi. . .int jaer 1544*. n.p., 1610.

Blesdijk *Christelijcke*   Nicolaas Meyndertsz van Blesdijk, *Christelijcke Verantwoordinghe ende billijcke nederlegginge des valschen onghegrondeden oordeels, lasterens ende scheldens, by Menno Symonsz in eenen Sendt-brief . . . niet bevonden werden als hy*. n.p., 1607.

Blesdijk *Historia*   Nicolaas Meyndertsz van Blesdijk, *Historia vitae, doctrinae ac rerum gestarum Davidis Georgii haeresiarchae*. Deventer, 1642.

Blesdijk "Oorspronck"   Nicolaas Meyndertsz van Blesdijk, "Van den oorspronck ende anuanck des sectes welk men wederdop noomt: dorch welck ende hoe en waer se in nederlant ingevort ende verbreydet . . . dorch M. van Blesdijck." Rare Book and Manuscript Department, University of Basel, *Jorislade* X, part 4.

Joris *Berichtinge*   David Joris, *Clare Berichtinge, Hoe die Mensch van Godt ghevallen ende jn wat manieren hy weder tot Godt gebrocht wert een claere ende leuendige opsluytinge*. n.p., 1543.

Joris *Boeck*   David Joris, *Neemt Waer. Dat boeck des levens / is mi gheopenbaert*. n.p., n.d.

Joris *Cort Bericht*   David Joris, *Cort Bericht vn schriftlyck Antwoort D.J. op den Brief des Eerwaardighen Heeren J.A.L.* n.p., 1544.

Joris *Ehestands*	David Joris, *Das Hemelschen Ehestands beginsel of trowinghe/ die Belofte of vereeniginge des herten.* n.p., n.d.
Joris *Eynde Coemt*	David Joris, *Dat eynde coemt/ dat eynde coemt over die vier hoecken der aerden.* n.p., n.d.
Joris *Gelouighe*	David Joris, *Hoe sich die gelouighe, die een suster ofte vrouwe tot hem neempt/ draghen of sy beyde haer tegen den ander hebben sullen.* n.p., n.d.
Joris *Hand-Boecxken* III	David Joris, *Dat Derde Hand-Boecxken.* n.p., 1614.
Joris *Hoert*	David Joris, *Hoert/ hoert/ hoert/ Groot wunder/ groot wunder/ groot wunder.* n.p., n.d.
Joris "Hydeckel"	David Joris, "Hydeckel," *Jorislade,* vol. 9, Sendbriefen, University of Basel.
Joris *Liedt-Boecxken*	David Joris, *Een Geestelijck Liedt-Boecxken.* Mennonite Songbooks I, Dutch Series. Nieuwkoop: B. de Graaf, n.d.
Joris *Lyeffde*	David Joris, *Een zeer zuuerlyck traectaet van de lyeffde, schoenheyt.* Deventer: Albert Pafraet, 1539.
Joris *Onderwysinge*	David Joris, *Eene onderwysinge ofte raet/ omme die gedachten in den toem tho brengen.* n.p., 1537.
Joris *Onschuldt*	David Joris, *Onschuldt Davids Jorisz. Gedaen unde gepresenteert an die Wolgeborene Vrouw/ Vrouw Anna.* n.p., 1540.
Joris *Ordeninge*	David Joris, *Van de heerlijcke ende godlijcke Ordeninge der Wonderlijker werckinghen Godes.* n.p., 1535, Reprinted 1614.
Joris *Salicheden*	David Joris, *Die Acht Salicheden.* n.p., 1539.
Joris *Salighe Leeringe*	David Joris, *Een salighe Leeringe voor die hongherighe bekommerde Zielen.* n.p., n.d.
Joris *Sendbrieuen* I	David Joris, *Christlijcke Sendbrieuen.* n.p., n.d.
Joris *Sendbrieuen* II	David Joris, *Het tweede Boeck der Christlijker Sendbrieuen,* n.p., n.d.
Joris *Sendbrieuen* III	David Joris, *Het derde Boeck der Christelijcker Sendbrieuen.* n.p., 1611.
[Joris] *Testament*	[David Joris], *Hier begint dat Testament dat Annecken Zaliger ge. Esaias haren sone bestelt heeft.* Deventer: Dirck van Borne, 1539.
Joris *Twonder Boeck* 1542	David Joris, *Twonder Boeck.* Deventer: Dirk von Borne, c. 1542.
Joris *Twonder Boeck* 1551	David Joris, *Twonder-boeck: waer in dat van der werldt aen versloten gheopenbaert is. Opt nieuw ghecorrigeert vnde vermeerdert by den Autheur selue.* n.p., 1551.
Joris *Vianden*	David Joris, *Een seer schone tractaet off onderwijs van mennigerley aert der menschen vianden.* Deventer: Albert Pafraet, 1539.

Joris *Wijsheit*   David Joris, *Seer goet onderwysinge der wijsheit . . .
                             Beyde vor ouden ende Jongen.* Deventer: Albert
                             Pafraet, 1539.

Joris *Wtroepinge*   David Joris, *Eyn wtroepinge van der brudegoms
                             kompst.* n.p., [1539] 1616.

Joris *Zielen*   David Joris, *Een salighe Leeringe voor die hong-
                             herighe bekommerde Zielen.* n.p., n.d.

Sources Cited by Author and Date

Arnold 1729   Gottfried Arnold, *Unpartheiische Kirchen- und Ket-
                             zer Historie.* Vol. 1-2. 1729 edition, reprinted
                             Hildesheim: Georg Olms, 1967.

Bainton 1935   Roland H. Bainton, ed., *Concerning Heretics: An
                             Anonymous Work Attributed to Sebastian Castellio.*
                             New York: Columbia University Press, 1935.

Bainton 1937   Roland H. Bainton, *David Joris. Wiedertäufer und
                             Kämpfer für Toleranz im 16. Jahrhundert.* Leipzig:
                             Archiv für Reformationsgeschichte, 1937.

Bergsma/Voolstra 1986   Wiebe Bergsma and Sjouke Voolstra, eds., *Uyt Ba-
                             bel ghevloden, in Jerusalem ghetogen. Menno
                             Simon's verlichting, bekering en beroeping.* Amster-
                             dam: Doopsgezinde Historische Kring, 1986.

Blouw 1991   Paul Valkema Blouw, "Printers to the 'Arch-
                             Heretic' David Joris: Prolegomena to a bibliogra-
                             phy of his works," *Quaerendo* 21 (1991), 163-209.

Boon 1988   K. G. Boon, "De Glasschilder David Joris, een Ex-
                             ponent van het Doperse Geloof. Zijn Kunst en Zijn
                             Invloed op Dirck Crabeth." *Mededelingen van de
                             Koninklijke Academie voor Wetenschappen, Let-
                             teren en Schone Kunsten van België,* 49 (1988), 117-
                             37.

Brandt 1720   Gerard Brandt, *The History of the Reformation.*
                             London: T. Wood, 1720-23 (translated from Dutch
                             original of 1674), reprinted AMS 1979.

Brouwer 1981   H. C. Brouwer, "De Verdwenen Kloosters uit de
                             Delftse Binnenstad," in R.A. Leeuw, ed., *De Stad
                             Delft. Cultuur en maatschappij tot 1572.* Delft:
                             Stedelijk Museum, Het Prinsenhof, 1981, 54-59.

Burckhardt 1949   P. Burckhardt, "David Joris und seine Gemeinde in
                             Basel," *Basler Zeitschrift für Geschichte und
                             Altertumskunde,* 48 (1949), 5-106.

Cramer 1844   A. M. Cramer, *Bijvoegselen tot de Levensbeschrijv-
                             ing van David Joris.* Leiden: 1844.

Deppermann 1987   Klaus Deppermann, *Melchior Hoffman: Social Un-
                             rest and Apocalyptic Visions in the Age of Reforma-
                             tion.* Trans. by Malcolm Wren and ed. by Benjamin
                             Drewery. Edinburgh: T. & T. Clark, 1987.

Droz 1965   Eugénie Droz, "Sur Quelques Traductions
                   Françaises D'Écrits de David Joris." *Het Boek*,
                   derde reeks, 37 (1965), 154-162.

Eeghen 1986   I. H. van Eeghen, "De inquisitie in Amsterdam," in
                   Margriet de Roever & Boudewijn Bakker, eds.,
                   *Woelige tijden: Amsterdam in de eeuw van de
                   Beeldenstorm.* Amsterdam: Gemeentearchief Am-
                   sterdam / De Bataafsche Leeuw, 1986, 73-82.

Fast 1962   Heinold Fast, ed., *Der linke Flügel der Reformation.*
                   Bremen: Carl Schunemann Verlag, 1962.

Furcha 1986   E. J. Furcha, ed./trans., *Sebastian Franck. 280
                   Paradoxes or Wondrous Sayings.* Texts and Studies
                   in Religion, Volume 26. Lewiston: The Edwin Mel-
                   len Press, 1986.

Hoogewerff 1930   G.C. Hoogewerff, *Liederen van Groot-Nederland.
                   Een Geestelijck Liedt-Boecxken.* Utrecht:
                   Koninklijke Vereeniging, 1930.

Horst 1972   Irvin B. Horst, *The Radical Brethren. Anabaptism
                   and the English Reformation to 1558.* Nieuwkoop:
                   B. de Graaf, 1972.

Horst 1986   Irvin B. Horst, ed., *Dutch Dissenters.* Leiden: E. J.
                   Brill, 1986.

Hullu 1897   J. G. de Hullu, ed., *Bescheiden Betreffende de Her-
                   vorming in Overijsel.* Deventer: 1897.

Hulshof 1920   A. Hulshof, ed., "Extracten uit de Rekeningen van
                   het Schoutambacht van Haarlem Betreffende
                   Wederdoopers (1535-39)," *Bijdragen en
                   Mededeelingen van het Historisch Genootschap*, 41
                   (1920), 199-231.

Jansma 1984   "Revolutionaire Wederdopers na 1535," in M. G.
                   Buist, et al., *Historisch Bewogen.* Groningen:
                   Wolters-Noordhoff, 1984, 49-66.

Jansma 1988   L. G. Jansma, "Crime in the Netherlands in the Six-
                   teenth-Century: The Batenburg Bands after 1540."
                   MQR 62 (1988), 221-35.

Johnston 1990   Colleen A. Johnston, "The Hymns of David Joris: A
                   Preliminary Study." *MQR* 64 (1990), 113-34.

Kirchoff 1963   Karl-Heinz Kirchoff, "Die Täufer im Münsterland.
                   Verbreitung und Verfolgung des Täufertums im
                   Stift Münster, 1533-1550." *Westfälische Zeitschrift*,
                   113 (1963), 1-109.

Koegler 1928   Hans Koegler, "Einiges über David Joris als
                   Künstler." *Öffentliche Kunstsammlung Basel,
                   Jahresberichte 1928-30*, 157-201.

Krahn 1981   Cornelius Krahn, *Dutch Anabaptism.* Scottdale:
                   Herald Press, 1981.

Lebensbeschreibung	"David Joris sonderbare Lebensbeschreibung aus einem Manuscript," in Arnold 1729, vol.2, 702-737.
Marshall 1984	Sherrin Marshall, "Women and Religious Choices in the Sixteenth Century Netherlands." *ARG*, 75 (1984), 276-89.
Marshall 1987	Sherrin Marshall, *The Dutch Gentry, 1500-1650*. New York: Greenwood Press, 1987.
McGinn 1985	Bernard McGinn, *The Calabrian Abbot Joachim of Fiore in the History of Western Thought*. New York: Macmillan Pub. Comp., 1985.
Mellink 1963	Albert F. Mellink, "Antwerpen als Anabaptisttencentrum tot 1550?." *Nederlands Archief voor Kerkgeschiedenis*, 46 (1963-64), 155-68.
Mellink 1981	Albert F. Mellink, *De Wederdopers in de Noordelijke Nederlanden*. Leeuwarden: Uitgeverij Gerben Dykstra, 1981.
Mellink 1988	Albert F. Mellink, "The Beginnings of Dutch Anabaptism in the Light of Recent Research." *MQR* 62 (1988), 211-20.
Nippold 1863	Friedrich Nippold, "David Joris von Delft. Sein Leben, seine Lehre und seine Secte." *Zeitschrift für historische Theologie*. Gotha: 1863.
Packull 1983	Werner O. Packull, "Melchior Hoffman—A Recanted Anabaptist in Schwäbisch Hall?" *MQR* 57 (1983), 83-111.
Packull 1986	Werner O. Packull, "A Reinterpretation of Melchior Hoffman's *Exposition* against the Background of Spiritualist Franciscan Eschatology with Special Reference to Peter John Olivi," in Irvin B. Horst, ed., *Dutch Dissenters*. Leiden: E. J. Brill, 1986, 32-65.
Packull 1987a	Werner O. Packull, "Anna Jansz of Rotterdam, a Historical Investigation of an Early Anabaptist Heroine." *ARG* 78 (1987), 147-73.
Packull 1987b	Werner O. Packull, "The Sign of Thau: The Changing Conception of the Seal of God's Elect in Early Anabaptist Thought." *MQR* 61 (1987), 363-74.
Packull 1988	Werner O. Packull, "Peter Tasch: From Melchiorite to Bankrupt Wine Merchant." *MQR* 62 (1988), 276-95.
Packull 1990	Werner O. Packull, "Melchior Hoffman's First Two Letters," *MQR* 64 (1990), 146-59.
Reeves 1969	Marjorie Reeves, *The Influence of Prophecy in the Later Middle Ages: A Study in Joachimism*. Oxford: Oxford University Press, 1969.
Rogge 1894	H. C. Rogge, "Een Band met tractaten van David

Joris," *Bibliographische Adversaria*, new series I, 1887-1894.

Rombouts/Lerius 1864
P. Rombouts and T. van Lerius, eds., *De Liggeren en andere historische Archieven der Antwerpsche Sint Lucas gilde*. Vol. 1-2. Antwerp, 1864-66, repr. Amsterdam, 1961.

Scheffer 1873
J. G. de Hoop Scheffer, *Geschiedenis der Kerkhervorming in Nederland van haar onstaan tot 1531*. Amsterdam: G. L. Funke, 1873.

Stayer 1976
James M. Stayer, *Anabaptists and the Sword*. 2nd ed. Lawrence, Kansas: Coronodo Press, 1976.

Stayer 1984
James M. Stayer, "Davidite vs. Mennonite." *MQR* 60 (1984), 459-76.

Stayer 1985
James M. Stayer, "David Joris: A Prolegomenon to Further Research." *MQR* 61 (1985), 350-66.

Stayer 1986
James M. Stayer, "Was Dr. Kuehler's Conception of Early Dutch Anabaptism Historically Sound? The Historical Discussion of Anabaptist Münster 450 Years After." *MQR* 60 (1986), 261-88.

Stayer/Packull 1980
James M. Stayer and Werner O. Packull, eds. *The Anabaptists and Thomas Müntzer*. Dubuque, Iowa: Kendall/Hunt Publ. Comp., 1980.

Stupperich 1970
Robert Stupperich, ed., *Die Schriften Bernhard Rothmanns*. Münster: Aschendorffsche Verlagsbuchhandlung, 1970.

Tracy 1982
"Heresy Law and Centralization under Mary of Hungary: Conflict between the Council of Holland and the Central Government over the Enforcement of Charles V's Placards." *ARG* 73 (1982), 284-307.

Tracy 1985
James D. Tracy, *A Financial Revolution in the Habsburg Netherlands*. Berkeley: University of California Press, 1985.

Voolstra 1982
Sjouke Voolstra, *Het Woorde is Vlees geworden: De Melchioritisch-Menniste Incarnatieleer*. Kampen: J. H. Kok, 1982.

Vos 1917a
Karel Vos, "Kleine bijdragen over de doopersche beweging in Nederland." *DB*, 54 (1917), 106-23.

Vos 1917b
Karel Vos, "Brief von David Joris, 1539." *DB* 54 (1917), 163-67.

Waite 1987
Gary K. Waite, "Staying Alive: The Methods of Survival as Practiced by an Anabaptist Fugitive, David Joris." *MQR* 61 (1987), 46-57.

Waite 1988a
Gary K. Waite, ed. and trans., "David Joris' Apology to Countess Anna of Oldenburg." *MQR* 62 (1988), 140-158.

Waite 1988b — Gary K. Waite, "David Joris' Thought in the Context of the Early Anabaptist Movement in the Netherlands, 1534-1536." *MQR* 62 (1988), 296-317.

Waite 1989a — Gary K. Waite, "From Apocalyptic Crusaders to Anabaptist Terrorists: Anabaptist Radicalism after Münster, 1535-1545." *ARG* 80 (1989), 173-193.

Waite 1989b — Gary K. Waite, ed. and trans., "The Post-Münster Melchiorite Debate on Marriage: David Joris' Response to Johannes Eisenburg, 1537." *MQR* 63 (1989), 367-400.

Waite 1990 — Gary K. Waite, *David Joris and Dutch Anabaptism.* Waterloo: Wilfrid Laurier University Press, 1990.

Waite 1991a — Gary K. Waite, "Writing in the Heavenly Language: a Guide to the Works of David Joris." *Renaissance and Reformation/ Renaissance et Réforme* n.s. 14 (Fall, 1990, date of issue December, 1991), 297-319.

Waite 1991b — Gary K. Waite, "Popular Drama and Radical Religion: The Chambers of Rhetoric and Anabaptism in the Netherlands." *MQR*, 65 (1991), 227-55.

Waite 1991c — Gary K. Waite, "The Longevity of Spiritualistic Anabaptism: The Literary Legacy of David Joris." *Canadian Journal of History / Annales Canadiennes D'Histoire*, 26 (1991), 177-98.

Waite 1992a — Gary K. Waite, "The Holy Spirit Speaks Dutch: David Joris and the Promotion of the Dutch Language." *Church History*, 61 (1992), 47-59.

Waite 1992b — Gary K. Waite, "The Dutch Nobility and Anabaptism, 1535-1545." *SCJ*, 23 (1992), 458-85.

Waite/Zijlstra 1992 — Gary K. Waite and Samme Zijlstra, eds. and trans., "Antiochus Revisited: An Anonymous Anabaptist Letter to the Court at The Hague." *MQR* 66 (1992), 26-46.

Zijlstra 1983 — Samme Zijlstra, *Nicolaas Meyndertsz van Blesdijk. Een bijdrage tot de Geschiedenis van het Davidjorisme.* Assen: Van Gorcum, 1983.

Zijlstra 1984 — Samme Zijlstra, "David Joris en de Doperse Stromingen," M. G. Buist, *et al.*, eds., *Historisch Bewogen.* Groningen: Wolters-Noordhoff, 1984, 125-138.

Zijlstra 1988 — Samme Zijlstra, "Menno Simons and David Joris." *MQR* 62 (1988), 249-56.

Scripture Index

Name and Place Index

Ham, 160
Hasselt, Hendrik van (alias the Norse-
man), 305
Hazerswoude, 45, 48, 299
Henry (of England), 48
Herberts, Herman, 25
Hertogenbosch, 71
Hesse, 156
Heuter, Jan de (sheriff of Delft), 303
Hillegont, (widow), 102
Hoffman, Melchior, 18, 20-22, 72-73,
110, 155-156, 184-186, 193, 197,
202-203, 207-208, 238, 247-248,
254-255, 262, 313
Holland, 18-20, 74
Hoorn, Damas van, 18, 46-47, 299

I

Isaac, 122, 129, 162
Isaiah, 88, 255
Ishmael, 160-162
Israel, 84, 111, 122-123, 136, 138-140,
160-161, 166, 171, 200, 221, 233,
237, 263
Israelites, 135
children of, 85, 224
house of, 221
spiritual, 136
Isselmonde, 101
Lord of, 101

J

Jacob, 111, 122, 128, 135, 138, 158, 160,
174, 259, 263
Jael, 115
Jambres, 280
James (apostle), 222, 225-229
Jannes, 280
Jans, Anna, 264, 294-295, 300, 311
Jeremiah, 233
Jerusalem, 135-136, 138, 158, 225
heavenly or new, 24
John (apostle), 250
John the Baptist, 86, 172, 225, 278
Joris, David, 274, 277
as Johan von Brugge, 24, 34, 297
as artist, 23, 36-37, 53-54, 59-60. See
also **Glass painting**
as servant of God, 59, 190, 196, 199,
210, 214-215, 277
as teacher, 46, 185-187, 190, 194-197,
205, 216, 218, 240-241, 243
authority (inspiration) of, 19, 22, 72,
79-80, 91, 117, 123, 155, 164, 184,
188, 191, 200, 202, 206, 217, 274

birth of, 34
children of, 34, 39, 53, 61, 82-83, 91,
94-96, 99, 304
conversion of, 41, 211
father of, 34, 36. See also Amersfoort,
Joris van
in Basel, 17
influence of, 48, 176
mental state of, 28, 31, 43, 47, 55, 127,
183, 242
mother of, 34, 36-37, 44, 49, 53, 62-63,
81-83, 85. See also Gortersdochter,
Maritje Jans de
name of, 34-35
punishment of, 18, 39, 264
relatives of, 40
teaching of, 69-70, 91-93, 220, 270,
274, 279-280, 292
wife of, 34, 39, 42, 44-45, 50, 53, 55,
59-60, 64, 71, 76, 83, 91, 94, 99-
100, 102
wife of, her trial, 96-98. See also Willem, Dirkgen
writings of, 20, 23, 25-27, 45, 48-49,
54, 56, 75, 77-78, 86-87, 90, 99,
149, 168, 185, 187, 192, 201, 235,
239, 242, 244, 275
youth of, 33, 35. See also **Anabaptism;
Spiritualism**
Joris, son of David Joris, 42. See also
David Joris, children of
Joseph, 138, 158, 161
Joshua, 122
Jost, Leonard, 42, 184, 193, 202-203, 235-
238, 241, 298, 313
Jost, Ursula, 156, 300
Judah, 127, 135, 138, 149, 158
Judas, 171, 273
Judas of Galilee (Acts 5:37), 240

K

Kaal, Heinrich, 68, 80-81, 302
Ketel, Jorien, 22, 96, 184, 186, 222, 292,
300, 302-303, 305, 308, 315
Kniepers, N., of Rotterdam, 41
Krechting, Heinrich, 19, 150, 175-176,
299-300, 310

L

Lasco, John a, 269, 315
Leiden, 91, 100, 305
Leiden, Jan Boeckelsz van, 19, 156, 175,
301, 303
Levi, 134
Lier, Cornelius van (the Lord of Ber-
chem), 23

Subject Index

secrets of, 167
testimony of, 203-204, 239, 260
Senses, 59, 85, 92, 105, 129, 143
five, 84-85, 114, 304
heavenly, 85
Serpent, 130, 132, 142, 158, 197, 256,
271. *See also* Devil; **Adam; Eve**
Servant of God, 134, 138, 140, 143, 152,
158, 208, 217, 231-232, 256. *See also*
David Joris, as servant of God
Sexual ethics, 23, 132, 172
and David Joris, 23, 66
Münsterite, 23
Shame, 55, 75-76, 129, 133-134, 137
Sheep, 55, 235, 253, 257, 266, 312
Sheriff, 80-83
Sickness, 71, 163, 178, 225-226
and David Joris, 35, 38, 45, 47, 60, 64,
66-67, 98
spiritual, 226
Signs and wonders, 203
Sin, 76, 93, 120, 144, 153-154, 223, 233
bewitching, 121
born in, 132
destruction of, 129
effects of, 41, 198, 202, 233
forgiveness of, 283. *See also* Confession; Flesh; Lust
renunciation of, 132-133
Soldiers, 42, 68-69, 102
Songs, 26, 52, 65, 119, 136, 173
of David Joris, 26, 32, 43, 52, 54, 105
of angels, 76
Spiritualism, 18
and David Joris, 17, 23-24, 269
Suffering, 63, 69, 93, 107, 114, 137, 197
Sword, 18, 21, 45, 47, 62, 65, 78, 81-82,
95, 132, 139-140, 142, 154, 222, 282,
293. *See also* Punishment;
Vengeance
of God, 261
of the Spirit, 282

T
Tau, sign of, 307
Taverns. *See* Inn
Teachers, 38, 41-42, 46, 159, 185, 205,
212, 259, 261
Temple, of God, 106, 111, 136, 152, 164,
167, 176, 180, 213, 267
living, 167
Temptation, 50-51, 86, 96, 117, 129, 256,
266
Toleration (religious), 269
Tongues, new (or strange), 85, 158

Torture, 91, 95, 97, 267
Transfiguration, 135, 140
Travel, 43, 62
by boat, 43-44, 50, 52, 83-84, 95, 100-
102, 244
by wagon, 52, 67-68, 100-101
over land, 47, 71, 96
Tribulation, 135, 147, 250, 267. *See also*
Anxiety; Suffering; Persecution
Trumpet, final or seventh, 141, 236, 248,
255
Truth, 34, 62, 70, 229, 240, 249, 253
eternal, 34, 92
love of, 45. *See also* Holy Spirit
of God, 128

U
Unchastity, 65, 222
Unity, 48-49, 70, 121, 134, 146, 180-181

V
Veil, 128, 143, 167
Vengeance, 26, 45, 48, 63, 73, 75, 151,
266
of God, 26
Victory, 68, 94, 113, 115-116, 118, 121,
123-124, 132, 135, 137, 140, 142,
204. *See also* Perfection
Violence, 114
Virgins, 124, 129, 173
Visions, 26-27, 62, 87, 90-91, 127, 185,
199, 201, 214, 219, 221, 311
and David Joris, 19-20, 26, 54, 56, 58,
77-78, 84-87, 90-91, 96, 126-127,
184, 186, 200. *See also* Dreams

W
War, 69, 118, 140, 160
Waterland conference, 18, 46, 109
Wisdom, 68, 130, 151, 157, 190, 193, 207
hidden, 163
human, 35, 119, 137, 191, 201, 207,
213, 256, 258
of David Joris, 51, 215, 217, 272
of God, 69, 86, 111, 215, 218, 232,
234-235, 257, 260, 289
of the Holy Spirit, 152
teachers of, 118
Witnesses, 277
two, 211
Women, 51, 54, 81, 116, 118, 120-121,
129-131, 151-152, 155, 160, 162,
169, 171-173, 175, 199, 211
abduction of, 68, 70, 80, 302
and David Joris, 66, 69, 150

The Editor

Born in Vancouver, British Columbia, Gary Waite grew up in Toronto, Ontario, with his mother and his brother, Brian. After studying theology in Toronto, he moved to Waterloo, Ontario, where he finished B.A. and M.A. degrees in history at the University of Waterloo.

His Ph.D., completed under the supervision of Werner O. Packull (Conrad Grebel College), was a groundbreaking study of the Anabaptist career of David Joris. After receiving the University of Waterloo Alumni Gold Medal, the dissertation was revised and published as *David Joris and Dutch Anabaptism, 1524-1543* (Wilfrid Laurier Press, 1990).

Gary has published numerous articles on David Joris and Anabaptism in several scholarly journals. He is currently engaged in a major project on the Dutch amateur acting and literary guilds, the Chambers of Rhetoric, and their activities for or against Reformation propaganda in the Low Countries of Charles V (1519-1556). He is also interested in the relationships between the Radical Reformation, popular culture of that era, the witch hunts, and the sixteenth-century rise of religious toleration in the Low Countries. He continues to conduct research into the writings of the enigmatic David Joris.

Since 1987, Gary has resided in Fredericton, New Brunswick. He is an associate professor at the University of New Brunswick, where he teaches Medieval, Renaissance, and Reformation history.

Gary is married to Katherine Hayward and they live with their daughter, Jessica, in a house near the University of New Brunswick campus.

GENERAL THEOLOGICAL SEMINARY
NEW YORK

DATE DUE

			Printed in USA